WINES OF SOUTH-WEST FRANCE

WINES *of* SOUTH-WEST FRANCE

PAUL STRANG

Illustrations by Jeanne Strang

Maps by Sally Maltby

KYLE CATHIE LIMITED

First published in paperback 1996 by
Kyle Cathie Limited
20 Vauxhall Bridge Road, London SW1V 2SA

ISBN 1 85626 222 7

Maps by Sally Maltby

Paul Strang is hereby identified as the author of this
work in accordance with Section 77 of the Copyright, Designs
and Patents Act 1988.

A Cataloguing in Publication record for this title is
available from the British Library.

Typeset by Heronwood Press
Printed by WBC Book Manufacturers Ltd.

Contents

Acknowledgements

My thanks to the hundreds of wine-makers I have visited for their unlimited generosity with their time and their wines. My appreciation also to Sophie Valléjo at SOPEXA in London, to Jacques Tranier, president of the Association of the Wines of the South-West, and to the Growers' Associations in the different wine-making areas, for their help and encouragement, and permission to use their material.

My gratitude also to *Editions Serg* for their permission to quote extracts from Zette Guinadeau-Franc's book *Les Secrets des Fermes en Périgord Noir*, and to Flammarion for allowing me to quote from La Mazille's *La Bonne Cuisine du Périgord*.

My thanks also to Aileen Hall for her help and enthusiasm, for being such a useful databank, and for her stamina on a tour of the Frontonnais.

I am grateful too to Kyle Cathie and her team for their patient and skilled *élevage* of this book.

Finally, my devoted thanks to my long-suffering wife Jeanne, for whom there can be few country lanes in South-West France remaining unexplored. Her skill as a chauffeuse is matched only by her enthusiasm in the tasting-room, and by the same meticulous care in proof-reading that she gave her own *Goose Fat and Garlic*, which covers in culinary terms the same area as this book.

NO APOLOGIES for occasional lapses into Winespeak. Phrases like 'big, fat buttery nose' may be risible, but say more in a few words than a whole paragraph of mainstream English.

NOTE

At the end of each chapter there is a list of growers. In these lists, an asterisk denotes those whose wines have given me most pleasure. Numbers against growers' names correspond with the maps, to give an approximate idea of location. Growers are listed in the alphabetical order of their vineyard names. Wines from growers listed in italics may be hard to find, particularly in recent vintages.

Co-opératives are open to the public except on Saturday afternoons and Sundays. Appointments to visit private growers should be made in advance wherever possible, as a matter of courtesy and to avoid disappointment. Telephone numbers, are, however, liable to change. From 18th October 1996, growers' telephone numbers must be prefixed by the additional digits 05 for calls made within France and by 00-335 for calls made from the United Kingdom.

For
Jeanne

Foreword

There are infinite variations in the technique of wine-making from one region of France to another. Nevertheless, it may be useful for the reader, particularly if visiting growers for the first time, to have an outline of the general process.

As is increasingly the practice nowadays, the wine-maker himself takes responsibility for rejecting any doubtful grapes from the bunches going into the *cuves*. It is mandatory under the rules of some areas for the grapes to be de-stalked before the wine is made. Pressing is nowadays mechanical, in the same machine that does the de-stalking.

For red wines, the length of the *cuvaison* varies enormously. It depends on the kind of wine the maker wants at the end of the day. A short vinification of as little as four days is quite common with co-opératives, for wines they want to market when young: whereas some growers give their red wines as much as five weeks. A short *cuvaison* makes for a wine which is elegant and quaffable, but the longer it is left to vinify, the tougher the structure it develops, and it becomes more complex with age.

Nowadays wine-makers have learnt from the oenologists the importance of temperature-control. Particularly in hot weather it is essential not to allow the must to overheat, otherwise fermentation stops and the wine is left with an unacceptable load of unconverted sugar. During the period of alcoholic fermentation it is also customary to stir up the contents of the vat, including the crust which forms on top of the wine and the must at the bottom of the *cuve*, by the process called *remontage*, a pumping operation carried out regularly throughout the fermentation. This extracts the maximum amount of colour from the skins and is considered particularly to benefit wines made from cabernet grapes.

It is usual for each grape-variety to be vinified separately. At the end of the alcoholic fermentation, it is drawn off its lees and transferred to large storage units for the first stage of the *élevage*. These may be either of concrete, stainless steel, fibre-glass or wood. During the first few months of its life, the wine is again drawn off its lees three or four times to oxygenate it, and at the end of the period the wine-maker blends the different varieties.

This operation, called *assemblage*, requires a great deal of discernment and responsibility because on it will depend the ultimate quality of the finished wine. Each grape-variety will have matured more or less successfully during the preceding year, and the precise amount of each going into the final blend will be fundamental to its quality and ageing

ability. After the *assemblage* the wines may be bottled, but increasingly
the practice is to give them more time in wood. Old barrels will not
affect the flavour, though they will improve the quality. New barrels
will lend a particular taste of vanilla and sometimes fresh sawdust to the
young wine, which, as the effect of the oak wears off, should develop an
enhanced bouquet and flavour, as well as a long finish and the capacity
to go on improving over the years.

With white wines, the pattern is totally different from that of the red.
For dry wines the vintage will take place several weeks before the harvesting of grapes for the sweet wines. Grapes for dry wines may be
given a short maceration before the fermentation takes place. This has
to be done at a temperature below that at which fermentation can start.
White grapes are always pressed as quickly as possible to minimise the
risk of oxidisation. The juice is then clarified by refrigeration, or sometimes, in the case of the dry wines, by actual filtration.

The temperature of the wine in the vat is controlled, usually by a
water-cooling system built into the fabric of the vats. This may vary
from between 18 and 25° for the sweet wines and 15 to 18° for the dry.
The latter are fermented through to the end of the conversion of sugar
into alcohol, but with the sweeter wines the process is arrested when the
balance between alcohol and sugar reaches between $12^1/_2$ and 13° and
$2^1/_2$ to 3° respectively.

Once fermentation is finished, the wines are fined, traditionally with
white of egg to draw to the bottom of the *cuves* all traces of sediment.
They are then filtered and may be bottled immediately, although nearly
a half of the sweet wines and an increasing proportion of the dry are
given ageing in wood for between three and six months.

The Wine Regions
of
SOUTH-WEST FRANCE
(except vin de pays)

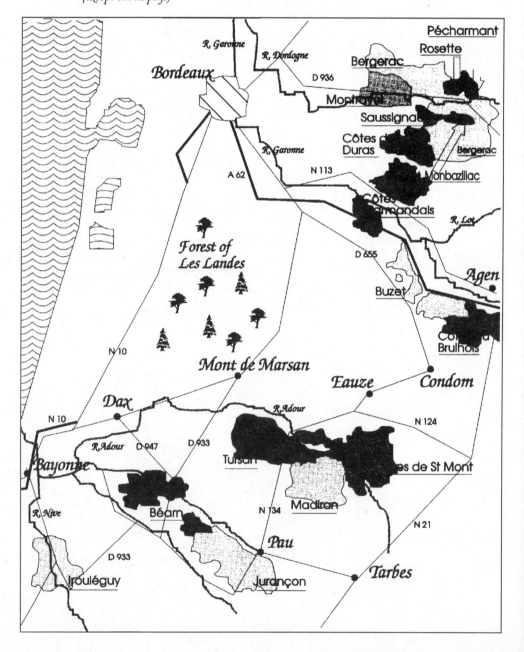

R. Garonne

R. Dordogne

Bordeaux

D 936

Pécharmant

Rosette

Bergerac

Montravel

Saussignac

Côtes de
Duras

Bergerac

R. Garonne

N 113

A 62

Monbazillac

Côtes
du marmandais

R. Lot

D 655

Forest of
Les Landes

Agen

Buzet

N 10

Côtes du
Brulhois

Mont de Marsan

Eauze

Condom

Dax

R. Adour

N 124

N 10

R. Adour   D 947   D 933

Tursan

Côtes de St Mont

Bayonne

N 134

Madiran

N 21

Béarn

R. Nive

D 933

Pau

Tarbes

Irouléguy

Jurançon

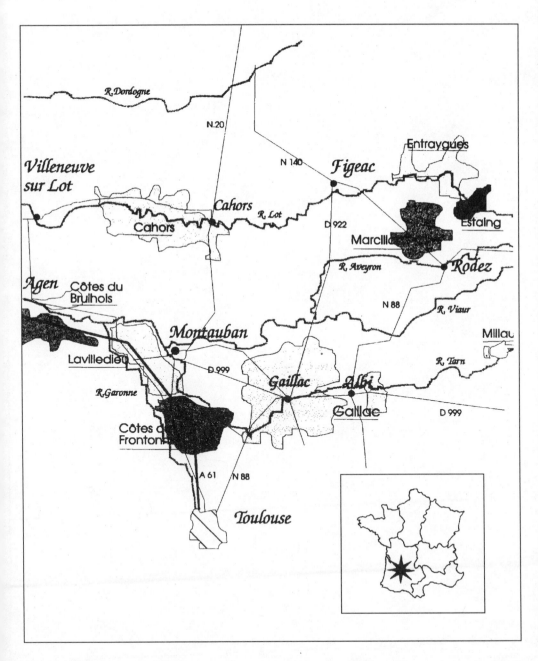

Upstream from Bordeaux: the Haut-Pays

Once upon a time, Bordeaux made very bad wine.

The merchants of that city learnt about wine-making from their country cousins upstream. The latter were making good, if sturdy, wines before the land round Bordeaux was anything but a marsh, and, as they had been among the first to export French wine beyond their region of production, it was these growers from whom the Bordelais learnt to identify their markets. It was the interdependence of Bordeaux and the *haut-pays* which guaranteed their joint commercial pre-eminence in wine-production, at least until the phylloxera disaster of a hundred years ago.

Nobody knows for certain how wine-making started in the South-West. My favourite explanation is the legend of the shepherd who set out from some far country with a small flock of sheep. After travelling perhaps thousands of miles over all types of terrain, he finally arrived at a piece of flat land where he could pasture his animals. One autumn day, when a storm had swelled the river, the shepherd marked the high-water mark by plunging his stick into the ground. He returned in the spring to find a vine sprouting leaves. So, it is said, was created the first vineyard, at the foot of a hillside and close to a ford over the river. The shepherd settled there with his family, having built a primitive stone hut – the first cellar as well as the first dairy.

This tale implies that the shepherd brought his wine-making know-how with him, but it still does not tell us where the shepherd came from: perhaps over the Pyrenees from Spain, where it is known that vines were introduced in the earliest days of antiquity. Certainly there was a lively traffic across the mountains because of the ancient trade in silver. Perhaps via central Europe, having started his journey from

Etruria and crossed the Alps into Switzerland. Certainly wine-making had, at an early date, reached an advanced state in the ancient Etruscan kingdom, for it was the Etruscans, not the Romans, who discovered the art of maturing and transporting wine in barrel.

The more generally accepted theory seems to be that the Romans, or perhaps the Greeks, brought the art of wine-making to Ancient Gaul. Certainly Caesar's centurions were encouraged to plant in the area of Narbonne what are believed to be the first extensive vineyards in France. They planted the grape-varieties which thrived back home, and the vineyards soon spread along the Mediterranean coast, up the Rhône valley, and as far as Gaillac. This was, however, the northern limit at which the Roman vines would survive the rigours of the French winter, so it is still not clear how the other vineyards of the South-West came into being.

From Narbonne it was an easy journey across relatively accessible terrain to the valley of the Garonne, where the vineyards of Moissac were one day to thrive. From there, downstream to Bordeaux was another easy step. But it seems that there was an interval of some years between the creation of the Gaillac vineyards and the planting of vines elsewhere in the Aquitaine basin. First it was necessary to develop a fully hardy stock which would withstand the Atlantic winters. The geographer Strabo, writing in the second half of the first century, does not mention any wine being made at Bordeaux although the town was apparently becoming a maritime outlet for the Gaillac growers. Seemingly, the Bordelais in those days drank beer . . . It was the profits from dealing in the wines of the hinterland that were to enable the Bordelais to carry out the necessary works of deforestation and drainage to create their own vineyards.

This hinterland – what we now call the *haut-pays* – was being colonised by the Romans at a rapid rate. They developed vineyards wherever they went, so the creation of tough grape-varieties was no problem. Vines gradually established themselves in a semi-circle from Libourne, along the Dordogne to Bergerac, along the Lot from Soturac to Cahors, and as far as the plains of Armagnac and the Béarn. By the beginning of the second century AD the future pattern for the development of wine-making in the South-West had been largely set, in a way that is little changed today.

Meanwhile Bordeaux flourished. It levied tolls on all the wines which were floated past its quays. The town itself became a centre for dealers in this new commodity, and one intrepid Englishman is on record as having come to Bordeaux to buy wine in the second century! The markets were evidently the Roman conquerors in the north of Europe, but so popular did wine become that the powers in Rome became concerned that the conquest of Gaul was not producing the wheat and other crops which were needed back home. It was little consolation that the inhabitants of their colony were growing fat on a scale of wine-production that was ruining the growers back in Rome.

In AD 92 the Emperor Domitian therefore ordered that all non-Italian vineyards be uprooted. Almost certainly, however, his ruling was flouted more than it was obeyed. Perhaps because this early attempt at prohibition was just as much a failure as it was to prove on the other side of the Atlantic 1800 years later, the edict was overturned by the Emperor Probus in AD 280. The event is commemorated today in the use of the name Probus as the premium wine from Clos Triguedina at Cahors.

Bordeaux meanwhile had become a favourite haunt of the Roman nobility and intelligentsia. The city stands proudly, like a concierge, at the mouth of the river Garonne. It has always been able to control the comings and goings of the river traffic passing its quays, policing it in its own self-interest and creaming off more than a little of the profits.

Nor are we concerned only with the Garonne, because flowing into it are some of the most important rivers of the South-West: the Lot, the Aveyron and the Tarn from the north and east, and the Gers and Baise from the other side; and only a few miles downstream from the city gates the Dordogne joins up with the Garonne to form the estuary of the Gironde, bringing with it the waters of the Vézère and the Isle.

Thus the city lies at the mouth of a huge basin comprising most of the South-West. The Garonne itself rises high in the central Pyrenees while its tributaries start life in the hills of the Limousin, the upland pastures of the Auvergne, the rugged *causses* of the Lozère and the granite mountains of the Cévennes. The hills of the old county of Armagnac form a small watershed of their own, the streams to the north running into the Garonne, the ones to the south into the Adour which flows into the Atlantic at Bayonne. Historically, Bayonne was the only French harbour south of Bordeaux to have any commercial importance.

It is therefore easy to understand why, in the days before railways and lorries, and when the roads were unsafe as well as inadequate, Bordeaux occupied such a powerful position in commerce. If all roads led to Rome, all rivers led to Bordeaux. Up them were transported, even in more recent times, all the goods which the inland and upland peasant farmers could not produce themselves: spices from the oriental French colonies, sugar from the West Indies, salt from the shores of the French coasts; and salted fish from as far afield as Norway in the days before refrigeration.

Downstream came timber from the mountain forests, in later days coal from the mines of Decazeville, and of course wine – in prodigious quantities. In the heyday of pre-phylloxera production, the quantity of wine shipped down the rivers to Bordeaux exceeded the total modern production of the Bordeaux vineyards. At its apogee Cahors alone accounted for 800,000 hectolitres (about 120,000 barrels) a year, one-third of the contemporary Appellation d'Origine Contrôlée (AOC) Bordeaux produced in a good year. In 1852 Gaillac was producing twice the current Bordeaux output, and in former times the vineyards of Moissac, which have disappeared along with their statistics, a probable similar amount.

It now becomes apparent that, whatever the truth about the legend of the old shepherd, the vineyards of the *haut-pays* developed not only in close proximity to rivers but at points where there was an established crossing. Libourne and Bergerac on the Dordogne, Cahors, Entraygues and Estaing on the Lot, Gaillac on the Tarn, Moissac, Marmande, Buzet and Duras on the Garonne, Tarascon on the Ariège, were all wine centres which had easy access to a navigable river leading to Bordeaux. What happened to their wine when it reached the quays of that city requires a little more historical explanation.

In 1152 Eleanor of Aquitaine married Henry Plantagenet, King of England. As dowry she brought with her most of the West and South of France. Henry was already Duke of Normandy, so the marriage made him a more powerful feudal monarch than the King of France in his own country. For the wine-growers of the South-West huge overseas markets were at once opened up. Sales to what are now the Low Countries, to northern France including Paris (the Seine was an easily navigable river then as it is today) and to the newly accessible Loire valley and Poitou all burgeoned, but it was above all the English market which spurred the merchants of Bordeaux to ever-growing trade.

Henry II and his successors had problems in administering such a huge kingdom, and inevitably his inclination to delegate government locally became a necessity. Bodies of local magistrates therefore took over many of the monarchical functions. In Bordeaux and in St Emilion they also not unnaturally concerned themselves with their principal trade – wine. To this day the Jurade of St Emilion, recreated in recent years but of course with no governmental powers, sits in judgement on the quality of wine produced within its area.

Bordeaux soon realised that its new powers could be used to solve their principal problem as growers of wine – quality. It is hard to believe that seven hundred years ago the wine produced in the immediate region of Bordeaux was thin stuff, pale in colour, lacking in body, and light in alcohol. The merchants were fully aware of the success of the wines of the *haut-pays* compared with their own. To enable their home-produced wine to travel by sea as far as England, the Bordelais invented the art of blending, liberally dosing their own inferior product with the sturdy wines from upstream:

> Thanks to the produce of Gaillac, we can give our wines the ripeness, strength, colour and flavour which please the English, who like their red wines strong and dark. So we can send to England wines which would otherwise get no further than Brittany. It is the same for the Dutch, who demand sweet white wine. The green wines which we produce can be stretched with the sweet white wines once again supplied by Gaillac . . . The interests of the King, the encouragement of trade and the public good call for the blending of our wines.
>
> (from a seventeenth-century report to Finance Minister Colbert from a Bordeaux merchant)

The merchants had one other difficulty. Until the end of the seventeenth century when the virtues of the glass bottle and the cork were discovered, wine would not keep for long. The thin wines of Bordeaux would sometimes not even survive until the next vintage. It was essential, therefore, for them to clear their warehouses as soon as possible after the new wine was made each year. Wine which was a year old would fetch only half the price of the new wine.

Although the Bordeaux merchants relied on the wines of the *haut-pays* for blending, the local growers needed to get their wine out of Bordeaux ahead of the Gaillac and Cahors wines which had their own direct access to overseas markets. So from the thirteenth century right through to the Revolution, Bordeaux enjoyed what it called the *grand privilège*, which it conferred on itself and managed to have ratified as often as necessary by the English and later the French kings. This ensured that the wines of the *haut-pays* were not allowed to proceed beyond the port of Bordeaux until after 11 November each year (the date later extended to Christmas in 1373 by our King Edward III). This not only gave the Bordelais the priority in the export queue which they needed but had the effect of totally depriving many inland producers of an overseas market, especially in the far distant but extensive colonies of France to which there were few winter sailings.

The growers of Cahors seem to have been particularly singled out for discrimination. Taxes were paid by the barrel irrespective of volume of content. Bordeaux required that Cahors barrels should be substantially smaller than the norm, thereby increasing the tax per litre and thus the ultimate selling price of the wine.

The canny inland growers, try hard as they might, were unable entirely to beat this fiscal and physical blockade. One dodge which was fairly successful was to ship wine down the Garonne as far as the little port of St Macaire, which was the limit of the writ of Bordeaux. The wine was then carried overland northwards to the Dordogne where it continued its journey downstream. The Dordogne does not join the Garonne until a point beyond Bordeaux, which therefore was not in a position to stop this deliberate attempt to flout its authority. Further progress was still difficult, however, without the facilities of the port of Bordeaux, especially the larger sea-going vessels based there.

By the end of the seventeenth century the know-how of the Bordeaux growers was beginning to undergo a basic if gradual development. Largely this was set in motion by a demand which was led by the London market for ever-increasing quality in red Bordeaux. The English importers started to develop techniques for conserving wines which previously had had to be drunk young. They were fortunate enough to have their wine shipped in new barrels, the cleanliness of which greatly helped to prevent the wine turning to vinegar within the year. They learnt from the Dutch the practice of sulphuring barrels to keep them sweet, and above all they developed the technique of bottling with good quality cork.

Furthermore, the end of the seventeenth and the beginning of the eighteenth centuries saw a new affluence in England. Those in high society were willing to spare no expense to ensure that they were able to offer only the best wines at their tables and at their coffee-houses.

In Bordeaux the growers began to devote the profits which they were amassing from this explosion in trade to improving quality. It was soon realised that the haphazard methods traditionally used were no longer valid. If it took ten years or more between the planting of a vine and the date when its produce could be consumed then there had to be some planning in the operation of a vineyard to ensure continuation of both quality and quantity. Smaller growers did not have the resources to structure their cultivation in this way. Thus larger quality estates, which we now call châteaux, came to be developed.

Experiments were carried out into the selection of the most suitable grape-varieties, having regard to variation in soil and micro-climate. Almost certainly at this time the now honoured cabernet, merlot, malbec and verdot varieties were identified as likely to produce the best quality wines. Some may have been in use before, but it is generally thought that the cabernet varieties at least were either a new introduction or were developed by some early form of clonage from older kinds. The merlot almost certainly arrived in the eighteenth century.

The Age of Enlightenment was a time of rising prosperity for the Bordelais. The Methuen Treaty between Portugal and England may have been intended to favour the importation of port rather than claret, but the duty on a bottle of first-class claret was the same as that on a similar quantity of ordinary table-wine from the *haut-pays*, so expansion of the quality châteaux was positively assisted. The growth of trade with the French colonies was a further protection against the effects of English legislation, as was the expansion of the export markets to the Low Countries, always buyers of Bordeaux. The French colonies were, incidentally, an important source of custom for the wines of the *haut-pays*.

The effect of the expansion of quality production in Bordeaux was two-fold for the wines produced upstream. First, Bordeaux was no longer so reliant on the inland growers for blending wines, because the Bordelais had learnt to produce wines of the required strength and quality themselves. Secondly, there was now no need to exclude the wines of the *haut-pays* from the port of Bordeaux, because the techniques of preserving the wine in barrel and bottle had long been mastered, and it was no longer necessary to steal a march on the competition.

Even so it was not until the eve of the French Revolution that the privileges of Bordeaux were brought to an end, as a result of intense pressure upon the authorities in Paris by the local growers in the upstream vineyards. Despite their success, conditions hardly improved for them, because of the outbreak of the Revolution and the trade blockades which were imposed on France during the Napoleonic wars.

*

It was in a greenhouse in Hammersmith, London, just as much as at the gates of the Bastille in Paris, that the modern history of South-West France was largely determined. The former unlikely location was the scene of the first European sighting, in 1863, of an aphid which, within a quarter of a century, was to destroy almost all the vineyards of France. Fat and tiny, it measures no more than a millimetre and can multiply itself twelve times in a year. It is indigenous to the eastern part of the United States, whence it first came. It is particularly partial to vines, feeding on the sap of the leaves and working down to the roots on which it produces nodules which eventually kill the plants. It then returns above ground to look for more food and so disseminates the disease.

Soon after its discovery in England the aphid was found near Tarascon in the Rhône valley. It spread rapidly throughout the South and was first seen in the Bordeaux area in 1866. Within sixteen years no less than 98% of the vineyards in the Gironde were affected. It reached Cahors in 1877, and by the beginning of the following decade it had infiltrated practically the whole *vignoble* of the South-West. It was named, appropriately, 'phylloxera vastatrix'.

The son of a family from the Lot, doing his military service in Bordeaux, wrote home in 1879:

I was very sad to learn that the phylloxera had appeared all over our district, it is a disease which is terrible for vines. As you say in your letter, if it continues the country people will be completely ruined for the vines are our main resource.

From home came the following reply:

The vines are not at all good, and we think that in two or three years we won't have any and we shall have to drink water. So be wise and prepare for tough times ahead.*

The tragedy of the phylloxera was that much greater in the South-West because such a large proportion of cultivatable ground was given over to vines. Over a period of centuries the area had become the most intensive wine-producing area in France. Bordeaux and the river country inland from it had become the vineyard of the civilised world. Vines were grown wherever they could thrive, and even in less favoured areas they represented a valuable cash-crop for the peasant-farmer.

The consequences of the phylloxera were so severe that it has taken almost a century for South-West France to recover. One immediate effect was the gradual depopulation of whole areas of countryside, especially the rough limestone *causses* where little could be grown except the vine. Whole communities were abandoned – for example, just north of Cahors, there was once a town called Toulousque which has now com-

* From the archives of a family in St Vincent-Rive-d'Olt, quoted in *Le Vin de Cahors* by Joseph Baudel, p. 46.

pletely disappeared. The younger generation moved to the towns in the hope of finding work there. Some went to Paris, and others emigrated.

The situation was not helped by the economic slump which followed the advent of the Third Republic in the 1880s. In these conditions few could afford to replant their vineyards with vines immune to the phylloxera. This involved grafting traditional French grape-varieties on to immune American stocks, and the expense in modern money is said to have been more than £4000 an acre, a sum which few country growers could command. Surprisingly enough, though, the amount of land under vine fell only gradually, because the immediate response of most farmers was to replant ungrafted stock. This fell prey to the disease almost immediately and even assisted the persistence of the plague by providing food for the aphids.

The dwindling country population was further reduced by the loss of so many lives during the First World War, and the economic conditions which followed simply compounded the problems. It was not until the recovery of the world economy in the 1950s that conditions were created in which the country wines of the South-West might flourish once again.

In France, in the middle of this century, the demand for everyday wine was largely being satisfied by the coarse wines from the Midi, often blended with others from North Africa. Elsewhere, wine-drinking as a habit had not extended beyond the relatively prosperous. Outside France the word 'wine' was largely synonymous with claret, Burgundy and the wines from the Rhône and Loire valleys. Rapidly increasing prosperity in the advanced nations of the world created a demand for wine which these traditional areas could not supply. Prices began to rise sharply, leaving a gap which the growers in less fashionable areas of France were quick to perceive. Suddenly there was a market for wines of decent quality at an acceptable price. The Midi wines were no longer acceptable, but classed growth claret was not affordable.

Other factors contributed to the rebirth. The coming of independence to Algeria stopped the flow of wine from that country, while many of its more skilful wine-makers returned to metropolitan France. They often brought with them a willingness to experiment and introduce new techniques not always to be found with the traditional peasant-growers. The European Commission had also offered substantial grants to growers willing to dig up the inferior grape-varieties which were planted in the wake of the phylloxera, and to replace them with quality vines.

Above all it has been the unquenchable enthusiasm of small numbers of local growers, working sometimes together with, and sometimes competing against, a new generation of wine-makers which is behind the renaissance. The story of the rebirth of the wines of South-West France is a modern romance.

The Wines of Cahors
and the Lower Lot

On a warm day in early summer, you may be tempted to sit down to a picnic by the river Lot in the small town of Douelle just west of Cahors. From the main village street steep cobbles lead to the water's edge and a weather-worn quay runs for two or three hundred yards just above the level of the river. Once the church bell rings for *midi*, there is silence except for the screaming of the swifts as they wheel in and out of the old buildings. Everything here moves at the same leisurely pace as the river, and you will feel that nothing has changed for centuries; that this water-side town has ever been a haven of peace and idyllic contentment.

As you unpack your lunch, you might hear the sound of footsteps approaching. A very old villager nears, who hesitantly introduces himself to wish you the traditional greeting of *bon appétit*. Enchanted with the spot you have chosen, you may be tempted to ask him about the deserted old quay where you are sitting, in which event he will soon launch into a series of reminiscences. As you nibble at your saucisson, he will explain how his ancestors had been boatmen on the river Lot and how his grandfather had spent the winter evenings round the fire-side with his family, telling them fantastic stories of life on the water.

Before the phylloxera, thousands of barrels of wine a year were sent downstream to Bordeaux for eventual export. The river boatmen were thus important people. They needed and possessed stamina and bravery: it was normal for thirty or so men to be drowned in a year, and more than 50,000 pounds weight of merchandise lost.

The old man may tell you how there used to be a pilgrimage to a nearby church just before the *vendange* each September. The purpose was to pray for the safety of the sailors. Legend has it that a master boatman, in danger of drowning in the waters of the Lot, had promised

God to donate the whole of his cargo to the restoration of the chapel if he safely reached dry land. He did and he kept his vow.

The sailors did more than navigate boats up and down the stream, they were also given the job of looking after the bed and banks of the river because, better than anyone else, they knew what was required. They made up the work-force of stone-workers, dredgers, carpenters and divers who created the infrastructure still in place today. They also took over responsibility for the tow-paths and drainage from absentee land-owners who spent as little on them as they could get away with. The tow-paths were often inadequate for the passage of horses, so men had to stand in for the animals, pulling with their bare hands from the riverbanks the heavily laden boats on enormous cables. No wonder that the little riverside churches at Velles, Vers, Douelle and Notre Dame de l'Isle at Luzech were endowed with votive offerings. These, in the shape of wooden models of the boats which plied the river, are still there.

Whole villages lived by the river trade. The children went aboard young to acquire the skills and learn the customs of life on the water. Thanks to the herculean efforts of all, the navigability of the river was gradually improved, a series of locks being built between Cahors and the confluence of the Lot with the Garonne at Aiguillon. Better tow-paths were excavated and the river could be reached by slipways, called *cales*, like the one you used in order to reach the water for your picnic.

You need only to scratch the surface of local history to discover how fascinating the story of the wine-trade throughout this part of France was. The history of the love-hate relationship between Bordeaux and the inland wine-growing areas has left its mark indelibly on the unique style of every wine made today in the *haut-pays*. Nowhere is this more true than with Cahors, whose history is one of the oldest of all.

Under the influence of the Romans, wine-making spread quickly to the Lot valley. The native Gauls were easily persuaded to abandon their taste for grain-based and sweet, sticky concoctions in favour of the fermented juice of the grape. During the Henry II/Eleanor of Aquitaine period, as early as 1225, the reputation of wine from Cahors had found its way to London, from where engineers arrived to establish the Lot as a commercial waterway. This made possible the transport of what they christened 'the black wine of Cahors'.

By the first half of the fourteenth century over half the wine being shipped out of Bordeaux came from the vineyards of Quercy, the province of which Cahors was the capital. Such was its reputation that, in the French merchant navy, officers were provided with Cahors while other ranks had to make do with Graves and other Bordeaux.

Exports were not confined to England. The Low Countries as well as Scandinavia were buyers. More surprisingly, Russia was an important market, because the Orthodox Church favoured Cahors as a wine for liturgical use.

The French themselves have always admired Cahors. The Avignon pope, John XXII, was a native of the Lot and had Cahors vines planted at the papal vineyards in the Rhône valley. François I engaged a grower from Cahors called Rivals to plant the royal vinery at Fontainebleau, whither Rivals set out with thirty mules laden with barrels and plants.

The stranglehold which Bordeaux exercised over the wines of the *haut-pays* lasted from the middle ages to the Revolution. Cahors probably came off worse than any of the other inland areas. The superiority which made the wines of the Lot so valuable to the merchants of Bordeaux was also a source of jealousy and fear. The formidable armoury of fiscal and commercial weapons to which the Bordelais had resort combined to depress and discourage the producers of the Quercy, who often had to agree to the disposal of their wines at sacrificial prices to speculators all too aware of their value and importance.

A merchant from Luzech, one of the principal wine ports on the Lot, issued a public warning in 1750. Writing about the so-called 'black' wines of Cahors, he saw with the clarity of a biblical prophet the need for some kind of control in order to safeguard standards. He wrote:

> . . . although the wines of Cahors manage to retain their reputation, they will lose it in the colonies and the export markets; prompt steps are needed to avert the disgrace which could overwhelm our region. We would be entirely impoverished if we lost our wine: it is our only resource because we do not have any of those other crops which make other provinces rich.

The classic account of the style of wines being made in the Lot before the phylloxera is that of a Monsieur Jullien, who wrote in 1816:

> Three kinds of red wines are made in this area: those which are called black because of the intensity of their colour; those which are called full-bodied red wines, and finally pink wines. The first are normally used only for blending; the second are good table-wines, and the third are ordinary wines, some better than others, which are the everyday drink of the local inhabitants.
> The black wines are made with grapes coming from the plant which is called in the area 'auxerrois': they combine a very deep colour, a good flavour and plenty of 'guts', and they are not really suitable for everyday use: but they are very useful for adding colour, body and strength to feeble wines, and they survive transportation well . . .

Then Monsieur Jullien comes to the point about the 'black wines'. He says:

> They make a point of baking a proportion of [the grapes] in the oven, or bringing to the boil the whole of the vintage before it is put into barrel for its natural fermentation . . . The first-mentioned process removes from the must quite a lot of the water content of the wines, and encourages a more active fermentation in which the colouring agents dissolve perfectly. The merchants who trade in these wines do not stop here: they blend with the must of the auxerrois a distillation at a strength of some 29 degrees, a kind of liquor which they add in the proportion of 1/5th, a quarter or even 1/3rd, according to the quality [sic] that they wish to produce.

Other cantons could make similar wine if they took the trouble to vinify the auxerrois separately: but they prefer to blend it with white grapes and other varieties, and they make what is called locally 'vin rouge dans tout son corps'. This is less deep in colour than the vin noir, but still quite a mouthful, sprightly in style and with good flavour.

It is not surprising that these wines were valued for their sturdiness and strength. Another commentator tells us that the fermentation continued for a whole month. Only the wines destined for the most expensive outlets were bottled, and then only when they had spent six to eight years in wood. This was regarded as the necessary period of maturity. They were then thought fit to drink after two years in bottle. Many producers today would keep their wine as long in the wood, were it not for the exorbitant cost of servicing the capital tied up in the stock.

Doctor Guyot, the first great expert in the pruning of vines, confirms the earlier account of Jullien and puts into perspective the roles of the unfortunate growers and wine-makers, whose lack of organisation in those days put them at the mercy of the counterfeit dealers:

> The table wines, much better than the black wines, are excellent and very clean, without too much alcohol. I have been surprised by the good effect of these wines on the digestion and on the well-being of body and mind. But the trade does not buy them, they are interested only in depth of colour. Today industry has created synthetic wines based on its great centres of blending and cooking. It abandons the wines of Quercy, offering for them little more than a pittance. It will always be the same where the land-owners and wine-makers are so ill-advised as to leave themselves unprotected from the fraudulent offers of the trade.

These accounts come from the first half of the nineteenth century and reflect in part the difficult effects of the immediate post-Revolutionary period. The breaking up of the larger estates put much of the land formerly in the ownership of the rich nobles and *grande bourgeoisie* into the hands of the small farmer and peasant-grower. Liberty and fraternity may have still been in short supply, but the dissolution of the feudal estates did bring about a relatively greater equality, making it possible for the first time for peasants to compete as *vignerons* with their former masters.

Nevertheless the wars with England had brought with them economic blockades, and there was no immediate expansion in the wine-trade. Exports had fallen from about 30,000 barrels to one or two thousand. As so often in the Quercy, economic hardship was accentuated by the fact that, in large areas of the countryside, nothing would grow except the vine. Even then the growers were able to extract a harvest of only a tiny yield. Without the wine-crop, the local population was reduced from poverty to destitution.

Suddenly in the 1850s the Cahors vineyards sprang into economic life. A disease called 'oidium', which was a parasitic mushroom, had dramatically affected the vineyards of Bordeaux as well as other regions, but for some reason spared Cahors. The ensuing demand for the wines of Cahors brought about a substantial expansion in the vineyard itself as well as a welcome boost in price. By 1866 there were 58,000 hectares under vine, as compared with the 40,000 when Jullien was writing in 1816. The price increase was even more dramatic, leaping from 9 francs per hectolitre in 1852 to 70 francs only three years later.

This period of expansion was fuelled, though not entirely caused, by the general expansion of the French economy under the Second Empire. The comparative well-being of the region is reflected by the number of fine farm and vineyard properties dating from this period. One cannot blame the local growers for making wine while the sun shone during this brief golden age. After so many centuries of being in thrall to Bordeaux, and the subsequent trials of the period immediately following their enfranchisement, they must have revelled in their relative prosperity. Although they could not have foreseen the disaster of the phylloxera which was soon to burst on them, there were nevertheless clouds on the horizon which were no doubt recognised by the more canny of a naturally canny peasantry.

The coming of the railways was to change life for the wine-maker. The growers in the Midi now had easy access to northern France and quickly took advantage to profit from their hot summer climate and the high-yielding grape-varieties which they used for their everyday wine. They turned most of their agriculture to wine-production so as to meet the requirements of the new industrial working class for cheap *vin ordinaire*. Similarly they were in a position to provide for the blenders a cut-price substitute for the finer wines of Cahors.

The competition from the Midi was a flea-bite compared with the advent of the phylloxera. The first areas to be hit were the vineyards on the plateaux above the river valley. In the shallower and poorer soil, the vine-roots were unable to penetrate as deeply into the ground as those in the valley, and were therefore much more prone to attack. The vines on the higher ground were entirely wiped out. At first the valley producers thought they would be spared, but eventually the whole vineyard was ruined, only a few parcels here and there surviving.

Some growers reacted by trying the most outlandish of remedies. Others tackled the problem by replanting more of the same grape-varieties, only to find that these vines too lasted but a few years in the face of the disease; some never even reached maturity. At least wine-making did not die out, because those who decided to replace the auxerrois with other kinds of vine made wine of some sort, though most of it hardly merited the name.

Others diversified into different crops: many ran into debt and failed. On the *causses* nothing else would grow – except the unpredictable and uncontrollable truffle. For many the lure of exotic lands overseas was irresistible, but they were to find that life in South America was just as disillusioning as life with the phylloxera, and many eventually returned embittered to their native country.

As the replacement of dead stocks with more of the same had failed, many growers took to planting American varieties, but all were unsatisfactory. The Cahors wine-makers then followed the example of other vineyards by grafting their traditional auxerrois grapes on to American rootstocks which were immune to the disease. This was a success in almost every other area where it was tried: in Cahors it failed.

The rootstock (*porte-greffe*), called rupestris, which was most generally used in the southern half of France, was naturally chosen for most Cahors. Some vines were grafted on to another stock called riparia gloire de Montpellier, mostly on the gentler slopes of the valley itself, and these were rather more successful. However the majority of vines, married to rupestris, did not succeed. The process of grafting is difficult enough on steep slopes at the best of times but rupestris has a long straggly root-formation which made grafting – the old auxerrois vines had been propagated by cuttings or layering – in this terrain even harder.

More importantly, rupestris proved too vigorous for the traditional auxerrois graft: it accentuated the vulnerability of the auxerrois to a disease called *coulure*, the effect of which was to cause the very young grapes to drop off the plants. The grafting process was, however, fully accepted as the only valid way of fighting phylloxera, so more and more growers applied it to their other traditional grape-variety, the Dame Noire or jurançon rouge. But this grape was no substitute for the auxerrois in terms of quality, so, to the extent that the Cahors vineyard survived, it was largely as a producer of a lowly *vin de pays* rather than a noble wine.

Wine-making was also kept alive, perhaps more importantly, by experimentation with Franco-American hybrid vines rather than grafting. For example, a direct cross between the auxerrois and rupestris continued to make viticulture in the Lot worthwhile, although the result could not bear comparison with the old-fashioned pre-phylloxera Cahors based on pure unblended auxerrois.

Meanwhile the replanting of the mass-producing rival vineyards of the Languedoc was an enormous success. Worse still, in the 1930s began the vast production of wine in Algeria, and much of it good wine at that, from quality vines such as carignan, grenache and cinsault, all varieties used in some of the better wines of the Midi. These wines were not only useful to the Midi to boost the quality and alcoholic content of its own rather poor stuff, but were exported direct to France, in tankers to Nantes and Rouen, feeding some of the markets which a hundred years before had been the happy hunting ground of Cahors.

The terrible frosts of 1956 and 1957 might have been expected to put paid to the wines of Cahors for ever. In 1958, the proportion of real Cahors grown in the Lot valley was as little as 1% of the total wine-production, which itself had fallen low enough. But it is strange how, throughout history, those with the inspiration or calling to defy all kinds of adversity manage to keep the flame of their faith alive. Just as the monks managed to protect the scholarship of the early Christian Church during the dark ages, so a handful of enthusiasts managed to keep real Cahors wine alive – just.

Their first task, in the face of the widespread fraud and adulteration which Cahors suffered in the early years of this century, and of the drop in quality which the adoption of inferior stocks had brought about, was to obtain the protection of the law for the name and standards of production of real Cahors. A band of the faithful obtained recognition for the name Cahors in some tentative legislation of the 1920s. In 1929 they created the Syndicat de Défense de l'Appellation d'Origine Cahors. But such was the low point from which they started that not even these enthusiasts were able to make their voices heard in Paris when the first of the appellations contrôlées were created in 1935.

The Second World War halted progress in its tracks, but in the late 1940s the movement gathered strength again. The cave co-opérative at Parnac was created in 1947, which gave great impetus to developing ways and means of re-creating the vineyards and reputation of Cahors. The grant of VDQS status in 1951 defined once and for all the geographical limits of the appellation, eventually to be repeated in the grant of full appellation contrôlée status in 1971 for forty-five communes stretching from Soturac in the west to Lamagdelaine in the east.

Following the course of the valley, the vineyard extends into the hinterland on both banks. Millions of years ago there was no river at all. The whole area formed part of a vast limestone plateau extending over the whole of Aquitaine, the fossilised bed of the ocean which formerly covered it. In remote history, internal convulsions within the earth's crust caused the Pyrenees and the Alps to burst forth, and this upheaval made the brittle limestone crack in various places. These faults gradually developed into the great rivers which now drain the plateau. The uplands which have been left behind are today called the *causses*.

The valleys created by this upheaval began to silt up with the deposits which were washed down from the mountains inland, and it is these valuable alluvial soils which now form the gently sloping terraces of the lower vineyards at Cahors. The characteristics of the soil on the *causses* and the valley are widely different, the latter relatively rich compared with the barren chalkiness of the higher ground. We have seen that this difference had a major impact when the phylloxera hit the region, and to this day the *causses* to the north of the river remain almost bare of vines. A hundred and fifty years ago the canton of Catus produced nearly a quarter of the red wine of the area; today there are only two independent producers in the canton.

Replanting on the *causses* has been almost entirely on the south side of the river in what, because of the bare chalk visible on the surface of the terrain, is called Quercy Blanc. Even before phylloxera, the wines made on the *causses* and in the valley were not as different in character as might be supposed. Each had their fierce supporters and there was keen competition to establish the supremacy of the small producers on the poor upland farms over the rich land-owners in the valley. But, as today, it was the grape-variety, the auxerrois, responding to the micro-climate of the region which could override what might elsewhere have been sharp contrasts in wine-styles between different terrains.

So the battle had been won for the protection of the name and for a legally delimited area of production. The harder task was how to re-introduce the auxerrois into an area where it had been rejected as ungrowable by most of the *vignerons*.

Here the newly born co-opérative played a vital role. The first task was to find better *porte-greffes* than the old rupestris and riparia vari-eties. An extensive programme of experiment undertaken by the cave co-opérative resulted in the selection of new hybrid *porte-greffes*. It did not take long to find out which new stocks would minimise the risk of *coulure*. In principle the auxerrois grape was quickly proved scientifi-cally viable.

The more difficult problem was how to revive the morale and moti-vation of the local producers. Over a period of hundreds of years the local auxerrois vines had undergone a process of gradual mutation so that by the middle of this century the greater part of the surviving plants were of little value for fine wine-making.

In 1955 the Parnac co-opérative discovered Monsieur Mallambic, a wine-maker near Blaye in the Gironde, who was particularly fond of the auxerrois grape. He had carefully nurtured a plantation of it in very good health on a property overlooking the Gironde estuary. Grafts were taken from these vines, and planted out in an experimental vineyard at Luzech back home in the Lot. In order to involve the Cahors growers in this experiment, a trip was organised to show them Monsieur Mallambic's model vineyard at Blaye.

Not daunted by the frosts of the mid-fifties which shrank the pro-duction of Cahors to its lowest point ever, work was put in hand to develop first-class auxerrois specimens clonally, on ground next door to the cave co-opérative. To ensure uniformity, only one kind of *porte-greffe* was used. A total of 2320 plants were created in this way, and from these have been developed slowly but surely much of the stock now used in the production of Cahors. The winning-over of local pro-ducers, conservative by nature and suspicious of scientific innovations, was the result of an extensive public relations exercise.

The prime movers in the revival of Cahors were also keen to mitigate the reputation of the district for producing black wines, or at least wines which took a very long time to mature. While retaining the dominance of the auxerrois variety, without which Cahors could never be Cahors, they obtained official sanction for the use of up to 30% of other varieties in their wines. Merlot was introduced for its roundness and fruit, as well as for its potential to produce more alcohol than the auxerrois, and tannat, a close relative of the auxerrois, for its backbone and spice. The planting of all other varieties has been phased out, and they will soon be nothing more than a memory so far as the AOC wines are concerned. Today there are still some growers who make wine with unblended auxerrois, but most have taken the opportunity to use a little of the other grapes to soften the austerities of the old-fashioned Cahors style.

At the beginning of the 1960s, Cahors was for once in luck. The revival of interest in quality wine and the buzz of excitement caused by the new research coincided with the beginning of the French economic revival. There was suddenly a demand for better quality table-wines which a wider population could afford. Indeed the *vignerons* of the Lot were caught on the hop because their meagre production was nowhere near enough to satisfy the sudden demand.

They responded with a programme of massive over-planting, over-production and over-pricing. A serious, if temporary, crisis arose in 1971, when many greedy growers decided to celebrate the grant of full appellation contrôlée to jack up the price of the wines. The market jibbed. There were then three poor years in a row, the growers were left with stocks of second-rate wine, and the prices fell back sharply again. In an effort to regulate the expansion of the vineyard, rules were introduced restricting the right to new planting in favour of young producers. This has ensured a lively, forward-looking attitude among some *vignerons* of Cahors. Over a third of the producers today are under the age of thirty-five.

Because Cahors is a *vin de garde*, producers need to carry substantial stocks . A vine takes five or six years to produce AOC quality wine. Add two years at least before it can be bottled, and already a vigneron must wait eight years for a return on his initial investment. Even then he will not, if he is wise, sell all his first vintage in case he has one or more lean years. To keep his name before the market, as well as his bank manager happy, he must always have some wine to sell. Thus, a new grower will not get his name much known until his vines have been in the ground for ten years. For this reason there are many new growers in the area whose wines are yet to become well-known. Today, many of the more famous wines still tend to come from estates where wine has been made for generations.

Take Jean Jouffreau at **Clos de Gamot (169)** for example. His wine is made exclusively from auxerrois. This is because his vineyards are some of the oldest in the region and date back to a time long before any other grape-varieties were even considered possible at Cahors. Jean really is one of the few (not more than half a dozen) who remained loyal to Cahors during the difficult years, and the story of his vineyard is witness to the struggle to keep Cahors alive. The family has been makng wine at Gamot since 1610, and Jean's great-grandmother kept a riverside auberge where she fed the boatmen who plied their trade down the Lot. After the phylloxera his great-grandfather was lucky enough to identify a *porte-greffe* called Herbemont which succeeded where the better-known kinds had failed, though he was able to afford to replant only half the previous vineyard. That was in 1885, and in 1995 Jean produced a special wine to commemorate the centenary of these now ancient vines. He told me not to open my bottles of his *cuvée centenaire* ahead of the millenium.

Gamot was typical of the local tradition of polyculture. The farmers grew a little of everything which might be needed in the family, and the surplus was sold at the local markets. Thus one hedged one's risks against bad weather; hail in this region can ruin a year's work in ten minutes, as it did for instance for some growers in 1995. After the Second World War, the family re-acquired a few more hectares of land; in the 1800's the farm had become reduced by division amongst heirs, and an opportunity arose to claw back some land for vine-growing. Higher production encouraged them to market the wine beyond their traditional customers, the local bourgeoisie and artisans. An imposing new clientèle included the three-star restaurant Lasserre in Paris and the late President Pompidou who had a home in the Lot and was no doubt an invaluable help in securing Appellation status for Cahors. He was particularly fond of Gamot 1962.

The Jouffreau family still has but 10 hectares at Gamot, but Jean won first prize in 1967 for the best VDQS wine France-wide. The great years for Gamot – and it must be remembered that many Cahors vine-yards making good wine today did not exist then – include 1947 (the first year in which 19-year-old Jean was entrusted by his father with the vinification on his own), 1959, 1964, 1971 and 1975. More recently 1978, 1982 and 1983 were all excellent. Vintages still available include the backward 1985 and 1988, the latter needing some cellarage; the more forward 1989 and the 1990 which is surprisingly precocious for the year. Tasted from the *cuve* after the first fermentation was over, the 1995 has tremendous fruit and promise.

Two bends in the river away is the **Château du Cayrou (174)**, which Jouffreau bought in 1971. His reluctance to borrow money persuaded him to fund this purchase largely through the sale of old vintages of Gamot, which he sent to auction in London. Able to put cash down for his purchase, it is said that he was able to pip to the post at least one pres-tigious competitor, who sent him a congratulatory bottle of champagne but has not spoken to him since. It is not surprising that Cayrou was much coveted, because it is one of the most beautiful buildings in a region which has more than its fair share of them. With it went 30 hectares of land, on which he planted a mix of 70% auxerrois, 20% merlot, 7% tannat and 3% jurançon rouge. The last-named has, under the rules, had to be dug up and was replaced by auxerrois. The size of investment implied in such an undertaking is vast. There is enough wire, according to Jean, to stretch from Cahors to Amsterdam. The most modern stain-less steel vats and the best Burgundian wooden *cuves* did not come cheap, even in those days. Part of his investment included the acquisition of a son-in-law, moreover one who was a fully-trained oenologist. To the traditional expertise of Jean, his wife and two daughters, Yves has been able to contribute the know-how which modern technology has given to wine-production. This splendid partnership, in which each recognizes and values the contribution which the other is able to make, symbolises in a way the renaissance of Cahors; the development and conversion of old traditions to suit modern times.

Now that the vines at this property are fully-grown, Cayrou is producing really fine wine. The *encépagement* differentiates it at once from Gamot; a little softer, quicker-maturing perhaps; the 1985 is already *à point*, while the Gamot of the same year has some way to go. The bouquet and flavour suggest strongly blackcurrants and prunes and the finish is very long. At both properties the production of the grapes is ultra-traditional. No chemical fertilisers are used, the vineyards are hoed regularly by hand, a labour which they keep in the family. Jean says that one hoeing is worth two heavy showers. Roses are planted at the end of each row, not, as I thought until Yves disabused me of the idea, to encourage the bees, but to keep off the *mildiou*. All picking is done by hand; the family believes that the clumsiness of the indiscriminate machine requires too much chemical over-correction of the juice. Jean says that his 'green' approach to viticulture enables him to bring in his auxerrois at a regular 12 degrees, while other growers have only too often to resort to chaptalisation. If the viticulture is classic, the vinification is modern, although no new wood is used at either property.

There is nothing stick-in-the-mud about the Jouffreau family. Their latest venture is to re-create a *caussenard* vineyard, overgrown for over 100 years, but where it is believed that some of the best Cahors was once made. For this purpose the family has developed clones from their very oldest Gamot vines and planted them on almost vertical slopes facing directly into the mid-day sun. A first trial wine was made in tiny quantities in 1995 and the Jouffreaus are over the moon about the potential for this vineyard, which they call Clos St. Jean.

Although many of Jean's older vintages were sold off to help pay for Cayrou, he still has his precious 'museum' where he keeps wines going back to before the phylloxera. These are his pride and joy, and he bestows on them the kind of affection which others reserve for their vintage cars. Malicious gossips have been known to challenge the authenticity of these amazing wines, but those who are fortunate enough to have tasted them require no convincing. If confirmation were needed of their quality, it was amply in evidence at a London tasting in 1995 of Gamot wines ranging from 1988 back to 1893, the older vintages being those bottled for the London auction nearly twenty-five years previously.

Jean needs of course to top up with wines of the same year the old casks in which these wines are still kept to prevent them from oxidizing. But he was keen to point out that this was not at all the same as another Cahors tradition called *perpétuelles*, which is rather like the Spanish solera system of sherry-making. A barrel is started with the vintage of a given year, perhaps a specially fine vintage, or a date to commemorate an important family event. After a few years of ageing in the wood, part of the wine, perhaps a quarter or a fifth, will be drawn off and bottled, its place being taken with wine of a more recent vintage of quality. Each year thereafter the process is repeated, hence the name *perpétuelle*. These wines have all the advantages and disadvantages of a blend, but wine from a really old *perpétuelle* is only poured for special family occasions. Sometimes rather oxidized, such a wine nevertheless goes well with the hearty food of the region.

Clos la Coutale (56) is another very old-established property; it has been in the Bernède family since before the Revolution. The family was winning medals in Paris when the Concours Générale was only in its third year, 1894. Philippe Bernède has modern plant, including temperature-controlled steel tanks, but does not use any new wood. The wine is matured in typical 225-litre casks for up to two years. Coutale also produces a small amount of white wine called Valmy, after the great victory of the Revolutionary armies at which no fewer than three Bernède brothers fought. The average age of the vines at this property is well over twenty years – perhaps this explains the round charm of the red wine. Certainly it seems to mature relatively quickly, though the style of the wine is by no means 'modern'. The colour is deep, and there is some toast on the nose. Big and powerful on the palate, it is quite fat with hints of liquorice. The finish is long and silky and the overall balance is good. This is a wine which often excels in lighter years, such as 1987 and 1992. Sadly, Coutale made little or no wine in 1995, because of the disastrous hail which hit parts of the western end of the Cahors vineyards during the first weekend of July, causing damage which may well reduce the crop for 1996 also.

Clos la Coutale is just in front of the rising ground to the south of Vire-sur-Lot, and the Bernèdes have a cluster of good wine-makers as neighbours; including the Durou family at **Château de Gaudou (58)**, where the wine is often spicy and peppery. Durou père is the mayor of the village of Vire. Until the revival of the Cahors vineyards in the 1960's, the family had to rely on other crops to eke out a living, growing lavender which they sent to Grasse and keeping cattle too. In recent years they have concentrated on wine, expanding the vineyards to their present 20 hectares. Like the Bernèdes, Durou fils, who has now taken over the running of the property, makes a little white wine too.

Other growers in this centre of excellence include Pascal and Jean-Marc Verhaeghe who have taken over the vineyards at **Château du Cèdre (68)** from their Flemish father. Ask any wine-maker in the area which other growers they respect, and almost all will instantly say Verhaeghe. The family has a manageable 25-hectare vineyard, planted with 80% auxerrois and 10% each of the other permitted varieties. Their mainstream wine is 90% auxerrois and 10% merlot, given a *cuvaison* of 17 to 18 days at a temperature of 30 degrees and then matured in old *foudres* for 16 months or so. Then there is their prestige wine, in which the merlot is replaced by the tannat, which may be given as much as

28 or even 30 days before being transferred to new oak, where the second malolactic fermentation takes place. It remains in the wood for up to 20 months. This is another property to have been devastated by the hail in 1995, which is very sad because it has to be numbered among the four or five best in Cahors.

A stone's throw away from these vineyards are two more properties of the first rank. **Domaine de la Pineraie (74)** is presided over by the jolly Robert Burc. His family have switched most of their attention to wine-production which they bottle at the domaine, although in the depressed days of the 1930's they did manage to find a market for their wine in barrel in Paris. Monsieur Burc is not a fan of the tannat grape, but he is devoted to the auxerrois, which represents a high 90% of his vines. He makes two wines, one from his vines on the lower slopes of the valley which he calls Pierre Sèche. The wine which you will come across in the region however is named after the Domaine, made from vines on the ground sloping upwards towards the *causse.* This is an altogether different proposition, a much tougher wine which needs bottle-age. The wine is aged in oak *barriques,* about a quarter of which are new each year, and the wood shows on the nose when the wine is young. His 1988 won a gold medal in Paris, a fine bright wine, the fruit masked on the nose by the wood, but wonderful on the palate.

His neighbour is Claude Vidal, whose great-grandfather bought **Château La Reyne (85)** in the 1860's, just before the phylloxera. Despite that disaster, the family persisted in making real Cahors without a break, so today some of the vines are 80 years old. There are twenty hectares, mainly devoted to auxerrois. Monsieur Vidal prefers concrete for *élevage*, but plans to change over to stainless steel for his vinification. He has in his private collection old bottles going back to 1865. Like the Burcs at Pineraie, the vines start on lower ground and rise gradually towards the *causse.* To even out any differences in the wine produced, the grapes from lower down are vinified a bit longer than the others. Vidal has 100 new *barriques* and some of his wine is raised in this new oak, the rest in cement for 14 months. Harvesting is by hand and all the grapes are hand-sorted before they go into the press. The wines of La Reyne are very high-class indeed and age magnificently in bottle. Monsieur Vidal gave me a bottle of his 1977 to take home, and after 18 years it was still full of fresh fruit and vigour.

In the hills above Albas, the brothers Jean and Claude Couture form what is becoming quite a common duo in the vineyards of South-West France. Claude looks after the vineyards and Jean makes the wine from their 25 hectares at **Domaine Eugénie (100)**, one of the most respected of the Cahors estates. The vines are on varying heights of ground so there are three distinct styles of wine. The premium wine is the Cuvée Réserve de l'Aïeul, which comes from the middle ground, so often the best, as in Burgundy for example. In a good year this can spend up to two and a half years in old wood, although there are always a few new barrels in which wine is allowed a short stay of up to three months. This very fine Cahors is made from 100% auxerrois, an applaudable reversion to traditional practice. Even the two other wines, called Etiquette Noire and the rather dearer Cuvée des Tsars, have 90% and 80% auxerrois respectively. The complement is in the first case all tannat, and in the second merlot. The Cuvée des Tsars also shows the influence of wood. This wine and the Réserve de l'Aïeul are both keepers, although the 1991 has developed quickly.

Another wine which ages well is that made by the Resses family at **Château la Caminade (125)**, which is at Parnac and on the doorstep of the Co-opérative. Up to the time of the revolution, this was a presbytery which housed several monks, and its quaint towers and covered gallery are typical of the Quercy architecture of former times. This is another property which flew the flag of real Cahors before 1960, and the Resses were founder-members of the Syndicat de Défense du Vin de Cahors. There are 33 hectares under vine, with a conventional 70% auxerrois content. As with some other Cahors there is plenty of pepper and spice on the bouquet of this wine: it is well-built and made to last. The premium wine, which is nowadays oaked, is called Clos du Commendery. Whether or not you prefer this to the unoaked wine of the property is a matter of taste, and either way you will not be disappointed. Cahors is a big enough wine to suffer marriage with new wood, and Le Commendery is a perfect example of this new fashionable style. Many properties are now developing the twin track of oaked and non-oaked wines, the former selling always for a premium price. Caminade also makes a second wine called Château Peyrouse.

Having discussed some of the Cahors veterans, it is time to meet some newcomers to the region. In the 1980's an American couple, Stephen and Sherry Schechter from New York bought up the **Château de Pech de Jammes (4)** which is up on the causse not far from Haute-Serre. The property had belonged to a prominent politician who was not interested in the vineyard, and was leased out on a *contrat de fermage* to the Vigouroux firm whom we will meet anon. The Schechters inherited this contract to which they negotiated some variations entitling them to market their own wine in English-speaking countries.

Pech de Jammes is, like the Vigouroux' Haute-Serre, on very stoney ground, high up on the *causse*. Small compared with its neighbour, it extends to only 9 or 10 hectares, enclosed within a dry stone wall typical of the region (where such walls are called *cayrous*). The Schechters have restored the very pretty château in the form of a chartreuse, which itself replaced an earlier building which had associations with Henri IV before it was destroyed during wars a hundred years later. The present buildings date from the latter part of the eighteenth century.

The *encépagement* at Pech de Jammes includes only 5% tannat, as at Haute-Serre, perhaps because the vines on the *causse* tend to mature later than those in the valley, and the tannat is a late-maturing variety anyway. Auxerrois accounts for 80% and merlot the remainder. As at Tertre-Rôteboeuf in St. Emilion, and Quarts de Chaume in the Loire, the Pech de Jammes vineyard sits in a natural south-facing amphitheatre which gives it maximum exposure to the late autumn sun and the warm south-east wind. These factors are said to account for the particularly tough structure of the wine and its full and generous character. There is a real middle to the wine which gives it perfect balance. Old wood, not new, is used to mature the wine for 18 months before it is bottled. The wine is then kept for a similar period in bottle before sale, when it is said to be mature. However the longer it is kept the better. The 1986 was showing very well in 1992 and suggested room for even further improvement. The 1988 at the same period obviously had a long life ahead of it, though even then displaying much charm. Even better than either of these is the 1990, which five years later showed huge promise of being ready just in time to usher in the next century. The colour of these wines is deep, the bouquet strongly suggests red fruits and grows in intensity with age, and the fanciful can also detect the scent of truffle, characteristic of the *causse* where it is made. Pech de Jammes is undoubtedly one of the best Cahors.

The Schechters are not the only Anglo-Saxons making Cahors wine. In the south-western corner of the appellation, and on a remote part of the *causse* near Mauroux, Colin and Penelope Duns acquired the small **Château Latuc (50)** in the late 1980's. Disillusioned by the poor prospects for his chosen profession, architecture, in Britain, Colin decided to make a complete break. He was lucky on two accounts: the vineyard was already fully planted, so he had neither the expense of starting from scratch nor the costly and frustrating time-lag between planting and production; also his first vintage was the magnificent 1990. The Duns were well-placed to exploit the custom of the many British expatriates who have settled in the Lot, and also to help finance his operation by taking in 'partners' who were willing to 'rent' a row or two of vines and thus assure themselves of a regular supply of Latuc. The Duns make two styles of wine, following the example becoming more and more general in the area; a *tradition* wine and an oaked *prestige* wine. If I express a preference for the former, it is because of my slight bias against new wood. An interesting novelty of presentation is that the prestige wine is available in 50 centilitre bottles at the same price as the full-sized traditional wine. The new bottles are so designed (they are tall and thin) that they can be packed alongside the normal 75 centilitre size. Good marketing you may say, and, yes, the Duns are good at promotion; they have to be, in an area where they have to fight hard to prove that that you do not have to be French to make good Cahors. And good Cahors it is: they thoroughly deserve their success in getting it into restaurants alongside well-established but not necessarily superior names.

Cahors seems to attract a wide variety of punters; none more enthusiastic than Alain Senderens, the celebrated chef at the Lucas-Carton restaurant in Paris. In 1991, Senderens bought, apparently on the spur of the moment, but not without first sounding out local expert opinion, the 30-hectare estate and the dilapidated buildings at **Château de**

Gautoul (175) just across the river from Puy l'Evêque. His priority was naturally to get the kitchen right, but now that that has been done he has turned his attention to the vineyards. Like the other rich investors in Cahors whom we shall meet presently, he has built a magnificent subterranean winery; he has his own resident oenologist, but also consults with other experts in the field. It is perhaps unfair to judge his efforts by his first two vintages, 1992 which was notoriously wet and difficult, and 1993 which was also brought in in far from ideal conditions. Is it also unfair to regret the fancy bottles in which he markets his prestige cuvée? Just let it be said that, on present showing, he has some way to go to bring the quality of his wines up to the level of his cooking.

More modest newcomers are the family who have taken over a small *caussenard* vineyard on the right bank near St. Médard-de-Catus, an area virtually abandoned by wine-makers after the phylloxera. The property is called **Manoir du Rouerguou (206)**, the name deriving from the safe haven given there to emigrés from the Rouergue at the time of the religious wars. The pretty manor house is being sympathetically restored; so are the vineyards. At present they are limited to 4 hectares, all planted with auxerrois, but the owners have planting rights which will enable them to have some merlot as well. Their wine is absolutely honest Cahors, and I can think of no other which displays better the bare taste of the grape from which it is made. It is unpretentious and has little complexity or sophistication, but that is no criticism. The property should have a good future.

Before turning to some of the bigger and better-known producers, there are three small growers on the left bank causse who are making very good wine. The **Domaine des Savarines (5)** lies just off the road from Cahors to Tournon, barely five miles as the crow flies from Cahors itself. It was bought by Danielle Biesbrouck back in 1970 when she planted 4 hectares on this barren ground. Although she was helped by experts, she admits to having had no knowledge or experience previously of growing grapes or of making wine. By 1978 she was already developing a discerning clientele, especially local restaurants. Instead of tannat, Madame Biesbrouck chose to plant some of the despised jurançon noir, which she has probably been obliged to root up by now. The soil is such that, particularly in the absence of any tannat in the mix, the fermentation period is only 12 days. On the other hand the wine spends at least a year in old wood, and the result is a supple, perfumed wine with enough tannins to require some ageing.

The fact that wines from *causse*-grown vines differ so little nowadays from the wines grown nearer the river leads one to think that it is not the terrain (widely different as it is from part of the region to another) which gives Cahors its *typicité*, but a combination of the micro-climate and the auxerrois grape, with its tendency to ripen late. The character of the auxerrois, though distinctive, is hard to describe. Often spicey and peppery on the nose, the flavour in the mouth sometimes reminds me of cherries or damsons with a touch of almonds.

The climate has an all-important part to play. The *causse* and the valley alike benefit from the late autumn weather which is so often fine and warm, with the auxerrois rarely ready to harvest before October 1st. The Cahors vineyards often avoid the rainfall which arrives in Bordeaux after the conclusion of the vintage there, as well as the autumn rains of the Mediterranean. In Indian summers, the auxerrois comes into its own and is able to thrive both on the stoney soil of the *causses* and on the richer alluvial deposits on the valley terraces.

Compare, for example, two quite different wines, both in the top flight: first the **Domaine de Paillas (43)**, grown at Floressas on one of the remoter vineyards of the *causse*, and incidentally another victim of the 1995 hail. For all its plummy colour and its slightly closed-up nose when young, the 1989, a year generally regarded as one of the best of recent vintages, was lightish. This is a *causse* wine which seems to be asking to be drunk young, though none the worse for that.

Contrast this with **Château Les Ifs (90)** at Pescadoires, where the vines almost have their feet in the river. It is (again in 1989) thicker in texture and fruitier in flavour, with more than a hint of cherries. The tannins too suggest more of a *causse* style of wine. The 1990 was a medal-winner at Macon, and this property deserves the success which it is making for itself.

Another quick-developing *caussenard* wine is made at the **Château** in the small village of **Lacapelle-Cabanac (46)**. The traditionally-flavoured wine of Alex Denjean was unearthed by Madame Miquel who maintains one of the best cellars in the region at the family hotel in Najac. A lady sommelier is somewhat unusual in the backwoods of the Aveyron, but Madame Miquel trained for a while with Georges Albert Aoust, the Burgundian oenologist who has helped so many restaurateurs build good cellars. Madame Miquel thinks so well of Lacapelle-Cabanac that she and Denjean have designed a personalised label for the hotel. The wine is bright and deep, quite drinkable a mere three years after the vintage. It has a good plummy nose and soft tannins for a *causse* wine; a very attractive bottle, probably not worth long keeping, but well made and ideal for a restaurant with a quick turnover.

Just to prove that there are still real country-style wines being made up on this causse, Gérard Decas makes a splendid example at his **Domaine de Trespoux-Rassiels (7)**. This is a really dark wine, and Decas does not need or use much tannat to give structure. It goes admirably with the winter stews of the region. He reckons the wine needs five years to prove its potential. Similar in style, but made from 100% auxerrois, is the wine made by Jean-Jacques Bousquet from his vines at Villesèque. He calls this **Domaine de la Garde (205)** . The *chais* is outside the Cahors appellation area, and Bousquet makes there an excellent vin de pays des Côteaux de Quercy.

Château de Bonnecoste is not a Cahors property at all, because it is well outside the AOC area up on the *causse* near Rocamadour. It is noteworthy because of its legendary reputation in earlier years for producing a one-off wine of old-fashioned splendour. Today the law prevents it from calling itself Cahors, and from being sold otherwise than a *vin de table*. It can be bought at the château, whose remote situation is well worth the detour. It can also be found in local restaurants.

Although there are today about 200 independent makers of Cahors, 45% of the total production is in the hands of the powerful Co-opérative at Parnac, a small village a few miles downstream from Cahors on the left bank. It has about 400 members. Among the wines which the Co-opérative makes and bottles for its members are some which are sold under the grower's name. Despite its important role in re-establishing Cahors, the Co-opérative is finding that its more adventurous members cannot resist the challenge of going their own way. The Queen of Denmark, who must surely have been the only reigning monarch to belong to a co-operative, has now built an elaborate *chais* of her own at her magnificent property the **Château de Caïx (151)**. Jean-Baptiste de Monpezat, the Queen's brother-in-law, is now also making wine under the tutelage of Georges Vigouroux at **Château Léret-Monpezat (101)**. Alain-Dominique Perrin had always intended to be his own wine-maker at the expensively-restored **Château de Lagrézette (147)**, where his premium wine is now being made, although the Co-opérative still makes some wine for him, as we shall see. Perrin is the Managing Director of the world-famous jewellers, Cartier. He did not come to Cahors in search of the black diamonds of the Quercy, but the Syndicat of growers clearly thought that his redoubtable skills at marketing would stand them and the appellation in good stead. After some polite resistance on his part, he was eventually made President of the Confrérie des Vins de Cahors. He it was who founded 'Les Seigneurs du Cahors', a group of prosperous and influential growers. Because this suggested a superior classification within the appellation, the title of the group had subtly to be changed by dropping the word '*du*'.

Lagrézette is an elegant renaissance château, now the country home of the Perrins. Originally it was built by rich bankers from Cahors, at a time when the town was an important financial centre. Since 1980 the Perrins have spent huge sums on restoring it and reconstituting the vineyard, which also has a history going back a long way. The *encépagement* includes 25% merlot, which is surprising because one would expect a softer style of wine. When it was made by the co-opérative, which Perrin endowed with new wood for the purpose, I was disappointed by the result which seemed mean and rather sour, short on fruit. Now that Perrin has completed his own magnificent winery, temperature- and computer-controlled, and engaged the services of a distinguished consultant oenologist, one will see whether the quality of the wine improves, but, as one grower said to me, 'you can't make good wine simply by throwing a cheque-book at it'.

Perrin's fellow-Seigneurs include three *négociants* who are among the most powerful in the South-West. The role of *négociant* is that of a combined wholesaler and distributor; his services are thus vital to growers, especially the smaller ones. Perhaps it was inevitable that, when the Cahors renaissance took the wine-market by surprise in the 1960's, the *négociants* would decide to become growers as well; with ready-made markets, they were ideally placed to jump one step ahead of the established vignerons.

Moreover their ready access to the media, fully exploited by Perrin, enabled them to create the cult of Cahors Nouveau, *fringant* as it is often called, and to spread the gospel that Cahors was no longer a wine which needed ageing, that it could be drunk young, and that that was the way which the growers were going to make it from then on.

This has created a political rift in Cahors, which is going through an unfriendly patch, aggravated by the failure of the dealers and the co-opérative to pay growers more than 7 or 8 francs a litre for their product. The older growers resent the newcomers, many of whom have never sat on a tractor, pruned a vine or picked a grape and who, with their smart packaging and advertising techniques, are able to sell their wines – and not always very good ones – in bottle at the door for up to ten times the price.

But what are their wines like? Georges Vigouroux is the biggest name in the region. In 1970 he acquired and restored the **Château de Haute-Serre (1)**, on the *causse* to the south-east of Cahors. It boasts the highest altitude of any property within the appellation. Haute-Serre has 62 hectares of vines, all grouped round the château in one holding. It was one of the earliest properties to fall victim to the phylloxera and was totally abandoned thereafter. Vigouroux was one of the first to replant on the *causse* and he started with the determination to make Cahors as it used to be in the last century. He spent a fortune fitting out the *chais* with ultra-modern equipment. The wine, matured without new oak, is well-made and supple. It is 'commercial' in the sense that it has plenty of ripe fruit and develops fairly quickly. The colour is not as deep as some, but the wine is always flavoursome and usually well-balanced. The tendency however has been over the last few years to go for a more generalized style, to the point where its identity as Cahors is getting lost. 1990 was perhaps its last good recent year. 1995 will show whether the house-style has indeed changed.

The best that can be said about the *nouveau*-style wine of this property is that it has more character than any others, which may be damning it with faint praise. Its name is liable to change from year to year.

The same remarks apply to the wines of **Château de Mercuès (142)**, the famous local landmark which dominates the Lot valley and is well-known from its many appearances on postcards and in tourist-books. Many years ago it was converted into a luxury hotel, and was then bought by Vigouroux in the 1980's. While continuing the hotel business, Vigouroux also replanted the vineyards from which once upon a time the bishops and counts of Cahors supplied the courts of Europe. There are 30 hectares of vines surrounding the château, 75% auxerrois, 20% merlot and 5% tannat. The first vintage to be commercialized was the 1987, and in a poor year its debut heralded great promise. This was not maintained after 1990, later wines having lost the grip of true Cahors, and sometimes being rather over-perfumed.

The Rigal brothers outdo the Vigouroux in one respect : they have three vineyards to the Vigouroux' two; **Château St.Didier (127)** near Parnac, where the wines of all three are made, **Prieuré de Cénac (127)** and **Château de Grézels (88)**. St. Didier is by far the biggest of these, having 70 hectares of vines just down the road from the co-opérative, and facing the Royal Danish property across the valley. I used to find this a rather hard and austere wine, no matter how long one kept it, but it has improved very much in recent years. There is also a Prestige Wine called 'Apogée' which would have a wonderful Cahors character, being from 100% auxerrois, if the fruit were not so heavily masked by new wood. The wine from Prieuré de Cénac is to my mind much to be preferred. This property, up on the *causse* on the left bank of the river above Albas used to be the home of oenologically-minded monks for whom the phylloxera was almost as potent an adversary as the devil. The Rigals bought it in 1979 and have gradually established it as a leading growth of the region. Being 80% auxerrois, it has authenticity, but it is supple for a *causse* wine all the same. It used to be more sophisticated and international in style, but the Rigals are going now for rather more local character.

The wine from the Château de Grézels, the most recent of the Rigal family aquisitions, I like the least. The property dominates the village of the same name where there used to be a small wine port. Medieval in origin, it owes its present appearance to a restoration in 1600. The first vintage here, as at Mercuès, was in 1987, but up until now at least the wine has been flabby and somewhat unstructured.

The Rigals seem now to be concentrating more and more on their role as vignerons, having hived off at least part of their business as *négociants*. But their name is still associated with a number of growers who do not belong to the Co-opérative. In the spring after the vintage, you can sometimes find the Rigal travelling bottling-plant at the *chais* of smaller producers.

The third *négociant* to have branched out into wine-making is Marc Delgoulet from Brive who bought the **Château de Chambert (42)** and replanted its vineyards up on the *causse* near Floressas. There are 55 hectares of vines on the most rugged of ground, almost all on one single plot round the château which dominates the undulating and barren countryside. No machines are allowed here; perhaps they would not be viable. Maintenance is by the plough. There are no chemical weedkillers or fertilisers either, only manure and compost. The grapes are not only picked and sorted by hand, but destalked also. Would that all this virtue received a just reward; the benefits are submerged in over-oaking. The wine is expensive to boot, but there is a cheaper second wine called Domaine des Hauts de Chambert, not exactly given away but more approachable.

Even further to the south, in the part of the country which is so chalky that they call it Quercy Blanc, are a pair of unexpected châteaux, joined together in a sort of corporate association which the French call a Société Civile. **Château Quattre (22)** was bought in 1974 by Monsieur and Madame Heilbronner, and the nearby **Château Treilles (22)** in 1980 by Monsieur and Madame de Portes. Each property has 18¹/₂ hectares of vines, planted in 1976 and 1980 respectively. Quattre has more auxerrois than Treilles, though the wines are similar in style; supple, fruity, with some elegance but somewhat in a modern style, intended for quick development rather than long ageing. The combination of the terrain and the low yield from it would lead one to expect a great deal more concentration. Whether these properties may be about to go their own way is not clear, but Quattre has left the Seigneurs, while Treilles is still one of them. Quattre makes a second wine called Domaine de Guingal, available for a time in UK supermarkets.

Clos Triguedina (70) is another property to have left the Seigneurs. Jean Baldès and his family have been making wine here since 1830 and are among the few to have persisted with real Cahors through its dark ages after the phylloxera. The vineyard enjoys a micro-climate which protected it from the worst of the frost in 1956, so to this day the estate, which covers 40 hectares of prime terrace site on the south bank near Puy l'Evêque, boasts a quantity of old vines. The overall *encépagement* is 70% auxerrois, 20% merlot and 10% tannat.

In addition to its mainstream wine, there is also a wine called Château Labrande and a premium wine under the name Prince Probus. All the wines share a bright, deep garnet colour, with a spicy nose, earthy too, reminiscent of mushrooms and dead leaves.

This property is among the most widely admired in Cahors, though I must say that my own experience has been mixed. I found that a range of their wines in several vintages, tasted at the Wine Society in 1992 were over-oaked, and the fruit was tending to dry out before the tannins had resolved themselves. On the other hand their mainstream 1990, tasted in a local restaurant, was sheer delight. I would not dispute the high ranking which Triguedina enjoys among Cahors enthusiasts.

M. le Comte André de Monpezat, the octogenarian father of Jean-Baptiste, has remained loyal to the co-opérative which he helped to found. His wine from **Château de Cayrou-Monpezat (99)** is, fittingly, more traditional in style than that of many others of his fellow Seigneurs. Noted for its peppery spice, the wine keeps well. The Comte has also generously lent his name to one of the co-opérative's better blends.

One wonders how he views the way in which Cahors has developed since the early days of its rebirth. Having set off down the road of re-creating a wine true to its *terroir* and the auxerrois grape, might he be concerned that the best growers, fighting hard to get their products into the market, are sometimes having to accept prices which belie the quality of their wines; while the great and the good, who seemingly dominate the market, are gradually changing the perceived character of the wine?

The critics of the big operators are right in regarding Cahors Nouveau, by whatever name called, as a heresy ; the auxerrois grape is incapable of producing a wine of that style which is true to its nature. The old 'black' wine is dead, but it is not necessary to go to the extreme of a *vin de l'année* to prove it. In other appellations, the best growers have emerged by merit; they are products of their *terroir*. In Cahors, the men from outside have taken over their role. The *négociants*, the managing directors and the restaurateurs may not surprise us by putting profit before authenticity, but they do not deserve to be excused. For them, wine-making is a business; for the dedicated wine-grower it is a way of life.

All the same, there are splendid wines being made in Cahors. It is inevitable that one day, with over 200 independent producers, a classification will be devised for the appellation. Here two dangers have to be faced; the powerful will be in a position to bring heavy influence to bear in their own favour; there are some names which the authorities will find difficult to exclude, whatever place they may deserve. Secondly, and perhaps more importantly in the long term, classifications in other appellations have so often been based on soil-analysis. In Cahors there is a wide divergence of soil-types, good wines coming from all kinds of ground. There is only one way to ensure that the best wines get the recognition they deserve; classification should be based on the wine in the bottle, and this means a system of rolling assessment, based on regular, blind and strictly independent tasting.

VIN DE PAYS DES CÔTEAUX DU QUERCY

The département of the Lot is not the whole of the old province of Quercy: for some reason, the post-revolutionary reform of French local government hived off the southern half of the province and concocted a strangely disunified area today called Tarn-et-Garonne. In both départements there is now made a *vin de pays* called Côteaux du Quercy.

Some of this comes from the Cahors AOC area, perhaps as one way of using de-classified Cahors produced in excess of the permitted quantity. Some growers find it a good way of using the wine from grape-varieties which are no longer permitted under AOC rules, such as jurançon rouge and syrah. Just as the French farmer cannot bear to throw anything away, so the wine-maker cannot bear to tear up producing vine-stocks if they can be made to earn a living for him. Some of the better wines also include auxerrois and tannat in their make-up.

Beyond the Cahors area itself, Côteaux du Quercy is to be found principally in a centre of production based on Castelnau-Montratier and Montpézat-du-Quercy. These old villages lie just over the southern edge of the Cahors boundary, and the latter has a cave co-opérative of small local growers. There is also an important centre of production at the co-opérative at La Ville-Dieu-du-Temple just to the west of Montauban. The work of this Cave is considered in the chapter on the wines of Toulouse (pages 129–30). Lavilledieu is a VDQS in its own right, but the Côteaux du Quercy from its co-opérative is the best of several *vins de pays* which it also makes.

As the price of AOC and VDQS wines increases there is a growing market for *vins de pays* such as Côteaux du Quercy. In the market they fill a gap which suits the *petite bourgeoisie* and the farmers who no longer produce their own wines. At their best these wines are extremely good value for money. The variation in quality is, however, substantial. They are something like a rustic version of Cahors, but since the vinification periods are always shorter, the wines are quicker to mature and less tannic. As a rule it is better to look out for wines which are not simply the second, third or fourth wines of an appellation vineyard, but are the first wine of a smaller country grower or a mini co-opérative.

In a rapidly developing field, I would pick out in particular the **Domaine d'Ariès**, near Puylaroque, where Pierre Belon ages his best wine – called Marquis des Vignes – in oak and manages a heady $12^{1}/_{2}°$ of alcohol. The bouquet is modest, but lightly perfumed. On the palate the wine shows good soft red-fruit flavours.

Other properties whose wines you are likely to find marketed locally include **Domaine de la Garde** and **Domaine de Lafage**.

A fair example of the co-opérative at **Montpézat** is the wine called Bessey de Boissy, 'Tradition'. The wine is dark, with little bouquet, but it is big, fruity and rustic in the mouth. Technically well made, the wine has good cabernet franc character, considerable impact and is at least not pretending to be a Cahors. It ages well too.

The Côteaux du Quercy produced by the négociants Vigouroux is good quality: it is also easy to find in shops and restaurants. By comparison, another blend from the Chais de la Barbacane in the town of Cahors is dull and smacks of a rather poor de-classified Cahors.

Côteaux du Quercy looks set for promotion to VDRS status in 1997.

VIN DE PAYS DE THÉZAC-PERRICARD

The present boundaries of the Cahors AOC were set just after the Second World War. It no doubt seemed administratively convenient to draw the line along the western boundary which separates the département of the Lot from its neighbour Lot-et-Garonne.

It is a fair bet that nobody at the time ever envisaged the possibility of replanting vines on the *causse* to the west of the delimited Cahors region, but in the days before phylloxera the wine of Cahors was not necessarily confined to the département of the Lot.

The small village of Thézac lies only one kilometre beyond the boundary, and the even smaller community of Perricard is only walking distance away to the west. In 1980, a group of local enthusiasts, well aware that the law would not allow them ever to grow vines and sell their produce under the name of Cahors, nevertheless examined the possibility of re-creating in this tiny area on the *causse* a vineyard with its own character. The terrain is arid indeed: there is very little soil as such, the ground consisting almost entirely of pebbles, flint and rock. As shown in similar conditions at Châteauneuf-du-Pape, the vine can thrive. No doubt the excellent suitability of the terrain explains why, a hundred years ago and more, very good Cahors indeed was being made at Thézac. The village is, after all, only four miles or so from Mauroux, which is home to some excellent Cahors-growers.

No doubt encouraged by the successful renaissance of Cahors, the would-be *vignerons* of Thézac set about re-creating the vineyard from scratch. They had to bring in powerful mechanical diggers to break up the stone so that space was made for the penetration of the vine-roots. The stones brought to the surface were broken up and cleaned, then young stocks were planted between the rows of these stones. In this way the roots were able to find the coolness of the small amount of soil beneath the ground, while the stone on the surface reflected the heat of the sun on to the grapes, providing excellent ripening conditions.

Marcel Calmette runs the front-of-house operation for what has now become an organised group of wine-growers, the **Vignerons de Thézac-Perricard.** He explained that it was necessary for an operation so close to Cahors to create its own image in the market-place. It was decided, therefore, not to make a virtue out of long ageing, but to make a lighter style of wine, which could be marketed young, but which had a *goût du terroir* deriving from the soil. They therefore adopted the traditional auxerrois, softened it with 20% merlot, and did not bother with tannat at all.

The wines are not vinified at Thézac but are made at the cave co-opérative at Goulens, just south of Agen, and the standard is remarkably high. The result of the Cave's efforts is brought back to Thézac where it is matured by the growers. They have built an attractive tasting- and sales-room in the middle of nowhere on the road D151 between Tournon and Puy-l'Evêque, where passers-by can stop and taste the wines.

Thézac-Perricard comes in two qualities: the first, called Tradition, is the basic product of the group, while its best barrels go to make a pre-mium wine called Bouquet. As may be guessed, the second aims higher, but both have a lively colour, clean nose and the characteristic scent of the auxerrois. The Bouquet wine is more flowery on the nose and has rather more finesse. In good years, such as 1988, they mature some of their best wine in oak, which not surprisingly gives it the characteristic vanillin quality that new wood brings, as well as a firmer structure.

Calmette has recently introduced another label under the title of

Domaine de Plaisance. Otherwise, looking for a name under which to market these wines, which when first made were entitled only to the lowly appellation of *vins de pays de l'agenais*, Maurice Calmette lighted on the happy title of Vin du Tsar. While reflecting and reviving the long Russian connection with the wines of the Lot valley, he has allowed two different explanations for the name to circulate. Quite possibly both are true.

The first, the official one, is that the renown of the wines of Thézac came to the notice of Napoléon III, and the French president Fallières. The latter, said to have been a fervent enthusiast for the gastronomy of South-West France, made a habit of offering the wine of Thézac-Perricard to his guests, and among others the Tsar Nicholas II. The latter, said to have been enchanted by the wine poured for him, immediately ordered a thousand bottles for a family celebration back in Moscow. However, Monsieur Pouzet, the grower who had produced the wine for the Paris banquet, was unable to satisfy this order and was constrained to inform the Tsar that his stock was exhausted.

Whatever the truth of this story, it is nevertheless undoubted that the wines of Thézac-Perricard won silver and gold medals at the time of the *belle époque*.

The second explanation of the title was offered me by Monsieur Laurent-Labourel, the patron of La Bonne Auberge at nearby Tournon d'Agenais, where I first tasted Vin du Tsar. According to him, the title was created by some White Russian would-be restaurateurs in Paris for their house-wine, which they were to buy from the *vignerons* de Thézac-Perricard. Unfortunately the restaurant went bankrupt before it opened and the wine-makers were left with a lot of stock on their hands labelled Vin du Tsar, and the name stuck. They also make a rosé which they market under the name Rosé des Pierres.

Thézac-Perricard was granted its own independent status as a *vin de pays* in April 1988. After the collapse of the Communist régime in Russia, the dynamic growers re-opened trading links with Russia direct, where they dispatched in 1991 the thousand bottles which Monsieur Pouzet had been unable to supply to the Tsar a hundred years earlier. It is to be hoped that the growers were paid for them – in French francs.

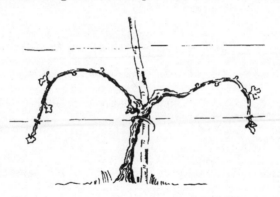

PRODUCERS

CAHORS

A second (exceptional) asterisk denotes wines which should head any classification of the wines of Cahors. The letter 'L' denotes those wines which travellers are likely to find in the shops and restaurants of the locality.

123.L.   GROUPEMENT DES PRODUCTEURS LES CÔTES
         D'OLT (CAVE CO-OPÉRATIVE DE PARNAC) 46140 Parnac
         Tel: 65-30-71-86.

47.   GAEC Tauriol, **Domaine les Acacias**, La Chambre, 46700 Lacapelle-
         Cabanac. Tel: 65-36-51-91

14.   René Couaillac, **Domaine d'Alary, Alary**, 46140 Cambayrac.
         Tel: 65-36-92-42

167.   Jacques Foissac, **Domaine des Albizzias**, Labrousse, 46220 Prayssac,
         Tel: 65-30-62-93

55.   Jeannette Alis, **Château Albret**, Les Bréziers, 46700 Vire.
         Tel: 65-36-54-71

195.   Ass. Ferme Expérimentale. **Château d'Anglars**, 46140 Anglars-Juillac.
         Tel: 65-36-28-93.

72.   *Philippe Bessières, **Domaine de L'Antenet**, Courbenac, 46700 Puy
         l'Evêque.   Tel: 65-21-32-31

34.   GAEC Bessières, **Domaine Argentelou**, 46800 St. Matré.
         Tel: 65-31-95-58

65.   Montagne et Fils, **Château d'Arquies**, 46700 Vire.   Tel: 65-36-52-75

44.   Jean-Jacques Aymard, **Clos d'Audhuy**, Le Bourg, 46700 Lacapelle-
         Cabanac.   Tel: 65-36-51-17

82.   Lamouroux et Fils, **Clos d'Auvergne**, (formerly Domaine de Gipoulou)
         La Pouline, 46220 Prayssac.   Tel: 65-21-30-68.

154.   *Nicole Bach, **Domaine de Bach**, Pech del Bras, 46150 Catus.
         Tel: 65-22-71-36*

148.   Didier Borredon, **Domaine de la Banière**, Caix, 46140 Luzech.
         Tel : 65-20-15-35

73. L   *Charles Burc, **Domaine des Bateliers**, Courbenac, 46700 Puy l'Evêque.
         Tel: 65-21-30-63

67.   *Jean-Paul Beaumont, **Château Beaumont**, Goulepdan, 46700 Vire.
         Tel: 65-24-62-74*

13.   E.A.R.L.Roucanières, **Château Bellecoste**, Trebaïx, 46090 Villesèque
         Tel: 65-36-95-43

63.   Loygues et Fils, **Cahors Bénéjou**, 46700 Vire.   Tel: 65-30-81-98

86.   Sylvie Bérenger, **Domaine de la Bérengeraie**, 46700 Grézels.
         Tel: 65-31-94-59

199.   Dominique Bessières, **Domaine Bessières**, Péjuscla, 46090 Villesèque.
         Tel: 65-36-95-49

198.   Philippe Souleillou, **Clos Bican-Ségur**, Bégoux, 46000 Cahors.
         Tel: 65-35-23-01

80.   Serge et Yves Bladinières, **Château Bladinières**, 46220 Pescadoires.
         Tel: 65-22-41-85

100.   IMP Boissor, **Domaine de Boissor**, 46140 Luzech.   Tel: 65-30-72-35

168.   Froment et Fils, **Domaine de la Borie**, La Borie Basse, 46220 Prayssac.
         Tel: 65-22-42-90

78. Michel Faille, **Domaine du Boscas**, Triguedina, 46700 Puy L'Evêque.
Tel: 65-30-80-70

36. Etienne et Francis Alleman, **Domaine des Boulbènes**, Les Boulbènes,
46800 Saux.   Tel: 65-31-96-27

92. Alain Oulières, **Chateau la Bourdette**, le Bourg, 46220 Pescadoires.
Tel: 65-22-44-66

143. Robert Vidal, Cahors Le Bourg, 46090 Mercuès. Tel: 65-30-93-44

161. Raymond Bouysset, **Domaine de Boutier**, Les Caris, 46220 Prayssac.
Tel: 65-30-61-74

144.*L* Les Côtes d'Olt, **Château les Bouysses**, 46090 Mercuès.
Tel: 65-30-71-86

23. *L* Jean-Claude Valière, **Château Bovila**, Bovila,468ƒ00 Fargues. Postal
Address: BP 26, 46001 Cahors Cedex.   Tel: 65-36-91-30.

129. Philippe Arnaudet, **Château la Brande Cessac (Domaine du Verdou)**,
Bourg, 46140 Douelle.   Tel: 65-30-91-34

29. Claude Séménadisse, **Château du Brel**, Le Brel, 46800 Fargues.
Tel: 65-36-91-08

184. Christian Bru, **Domaine Bru**, Le Bourg, 46090 Trespoux-Rassiels.
Tel: 65-35-33-30

57. Jean-Claude Dumeaux, **Domaine de Bru-Haut**, Bru, 46700 Vire,
Tel: 65-24-60-79

21. Eloi Brel, **Château Bru-Lagardette**, 46800 Bagat-en-Quercy. (made at
the Parnac co-opérative).   Tel: 65-31-83-61

200. Francis Grialou, **Domaine du Buis**, 46700 St. Martin-le Redon.
Tel: 65-35-33-30

151.*L.* The Prince Consort of Denmark, **Château de Caïx**, Caïx, 46140 Luzech.
Tel: 65-20-13-22

145. Colette Delfour, **Cave Delf**, 46140 Caillac.   Tel: 65-20-00-51

183. Odette Souveton, **Château de Calassou**, Calassou, 46700 Duravel.
Tel: 65-36-51-61

125.*L* **Resses et Fils, **Château la Caminade**, 46140 Parnac.   Tel: 65-30-73-05

107.*L* Georges Souque, **Château Camp d'Auriol**, 46140 Luzech.
Tel: 65-20-12-90

164. Delbru et Fils, **Domaine Camp del Saltre**, route du Collège,
46220 Prayssac.   Tel: 65-22-42-40.

126. Jacques Dauliac, **Domaine de Capalanel Fages**, 46140 Luzech.
Tel: 65-20-10-15

119. GAEC La Fumade, **Domaine du Cap Blanc**, 46090 Villesèque.
Tel: 65-36-94-58

170. Lacombe et fils, **Cahors Les Caris**, 46220 Prayssac.   Tel: 65-30-63-36

201. Hartmann-Dulac, **Domaine de Carreyrès**, Carreyrès, 46700 Vire.
Tel: 65-36-53-61

49. Guy Delbès, **Château de Castella**, Castella 46700 Mauroux
Tel: 65-36-51-18

117. Roucanières et Fils, **Château le Castellas**, Cournou, St. Vincent Rive-
d'Olt.   Tel: 65-20-17-48

165. Charles-Michel Maratuech, **Cuvée Cathare**, Les Fourqueries,
46220 Prayssac.   Tel: 65-30-60-86

*124 . Michel et Bernard Lafage, Domaine de Caunezil, 46140 Parnac.
Tel: 65-20-12-89*

187. Messieurs Durou et Costes, **Domaine de Cause**, Cavagnac, 46700 Soturac.
Tel: 65-36-57-69

3. Gérard Oulié, **Domaine des Cayrasses**, Combe de l'Aze, 46090 Flaujac-
Poujols.   Tel: 65-35-22-61 or 65-35-69-59

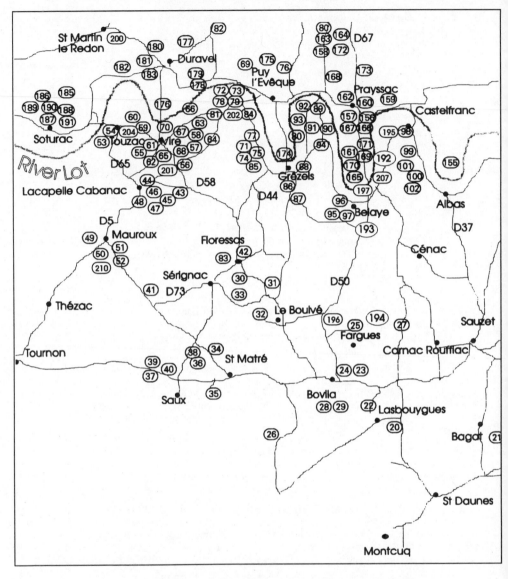

174.*L* **Jean Jouffreau,**Château du Cayrou**, 46700 Puy L'Evêque,
Tel: 65-22-40-26

9. *L* Comte André Monpézat, **Château de Cayrou-Monpezat**, 46140 Albas.
Tel: 65-36-20-12

192. Alain Dumeau, **Château de Cazérac**, 46140 Anglars Juillac.
Tel: 65-36-20-81

8. *L* **Verhaeghe et Fils, **Château du Cèdre**, Bru, 46700 Vire.
Tel: 65-36-53-87

155. Pelvilain et Fils, **Château Port-Cénac**, Circofoul,46140 Albas.
Tel: 65-20-13-13

7. Jean Delseries, **Château Cerinne, Sarlat**, 46700 Puy L'Evêque.
Tel: 65-30-80-68

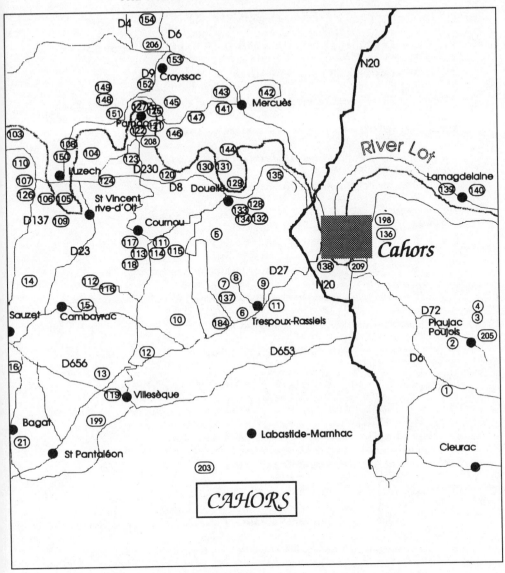

42 .*L*   Marc Delgoulet, **Château de Chambert**, 4670 Floressas.   Tel: 65-31-95-75

146.   Brunet et fils, **Domaine Chantelle**, Chantelle,46140 Caillac.
Tel: 65-20-04-66

113.   Pierre Ilbert, **Domaine du Charron**, Cournou,St. Vincent Rive-d'Olt.
Tel: 65-30-71-34 (made at the Parnac Co-opérative)

181.   Jean-Paul Roussilles, **Clos du Chêne**, 46700 Duravel.   Tel: 65-24-60-81

131.   Jean-Luc Cagnac et Josiane Alibert, **Domaine du Chêne** Rond , Cessac,
46140 Douelle.   Tel: 65-20-02-92

38.   Bernard Pouchet, **Château des Cloutous**, Sanayre, 46800 Saux.
Tel: 65-31-97-33

61.   Claude Labruyère et fille, **Domaine du Colombier**, Le Colombier,
46700 Vire.   Tel: 65-36-58-33

205.   Jean Jouglas, **La Ferme du Colombier**, 46090 Flaujac- Poujols.
       Tel: 65-35-22-52

6.   Jean Combarieu, **Château Combarieu**, Le Bourg, 46090 Trespoux-Rassiels.
       Tel: 65-35-41-96

16.   Roger Couaillac, **Château Couaillac**, La Séoune, 46140 Sauzet.
       Tel: 65-36-90-82

118.   *Claudine Vincent, **Domaine du Coustalou**, Cournou, St. Vincent Rive-d'Olt.   Tel: 65-30-71-45 (formerly made at Parnac a Co-opérative).*

162.L *Michel Cassot, **Château la Coustarelle**, 46220 Prayssac.
       Tel: 65-22-40-10

56. L **Bernède et Fils, **Clos la Coutale**, La Chambre, 46700 Vire.
       Tel: 65-36-51-47.

98.   François Pélissié, **Croix du Mayne**, 46140 Anglars-Juillac.
       Tel: 65-36-27-34

196.   GAEC du Chêne Vert, **Château La Croix du Roy**, Farguettes,
       46800 Fargues.   Tel: 65-36-90-67

66.   Roche et Fils, **Château de la Croze de Pys**, Pys Bas, 46700 Vire.
       Tel: 65-21-31-99

110.   Josette Rességuier, **Domaine de Dauliac**, 46140 Luzech.
       Tel: 65-30-72-38 (made at Parnac Co-opérative)

7.   *Gérard Decas, **Domaine de Decas**, Lannac, À46090 Trespoux-Rassiels
       Tel: 65-35-37-74

111.   Dolorès Bénac, **Château de l'Eglantier**, Cournou, St. Vincent Rive-d'Olt.
       Tel: 65-30-71-48

28.   Odette Saurt, **Domaine de l'Eteil**, Le Brel, 46800 Fargues.
       Tel: 65-36-91-19

100.L **Jean et Claude Couture,**Château Eugénie**, 46140 Albas.
       Tel: 65-30-73-51

15.   Jean-Paul Lamberty, **Domaine Eustache**, Les Grèzes, 46140 Cambayrac.
       Tel: 65-30-72-01

106.   Jean Bel, **Domaine de Fages**, Fages, 46140 Luzech.   Tel: 65-20-11-83

156.   *Guy Bouysset, **Clos de Fantou**, 46140 Castelfranc. Tel: 65-30-61-46*

157.   Bernard Aldhuy, **Domaine de Fantou**, Fantou, 46220 Prayssac.
       Tel: 65-30-61-85

69.   *Jean-François Baldès, **Château de Flore**, 46700 Puy L'Evêque.
       Tel: 65-21-37-92.*

81.   Pierre Johnstone, **Château Fontaine**, Inganels, 46700 Puy L'Evêque.
       Tel: 65-21-32-64

8.   René Deilhès, **Château des Fontanelles**, Lannac, 46090 Trespoux-
       Rassiels.   Tel: 65-35-10-50

152.   Marcel Mouly, **Château Fontenille**, Mas de Greffier, 46150 Crayssac.
       Tel: 65-20-03-52

89.   Francis Benech, **Château de la Fore**, 46220 Pescadoires.
       Tel: 65-22-42-65

173.   Salvador et Fils, **Domaine de Fourqueries**, route du Collège,
       46220 Prayssac.   Tel: 65-22-43-10

169.L **Jean Jouffreau, **Clos de Gamot**, Gamot, 46220 Prayssac.
       Tel: 65-22-40-26

94.   Odile et Claude Teulet, **Château de la Garde**, 46220 Lagardelle.
       Tel: 65-22-42-84

203.   *Jean-Jacques Bousquet, **Domaine de La Garde**, Le Mazut,
       46090 Labastide-Marnhac.   Tel: 65-21-01-61

32.   *Alain Pion, **Château Garinet**, 46800 Le Boulvé.   Tel: 65-31-98-10*

102.   Christian Lacam, **Château Garrigou**, 46140 Albas.   Tel: 65-36-96-63

62.   Roger Labruyère, **Domaine de Garrigue**, *(Château la Trompette)*,*46700 Vire.   Tel: 65-36-54-58*

58.L *Durou et Fils, **Château de Gaudou**, Gaudou, 46700 Vire.
      Tel: 65-36-52-93

175.L Alain Senderens, **Château de Gautoul**, 46700 Puy l'Evêque.
      Tel: 65-30-84-17

71.   Guy Besset, **Château la Gérie**, route de Montcuq, 46700 Puy l'Evêque.
      Tel: 65-21-34-75

182. SCEA La Gineste, **Château la Gineste**, 46700 Duravel.   Tel: 65-36-50-09

59.   Francis Ferréro, **Domaine de Goulepdan**, Goulepdan, 46700 Vire.
      Tel: 65-36-54-51

97.   Jacques Heurtier, **Château du Grand Chêne**, 46140 Belaye
      Tel: 65-72-09-86

171. L*Francis et Philippe Pontie, **Château des Grauzils**, Gamot,
      46220 Prayssac.   Tel: 65-30-62-44

91.   Fabbro età Fils, **Domaine des Gravalous**, 46220 Pescadoires
      Tel: 65-22-40-46

136. Alain Belon, **Domaine des Gravettes**, Bégoux, 46090 Cahors.
      Tel: 65-35-57-46

88.L Rigal SA, **Château de Grézels**, 46700 Grézels.   Tel: 65-21-37-61 (see
      Ch. St. Didier-Parnac)

191. *Jean-Marie Sigaud, **Domaine Haute-Borie**, 46700 Soturac*
      Tel: 65-22-41-80

60.   Filhol et Fils, **Domaine de Hauterive**, 46700 Vire.   Tel: 65-36-52-84

210. Bernard Magret, **Domaine des Hautes-Combes**,46700 Mauroux

1. L *Georges Vigouroux, **Château de Haute-Serre**, 46230 Cieurac.
      Tel: 65-20-80-20

190. Guy Rey, **Château des Hauts d'Aglan**, Aglan, 46700 Soturac.
      Tel: 65-36-52-02

39.   Jean-Claude Salles, **Domaine Les Homs**, 46800 Saux.   Tel: 65-31-96-21

202. Jean-Pierre Ichard, **Domaine Ichard**, Le Caux, 46700, Puy l'Evêque.
      Tel: 65-22-42-71

90. L **Buri et Fils. **Château Les Ifs**, 46220 Pescadoires.   Tel: 65-22-44-53

84.   Nicole Maléta, **Domaine de Kanijo**, La Brande 46700 Puy l'Evêque.
      Tel: 65-21-35-89

46.L *Alex Denjean, **Château Lacapelle-Cabanac**, 46700 Lacapelle-Cabanac.
      Tel: 65-36-51-92

37.   Jacques Marès, **Domaine de Laetitia**, Les Clauzades, 46800 Saux.
      Tel: 65-31-96-19 (formerly Domaine des Rocailles)

149. Jacques Lafon, **Domaine Lafon**, Caïx, 46140 Luzech.   Tel: 65-20-14-97

27.   Antoine Pérez, **Clos de Lagarde and Les Poujols**, 46800 Fargues.
      Tel: 65-36-93-04

139. Christian Lagarrigues, **Domaine Lagarrigue**, 46090 Lamagdelaine.
      Tel: 65-30-00-54

147. L Alain Dominique Perrin, **Château Lagrézette**, 46140 Caillac.
      Tel: 65-20-01-70

41.   *Pierre Bonnafoux, **Domaine de Laguille**, 46700 Sérignac.*
      Tel: 65-31-97-98

95.   Bargues et Fils, **Domaine de Lalande**, Lalande, 46140 Belaye.
      Tel: 65-21-35-39

48.   René Vessié, **Domaine de Lalbatut**, Lalbatu, 46700 Lacapelle-Cabanac.
      Tel: 65-36-51-52

103. Christian Armagnat, **Domaine de Lamarie**, Lamarie, 46140 Luzech.
      Tel: 65-30-74-24

188.*L* *Gayroud et Fils, **Château Lamartine**, 46700 Soturac. Tel: 65-36-54-14

54. S.C.A. de Ferrières, **Domaine de Landiech**, Landiech, 46700 Touzac.
Tel: 65-36-52-11

166. Pierre Florenty, **Domaine de Lasserre**, 46220 Prayssac.
Tel: 65-30-63-31

50.*L* *Colin et Penelope Duns, **Château Latuc**, Laborie,46700 Mauroux.
Tel: 65-36-58-63

83. Maurice et Patrick Laur, **Château Laur**, 46700 Floressas. Tel: 65-31-95-61

33. Guy Philip, **Château de Lavalette**, Rials, 46800 Le Boulvé.
Tel: 65-31-97-15

186. Renée Delpech, **Domaine de Lavaur**, 46700 Soturac. Tel: 65-36-56-30

96. Eric Froment, **Domaine de Lavergne**, Lavergne, 46140 Belaye.
Tel: 65-36-21-09

101.*L* Jean-Baptiste de Monpezat, **Château Léret-Monpezat**, 46140 Albas.
Tel: 65-36-26-34

209. Marcel Cambou, **Ma Petite Vigne**, 24 rue des Neuve-Badenat,
46000 Cahors. 63-35-06-46.

30. Bernard Delmouly, **Domaine de Maison Neuve**, Maison Neuve,
46800 Le Boulvé. Tel: 65-31-95-73

206. *Le Rouergou, **Manoir du Rouergou**, 46150 St. Médard de Catus.
Tel: 65- 21-42-59.

120. Séverine Martin, **Ségala Cazes**, 46700 Puy l'Evêque. Tel: not available.

120. Dominique Delcros, **Domaine de Massabie**, 46140 Parnac.
Tel: 65-20-12-67 (made at Parnac Co-opérative).

142.*L* *GFA Georges Vigouroux, **Château de Mercuès**, 46090 Mercuès.
Tel: 65-20-09-20

11. Roger Vincent, **Domaine de Mériguet**, Le Bourg, 46090 Trespoux-
Rassiels Tel: 65-22-61-11

207. EARL des Colombiers, **La Métairie-Haute**, 46140 Anglars- Juillac.
Tel: 65-36-23-36

31. Claude Lalabarde, **Domaine de la Molinie**, La Molinie, 46890 Le Boulvé.
Tel: 65-31-97-02

179. Jacques Lamoulie, **Domaine des Noyers**, Girard, 46700 Duravel.
Tel: 65-36-52-69

64. *L.* *GAEC Maradenne-Guitard, **Château de Noziéres**, 46700 Vire.
Tel: 65-36-52-73

197. Geneviève Dulac, **Château Onésime**, Les Cambous, 46220 Prayssac.
Tel: 65-30-61-68

79. Dominique Henry, **Domaine la Paganie**, La Paganie, 46700 Puy
l'Evêque. Tel: 65-21-36-08

51. Jean-ClaudeLandiech, **Château de Paillargues**,Paillargues,
46700 Mauroux. Tel: 65-36-51-19

43.*L* **SCEA de St. Robert, **Domaine de Paillas**, 46700 Floressas.
Tel: 65-36-58-28

122. Georges Delmas, **Château Parnac**, 46140 Parnac.Tel: 65-30-73-84

130. Thierry Baudel, **Domaine le Passelys**, 46140 Douelle, Tel: 65-20-05-76

172. Monique Rodriguès, **Château de Patrounet**, 46220 Prayssac.
Tel: 65-30-64-58

52. Charles Péchau, **Château de Péchaussou**, Péchaussou, 46700 Mauroux.
Tel: 65-36-51-12

140. Antonia Valette-Clary, **Domaine du Pech de Clary**, 46090 Lamagdelaine.
Tel: 65-35-37-08

4. **Stephen and Sherry Schechter, **Domaine du Pech de Jammes**,
46090 Flaujac-Poujols. Tel: 65-22-02-95

87.   Didier Ibre, **Domaine Pech d'Estournel**, 46700 Grézels. Tel: 65-30-82-43

17.   Jean-Luc Daubanes, **Domaine du Pech des Vignes**, Montplaisir,
        46140 Sauzet,   Tel: 65-36-90-39

185.   Robert Bru, **Domaine de Péclair**, Cavagnac,46700 Soturac.
        Tel: 65-36-55-56

150.   Robert Siutat, **Domaine du Pécot**, Avenue d'Uxellodunum,
        46140 Luzech. Tel ; 65-20-10-73

93.   Gérard Perié, **Domaine Perié**, 46220 Pescadoires.   Tel: 65-22-42-75

178.   Christian Lamoulie, **Domaine du Peuplier**, Girard, 46700 Duravel.
        Tel: 65-24-60-85

159.   Henri Bessières, **Cahors Peyrebos**, 46220 Prayssac. Tel ; 65-30-62-74

204.   GAEC des Combes. **Domaine de Peyreboy**, 46700 Touzac.
        Tel: 65-36-56-48

75.   Jean-Pierre Cantagrel, **Domaine du Peyret**, Le Peyret, 46700 Puy
        l'Evêque.   Tel: 65-21-32-30

189.   Gilis et Fils, **Domaine du Peyrié**, Peyrié, 46700 Soturac.
        Tel: 65-36-57-15

133.L   *José Roucanières, **Domaine du Pic**, 46140 Douelle.   Tel: 65-20-04-28

74. L   **SCEA Burc et Fils, **Domaine Pineraie**, Leygues, 46700 Puy L'Evêque.
        Tel: 65-30-82-07

112.   GAEC Bezières, **Château du Plai Faisant**, Les Roques, 46140 St. Vincent
        Rive-d'Olt.   Tel: 65-20-16-34

2.   Michel Imbert, **Domaine des Plantades**, Bourg, 46090 Flaujac-Poujols.
        Tel: 65-35-02-16

76.   *André Cirech, Cahors Le Pommier, 46700 Puy L'Evêque. Tel: 65-21-34-88*

194.   André Séménadisse, **Château de Pons**, Pons, 46800 Fargues.
        Tel: 65-36-91-32

176.   Jacques Duchamp, **Domaine du Port**, Le Port, 46700 Duravel.
        Tel: 65-36-54-27

121.   Je÷an-Claude Delcros, **Château Port de l'Angle**, 46140 Parnac.
        Tel: 65-30-73-06 Les Poujols, see 27. Antoine Pérez,**Clos de Lagarde**.

153.   René Mouly, **Mas de Pouzat**, 46150 Crayssac.   Tel: 65-20-08-73

116.   Gérard Maerten, **Château le Pradel**, Les Roques, 46140 St. Vincent
        Rive-D'Olt.   Tel: 65-30-71-55

114.   Jacques Jouves, **Domaine du Prince**, Cournou, 46140 St. Vincent Rive-
        D'Olt.   Tel: 65-20-14-09

127.L   *Rigal SA, **Prieuré de Cénac**, Albas (see Ch. St. Didier-Parnac)

22.   S.C. de Quattre et Treilles, **Château de Quattre**, Tel: 65-36-91-04 and
        Château Treilles, Tel: 65-36-93-56. Both at 46800 Bagat-en-Quercy.

45.   Louis Cure, **Domaine des Quatre Vents**, Frayssi, 46700 Lacapelle-
        Cabanac.   Tel: 65-36-55-68

10.   Monique Raynal, **Château Raynal**, Le Bournaguet, 46090 Trespoux-
        Rassiels.   Tel: 65-35-18-97

18.   GAEC Les Espinasses-Rességuier, **Clos Rességuier**, 46140 Sauzet.
        Tel: 65-36-90-03

85.L   **Jean-Claude Vidal, **Château La Reyne**, also **Clos des Batuts**, Leygues,
        46700° Puy l'Evêque.   Tel: 65-21-30-26

160.   André Bouloumié, **Château Les Rigalets**, 46220 Prayssac. Tel: 65-30-61-69

25.   Martial Andrieu, **Domaine Lou Roc**, Farguettes, Fargues, 46800
        Fargues.   Tel: 65-36-91-24

80.   Claude Rigal, **Domaine La Roseraie**, La Gineste, 46700 Duravel.
        Tel: 65-36-52-98

19.   Jean-Claude Vincent, **Domaine Les Rosiers**, 46140 Carnac-Rouffiac.
        Tel: 65-36-95-81

Rouergou see Manoir du Rouergou

177.   Philippe Ducoum, **Château de Rouffiac**, Rouffiac, 46700 Duravel
Tel: 65-36-54-27

127 L   *Rigal SA, **Château St. Didier-Parnac**, 46140 Parnac.   Tel: 65-30-70-10

208.   Dominique Cavalié, **Château St. Sernin**, 46140 Parnac.   Tel: 65-20-13-26

12.   Philippe Lasbouygues, **Domaine des Salles**, Les Salles, 46090 Villesèque.

5. L   * Danielle Biesbrouck, **Domaine des Savarine**s, 46090 Trespoux -
Rassiels.   Tel: 65-22-33-67

24.   GFSA Merlo et Pondepeyre **Domaine Serre de Bovila**, Bovila, 46800
Fargues. Te l: 65-22-21-15. Postal address: BP 161, 46003 Cahors Cedex.

134.   Jean Sers, **Domaine de Sers**, 46140 Douelle.   Tel: 65-20-02-18

20. L   Simon Bley, **Clos Siguier**, Lasbouygues, 46800 Bagat-en- Quercy.
Tel: 65-36-91-05

135.   Francis Alazard, **Domaine du Souleillan**, Flottes, 46090 Pradines.
Tel: 65-35-61-72

132. L *Jean-Pierre Raynal, **Château de Souleillou**, 46140 Douelle.
Tel: 65-20-01-88

*137   GAEC Foissac, **Domaine de la Souque**, Le Bournaguet, 46090 Trespoux-
Rassiels. Tel: 65-22-06-30*

108.   Jean-Marc Tanays, **Domaine Tanays**, Avenue Docteur Pélissié,
46140 Luzech.   Tel: 65-30-71-12

163.   Jacques Combarel, **Domaine du Théron**, 46220 Prayssac.
Tel: 65-30-64-51

158.   *Liliane Barat-Sigaud, **Métairie Grande du Théron**, 46220 Prayssac,
Tel: 65-22-41-80

128.   Pierre Alibert, **Domaine des Tilleuls**, Rue de l'Eglise, 46140 Douelle.
Tel: 65-30-91-92

105.   Didier Davidou, **Domaine des Tilleuls**, Fages, 46140 Luzech
Tel: 65-20-13-16

Château de Treilles . see 22. Domaine Quattre

70 L   **SCEA Baldès et Fils, **Clos Triguedina**, Triguedina, 46700 Puy
l'Evêque.   Tel: 65-21-30-81 or 65-21-34-64.

9.   Francis Pouderoux, **Domaine des Trois Cazelles**, Le Pech,
46090 Trespoux-Rasiels.   Tel: 65-30-05-17

*26.   Daniel Chabert, **Domaine du Vieil Amandier**, Mascayrolles,
46800 Fargues. Tel: 65-36-90-64*

35.   Annette Godin, **Château Vent d'Autan**, Moustans hauts, 46800 Fargues.
Tel: 65-31-96-75

*115.   André Labrande, **Domaine des Vignals**, 46140 St,. Vincent Rive-d'Olt.
Tel: 65-30-73-92*

53.   Claude Demeaux, **Les Vignals**, Le Roc,46700 Touzac.   Tel: 65-36-52-24
(made at parnac Co-opérative).

40 .   Joel Vigouroux, **Domaine de Vigouroux**, 46800 Saux Tel: 65-31-96-07

109.   Michel Vincens, **Château Vincens Foussal**, 46140 Luzech
Tel: 65-30-74-78

141.   Raymond Delfau, **Domaine de Vinssou**, Route de Caillac, 46090 Mercuès.
Tel: 65-30-92-84

VINS DE PAYS DES COTEAUX DU QUERCY
At or near Puylaroque 82240

Pierre Belon, **Domaine d'Ariès**   Tel: 63-64-92-52
Cavaillé Père et Fils, St Hugues   Tel: 63-64-90-60

Michel et Pierre Andrieu, **Domaine de la Fourniol**, St Georges Tel: 63-64-90-68
Fernand Carles, **Domaine Mazuc**   Tel: 63-64-90-91

At or near Montpézat-de-Quercy 82270

Les Vignerons du Quercy (Cave Co-opérative), Monpezat-de-Quercy
    (dir.Francis Jeansou)   Tel: 63-02-03-50
Domaine de Pech-Bèly, Couloussac   Tel: 63-94-47-28
Xavier et Laurence Dieuzaide, **Domaine de la Combarade**, 46170 Castelnau-
    Monratier   Tel: 65-21-95-95
Guy Cammas, **Domaine de Gabachou**   Tel: 63-02-07-64
Bernard Bouyssou, **Domaine de Lafage**   Tel: 63-02-07-09
Jean-Jacques Bousquet, **Le Mazut**, 46090 Labastide-Marnhac   Tel: 65-21-01-61
    (Domaine de la Garde)

At La Ville-Dieu-du-Temple 82290

Cave Lavilledieu-du-Temple   Tel: 63-31-68-48

The Wines of the High Hills: Aveyron and the River Gorges

Lo vin lo cal beure
lo matin tot pur,
à miègjour sans aiga
e lo ser tal que lo Bou Dius
l' a donat!

Wine should be drunk neat
in the morning, without
water at mid-day, and in
the evening just as the
the Good Lord gave it us!
(Old Aveyron proverb)

The city of Rodez is built on a hill and it cannot be hid. The huge Gothic cathedral dominates the old quarters of this capital of the Rouergue and church and buildings try in vain to draw under their mountainous skirts the sprawling ugly suburbs so typical of modern *préfectures*.

Rodez is the county town of Aveyron, the fifth largest département in France, which is nearly co-extensive with the old province of Rouergue. Rouergue literally means 'red earth', the very typical soil which gives the local wines their hallmark.

To the north are the high pastures of the Auvergne, and the inhospitable barren plateaux called the *causses* lie to the east. Until the coming of modern communications the Rouergue was almost cut off from the rest of France. Its wild frontiers were the home of robbers and worse, who made overland communications extremely hazardous: its rivers flowed westwards through unnavigable gorges so that contact with the outside world was denied in that direction also. Only to the south was the Rouergue more accessible, but until modern times the south too offered little real connection with the mainstream of French culture or commerce.

The Ruthénois, as the inhabitants of Rodez are called, were no wine-traders in the sense of the growers in Quercy or Gaillac, because they had

such limited outlets for their wines. But from the earliest times pestilence
and plague were rife in Rodez, due to a large extent to the polluted water
supplies of the city. Wine was regarded as a healthy substitute, and, even
more positively, as a medicine. The hospitals and convents needed a plentiful supply of wine for the well-being of the inhabitants. Until the coming of the phylloxera, vines were widely grown in the suburbs of Rodez,
where today stand the out-of-town hypermarkets, flats, factories and
other appurtenances of the modern city.

But the climate of Rodez, which is over 2000 feet above sea-level, was
intemperate and rude compared with some of the nearby countryside
where the soil and weather were more favourable to the cultivation of
the vine. The virtues of the sheltered valleys to the north-west of Rodez
had been discovered by the monks of Conques who had founded their
now celebrated abbey in the ninth century. Conques was one of the
principal staging posts on the way from eastern France to St Jacques de
Compostelle. The monks are thought to have come from Burgundy and
to have brought with them the wine-making skills which had been
developed there under the auspices of the Church. Certainly their pioneering interests in the region of Marcillac are well proven, and their
influence on the other wine-growing areas of the Aveyron was no less
important.

MARCILLAC AND THE WINES OF THE VALLON

Conques stands close to the confluence of the river Lot and its tributary
the Dourdou. The latter has two tributaries of its own, which rise in the
high ground of central Aveyron. One spurts from the rocks of the
Causse de Comtal at the pretty village of Salles-la-Source only a few
miles from Rodez: the other river is parallel and a little to the west: it is
called the Ady and gives its name to the village of Valady, today the
home of the Marcillac cave co-opérative. Their valleys are steep-sided,
clad with the brilliant red earth of the region and a generous dose of
stones washed down from the *causses*, and they are sheltered from the
cruel winter winds of the Auvergne. In summer and autumn they bask
in the sunshine provided by a partly Mediterranean climate. They are
particularly suitable for the growing of vines, especially the slopes
which face to the south and west.

This small river network is called Le Vallon and the wine made there
has always been called Marcillac after the small country town of that
name, which is halfway between Conques and Rodez. The monks of
Conques set up a small satellite monastery nearby to develop the vineyards, and one local grower told me that some of the ruins can still be
seen in winter amid the scrub and undergrowth of the hillsides.

The renown of the Vallon's micro-climate had certainly spread to
Rodez by the late middle ages. The hospices and convents of the city
had already acquired substantial holdings of land between Valady and
Clairvaux, where they created extensive vineyards. The villages of the

Vallon even today bear witness to the scale of medieval wine-making: many have kept their town gates and miniature fortifications, and there are still whole streets of houses with characteristic pointed Gothic arches carved out of the local red sandstone, which glow like coals in the evening sun. There are solid but pretty Romanesque churches here, whose size reflect a once healthy attendance at worship. The church at Clairvaux is clearly modelled on the Abbey of Conques itself.

The emergence of a wealthy bourgeoisie in Rodez gave further impetus to the expansion of these vineyards. The richer local merchants began to plant their own and to build country houses in the middle of them. It became socially *de rigueur* to have a *maison secondaire* in the Vallon, to which whole families would repair in the summer until the end of the vintage in October. Some of these handsome houses still stand today among the now abandoned terraces on the hillsides: others line the streets of the wine villages of Salles-la-Source, Marcillac, Bruéjols, Clairvaux and Valady, some sadly abandoned and given over to ducks and hens, the occasional example renovated by a latter-day Rodez businessman or perhaps a Parisian weekender. The whole of the medieval centre of Clairvaux is derelict; I met an elderly lady walking her dog among the silent streets and she told me that the imposing houses all around had huge underground cellars where the wines of Marcillac were once stored. Their architectural detail is impressive: sometimes even the dung-heaps for the cattle have roofs made from the pretty scalloped slates of the region, which would have been an impossible indulgence at modern prices.

It was usual for these city *vignerons* to employ a full-time manager to run the vineyards for them. Sometimes these privileged servants had their own small house built quite apart from their masters'. They were like stewards and acted as a buffer between the proprietor and the vineyard workers, rather after the manner of an English country-house butler. They had their own unofficial *confrérie*, which spurred competition between the growers and introduced the concept of quality into winemaking. Until that time wine had been merely a beverage, a substitute for water, and quality had meant little: as long as it was cleanly made, little notice was taken as to whether it was good or bad. But the bourgeoisie began to vie with each other to produce wine which was better than their neighbours', and so the quality of the wines of the Vallon rose.

The local historian, Alexis Monteil, writing just after the Revolution, described the village of Marcillac in this way:

> This place is languid in the spring, but brilliant in the autumn. During that season, the inhabitants of Rodez, owners of virtually all the vines in the area, come with their families for the harvest. Most are middle-class and well off. They are not prepared to forego any of the benefits of town-life, so bring with them a large quantity of equipment and food. As they pass you on the road, you might well think they were going off somewhere to found a new colony.

This all sounds rather familiar, like any Channel port in August.

Vintage-time must have been more than usually frenetic in Marcillac in those heady days of its golden age. The stewards and staff would work together day and night to prepare the huge old *cuves* for the newly pressed wine, for in those days all the fermentation took place in ancient wooden barrels: there was no cement, let alone stainless steel or fibre-glass. The whole community was engaged in the grape-harvest, because there was only one other crop in the Vallon, the soft fruits from the orchards which had long been gathered before the vintage began. The jobless from Rodez walked from the city to the Vallon to be hired for the duration of the grape-harvest. Accounts of the local markets remind one of the fairs described by Thomas Hardy. Every able-bodied person had a part to play: even the town-crier, a job now sadly lost to French village life, made his contribution. A young school-mistress, arriving to take up her post at the village school in Salles-la-Source was surprised to find him beating his drum beneath her window and chanting in a stentorian voice: 'Oyez! Oyez! Will whoever it was who borrowed Monsieur X's funnel please bring it back, because he needs it urgently.'

The vintage naturally ended with all-night dancing to the sound of a flute or a panting bagpipe. When it was all over, the families from Rodez packed up and went home, the pickers went back to their family farms, and only the stewards were left to deal with the *élevage*: controlling the maturing of the new wine in barrel, racking it every six weeks or so, so that in the spring it could be sold on before work began on the next year's vintage. The money would be needed to finance the next *vendange* and to give the Rodez businessman a return on his investment.

This prosperity disappeared almost overnight with the phylloxera. As elsewhere, the vineyards were wiped out and sudden decline over-took the Vallon. The rich citizens of Rodez abandoned their country-homes, thousands of country-dwellers were left destitute, and the once thickly populated valleys started to empty of people, some drifting to find employment in the big towns and cities, others emigrating. The story is a familiar one in the South-West, but in the Vallon it was to have a different ending.

Few would describe the murky town of Decazeville as a silver lining (except perhaps the English duke who spent his honeymoon there), but to the people of the Vallon it was just that. Beneath the hills adjoining the valley of the Lot lay deep seams of coal. The Industrial Revolution duly came to the Aveyron and the coal-reserves were only opened up in the middle of the nineteenth century. Decazeville and its satellite towns became a magnet for those who had lost their livelihood with the phylloxera, and who were driven away from the countryside by the threat of starvation.

The conditions in the mines of Decazeville were no better, perhaps worse, than in other French mining towns. Danger, filth and long work-ing hours for very little pay provided only the poorest quality of life for the miners. Conditions such as those described in Zola's *Germinal* were

general, crime and riots frequent and the suffering labour force and their families needed alcohol to provide their only solace.

The Vallon was on hand to supply it. No sooner had the phylloxera emptied the vineyards than replanting began. Some growers who had taken jobs in the Decazeville mines eked out their wretched livings by returning home to their old vineyards with their miners' lamps at night and on Sundays. New, grafted, and therefore immune, vines were planted: not on the high terraces where the best wine had come from in the old days, but on ground lower down the slopes which was easier to cultivate. The accent switched from quality to bulk: the old stewards had left with their bourgeois masters; and mass-production of cheap and cheerful wine was taken over by the peasants who picked up ownership of the abandoned vineyards for a song. But in one respect Marcillac succeeded where Cahors had failed: the traditional grape-variety, the mansois, grafted well, and was easy to propagate. Although the thoroughbred juice from it was blended with that of inferior varieties, the distinctive grape of the region survived. This made the later renaissance of Marcillac easier to bring about.

The thirsty coal-miners kept the peasant-growers in the Vallon going for as long as the numbers in the mines kept up. The loss of life in the First World War caused a sharp fall in the male population and the Second was followed by a general drift to the cities, which reduced both the numbers working in the mines but, just as importantly, the vineyard-workers, who were consumers as well as producers. At this time the real decline in Marcillac started, just when other vineyards in the South-West were beginning to come out of their doldrums. The death-knell of Marcillac as cheap plonk for the poor finally sounded when the Decazeville mines were closed in 1962. Conditions had become too dangerous to work them, and the quality of the coal had fallen to the point where further production was uneconomic. The closure of the Decazeville basin killed overnight the market for Marcillac as it was then produced.

The growers, drastically reduced in numbers, were immediately faced with the task of finding new markets. The most imaginative realised that they needed to seek a unified image for the wine, even if this meant sinking their individual identities. So there came about the first tentative moves towards a co-opérative. Nine growers joined together and, in an old barn, pooled their wine and their resources to make a Marcillac which would become the style for the future. In their first year they made just 80 hectolitres between them. To enhance the name of Marcillac, and to help them obtain a better price for their product, they applied for VDQS status in 1966 and when this was granted in 1968 the formation of a real cave co-opérative followed immediately.

The 'new' Marcillac was to represent a return to the pre-phylloxera standards of quality. The grant of VDQS status brought with it the right to add small amounts of the two cabernets and merlot because the authorities doubted whether the local grape on its own would be commercially successful. No one I have met has taken advantage of this facility, even though those other varieties ripen early. The mansois of Marcillac is something of a viticultural curiosity, seemingly confined to the South-West of France. It crops up as a minor ingredient in many wines of the region and under a variety of different disguises. We shall find it in Gaillac under the name of braucol, in Gascony and the Béarn as pinenc, while its general name in occitan is fer servadou, under which title it will be recognised everywhere it is grown. The title mansois derives from the patois saoumensès.

In the Vallon the grape is not just grown: it *is* the wine. Nothing else goes into Marcillac, which is the only appellation which adopts mansois not just as its principal variety, but uniquely. André Metge, who runs the cave co-opérative says that only 2 or 3% of the grapes which come into the Cave are cabernet or merlot. The mansois is said to be related to the cabernet franc, and certainly the two grapes share the same grassy sappiness and have a distinctive flavour of soft red fruits, currants, raspberries and sometimes blackcurrants. It is this very unusual grape, unblended and married to the local soil, which has a great deal of iron in it, which gives Marcillac its unique and unmistakable *goût du terroir*. Not everybody likes it: some people find the flavour too pronounced, but it certainly resembles no other wine of the South-West and can be picked out immediately, even by a novice at a blind tasting.

The resulting wine is always dark, but clear and bright, shot through with violet lights. The fruits are balanced by tannins which are full but not aggressive. Marcillac matures quickly, and, though it will last for five or six years if it is well made and from a good vintage, even the special *cuvées* do not improve much after three years. For the most part the wines are drinkable one year after the vintage. They are best drunk at 16°.

Today the vineyard covers about 130 hectares, and annual production averages 5000 hectolitres. There are seventy or so growers but all, bar ten, and a handful of others who have virtually stopped production,are members of the co-opérative, which is called the **Cave des Vignerons du Vallon (3M)** and is to be found just to the south of Valady on the road from Decazeville to Rodez. The Cave has been run by the passionate and energetic André Metge ever since its inception in 1968, and today it is responsible for about two-thirds of the total production of Marcillac. This is about the same scale of production as is achieved, say, by a château in the Bordelais, so André is able to adopt an artisanal rather than an industrial approach. He has only three staff and he does all the marketing himself as well as supervising the vinification and *élevage* of the wines. André is forever trying to improve quality and standards and he does not hesitate to reject members' wines if they are below par. '*La cave n'est pas la poubelle,*' he maintains.

The vinification process is simple. *Egrappage* is now total, the grapes then being fermented in stainless steel for fifteen days. The problem in this area is not to keep the temperature down but up, so water-cooling is not needed. Picking never takes place before October, by which time there can be a distinct chill in the air. Sometimes the must has to be heated, particularly if picking has been late.

None of the Marcillac growers I met will be heard to preach the virtues of new wood: André has been persuaded by siren voices ('the accountants,' he says) to experiment with it. So far as I know he is alone. A small part of the best *cuvées* is set apart and given six months in new barrels from the Gaillac *tonnelier*, Alibert. Metge is anxious not to be left behind by the market, but he seemed to have little personal enthusiasm for this venture. Marcillac is such a distinctive wine that new wood is more likely to detract from its originality than enhance it. This is certainly the impression I get from his *cuvée boisée*: it is an excellently made and high-quality product, but the hallmark of Marcillac is completely hidden. The wine could have come from any wine-district in the world – one expert taster given it blind guessed it as a South African cabernet sauvignon!

The wines of the co-opérative are better judged by their two *cuvées* of unoaked red wines and their rosé. The latter has a distinctly Loire character to it, the scented fresh fruit reminiscent of the related cabernet franc grape. The reds show a typically mainstream style for Marcillac: the basic wine, called Tradition, has all the characteristics of the appellation at a very reasonable price. The Cuvée Réserve is just that much better because it comes from better-sited vines on the higher terraces, and perhaps also from members who are known to be more careful producers. This wine is very dark, with good extract even in a poor year like 1992. There is a lot of fruit on the palate and the wine has considerable structure and impact. It is easy to see that there are already enough tannins without adding any more by the use of new wood.

Not even the more modern of the private growers seem to have any interest in new wood either. Philippe Teulier at the **Domaine du Cros (5M)** won't hear of it. For him, Marcillac is not a wine for long keeping and its fruit would start to dry out before the wood had had time to finish its work. Instead he has a wonderful array of ancient *barriques* which he maintains carefully and lovingly. He is fortunate that, in the village of Clairvaux, there is still a cooper who is prepared to provide replacement staves and other spare parts. These barrels are a legacy from the days of his great-grandfather who started to assemble the present family vineyard immediately after the phylloxera. Today it consists of a number of parcels of land mostly on slopes facing south-east: but there are also 2 hectares on the other side of the valley looking back towards the domaine. There are 13 hectares in all which make Teulier the largest single producer, responsible for about 10% of the total Marcillac production, a reminder of how small the whole *vignoble* is today, even after twenty-five years.

Marcillac is particularly hard hit by the present ban on the planting of further vines in appellation areas. This seems to defy any element of logic or continuity on the part of those responsible for making decisions on agricultural policy, whether in Brussels or in Bordeaux. During the 1970s the rebuilding of the old terraces at the top of the slopes was encouraged by substantial financial help from the local equivalent of the County Council and the Chamber of Agriculture, who recognised that the Vallon was unlikely to have any economic future without the wine of Marcillac. Production would be encouraged to grow, and the quality would rise too because historically the finest wines had always been made in the difficult terrain of the terraces which had been the first to be abandoned after the phylloxera.

Now, twenty years later, a short time in the history of a vineyard, the growers are forbidden to plant new ground at all. The surplus of wine in the European Community has meant that each wine-producing country has had to find ways of capping its own production. In France, the Government has delegated this task to the industry itself, so it is not surprising that powerful lobbies have protected themselves at the expense of the smaller appellations. At a time when Bordeaux has several years' stocks of wines which it cannot sell, André Metge has a ready market for twice as much Marcillac as he can produce, but his members are not allowed to plant any more vines, unless they are younger growers starting up.

This is a grievance which you meet everywhere in the country vineyards of the South-West. Present policies threaten to stop in its tracks the revival of quality wine-making in those areas which had at one time received both the blessing and financial encouragement of the politicians. André Metge feels that it is extremely unlikely that the latter will intervene to help the smaller growers, having passed the buck in the first place, although small relaxations in the rules are sometimes decreed for AOC areas which have no problems in commercialising their wines. Even so the whole of the Marcillac area will get only an extra 8 hectares of vines from the latest concession.

Teulier's postal address is the small village of Goutrens, set in the middle of a plateau of park-like pasture, and as you set off in search of Le Cros, you have no hint of the surprise in store. As you round a bend in the road, the landscape is suddenly transformed as the Vallon comes into view 700 feet below you. Where for miles there had been no farming except cattle, now there is nothing but architected vine-terraces, some planted, others still abandoned. The views across to the other side are stupendous, especially in the late afternoon sunshine. So is the vista looking northwards down the narrow rift in the hills. The green vegetation is in sharp contrast to the purply red soil, called locally *le rougier*.

You can hardly believe that this sparsely populated countryside was once the homeland of thousands of people, much of whose lives was devoted to hewing out the sides of the hills, building retaining walls for the vines against erosion by the rains, or otherwise banking up the plants to prevent their being washed down the hillsides. In such a landscape the mansois terraces could not be reached by plough or oxen: all the work had to be done by hand. The stones and earth washed down in the storms had to be carried back uphill in baskets on the backs of men, some of whom had living quarters in primitive huts in the hills to which their womenfolk would bring their midday meal.

In those days the terraces were sometimes wide enough to take six or seven rows of vines, and there would be a stone wall seven or eight feet high before the next terrace, with a stairway built into it to give access to the next level. A good example of this can be seen today above the hamlet of Cougousse, where there is a vineyard with eight such terraces.

Nowadays, where the terraces have been replanted, the rows of vines have been set far enough apart to enable small tractors to pass between them, although the *vendange* itself still has to be done by hand. The yield from such a vineyard is relatively low, and the quality of wine correspondingly high. On the gentler slopes, terracing can sometimes be dispensed with altogether. Generally speaking the wine from the lower vines is not as good, because the yield is higher and there is a smaller proportion of schist in the soil than on the higher terraces. The lower ground is also more at risk from spring frosts.

In the shock of arriving at the edge of the valley, it is easy to miss Teulier's domaine, Le Cros, which is itself set into the hillside. The *vignerons* in this sort of terrain can make the maximum use of gravity. As the grapes come in from the vineyards, the *égrappage* and the pressing is done on the top floor, as it were, and the juice goes into the *cuves* on the next level down. When the fermentation is finished, the wine goes down another floor to the Cave where the *barriques* are. This system has the advantage of avoiding sideways and upwards pumping to a very large extent, which in turn reduces the amount of disturbance to the wine.

De-stalking at Le Cros is total, and the grapes, once crushed, are vinified in stainless steel for between fifteen and twenty days at 30–32°: beyond this point fermentation is in danger of stopping. After racking, the wine is transferred into the old *barriques*, where the second malolactic fermentation takes place. Philippe Teulier makes two red *cuvées*: his basic wine is matured for six months, but the better wine, made largely from the very old vines planted by his great-grandfather, is given another twelve months in the old wood.

Marcillac is little seen outside its region of production, where it is popular in the local shops and restaurants. Teulier has succeeded in interesting some famous restaurants such as Les Jardins de l'Opéra in Toulouse and the two Thuriès restaurants in Cordes in his wine, and it is also available in the United Kingdom. He can justly claim that his is some of the best Marcillac made. His 1992, tasted just after it had been bottled, was highly successful seeing that the vintage had taken place in pouring rain and deep mud. The 1994 was a good follow-up; in addition to the usual range of red fruits, it had a spicy nose and quite a powerful almond character. The *cuvée spéciale* was more sophisticated and beginning to taste closer to a cabernet franc wine. It was less grassy and the marzipan was missing, but it was rounder, suppler and longer, partly because of its greater maturity, but also perhaps because it had spent longer in wood before being bottled. Teulier's 1994 is good too, and the prospects for 1995 are better still.

Teulier could not be more different from his friend and rival-producer, **Jean-Luc Matha (6M)**: the former is quiet and reflective, polished perhaps by his oenological training at Montpellier, whereas Matha is the opposite, ebullient, outgoing and with a mischievous twinkle in the eye. He is a big man, and this makes more beguiling his romantic fanaticism for the wines of the Vallon. He waxes lyrical over the old-style *vendanges*, even about the hardships of tending such difficult vineyards without mechanical aids. The Aveyronnais are not given to blarney, but one might be excused for taking with a pinch of salt his claim that, in the old days, the pickers used to drink up to 14 or 15 litres of wine a day at the time of the *vendange*. In the cellar, he has developed with Teulier a technique for breaking up the *chapeau* which forms on the top of the must with a system of wooden sticks which, he says, simulates the treading of the grapes with the feet.

Matha must be a throw-back to an earlier generation, because his father gave up most of his land to take a job in Rodez to support the family. Matha always nurtured a passion for the family vines. He started by joining the co-opérative, but his desire to look after the making of the wine as well as the growing of the grapes persuaded him to set up on his own. He regards each aspect of the production as complementary to the other: it is the grower's job to concentrate as much as possible on the grapes, and the wine-maker's to extract as much as possible from them. Only one thing matters and that is quality, which he says is the key to the future of small appellations like Marcillac. He claims that each year he pushes back the frontiers of quality a little further, though, given a year like 1992, he concedes that all the efforts in the world will not make up for a cold, grey summer and a drenched harvest.

His landholding has grown to 11¹/₂ hectares: Matha sees no future for the part-time polycultural wine-grower in Marcillac, a view with which Teulier but few others of the independents would agree. He grows nothing but mansois officially, though he likes to have a row or so of auxerrois and some jurançon noir for his own amusement. At the drop of a hat he will shovel you into his Land-Rover and take you on a hair-raising conducted tour of his terraces, which is quite an alarming experience. Perhaps this is the best way of appreciating the amazing gradients at which these grapes are grown. They are all on south-west facing slopes above the village of Bruéjols, towards the head of the valley of the Ady. He talked a great deal to me about the mansois: he said it was important to limit the height of the vines otherwise the grapes would not ripen. Because the variety had become so established in the particular soil and micro-climate of the Vallon, it was more resistant to malady than most other varieties, so sulphating was not necessary as often as elsewhere. He did, however, point out to me a nasty bug which curled the vine-leaf round itself into a neat tight roll, the better to suck out the juices: this is called, appropriately enough, *le sigarié*.

Matha produces a little rosé because it sells well during the season following the vintage and helps the cash-flow: so does Teulier, but both of them concentrate on the red wines which represent 90% of their output. Both men make their wine in very similar ways, except that Matha gives the grapes an even longer *cuvaison* of 25–30 days after total de-stalking of the grapes. Matha claims to have been the first wine-maker in the Vallon to have destalked his bunches of grapes, and now it is the recommended practice throughout the appellation. In his case it is essential in view of the long vinification. Wine left as long as this on its stalks and pips would become green, woody and bitter if vinified out fully. His old *barriques* are worthy rivals to those of Teulier: they include one which holds no fewer than 1735 litres. Matha stresses the utmost importance of hygiene, but with only the minimum use of sulphur.

Like Teulier he makes two reds with the same periods of *élevage* in wood. It was interesting to compare their wines, and it would be difficult as well as invidious to prefer one to the other, since they are such good friends. Matha's new wine is more restrained than Teulier's, lighter too, but it is very fruity and forward and makes delicious drinking in the short term. It has minimal ageing prospects. The special *cuvée* which Matha opened was his 1989 and it was just about at its peak after four years. It had splendid legs, the gothic arches mirroring those which I had seen in the houses of Clairvaux earlier the same afternoon. The colour was a deep intense garnet, and the nose spicy like Teulier's 1992. The fruit was amazing with plums and currants and the finish was really long. The 1994 and 1995 should be good too. Both these growers make a sophisticated premium wine. Perhaps in the process some of the typical Marcillac character gets lost. True Marcillac fans may often prefer the basic wines to these special *cuvées*, but for those who find the Marcillac taste a bit too much, the softer, more sophisticated style of the premium wines may be preferred.

I have not been able to find any other growers in the Vallon who produce more than one red *cuvée*. That may not be surprising when the other eight have only about 15% of the total Marcillac production between them. Some of the wines which they make are however excellent, many in perhaps a more authentic rustic style than the wines from the larger growers.

Take **Pierre Lacombe (7M)**, for example. He is to be found in the town of Marcillac, close by the railway viaduct on the road going south to Rodez. The *salle des fêtes* is next door with a large car park and many visitors are tempted into believing that this is Monsieur Lacombe's Cave. The real Cave is out of town, but Monsieur Lacombe is usually on hand to enable visitors to taste his wine in Marcillac itself. With 3¹/₂ hectares he is the largest of the smaller independent growers. Like everybody else he makes a little rosé for the summer trade, but, as he says, '*Marcillac est surtout un vin rouge.*' Even so he makes also a modest white *vin de pays* from chenin blanc and aligoté.

Monsieur Lacombe is a little older than some of his fellow-growers, but then his father was making Marcillac when most had given up, winning a first prize in Rodez as long ago as 1933. His all-mansois vineyard is in small parcels dotted about the region, but all the vines face south-west and enjoy a good position on slopes just outside town.

I was to find a similar pattern with all the small growers I visited: no *égrappage*, fermentation in open wooden barrels, though the vinification period may vary from eight to fifteen days. With Lacombe, it is longer rather than shorter: after racking, the wine is transferred to old *barriques* of which Lacombe has a collection to vie with the best. This is done as close as possible to the shortest day, which Lacombe says is ideal. The new wine does not like the light, in his view. There it stays for six months until the longest day, when it is bottled.

The wine-making may be simple, but it is spotlessly clean, and growers like Lacombe make one wonder whether all the expense of modern plant is not an example of the law of diminishing returns. Certainly the new wine, tasted just after bottling, has the typical deep garnet colour, shot through with purple glints. The style is entirely natural and *artisanale*. Lacombe makes no attempt to push up the alcoholic content with extra sugar: he is quite happy that it measures only 10¹/₂°. Perhaps this was how Marcillac always used to be, and the modern wine is a shade too complicated? Again, 1994 and 1995 will be good.

Claudine Costes (2M) at Combret is another who does not mind that her wine does not reach too dizzy a height in terms of alcohol. Her 1992 measured only 10.8° but delicious it was. She has just taken over from her father their farm in this hilltop village at the northern end of the appellation. It has wonderful views down the Dourdou valley to the gorges of that river as they plunge downwards into the Lot. Her partner, who is in charge of the wine-making, explained that, while Decazeville was a thriving industrial centre, they sent all their wine there *en vrac*. After the collapse of the *bassin houillier*, when it became official policy to encourage Marcillac to revert to being a quality wine, her father started to bottle his wine for sale. In the old days there had been quite a lot of jurançon noir in the vineyards, but the coming of VDQS and later AOC status outlawed its retention, so that today there is only mansois. Some of the vines are therefore relatively young.

The wine is made exactly as at Lacombe, though the vinification may be a little shorter and bottling takes place in the spring without fining. The wine is drawn off its lees and bottled with simple filtration. It will have been racked twice during the late winter and spring.

Although the Costes' farm enjoys such a superb position, it faces the wrong direction for wine-growing. The vines themselves are in two quite separate parcels round the other side of the hill, facing of course towards the afternoon sun. The soil is nearly entirely *rougier*, with very little chalk or stone, so you might expect that the wines would be coarser and more acidic than some others. This is not the case: the red which we tasted was deliciously fresh and fruity and could stand comparison with any others. It was wonderfully bright and clear despite conditions which might have caused eyebrows to be raised in more sophisticated wineries. The bottling is all done by hand, we were told with an apologetic smile. No apology was necessary.

A feature of the farm is the wonderful vaulted cellar which the Costes bought from the Marquis de Valady, whose family own the medieval château which crowns the village. When he needed to raise some money he sold off some of the village buildings, including this natural, cool and moist cellar where Claudine Costes keeps her *barriques*. These are now so old and hard that they need no maintenance.

The barrels of **Jean-Marie Revel (14M)** are nearly as tough as their owner. Jean-Marie has a farm at Mernac on the Côte des Austremoines, just above the valley running down from Salles-la-Source. A high proportion of the smaller growers live in this part of the Vallon, where the soil is more characteristic of the *causse* than of the usual red soil of Marcillac. Jean-Marie is an enormous fellow, everybody's idea of a second-row rugby forward. He is the fourth generation of Revels at this farm, and he has a worthy successor in his two-year-old son who promises to be as big and tough as he is. His grandfather was a stone-mason as well as a *vigneron*, so was able to build his own wine-making plant himself, including a magnificent stone wine-press.

Jean-Marie likes to concentrate on his 3 hectares of vines, but the family also keeps 200 ewes up on the *causse* above the farm. Every day a van comes to collect the milk and take it to the Caves of Roquefort where it is transformed into cheese. The Revels thus have a continuous source of cheap cheese, and the family eats a quarter of a whole cheese a day, which may account for Jean-Marie's robustness.

In the old days, Salles was the nearest wine-making village of the Vallon to the town of Rodez, and Jean-Marie explained that the hillside above the village was riddled with old Caves in the rock from the pre-phylloxera days. He himself still has a Cave at Salles two or three miles away, as well as the one at his farm at Mernac.

He told us that, because of the difference in soil, the wines of Salles tended to be more rustic in style than those made lower down the Vallon. His own wine was certainly ultra-typical of Marcillac, with loads of soft fruit and plums, the wine showing well after only nine months from the vintage. Again one marvelled at such a characterful wine emerging from such an unsophisticated source. Jean-Marie Revel was surprisingly modest about his wine and almost needed reassuring that it was good. He is concerned about the return he is getting for it, and we agreed that there could be no breakthrough for Marcillac until they were allowed to plant more vines and make more wine, so that there was enough to command a market outside the region of production. Consumers perceived it to be a *petit vin* because there was so little of it, and it does not enjoy the historical links with the outside world, like Cahors and Gaillac for example. Nor were the growers helped by the disastrous frosts of 1991 which had reduced their crops by up to 90% of normal. (Philippe Teulier had told me that, in a good year, he produced as much wine as the whole appellation had made in 1991.)

There is no shortage of optimism though. Many of the best growers are young and very enthusiastic, as well as respectful of a long rural tradition. Marcillac may have had its ups and downs and the *vignoble* is but a fraction of its former size: but the old folklore survives. Every Whit Sunday there is a pilgrimage to the little chapel of Notre Dame de Foncarrieu just above the town of Marcillac: after Mass the trestle tables are set up for an open-air fête to celebrate the new wine. The old country costumes are worn and there is dancing to the *cabrette*, a kind of bagpipe still played in the Auvergne. The casks run free, the phylloxera is forgotten, as are the names of the families whom it forced to emigrate. The people of the Vallon celebrate a saint whom they have created and canonised themselves: a mythical Saint Bourrou, a word in patois meaning the bud of the grape, which at that season is shooting while the country people drink its health. The modern French for Bourrou is *bourgeon*, and the chapel on the hill is locally called Notre Dame des Bourgeons.

The medieval citizens of Rodez who took Marcillac because it was good for their health have a modern echo from Pascal Monestier, the son of the pharmacist in Marcillac. Pascal took as the subject of his thesis for his degree at Montpellier the prevention of cholesterol by a modest consumption of red wine. Taking up the research of others, which tended to show that red wines were beneficial in this respect, especially for those whose diets contained more rather than less fat, he showed that the wines of Marcillac in particular contained naturally more therapeutic qualities than any other, especially compounds called procyamidol and cathecine, both of which have proven anti-cholesterol properties. The local wine-makers are the first to agree that a bottle of red Marcillac is the best possible prescription that Pascal Monestier will ever hand over the counter of his chemist's shop.

ENTRAYGUES ET LE FEL

The vineyards of the Aveyron and the upper valley of the Lot have boundaries which nearly adjoin, but to get from one centre of production to the next is quite an undertaking.

The town of Entraygues is an hour and a half away from Marcillac by car, down winding but outstandingly beautiful roads. It stands at the point of confluence of the rivers Lot and Truyère: in local patois the name means 'Entre Eaux', rather like 'Entre-Deux-Mers'. The Lot here curves from the south-east, off the limestone *causses* of the upper Rouergue, while the Truyère derives from the mountain waters of the wild country of the south-west Cantal. Entraygues therefore stands at the frontiers of the Auvergne: traditionally the wine was largely sold to the Auvergnats, the creators of so many of the bistros of Paris.

Le Fel is the name given to a tract of hill-country to the north-west of the town. It projects a narrow ridge parallel with the Lot valley, and the slopes running down from it to the river produce red wine – no white because of the stony nature of the soil. The terracing is even more dramatic than at Marcillac, just the occasional row of vines here and there, clinging to the sides of the mountain: one of the growers told me that you have virtually to rope yourself to the vines in order to pick the grapes. This must be the most dramatic of all French wine-landscapes, the sinuous river Lot curving its way through the gorges 1500 feet below.

The sun-baked terraces of Le Fel make a bizarre contrast to the northern slopes of the ridge facing the other way towards the Auvergne. Here goats have nibbled for a hundred years at the scrubby remains of the chestnut plantations. The region is still called La Châtaigneraie, but the chestnut crop is now of no importance because of disease which afflicted the forests at about the same time as the phylloxera struck at the vineyards. In former times, the two crops were as important as each other, the chestnut trees being as carefully tended as the vines. Today the northern slopes of Le Fel are bare, while the once magnificent vine-terraces on the southern side are but a shadow of their former selves.

I have found only two small producers still making wine on a commercial scale at Le Fel. Most of the wine from the tiny Entraygues appellation is made on the outskirts of the small town itself, on much lower and more easily cultivable ground, where white as well as red and pink wine can be made, and where the white is the most successful.

The vineyard is an ancient one, records going back as far as the year 902, showing that the Abbey of Conques was just as influential at Entraygues as at Marcillac. In feudal times much of the land was in the fiefdom of the bishopric of Rodez, and later the bourgeoisie of Aurillac became keen buyers, as did the mountain farmers of the high Aubrac plateau where vines would not grow. The vineyards at one time extended to over 1000 hectares, and there was scarcely a corner of the south-facing slopes of the river gorges that was not planted with vines if capable of nurturing them.

The working of vineyards in such terrain was even harder than at Marcillac. Even today machines cannot deal with the old terraces and the gradients. Every operation has to be done by hand, except in the few places where replanting has taken place with enough space between the rows. The rapid depopulation of the area which followed the phylloxera, here almost total in its destructive effect, meant that there was no labour for the replanting, even if there was the will or the resources. The decline was rapid and complete. Today the vineyard is no more than 20 hectares in all. Marcillac may be a relatively small vineyard, but Entraygues is tiny, producing only about 600 hectolitres a year to Marcillac's 5000.

There is no cave co-opérative, but **François Avallon (2EN)** has taken it upon himself to form an unofficial *syndicat* including all the six other growers, for there are only seven of them all told. François' own vineyards are just behind the town of Entraygues, over which they have a panoramic view. It was his father who started planting vines as recently as 1955, when he arrived in the small suburb of St Georges. He now has just 4 hectares, half of which is given over to chénin blanc, the only grape that nowadays goes into the making of white Entraygues. In the old days they used to use small quantities of mauzac and barroque, but neither has remained in favour.

François Avallon has just started to make a *cuvée spéciale* of white wine, the first year being the unfortunate 1992. His equipment certainly justifies it, because it is very up-to-date in such a small property. The grapes are rapidly stripped of their stalks and pips at a low temperature, and the vinification is allowed to proceed only at 18–19° in water-cooled stainless or enamelled steel. The *cuvée spéciale* was a very good wine indeed: it does not need to be too cold, because the character seems only to be released with a slight aeration at room temperature: a flinty bouquet gives way to apples and almonds. The wine is bone-dry and gives that slight tingle on the lips which you get with a white Loire. 1993 was a better year – that extra fruit on the palate making it very exciting. 1995 should be better still.

The red and rosé wines come from an *assemblage* of mansois and the two cabernets, together with a little gamay for the rosé, which gives it a little extra fruit. Monsieur Avallon makes two reds as well as two whites. The basic version comes from mansois and cabernet sauvignon. The *cuvée spéciale* is nearly all cabernet franc with just a little gamay. It would be difficult for the reds to come up to the quality of the whites, and one can hardly say they do. They have more rusticity, but match well the style of the local cuisine.

Not all his colleagues would agree with Avallon's view that Entraygues needs promotion to AOC status, but there is pressure being brought to bear by the authorities to adopt a 100% mansois style for the Entraygues reds and rosés. Some see this as an attempt to push a reverse take-over into Marcillac, whose growers are jealous of the independence and good name of Entraygues.

Jean-Marc Viguier (7EN), the other main producer at present, says that there is little point in promotion because Entraygues cannot meet even the existing demand for its wines. If there were an expansion of the vineyard, then it might be necessary to find markets away from the Aveyron and the Auvergne, but, because of the restrictions on new planting, this seems a low priority at the moment. The tiny total production explains why, although Entraygues is much admired locally, you are unlikely to find it more than 50 miles from its source. But visitors to the region will find it easily available in shops and restaurants.

You will find Jean-Marc Viguier's *chais* as you come down into Entraygues on the main road from Aurillac: it is also signed off the valley road which runs along the Lot. His 5 hectares, which make him marginally the largest grower, are on sloping ground, but nothing like as hilly as the vineyards at Le Fel. He has now taken over from his father, and it is good to see such a small appellation largely in the hands of younger men. He comes from an old local family and a somewhat urban polish has done nothing to diminish his Aveyronnais passion for his vines. He nowadays has no other crop, but his family used to have cows and goats as well as extensive chestnut plantations: in those days the farm was an extended family with some six or seven employees working in the vines and woods. The farmer could at that time hedge his bets against a bad summer, but, as Jean-Marc said, nowadays it is the banks which carry that risk.

Viguier's production is half white and half red and rosé. Like Avallon, Viguier de-stalks his white grapes (all chenin) *à froid*, and the fermentation is long and cold, perhaps 21 days at 18–19°. The wine is bottled in March after the lightest possible sulphuring. I did not like his 1992 as well as Avallon's: it had less acidity, but less character too. The 1990 *cuvée spéciale* was excellent though, with a bouquet of quinces and, according to Jean-Marc, ground almonds. The fruit was well developed which prompted me to ask Jean-Marc whether his white wines kept, as Vouvray does. He said that he has some 1975s which are still in excellent condition, and he rates his 1987s highly. He disagreed with most commentators who find it all too easy to dismiss Entraygues as a wine to be drunk within the year.

The red wines from his vineyards, which are called Le Buis, derive from a bewildering array of grape-varieties, quite astonishing for only 2¹/₂ hectares of land. His basic red and his rosé come from a blend of gamay, a touch each of jurançon noir and cabernet franc, and quite a lot of a grape called négret. Viguier was adamant that this is a purely local variety and is not related to the négrette of Fronton. I found it again in Estaing, where it was called négret de Banhars, the latter being a small village a few miles up the Truyère from Entraygues. One grower told me he thought it was related to the abouriou grape of Marmande, which seems rather improbable. When I asked the director of the Fronton co-opérative whether he thought that the négrette, which he said was to be found nowhere in France but in and around Fronton, could have a country cousin in the hills of the Aveyron, he seemed amazed: he agreed, however, that it was possible that the two grapes, if not identical, could be related. Anyway it is a good part of Jean-Marc's basic red, from which he draws off his rosé after it has attained the required colour.

Viguier de-stalks most (80%) but not all of his grapes, and fermentation is partly in cement and partly in fibre-glass. He prefers the latter material for his *cuves*, because these can be used for the cold de-stalking of the white grapes as well as the longer-term storage of red wine. The mainstream red spends six months in the *cuves* before bottling.

The red *cuvée spéciale* is 50% mansois and 50% cabernet franc. It gets twelve months in barrel. All the wood is old, and he says he has no intention of experimenting with new. He aims to make wines which have a commercial span of one to four years, so new oak is of little use to him.

It was interesting to compare his range of red and rosé wines with those of Marcillac. The pink was less grassy than its counterparts from the Vallon, perhaps because of the gamay content. Of the red wines his mainstream is light and what the French call *gouléyant*, easy to drink like a *vin nouveau*. The gamay is not however prominent, well masked by the other varieties. The *cuvée spéciale* needs only a few more months to become a quite impressive wine. The mansois dominates, but the cabernet franc prevents this red Entraygues from being a Marcillac lookalike.

A trip to Le Fel is a must for visitors to Entraygues, although it takes longer to get there than you would expect from the map. Whether you approach from the main Aurillac road, or from the floor of the valley of the Lot, you will have earned a glass of cool white wine at Madame Albespy's excellent *auberge*, which will prepare you for a visit to the youngest grower in this area. **Laurent Mousset (5EN)** is only a few yards up the road from the pub at a farm called Cassos, where they sell goats' cheese at the door. Young Monsieur Mousset's aunt has a little restaurant nearby which serves as an outlet for the Mousset wines.

There was no vineyard on the Mousset farm until Laurent returned from his studies at Angoulême, bent on creating one. He is serious about his chosen task, shy and quietly spoken, but there lurks somewhere inside the passion of the *vigneron* which you find all over this region. In 1988 he rented 3 hectares from a neighbour, built his own terracing and planted some vines, mansois and cabernet franc for the most part with a little cabernet sauvignon for good measure. Even though Laurent enjoys some security of tenure, he is happier now that he has been able to plant two more hectares which he has bought outright. His 5 hectares will put him in the big league in Entraygues when the new vines are producing.

Laurent Mousset was lucky that, as a young grower starting out on his own, he was not barred by rules from going ahead with his planting plans. He thinks it may be a good thing that the French Minister of Agriculture comes from the Aveyron! He is also lucky in having Jean-Marc Viguier as a cousin, because the latter's father, now retired at Le Buis, has had time on his hands to help his enthusiastic young nephew in the creation of this new vineyard. The situation of the vines is classic: directly south-facing with plenty of protection against the cold weather from the north. The rows are planted wide enough apart in their brand-new terraces to allow the smallest tractors to pass up and down, but all the harvesting is done by hand. He is helped by his father, his brother who has just taken over the running of the rest of the farm, and any other family arms he can twist.

1992 was his first vintage – a difficult year on the flat, let alone on the slopes of Le Fel. The vines too are still young, but he felt obliged to make some wine, if only to placate the bank manager. He follows the Viguier red-grape pattern. One-third of his production is rosé, and highly attractive it is too. Very fresh, with a strong almondy character, this must be one of the best Aveyron pink wines I have come across. Because of the poor quality of the 1992 vintage, the red wine was not as successful, but Laurent Mousset tells me that, in 1995, he has at last made red Entraygues of which he is already proud.

Apart from the three growers I have mentioned, you will be lucky to find any other Entraygues on sale even locally, except perhaps for those of **Auguste Abeil (1EN)** and **Raymond Fau (3EN)**, whose 1 hectare of vines is just over the border into the Cantal. When we met Monsieur Fau, he did not seem very hopeful that he would be producing wine for much longer, since he did not have a son to follow on after him. He was, however, proud of his daughter who was responsible for a herd of sixty-five goats. From these she made a cheese which she sells as far afield as Paris and Cannes, a far cry from the terraces of the Cantal. Perhaps one day her husband will want to take over the vines?

Another elderly grower with no one to take over after him was Monsieur Ferrary, whom we found perched vertiginously, himself rather like a mountain goat, hundreds of feet above the river Truyère at Haut-Couesque. He has retired now, or rather it would be more correct to say that he has abandoned his vines to the weeds. He no longer pays his subscription to the *syndicat* run by François Avallon but, he says, this does not prevent him from turning up to their meetings and giving them the benefit of his long experience.

ESTAING

The third of the wine-growing areas in the Aveyron which were spawned by the monks of Conques is a little further up the Lot from Entraygues, centred on the small town of Estaing. The castle, built by a member of the eponymous family who was a bishop of Rodez in the sixteenth century, dominates a cluster of quaint, slated buildings at the centre. As at Entraygues downstream and Espalion upstream, the river is spanned by an especially handsome Gothic bridge which here connects the town with the road to Marcillac. Everything about Estaing is picturesque, except for the seemingly endless convoys of large lorries grinding their laborious way from Rodez to Aurillac and back.

The wine-records go back a mere six hundred years and the first mention of Estaing wine is found in the archives of the tiny mountain monastery of Cabrespines. Equally tiny is the extent of the modern production of Estaing wine, even smaller than that of Entraygues: Estaing claims to be the smallest VDQS in France. Today the growers have but 15 hectares between them, and make only 400 hectolitres of VDQS wine, about 53,000 bottles each year.

The presiding genius is Monsieur Pierre Rieu who has a delightful farm up in the hills on the road to Laguiole, but is more likely to be found at the mini cave co-opérative, which he directs. Just outside the town to the north-east in a pretty sheltered valley, it is called **Le Caveau du Viala (1ES)**. His story of the local wine corresponded in large measure with the history of Marcillac. Before the First World War there were 1000 hectares under vine, but mostly on unsuitable ground and planted with inferior varieties. A handful of local growers managed to get VDQS status for Estaing in 1979, and a little later in 1983 SAFALT (Société Agricole Foncière de l'Aveyron, Lot et Tarn) helped them to reclaim some of the terraces at the top of the slopes. More land still was recovered from the forest and the undergrowth in 1985. Monsieur Rieu told me how the woods were infested with honey-fungus, which can still be a menace to the vines.

The rebuilding of the terraces was experimental in another sense. The land was acquired in common by four of the six members of the co-opérative; the other two are apparently kicking themselves that they did not join in, because it is on this land that the grapes which go into the Cave's best *cuvée* are grown. Monsieur Rieu says that it is unique in France for a vineyard to be owned in this way. The 5 hectares in question are all planted on the hillsides opposite the Cave. They still have problems with erosion, and it seems that physical removal of the weeds can accentuate the difficulties by destabilising the soil. Monsieur Rieu jokingly wondered whether it might be possible to apply a good dose of weedkiller on a Sunday morning when everyone was at Mass.

The move to get VDQS status was initiated by the ten independent growers who were operating in 1979. Six of them eventually formed the co-opérative which has 10 hectares in all. Monsieur Rieu is expecting three new young members to join, each bringing with them 1 hectare with planting rights. The Cave has capacity to make 500 hectolitres of wine, so they can easily accommodate this modest expansion.

The Cave makes wine in all three colours, though 60% of the production is red. The soil is 80% *schiste*, much more stony than in the other Aveyron vineyards, so the mix of grape-varieties is not the same. For their basic *cuvée*, they use about 60% gamay, a tiny bit of négret and nearly 40% pinotous d'Estaing, probably a locally bastardised sub-variety of pinot noir. For the premium wine, an *assemblage* is made from the two cabernets, merlot and mansois. The rosé is made by *saignage*, that is to say, drawing it off from the basic red wine after about twenty-four hours on the skins. The white wine is a relatively small part of the output and is made from 70% chenin blanc and 30% mauzac.

At present the Cave does not practise *égrappage*, but they plan soon to acquire the necessary plant. The *cuvaison* is short, only four to six days according to the vintage. Surplus production goes into a *vin de table*: Monsieur Rieu says that in good years this can be of the same standard as the VDQS wine; in bad years it is rather ordinary.

Monsieur Rieu thinks that at the Cave they make a better wine than that of any of the three independent producers, but then he would, wouldn't he? I have to say that I did not like his white as much as Madame Fages', nor the red as much as Michel Alaux's, but the range was generally well made and of pleasing quality. The rosé is perhaps the best. The wines are quite widely available in the region of production, but would be difficult to find outside the Aveyron. The problem with them is that, although they have a certain rustic charm, they lack the individuality either of the Marcillac reds or the Entraygues whites, so it was particularly interesting to visit some private producers who are still making and bottling their own wines.

Halfway along the valley to Espalion, a narrow twisting lane leads up past the Romanesque church of Vinnac to a small farm called **La Ponsarderie (3ES)**, the home of Monique Fages. Her husband has retired and passed the vineyards over to her, and she is resigned to the fact that none of her four children is interested in taking them on, though one of her sons works in Pommard. She is pleased, though, that the family was instrumental in getting the VDQS status for Estaing in 1979. Before that they had a variety of inferior grapes – and they made more wine than they do today, but it was all sold *en vrac*, and fetched a pittance. Now she has only 2 hectares of the permitted varieties, and has grubbed up the rest, though she still has some very old vines planted by her husband's parents. She had thought of joining the Cave, but decided not to because she had a number of old customers whom she wanted to go on supplying herself. She is the only independent grower to make white Estaing, and very good it is too, the best we tasted, made from chenin blanc with just a little mauzac. I am not convinced that the addition of mauzac does much for chenin blanc, at least in this terrain. It is traditional in the region, but at Entraygues they phased out mauzac and the wine may be all the better for it. Certainly it dominated the flavour of the Estaing co-opérative's white, which is probably why I preferred Madame Fages', which had only a hint of the grape and was bone dry.

She makes her red from gamay (60%) and mansois (40%), and for the rosé she adds a little jurançon noir, because the wine is not left on the skins and the jurançon noir adds the necessary colour. She also adds a little pinotous. All the *égrappage* is carried out in the vineyard. The *cuvaison* is short – seven days – and the wine is transferred to the barrels before the malolactic fermentation. I asked her about the age of the barrels and she looked at me as though I were a bit stupid. Of course they were old, 'New ones would give an acrid taste to the wine, wouldn't they?'

Madame Fages' vines are situated immediately up the hillside from those of her neighbour Michel Alaux, whose farm, **La Frayssinette (2ES)**, is two or three hairpin bends down the road. The farmhouse was built into the hillside, and we were welcomed by Madame Bilières, Monsieur Alaux's mother-in-law. They have only a tiny holding, less than 1 hectare of vines. They also grow some maize, and have some cattle, most of which had gone up into the mountains for the summer.

They make only red and rosé wines. The red is mostly from gamay and mansois, but they also have a little merlot and jurançon noir, and for the rosé a little pinotous and mauzac. Certainly the rosé which we tasted had the unmistakably appley flavour of the mauzac. The vinification is simple, without *égrappage*, and the red wine is stored in 550-litre *barriques* for six months or a bit more before being bottled. These are housed in a splendid vaulted cellar, which Madame Bilières thought was probably more than 150 years old. There is plenty of space and she explained that, in the old days, they used to make quite a lot of *vin ordinaire* from vines which they had in the valley. She is not sorry they have given that up because it brought in very little money. Anyway, because of the VDQS rules, they had to dig up all the inferior stocks.

I was particularly struck by Monsieur Alaux's red wine. They were lucky to have harvested early in 1992 and so missed the torrential rain which set in on 24 September. The wine was exceptionally fruity, with the mansois exercising a strong minority voice and giving the wine a real *goût du terroir*. I certainly preferred this to the red wine from the third independent producer, **Germain Nayrolles**, whose vineyards at **Majorac (4ES)** are on the other side of the river, some 5 kilometres westward up into the hills. His wine is quite well made, and in fact complements very nicely a plate of *aligot*, the local potato dish made with butter, garlic of course, and the unfermented local cheese from Laguiole. Monsieur Alaux's red remained my firm favourite, however.

The three independent growers produce so little wine between them that they have clubbed together to produce a common label, the only difference being the names and addresses at the bottom. Since they manage to sell all of their wine before the succeeding vintage, they never bother with vintage years on the label.

Vins des Gorges et Côtes de Millau

The ruins of the citadel of Compeyre cut into the skyline of the limestone *causses* which guard the western approaches to the famous Gorges du Tarn. They also guard the access to Millau from the north, frowning on the road which flanks the narrow twisting river and on the larger highway which links Millau to the North of France.

Compeyre was once the most important fortified city of the area. Apart from its military significance, it was also the natural site of hundreds of caves eroded out of the chalky cliffs by the rains and snows of the cold winters. These caves were home to thousands of barrels of quality wine: Compeyre was the warehouse for the very considerable and important production of good wine in this most easterly part of the county of Guyenne. As with the caves at Roquefort on the other side of Millau, fissures in the rocks assured the passage of air which maintained the wine at a perfect temperature, winter and summer. Even today you can see the remains of the rows of Caves, sometimes three storeys high, their now open doors giving on to the open air and looking from afar like a huge gruyère cheese.

For many centuries this was the centre of a rich and extensive vineyard bringing a degree of prosperity and civilisation to this wild country. The vineyards extended from Peyrelau, the gateway of the gorges, as far downstream as Connac, a good deal west of Millau. The region of Millau itself and the parts of the lower valley of the Tarn which run below Montjaux and past St Rome to Broquiès must have looked rather like the vineyards of French Switzerland today, thousands of almond trees decking the vines in spring with their white blossom.

The grapes which made the local wines were called gamay St Laurent, a grape which crops up later in the Garonne valley under its more usual name, abouriou. Clones of this wine are today still called gamay du Pape, because one of the Avignon popes appointed a cardinal who came from Mostuéjols in the gorge of the Tarn, who is said to have entertained His Holiness every year in his native village as a respite from the mosquitoes of the Rhône valley. Naturally the Papal entourage took back to Avignon a plentiful supply of the good wines of Mostuéjols.

The fortress of Compeyre, taken with terrible bloodshed by the Huguenots in the Religious Wars, was largely demolished by the troops of Cardinal Richelieu in the late 1600s, and there followed a decline of the Millau vineyards. Nevertheless they did survive as an important area of production right up to the time of the phylloxera, thanks largely to the coming of the railway. The purpose-built station at Aguessac was connected directly to Paris and the French ports beyond. The local producers had replaced the Caves of Compeyre with others scattered about in the villages betwen Aguessac and Mostuéjols. Travellers can still see on the lintel of a Cave at Contre Pinet a carved figure of Bacchus astride a barrel carousing with his girlfriend Jeanne. Folkloric traditions maintain that the owners of these Caves would have parties outside the doors to which they would invite their neighbours to taste their good Rouergue wine, with dried and salted sardines nicknamed 'gendarmes', a fearsome cheese made from a blend of Roquefort and local eau-de-vie, and the local cake called *fouace*, guaranteed to dry out the tastebuds of even the thirstiest guest. Ribald songs and the most unlikely tales would accompany these tastings which went on for the whole of a Sunday evening, while the womenfolk prayed piously in church that the men would not get too drunk.

In 1850 Doctor Guyot recorded that the vineyards of the Tarn gorges extended over 15,000 hectares and produced 500,000 hectolitres of wine a year. This is rather more than the whole of the vineyards of Bergerac produce today, which gives one a vivid idea of the importance of Millau as a wine-centre before the phylloxera. The sinister aphid was no less successful in its deadly work here than elsewhere: faced with the decision as to how the vineyard might be re-structured the growers took a wrong turning – as at Marcillac they went in for bulk-production, only replanting the easiest of terrains, abandoning the choicest slopes and terraces and covering the lower slopes with poor hybrid vines. The reasons for this policy were much the same as elsewhere: the demand of the expanding working-class for cheap everyday wine, the clamour for an immediate cheap product to replace the sources lost to the phylloxera and the poor return offered by the traditional grape-varieties compared with the high-yielding plants of the Midi. Even this modest renaissance was brought to a sharp end by the two world wars: all the horses which worked the vineyards were requisitioned, and those few soldiers who came back from the battlefields returned to vineyards overgrown with brambles and weeds. Properties fell into ruin, there was a mass exodus of population and it seemed that the vineyards of the Gorges du Tarn were finished. It needed only the frosts of 1956 to deliver the *coup de grâce*.

In this part of the Rouergue the revival of interest in wine-making came about through the pioneering efforts of the local Chamber of Agriculture. After some attempts to introduce fruit-production to the region, it was recognised that the only plant which could succeed the vine was the vine: but this time there would be only the best varieties and the production would be properly planned. A *syndicat* was formed of experimental growers, and an appellation simple was granted. This was soon followed by the stricter discipline of the VDQS: growers who would have to face restaurants and the wine-trade in the wider world needed to persuade potential buyers that the wine from a region which had until recently been producing only plonk was now making a serious wine. Their best prospect lay in the creation of a co-opérative in 1980: it is still one of the smallest in France, but is thriving under the leadership of Louis Valès, and having great success locally with its wines.

One of the problems which faced the producers was the proper title for the appellation, because the vineyards lay mostly in the département of Aveyron, and the rules did not therefore allow them the use of the name of the neighbouring département, Tarn: in any case the *vins de pays des Côtes de Tarn* had already pre-empted the use of 'Tarn' in the title. Eventually the Cave settled for the name Vins des Gorges et Côtes de Millau, accurate if not exactly memorable.

The co-opérative, which is based at Aguessac, is called **Cave des Vignerons des Gorges du Tarn (1G)**. They make four wines from just 100 hectares of grapes: a dry white after the style of Entraygues, from 70% chenin and 30% mauzac; a rosé from equal quantities of modern (real) gamay and cabernet franc; and a red from 40% gamay, 30% syrah, 20% cabernet and 10% from a range of local grapes such as our old friends tannat, malbec, duras and négret. There is also a premium grade of red from 60% cabernet, 10% each gamay and syrah and 20% the other local varieties. The reds I find particularly attractive, the unusual *encépagements* giving them a distinctive personality which goes well with hearty country food.

CÔTEAUX DE GLANES

The market for Aveyron wines in the old days was the mountain farmers of the Aubrac and the Auvergne who could not cultivate their own vines. These customers also had another source of supply, the growers in the upper valley of the Dordogne near Argentat. Vines have long disappeared from the region of that pretty town, but in recent years there has been a revival of wine-making a little further downstream in the hills above Bretenoux in the Lot. Based in the village of Glanes, eight growers have together formed a small co-opérative where they are making a *vin de pays* which is very attractive indeed. When they applied for official recognition as a *vin de pays*, the rules allowed the wine to come from six communes, spread over quite a wide area, but in the event only the farmers in the village of Glanes have availed themselves of it.

There are no terraces here. The descent from the western edge of the Châtaigneraie to the Dordogne is relatively gentle, the countryside being divided between the vine, the walnut and the peach, with a little cattle-growing mixed in. Vines have the first call on the best parcels of land, which are those facing south-west on a soil which is a mixture of clay and sandstone: there are a lot of rough stones which reflect the hot summer sun back on to the lower surfaces of the grapes. The landscape is as peaceful and breathtakingly beautiful as you would expect in these upper reaches of the river.

Monsieur Quercy is not, as you might imagine from his name, the president of the **Vignerons du Haut-Quercy**, which is the full title of the co-opérative: but his farm is exactly opposite the buildings of the Cave, so he seems to get the job of showing most of the visitors round. Like all the other members, he exhibits a plaque at the entrance to his house, indicating his name and membership of the co-opérative. The organisation is highly democratic, having started as a partnership (GAEC) in 1976, developing juridically into a co-opérative in 1992. They employ no manager, let alone other labour: all the work in the Cave is shared between them, even the bottling, for which a rota is drawn up by lot and pinned up in the cellars. All the paperwork is done by the members' wives.

The economy on staff is hardly surprising because the eight members have only 20 hectares between them. Production is at the rate of 50 hectolitres per hectare. The rules permit 70, but in the interests of quality the members discipline themselves by severe pruning in the summer – what is called a *vendange verte* – and they elect a small group of three to supervise quality and best practice in the vineyards.

Vines have been grown at Glanes for hundreds of years, but it was only in the 1960s that quality vines began to be planted. Before that, the

production which was surplus to the growers' own domestic requirements was sold off *en vrac* as *vin ordinaire*. The Auvergnat customers
seemed only to want red wine, perhaps because their demand for white
was met by the vineyards of Entraygues. This explains why today the
Glanes vineyards only produce red wine, and only one *cuvée* of it at that.
It comes from 40% gamay, 40% merlot and 20% ségalin. No, that is not a
misprint: ségalin is a new cross between jurançon noir and portugais
bleu, both of which were once common in the Cahors vineyards until the
Second World War. The Glanes growers like the gamay for its fruit and
the merlot for its alcohol and roundness, but they needed something to
give their wine a distinctiveness, an element of rusticity and depth of
colour. The ségalin was therefore specially created for them by experts
in Bordeaux, and they are the only officially denominated vineyard to
use it. It is also said to be resistant to rot and *coulure*, the principal drawback of merlot.

It will be noticed that all these varieties are early maturing, so could
be harvested before the rains in years like 1992 and 1994. The wine
from them is also quick to develop, which reflects the policy of the
Cave: to make a wine which they can turn round fast for their members
without tying too much capital up in stocks. At the same time they are
very conscious that the French are nowadays drinking less wine, but
expect it to be good: so it is important that *vins de pays* such as theirs are
of the best possible quality. For this reason they are not enthusiastic
about expanding either their membership or production.

Fermentation can be either in cement or stainless steel: they have
both, including a very expensive-looking brand-new outdoor steel *cuve*.
They need water-cooling at Glanes, especially since they prefer a cooler
temperature than some other wine-makers: 25–27°. Once the wine has
been racked off its lees, the *cuves* are cleaned and used for the malolactic fermentation. As soon as this is finished the *assemblage* is made.

Like the other wines of the hill-country, distribution is very largely
local. Monsieur Quercy claims a high 70% of private customers living in
the district, with most of the rest taken up by restaurants, shops and
hotels. In fact there are few restaurants in the region which do not feature
the wine of Glanes on their lists, so travellers will have no difficulty in
sampling it.

What of the wine itself? The general impression is of a softened version of Marcillac. Red summer fruits on the nose and a slightly raspberry
flavour, but without the pronounced grassiness of the other wine, and
with much softer tannins. It has good style and finishes well – it comes as
no surprise that it has won strings of medals in Paris from 1980 onwards.

VIN PAILLÉ DE QUEYSSAC

My first visit to the Dordogne was in 1960, and I stayed in a modest
country *auberge* at Queyssac-les-Vignes, tucked away in the hills between
Beaulieu and Vayrac in the Corrèze. It was called Au Vin Paillé, and I

kept for many years a vague recollection that they served as an apéritif a sweet dark wine after which the pub was named.

Over thirty years later, I went back to Queyssac for a trip down memory lane – more specifically lunch. The meal was fine, but alas the eponymous wine was no longer available. I was in luck, however, a couple of days later, when staying at the Central Hotel in Beaulieu, where Madame Fournier not only served the wine but was kind enough to give me the address of the maker, a Madame Soursac, who lives in the lower part of the village of Queyssac.

One must worry that, when Madame Soursac retires or gives up her 1 hectare of vines in the back of beyond at Queyssac-Bas, the traditional *vin paillé* will die out. Similar wines are made by farmers and local artisans for their own consumption, but I know of no other maker on a commercial scale. The wine is made by putting the grapes to dry indoors on a bed of straw with plenty of ventilation. By midwinter the grapes have shrivelled almost completely, what little juice there is having become very concentrated. The grapes are pressed and slowly fermented for a few months and the resulting wine is then matured in cask for a year or two. By this time it has become really dark, dense and sugary, but with a redeeming twist of acidity which makes it delicious before a meal, or as a substitute for port with melon. If you are lucky enough to find this wine, don't miss the chance of trying it: it might be your last.

VIN DE PAYS DE CORRÈZE

A little further to the west, at the village of Branceilles and still in the hills of Corrèze, is a new *vin de pays*, developed under the aegis of Monsieur Perrinet, who is a friend of Monsieur Quercy from Glanes. It too consists of a small co-opérative of growers (tel: 55-84-09-01) in the attractive hill-country between Brive and the Dordogne valley, described on their wine label as 'terrain truffier'. They have not been helped by frost and hail in recent years which combined almost to halt production in its tracks. They also hit a marketing problem when the name they chose for the product – Mille Pierres – turned out to have already been registered by someone else. They have now decided to call the Branceilles wine Mille et une Pierres. It would be a pity if bad luck continued to plague such a new and enterprising venture. Their 1991 was very attractive indeed, with a forward merlot character and much in the same style as Côteaux de Glanes. Another example of *vin de pays de Corrèze* is called Domaine de Mégénie and comes from Voutézac. It is the house red at the popular Parisian brasserie, Thoumieux, between the Hôtel des Invalides and the Eiffel Tower.

PRODUCERS

MARCILLAC

3***CAVE DES VIGNERONS DU VALLON**, 12330 Valady Tel: 65-72-70-21
　9M　*Marcel **Bardou**, La Boutique, 12330 Salles-la-Source Tel: 65-71-82-34*

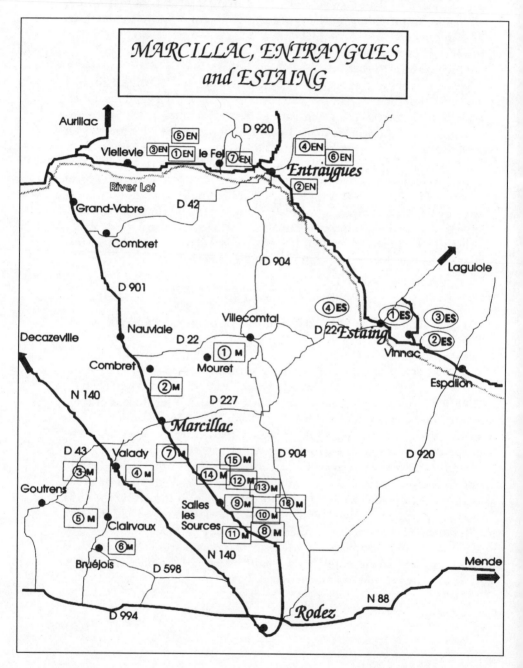

10M *Gabriel **Barre**, Alseroque, 12330 Salles-la-Source Tel: 65-46-34-56*
11M *Adrien **Cabrolier**, Limagne, 12330 Salles-la-Source Tel: 65-71-87-77*
8M Pierre **Carles**, Limagnes, 12330 Salles-la-Source Tel: 65-71-74-33
2M *Claudine **Costes**, Combret, 12330 Nauviale Tel: 65-69-81-67
1M Francis **Costes**, La Baronie, 12330 Mouret Tel: 65-69-83-05
12M Philippe **Croizat**, St Austremoine, 12330 Salles-la-Source
Tel: 65-71-82-13
13M Michel **Durand**, Le Monteil, 12330 Salles-la-Source Tel: 65-71-80-96
4M Joel **Gradels**, La Carolie, 12330 Valady Tel: 65-71-80-20
7M *Pierre **Lacombe**, Avenue de Rodez, 12330 Marcillac Tel: 65-71-80-05
6M *Jean-Luc **Matha**, Le Vieux Roche, Bruéjols, 12330 Clairvaux
Tel: 65-72-63-29
14M *Jean-Marc **Revel**, Mernac, 12330 Salles-la-Source Tel: 65-71-76-01
15M *Léon **Romieu**, Mernac, 12330 Salles-la-Source Tel: 65-71-71-49*
16M *Henri **Sanhes**, Limagnes, 12330 Salles-la-Source Tel: 65-71-80-21*
5M *Philippe **Teulier**, Domaine du Cros, 12390 Goutrens Tel: 65-72-71-77

ENTRAYGUES ET LE FEL

1EN *Auguste **Abeil**, Le Fel, 12140 Entraygues Tel: 65-44-58-35
2EN *François **Avallon**, St Georges, 12140 Entraygues Tel: 65-48-61-65
3EN Raymond **Fau**, La Vidalie du Port, 15120 Montsalvy Tel: 71-49-94-13
4EN Fréderic **Forveille**, Méjanassène, 12140 Entraygues Tel: 65-44-54-76
5EN *Laurent **Mousset**, Cassos, Le Fel, 12140 Entraygues Tel: 65-44-52-35
6EN Alain **Souton**, Lavernhe, 12140 Entraygues Tel: 65-44-55-05
7EN *Jean-Marc **Viguier**, Les Buis, 112140 Entraygues Tel: 65-44-50-45

ESTAING

1ES **Le Caveau du Viala**, 12190 Estaing Tel: 65-48-20-96
(cave co-opérative)
2ES Michel **Alaux**, La Frayssinette, 12190 Estaing Tel: 65-48-05-17
3ES Monique **Fages**, La Ponsarderie, 12190 Estaing Tel: 65-44-06-84
4ES Germain **Nayrolles**, Majorac, 12190 Estaing Tel: 65-44-70-41

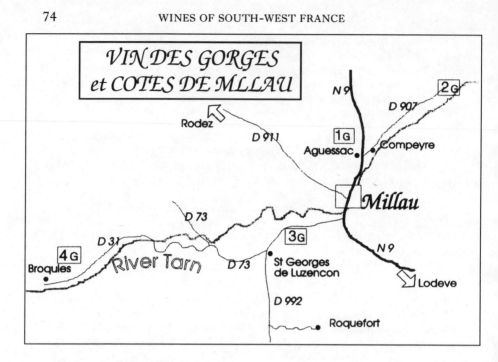

VINS DES GORGES AND CÔTES DE MILLAU

1G   CAVE DES VIGNERONS DES GORGES DU TARN, 12520 Aguessac
       Tel: 65-59-84-11

2G   Xavier **Baudonet**, Place de l'Eglise, 12640 Rivière-sur-Tarn
       Tel: 65-59-86-34

3G   Dominique **Pottier**, Creissac, 121000 St Georges-de-Luzençon
       Tel: 65-62-38-73

4G   Raymond **Toulouse**, La Salvanie, 12480 Broquiès Tel: 65-99-42-36

The Wines of Gaillac

Gaillac was the first inland vineyard which the Romans planted after they had colonised the coast in the area of Narbonne, long before other areas in the South-West, and before even the Rhône valley and Provence where their influence was already well established. By the end of the first century AD the vineyards of Gaillac were already thriving. The discovery of an extensive pottery for making wine-containers in the small town of Montans, and of mosaics depicting wine-harvesting at a nearby Roman villa, conclusively prove the age of the vineyard. Gaillac, whose situation on the banks of the Tarn destined it to take over the primacy of the area from Montans, is on the way north-east from Toulouse towards Albi. Approaching from that direction the vineyards begin at the old town of Rabastens and continue on either bank of the river into the hills on the north bank as far as Cordes.

Today Gaillac is one of the most innovative wine-growing areas of France: but since its Roman beginnings it has had its ups and downs. The collapse of the Roman Empire and its replacement by successive barbarian hordes would have wiped out the vines but for the persistence of the Church. The monks of the abbey at Gaillac laid the basis for a flourishing trade throughout the middle ages. As land-owners, the Church developed a kind of leasing contract under which land was made available to anyone prepared to clear it and plant vines. The tenant paid a tax based on the revenue of the land, a concept reflected later in the much-hated *dîme* tax.

It was not long before local producers started to ship wine down the river Tarn to Bordeaux, where it was either bought for blending or exported. The English connection, which began with the marriage of Henry II to Eleanor of Aquitaine, lasted until the final English defeat at the end of the Hundred Years' War in 1453. During this time, Gaillac wine was a favourite at the English court.

The Gaillacois soon learnt that their biggest enemies were fraud and adulteration. They needed to devise means of maintaining standards common to all wines claiming the name of Gaillac. Rules came into being, policed by the producers themselves under a kind of delegation of authority from the feudal lords. In a primitive system of appellation contrôlée it was decreed, for example, that pigeon droppings were the only permissible fertiliser, a rule which persisted until the nineteenth century, and which explains the presence of so many *pigeonniers* in the region. To prevent adulteration, the importation of other wines into the Gaillac area was forbidden, so that growers should not be able to stretch their wines with others of inferior quality; and the device of a cockerel was used to brand containers as a guarantee of origin. The cockerel is still the local logo.

The planting of a vineyard implies a fifty-year programme: viticulture as a way of life calls for continuity and civil peace. The intermittent wars between the feudal rulers of the region and, in Gaillac's case, the pitiless crusade against the Albigensian heretics had a devastating effect on the countryside. The long struggles between France and England brought in their wake spasmodic periods of plague which decimated the local population. Not until the sixteenth century did local prosperity return. By then the English had left, and the wines of Gaillac were bought almost entirely by the blenders in Bordeaux, whose demand was for robust and alcoholic red wine which was then Gaillac's style. The amount of white wine made in those years was tiny. As the local magistrates themselves proclaimed in 1509:

> In the administrative area and vineyards of Gaillac, we make strong, powerful wines of good quality, of a style which ensures that, the further they travel by land or by sea, the better they are . . .

Certainly the fifty barrels of Gaillac which François I gave Henry VIII when they met at the Field of the Cloth of Gold had not suffered from the journey, because the English King became a regular buyer.

It was at about this time that local producers joined together to establish one of the oldest of the French wine-fraternities, La Companha de la Poda, literally 'the Company of the Pruning-Knife'. Its present-day counterpart is L'Ordre de la Dive Bouteille. Their ceremonial dress consists of a red cloak, edged in black, a red hat in the style of that which Rabelais might have worn, the whole costume touched off with a long red and black chain round the neck from which hangs the Divine Bottle in bronze.

The quantity of wine produced by Gaillac during the *ancien régime*, compared with today, is difficult to establish. Two hundred years ago, there was no standardisation of measures, which varied from locality to locality: the situation is also confused by the modern division of production into three qualities – Gaillac AOC, the *vin de pays des Côtes de Tarn* and *vin de table*; until this century Gaillac wine was simply Gaillac wine.

By 1852 the total volume of wine (of all qualities) produced at Gaillac had reached the huge figure of 4.5 million hectolitres, of which only 12,500 were white. Today the situation is very different. The AOC Gaillac figure for 1989 was a mere 99,000 hectolitres, divided almost two to one in favour of red wine. In addition, there were 173,000 hectolitres of *vin de pays des Côtes de Tarn* and 528,000 of *vin de table*. The total is impressive, but still less than 20% of the 1852 figure.

The scale of Gaillac production in the period immediately before the phylloxera suggests that the vineyard covered at least twenty times the area it does today, taking into account the vastly increased yields in modern times. In the eighteenth century this would vary between 7 and 14 hectolitres to the hectare (according to the quality of the vintage). By the middle of the nineteenth century this had risen to 20, compared with the modern AOC norm of 45. At the level of *vins de table* the modern figure is 120! Even so, the area of land under vine has shrunk dramatically. Today the figure stands at about 10,000 hectares.

Another interesting change is in the pattern of land distribution. In the days before the Revolution, there was a gradual tendency for the units of land-holding to grow, as the number of small producers fell. Afterwards, the trend was sharply reversed, and today there are hundreds of small growers selling their wines through the co-opératives, while the best quality wines are concentrated in the hands of relatively small growers too.

The decline of the Gaillac vineyard, after its golden age in the middle of the last century, was due to the same influences which nearly destroyed Cahors: the creation of the French rail network opened up the Midi to Bordeaux; the mass-production of cheap coarse wine in the Hérault made a serious impact on Gaillac's ability to compete in the market-place; and the building of the Canal du Midi would have provided the *coup de grâce* had not the phylloxera done so even more effectively.

In 1885, a Monsieur Timothée Bousquet published a pamphlet locally in which he wrote:

> During the nine years since the phylloxera invaded our area, I have worked hard to beat it. I have used all known insecticides: sulphate of carbon, of potassium, phenol, all kinds of oils and even distemper. None of these has saved my poor vines, so I have resorted to American stocks which I have

been growing successfully for five years now. We were very lucky to have
found the way ahead after the oidium in 1855/60, when our vineyards were
nearly as sad as they are today. People in the south said 'Sulphur your vines
and you will be saved.' We did it with great hesitation, but we had been well-
advised, because we *were* saved by sulphur. Today it will be the same with
the American vines.

The production statistics show that, after the phylloxera, the
Gaillacois shrewdly decided to switch partly to white wine production,
because they could not compete with the flood of cheap red wine from
the Midi. They favoured the development of the mauzac and muscadelle grape-varieties, preferring them temporarily to the other traditional local variety called len de l'el.

On the other hand, the re-establishment of the red wine vineyards
was largely based on inferior hybrids which were found to be resistant
to disease and frost, and involved fewer man-hours in the vineyards.
The resulting wine was inferior too, which explains why the grant of
AOC status was at first awarded to the white wines exclusively and why
the grant of similar privileges to the red wines took longer.

It was not long before Gaillac was on the road to recovery. Between
1890 and the turn of the century, production had increased from 40,000
hectolitres a year to over 200,000.

What sort of wines were these? Accounts from the end of the last century are not easy to reconcile with those of present-day growers whose
knowledge comes by word of mouth from their grandparents. Certainly
there was a curious sweet white wine primeur. The musts from the
pickings of the earliest white grapes were transferred to barrel while
still in a state of fermentation and delivered direct to the buyers, bub-
bling away, often cloudy and still full of yeasts. This wine was highly
fashionable in the bars of Paris in particular, and the growers extracted
a contract from the railway company which guaranteed delivery to
Paris within 56 hours. This type of wine would have been no good after
a month or so. The market for it died during the Second World War
when France was divided into two. You can still sometimes find the real
thing in the district under the name *le moustillant*. In the old days it was
called *vin bourru* or *vin Macadam*.

In addition to the *vins bourrus* there seem to have been sweet whites
both still and sparkling and a large quantity of ordinary red. I was to
learn from the local growers that the dry white wine was allowed to
mature in barrel long enough to enable it to oxidise and take on the
colour of a *vin jaune*.

With the turn of the century, the newly planted vines were mature.
This caused temporary over-production, which in turn led to frauds,
particularly through sugaring and other adulteration. More difficult
was the battle to protect the name of Gaillac. Since historically much of
the wine sold as Bordeaux had been blended with the wines of Gaillac,
there were many who wished to define Bordeaux as including the traditional areas of the *haut-pays*. The eventual grant of AOC status for the

white wines sealed the success of those producers who sought to preserve their local identity.

In the immediate post-phylloxera period, most of the wines were sold
to *négociants*, of whom there were fifteen with premises in the main
square of Gaillac alone. The idea of single-vineyard Gaillac wines was
unknown, and bottling at origin was unheard of. The prevalence of
fraud and the struggle to maintain the individuality of Gaillac led to the
creation of the first of the local co-opératives, the Abbaye St Michel,
one of the earliest in France. Starting with about 100 members, the co-
opérative had grown to about 500 by the outbreak of the Second World
War, despite the fact that in 1926 a breakaway group had formed the
Union Viticole. Both these groups were marketing organisations – they
did not make the wine: the members did that. What these earlier co-
opératives did achieve was partly to take the place of the local *négociants*
of whom there are only a handful left in the area. The wine, which
today is sold *en négoce*, is also bought by large firms based elsewhere,
which handle wines from other areas in the South-West as well as
Gaillac, such as Vigouroux in Cahors and Arbeau in Fronton.

The period after the Second World War was another crisis-time for
Gaillac. Stocks had been run down, and the first few post-war vintages
were small. Prices rose sharply, but the war had destroyed the market.
It often paid growers to forget about the appellation and de-classify
their wines. Between 1950 and 1970 the production of wine declared as
AOC fell dramatically. Furthermore the pending introduction of rules
for AOC red wine required the elimination of two grape-varieties, the
jurançon noir and the portugais bleu. Why should growers be willing to
dig up these plants when they might well have many years of life left for
making *vin de pays*?

Full appellation status was granted to the red wines in 1970.
Recognition has meant a huge increase in the production, to the point
where the amount of AOC red being produced today is half as much
again as the amount of the white. Compliance with the new rules has
meant that growers are encouraged and obliged to plant only the better
quality grape-varieties.

The powerful influence of the policy of the European Community
has had a similarly profound effect. Growers have been financially
encouraged to cut production of inferior wine. Thus, in the decade to
1988 the total area under vine fell from 20,000 hectares to 11,000. The
number of registered growers fell during the same period from 14,000
to 6000. By contrast the area of land planted to produce AOC wine has
increased by a quarter, even though it is still only 15% of the total
planted vineyard.

There have been corresponding changes in the size of individual
vineyards. After the Revolution, and the ensuing compulsory sale of the
large estates, buyers bought land wherever they could. They did not
mind that their holdings were scattered over the countryside, because
this spread the risk of damage from hail and frost, often highly

localised. The smaller growers tended to expand. Working as families, taking on occasional labour when needed, was cheaper than running the large estates with full-time staff. Some of the smallest growers had other jobs elsewhere: they were called 'the four o'clock bells', because it was a long-standing custom of the country to permit these workers to down tools at four o'clock in the afternoon so that they could go home and tend their vineyards.

In the days immediately after 1945, small vineyards of between 6 and 15 hectares were the norm. A holding of 20 hectares or more was regarded as a large estate. On the lower ground in the valley there were only ten properties as big as that. The tiny holding of 2 or 3 hectares was common, many tradespeople and artisans still having retained some vines. Generally speaking, resources were lacking and there was little hired labour because it was badly paid. The product sold for little money, and a better living could be earned in the expanding local industries.

The sixties saw a rapid change. It was a time of general discontent among the peasants, and many realised that they had either to expand their holdings or leave the land. This was also the era of the return from Algeria of skilled wine-makers, who were motivated, prepared to take risks and technically well equipped. They were in a position to give a new push to local wine-making. Nevertheless, although the average size of the vineyards which produce and bottle their own wines has grown, it is still no more than 27 hectares, and even some of these may be partly given over to other crops. Many of the quality estates are smaller still.

Today's wine-maker has to run his holding like a business. He has to understand concepts like profit, investment and depreciation; and he has to have the skills of a business manager. No wonder that many country people have turned to the co-opératives to take their raw materials off them and then to make the wine and market it on the growers' behalf. In this way a small-holder can still profit from his vines, which need not represent a monoculture, so he can earn a living in other ways, either by growing other crops or by getting a local job.

Only about a tenth of today's growers devote more than two-thirds of their property to the vine. There are about ninety who make and market their own wine, compared with only ten or so back in 1970. For the rest of the vine-growers there are the co-opératives, which between them share the bulk of the trade in Gaillac, representing some 60% of the AOC production and 70% of the remainder.

For a *vignoble* which has had such a dramatic history, it is surprising how little change has occurred in the varieties of grape grown in Gaillac. Doctor Guyot, the famous nineteenth-century viticulturist reported the following main kinds in the immediately pre-phylloxera period:

red wines:
pignol, brocol, prunelar, négret, duraze

white wines:
len de l'el, ondenc, mauzac blanc, jurançon.

A century later braucol and duras are still the mainstay of the reds, although modern practice is to soften them with merlot, cabernet or syrah. The mysterious négret may or may not be the same as the modern négrette: if so, it is now more or less confined to the wines of Fronton. Prunelar and pignol disappeared with the phylloxera.

In the South-West each regional wine derives its particular character from one or two local grapes. The duras is exclusive to Gaillac. It is a very old variety, preferring a light sand or a poor chalk. On clay soil it tends to excessive acidity. It gives finesse, good colour and alcohol. With age duras develops a fine bouquet, its tannins are soft and elegant, and it gives roundness and a long finish to the wine.

Braucol crops up all over the South-West and under a variety of names. It is the mansois or fer servadou which we have met in the Aveyron, and the pinenc of the Béarn. In the river valley spring frosts are more common than in the hills and the braucol withstands them better. The plant bears conical bunches of grapes which make a good-coloured and well-built wine, which can be drunk young but equally will hold up well in bottle.

The syrah grape is best-known for its contribution to the wines of the Rhône, so its use in Gaillac is, not surprisingly, to give structure and colour and something of a southern toasted taste.

A modern and different style of red wine, to be drunk *en primeur* like a Beaujolais, is made from the gamay grape sometimes mixed with syrah. The *vin de pays* version may be released on the third Thursday in October, but, so as not to jump the Beaujolais Nouveau gun, the AOC version may not be sold until a month later. The better growers claim, with a justification evidenced by the medals they have won, that their *vin de l'année* is often much better than even the best of Beaujolais. The same grapes are used to make an attractive rosé which enjoys a *vin de pays* appellation all of its own.

The only white varieties permitted for white Gaillac are mauzac and len de l'el – the two most important – ondenc, muscadelle, sémillon and sauvignon.

Mauzac is also the basis of Blanquette de Limoux, but otherwise it is only to be found outside Gaillac as an occasional supporting variety, or at *vin de pays* level. The vine has small leaves, and the foliage makes the plant look as if it is draped in white cotton. It is tough and rustic, resists frosts and disease well and favours a chalky soil, where it ripens well and late. The wine it makes is aromatic with a scent of apples.

Len de l'el is found nowhere but in Gaillac. The unlikely name has an equally unlikely explanation. In the language of the Languedoc it means 'far from the eye' (*loin de l'oeil*). The grapes are on very long stalks, and thus further from the eye of the picker than other varieties, growing in long and loose bunches. The plant, though susceptible to the spring frosts, is nevertheless on the increase at the expense of the mauzac. In 1960 mauzac represented 94% of the white wine vineyard, the len de l'el only 1.6%. In 1990 the percentages were respectively 67%

and 20%. Other grape-varieties to increase their representation are muscadelle (4–8%) and sauvignon (0–5% and gaining ground fast). Under the rules of the appellation, all white wine-growers are required to have at least 15% of their vines in sauvignon and/or len de l'el.

The ondenc grape all but disappeared after the phylloxera. The fashionable Robert Plageoles (see page 87) has 2 hectares planted with it, but is the only private grower I know who has any left. Two members of the Rabastens co-opérative have about 1 hectare of ondenc between them. The grape used to give a pretty pale yellow wine said to have an attractive bite, but Plageoles uses it to make a formidable *vin doux*, as we shall see.

Muscadelle plants persist mostly where the sweeter wines are made and was much used in the production of the old *vin bourru*. Its problem is that it is liable to oxidise. It is more generally to be found in vineyards on lower ground, for example Domaine Clément-Termes where it represents as much as 80% of the white wine *encépagement* and is particularly suited to the rather acid and sandy soil.

The sauvignon grape is a controversial newcomer. It has been grown all over France because of its high quality and yield. In Gaillac it is being increasingly used to give the freshness and typically grassy style with which it is associated. When blended with the mauzac or len de l'el, it makes up for the acidity sometimes lacking in the local grapes. It is also popular with the growers because it ripens early, thus reducing the weather risks at vintage time. Some Gaillacois maintain however that there is no place for sauvignon in the appellation: they say it neutralises the character of white Gaillac, turning it into just another dry white wine.

The mainstay of the red *vins de pays* and *vins de table* are the jurançon noir and portugais bleu, both now banished from the AOC wines. These varieties have a long history in the South-West – the former is also known as *folle noire* or *dame noire*. We have met it in Cahors, from which it has now been phased out too. It gives a wine somewhat lacking in individuality, and the plant is liable to rot in a wet year. The portugais bleu has a much fruitier character, but it ages quickly and is therefore only suitable for *vins de pays*.

The range of wines produced from this formidable array of grape-varieties is very large. There are two main styles of dry white wine. First the so-called *perlé*, which has a slight tingle or bubble on the tongue – the only grape which produces this quality is the mauzac. Gaillac *perlé* is said to 'jump in the mouth'. The prickle adds a clean freshness to the taste and brings out the fruit. *Perlé* does not have a long history in Gaillac, and some growers are tending to drop it. It is produced at the Labastide co-opérative under the name Gaberlé. They told me that they have stopped using the name Perlé which has apparently been registered in Germany as a trade-mark for something else. The Labastide version went through a bad patch but is now very good indeed and exceptional value. The correct way to make *perlé* is to retain some of the carbon dioxide from the second fermentation at the time the wine is bottled. It is a poor short cut to add gas artificially at any stage.

The second widely produced dry white Gaillac is a still wine, low in acidity, and best when drunk young. Here the presence of the len de l'el and sauvignon are ever on the increase. Characteristically these wines have a less apple-and-pear taste than wines based on mauzac and retain a light, rather low-alcohol style. The introduction of sauvignon tends to neutralise their distinctive character.

To complete the range of dry whites, mention must be made of a minority production of a kind of *vin jaune*, said by its makers to be the only truly authentic dry white Gaillac wine. It is made exclusively from the mauzac grape. Some old-timers in the region maintain that all other dry white Gaillacs are modern creations, and that in the old days practically all the white wine made was sweet and/or sparkling. This would certainly explain the virtual monopoly of the mauzac grape until very recent times.

Today the sweet white wines are variously called *doux* or *moelleux*. The word *doux* is reserved by law for wines which develop 75 grams of sugar per litre. The more general description *moelleux* leaves the degree of sweetness to the grower's discretion and taste. These sweet wines are made principally in the hills north of the town of Gaillac, where many growers use nothing but mauzac. It is the wine which local farmers and their families have traditionally drunk round their farmhouse fires when gathered with their neighbours to strip the maize and shell the chestnuts. Nowadays it is a fashionable match for *foie gras* and blue cheeses as well as pâtisseries. It is made by allowing the grapes to become overripe on the vine although the generally dry autumn climate prevents the development of botrytis, the 'noble rot' which is deliberately encouraged in Monbazillac (see page 148). Sweet Gaillac, unlike the dry, can age well.

There are two types of sparkling wine. One made by the *méthode gaillacoise* develops itself naturally in bottle without the addition of extra sugar. Gaillac shares a claim with Limoux to have made sparkling wine before Dom Pérignon was born. The wine is made from grapes that are quite sweet to start with, so a wine made by this method is rarely wholly dry. The fermentation is slowed down usually by several rackings which wear out the yeasts, or sometimes today by refrigeration. The wine is bottled before all the sugar is converted into alcohol. Next spring, the sugar starts to re-ferment and it is this which produces the sparkle in the wine. This is a difficult process and is strictly local to Gaillac and to Limoux where it is called *méthode rurale*. Sadly it is on the decline, and is gradually giving way to the champagne method, which often includes dosage with extra sugar to produce the bubbles. This is a much easier way of proceeding, but does not produce wine of such originality.

The range of white wine is completed by *le moustillant*, already noted. You may still find this at vintage time, sometimes under its old name, *vin bourru*. It is commercialised at the Manoir d'Emeillé by Monsieur Poussou.

Red Gaillac comes in three different styles in addition to the Beaujolais lookalike already noted. The first, often referred to as *classique*, is not intended for long keeping, though it will last satisfactorily in bottle for up to five years. It is usually given a relatively short fermentation of eight to ten days and bottled in the spring after the vintage. A second style is made from specially selected grapes, perhaps coming from older vines: it is given a longer fermentation and may be aged for a year before bottling. The third style is matured wholly or partly in new oak barrels for anything between six and twelve months.

The combination of these different styles with infinite permutations of grape-varieties in different proportions makes it hard to define what the consumer might fairly expect a red Gaillac to taste of. Where there is a strong complement of merlot or cabernet, or where the wine has been oaked, it can be particularly hard to identify it as Gaillac at all. One producer summed up the problems which face the wine-maker. The wine-buying public is conservative, he said; it has a clear idea of what it expects a red wine to taste of – typically it should approximate to Bordeaux. When faced with a country wine such as Gaillac, the more it tastes like Bordeaux the easier it is to sell. The more a wine sets out to preserve a specifically local style, the less Bordeaux-like it will be, and the harder it will be to sell. There are two schools of thought: one which believes that red Gaillac should approximate to a style which the public already knows. The other maintains that Gaillac can only survive if it maintains its *goût du terroir*, even if the customer has to be educated gradually to appreciate it. This is the dilemma which faces all the appellations of the South-West.

A great deal of wine of all three colours is made either as table wine or *vin de pays des Côtes de Tarn*. Wine cannot call itself Gaillac if it does not both derive from the AOC grapes and come from the appellation area. The Côtes de Tarn area stretches further south than Gaillac AOC, as far as the river Agoût and east to the little enclave of Cunac to the east of Albi. The *vin de pays* can be extraordinarily good value, and is usually available at growers' cellars as well as at the co-opératives, if you think to take a plastic *bidon* with you.

There is a superior appellation Premières Côtes for white wines, limited to a few communes to the north of the town of Gaillac, and to the area of Lisle-sur-Tarn. Many of the finest white wines come from the Premières Côtes, but in practice the growers find that the superior appellation does not benefit them. Why cut back on the yield, as the law requires, and why push for the statutory 12% alcohol from grape-varieties which usually yield less?

For red wine, a minimum of 60% *must* consist of any one or more of the principal growths, duras, braucol, syrah and gamay. Up to 40% *may* consist of one or more of the two cabernet varieties and merlot. White mauzac and sauvignon are also allowed but not used: the practice of using white-wine grapes in red wine seems to have died out, though, as we have seen, it was once common in Cahors.

Red wines must reach at least 10.5° alcohol by volume and the maximum permitted yield is 45 hectolitres to the hectare. White wines must reach 10° (12° in the Premières Côtes) and the maximum yield is again 45 hectolitres to the hectare (40 in the Premières Côtes). In practice all the wines reach at least 11° alcohol, the red usually 12° or more.

The wide variations in *encépagement* between one property and another are not wholly explained by the different soil conditions within the area, although contrasts in terrain are not without effect. In the hill country between Gaillac and Cordes, the northern frontier-town of the appellation, the soil is high in chalk, while on the terraces on the rising ground above the banks of the river Tarn, rich alluvia rest on strata of sand and pebbles with some clay. In the plain, only the gravelly soil enjoys the benefit of AOC, yet throughout the appellation one can find all of the authorised grape-varieties planted. At the Château de Salettes, for example, there is no braucol at all, whereas the same proprietor until recently made wine at the Domaine de Bosc Long with a generous amount of it, and not far away at the Manoir de L'Emeillé, it is the most planted of all the red grapes.

Generalisations are dangerous in this appellation, but it is safe to say that most of the finest white wines are made on the right bank of the river. East of Cahuzac, tucked away in the hills close to the village of Castanet is the **Domaine de Labarthe (90)**, one of the pioneer estates in Gaillac. Jeanne and I first visited the property in the early seventies after tasting their delicious *perlé* at a local restaurant. Jean Albert and his son today make the wine there, but in those days it was Jean's father who shared with us a most agreeable afternoon in his shuttered kitchen tasting the range of his wines. It was a very hot day, and the first time that we had tasted a sweet white Gaillac. Beautifully restorative it was too, pale in colour, not at all cloying but having a lovely finish of honey, apricots and nuts. We became devotees of this wine, and remember particularly the 1983, which was still showing beautifully nine years later.

The Alberts make two red wines. Their premium red is called Cuvée Guillaume, named after a distant ancestor to celebrate the fact that the property has been in the family for hundreds of years. This wine is very dark in colour and definitely a keeper. It has plenty of cabernet in the mix, which is probably what gives it the extra finesse and capacity to age. It is discreetly oaked, and the wood masks only a little of the distinctive taste of pepper and spices.

Some of the mauzac vines at Labarthe are used as the base for the *perlé*. It is one of the best you will find in Gaillac, although, because of the legal difficulties surrounding the name 'perlé', Jean has only recently started again to market it freely. Jean's father explained to us that, in a good year, he would leave some of his mauzac to dry out on the vine, vinifying it separately and adding it to the main blend to give it a little extra richness.

As if to accentuate the distinction between the two styles of white wine, the non-*perlé* wine is nowadays sauvignon-based. Good though it is, it has less personality, less of what the French call *typicité*, than the *perlé*. There is also an ambitious oaked version called Héritage. Jean Albert is not slow in moving with the times. He is able to dominate the local restaurant market, having identified the need for a substantial production of half-bottles, which are relatively rare from other producers.

Domaine de Labarthe also makes a fine *mousseux* and those with a taste for the *vin de pays des Côtes de Tarn* can take their plastic *bidons* along to Monsieur Albert, who seems to have an endless supply of good quaffing wine from the area.

The syrah grape is increasingly fashionable in Gaillac, but Jean Albert grows little of it, and what he does produce is mostly reserved for his rosé. There is a great deal of pink wine made at Gaillac, usually from a mixture of syrah and gamay, but it does not enjoy AOC, so rosé can also be made with the jurançon and portugais bleu as well as some admixture of the other mainstream red grapes.

Labarthe, with its 35 hectares, is quite a large property. The Alberts compete successfully for the excellence of their red *primeurs*, which invariably have a fresh bouquet of cherries and blackcurrants. They have won prizes for producing the best of all French *primeurs*, beating the best of the Beaujolais growers. One of their chief rivals in Gaillac was **Domaine Jean Cros (69)**, whose once excellent production just to the east of Cahuzac has been overshadowed by family division and the death of Jean himself. This double calamity is a blow for the appellation as a whole, which Jean Cros had done so much to bring to life in the 1960s and 1970s. His wines were fairly easily available in London, and even after his death some earlier years are still to be found on merchants' lists. From 1990 onwards, however, the red wines have been marketed *en négoce* and show little of their former quality.

The Alberts have other rivals, however. A whole range of particularly attractive wines is made not far away at the **Mas d'Aurel (72)**, a smaller estate of some 14 hectares in the small village of Donnazac. In the tenth century the land was given by the local diocese to monks specially for the cultivation of vines. The Mas stands on top of a gentle hill, flanked by a particularly attractive *pigeonnier* which makes it hard to miss. Monsieur Ribot is always pleased to welcome visitors and to show them his range of wines, which feature often on the wine-lists of local restaurants. His red wines age particularly well. His *classique* is made typically from 50% duras, with the balance coming from a cocktail of the other permitted varieties, while his *cuvée spéciale* is half braucol and half cabernet sauvignon. The latter and his dry sparkling wine, which is particularly good, both deservedly won gold medals at the Gaillac wine-fair in 1993.

To the north of the Mas d'Aurel is the famous medieval town of Cordes. Although Cordes is a hill-town and on top of a steep pinnacle, the plateau separating the town from the Tarn valley is even higher than the town itself. The vineyards are on the highest ground in open countryside, very gently undulating with magnificent views over to the forest of Grésigne to the west. You really feel on the roof of the world here, in a countryside of skylarks and wind-borne hawks, and vines as far as the eye can see: yet you are only 1000 feet above sea-level.

It is surprising that there are relatively few private producers in this part of the *vignoble*. They account all told for only 4% of the total AOC production. Three-quarters of the wine they make is red, and one of the larger of these producers is the Brun family at **Le Domaine le Payssel (74)**, but even they have only 20 hectares of AOC vineyard. Louis Brun was one of those wine-makers who came back from Algeria in the early 1960s: he bought the present domaine in 1962 and replanted it entirely. Nowadays he runs the vineyard in partnership with his son Eric. Their best white is an all-mauzac wine. They have quite a lot of syrah, and their red *classique* is completed with duras and braucol. The prestige red has cabernet and merlot too and tends to be over-oaked. The domaine is in the village of Frausseilles, and Monsieur Brun has two splendid *pigeonniers*, like watch-towers guarding the long low *chais*. There is also a real little medieval Château de Frausseilles, where they used to make a very good dry white wine. Some years ago, I called at the cellar one day in September, only to find nailed to the door a notice saying, '*Fermé, à cause de départ pour champignons.*' Even a *vigneron* has his priorities. Sadly the wine is no longer available.

The sleepy little town of Cahuzac is back on the main road south, in the direction of Gaillac. Production in the area was, until recently, dominated by Monsieur Willenborg who had 65 hectares of vines within the appellation. His **Château de Salettes (61)** has already been mentioned (page 85) and was built in the eighteenth century in feudal style by the Comte d'Hautpoul, whose ancestors, originally from Mazamet further south, took refuge in the region to escape the fury of the Albigensian crusaders. This vineyard is sufficiently remote from the outside world also to have escaped the ravages of the phylloxera, and in this respect it is unique in the region. The château is particularly noted for its white wine, based on len de l'el rather than mauzac. It is given some ageing in wood and enjoys a high reputation, though it may by now have changed hands.

Monsieur Willenborg's other property, **Domaine de Bosc Long (55)**, is over to the west and nearly three times the size of Salettes. The vineyard was developed at the height of the Gaillac boom of the 1850s by a Monsieur Abadie, who had built for him two huge vaulted cellars under his rather grand house. These are still used today, although the impressive span of the arches is largely concealed by the gleaming stainless-steel vats which have recently been installed. Monsieur Abadie also employed a full-time barrel-maker, such was the importance of his estate. Today the production is divided equally between red and white wines, of which Monsieur Willenbourg produces a complete range.

A near neighbour is Robert Plageoles, who has two small vineyards at

Les Trés Cantous and Roucou-Cantemerle (44), which together add up to only 15 hectares of vines. His house and *chais* make up one of the three *cantous*, meaning hearths, which constitute this tiny hamlet. The other two are on the west side of the main road which splits the place down the middle, and the signposts point to the west rather than the east side of the road. To avoid confusion with the wines made over the way, Plageoles labels his wines Vignobles Robert Plageoles et Fils. These vines are set in some of the most beautiful countryside in the South-West, a landscape on a grand scale with gentle slopes stretching for miles. In autumn the vivid maroon-coloured leaves of the dying gamay appear as vivid stripes amongst the golden duras and braucol vines, which live on much later into the season. The setting could not be more appropriate for some of the most authentic wines of the region.

Robert Plageoles is at once a traditionalist and an inventor. He insists on using only the historic Gaillac varieties, although obliged by the rules of the appellation to have 15% of his white grapes in sauvignon. Being the perfectionist he is, he sets out to make a better version than anyone else, even if he does not regard the result as a true Gaillac. It is naturally 100% sauvignon, though Gault-Millau said of this wine, '*Ce n'est pas un sauvignon, c'est un Plageoles.*'

His basic dry and sweet wines have the same blend of flair and pedigree, and are made wholly from mauzac. The dry wine is not all that generous on the nose with the apples and lime which Plageoles claims for it, but in the mouth it is rich, but never blowsy, and always bone-dry. Plageoles says it should be kept for three to five years, but he seems keen on long ageing. This is a refreshing feature in a world where wine-makers say a wine is already going downhill when, for the average drinker, it is nowhere near ready. The *doux* is more of a *moelleux* really, light in texture and in alcohol. Plageoles says he is more interested in depth of fruit than in the alcoholic degree. He describes this wine as 'a *moelleux* for those who don't like *moelleux*'. He reserves some of his best *cuves* of this wine to mature in new wood. He says that in principle he is neither for nor against the use of new oak, but I got the very strong feeling that he was not all that enthusiastic about it. He acknowledges that wood gives something to a wine, but 'it is always the same thing. It is like dressing a wine up in clothes: I prefer my wine naked'.

His dry sparkling wine is also 100% mauzac, but he does not call it *mousseux*, simply 'mauzac nature', making it as his father did by the *méthode rurale*, or *gaillacoise*. He describes this as the oldest and most traditional of all Gaillac wines, and it must be drunk young. It is sad that the number of growers who are making it this way can now be counted on the fingers of both hands. He pours it in his tasting-room from an old-fashioned lemonade bottle, complete with marble stopper. The colour is rich, and the *mousse* reminds one of a *crémant*: the bubbles are tiny but persistent. The nose is beautifully yeasty because the wine is bottled on its lees, which may also explain why there is a hint of sweetness behind the sparkle.

The fourth of Plageoles' unblended mauzac wines is perhaps the most unusual of them all, but also entirely traditional. Using only the juice from the first pressing, the wine is fermented in old oak, and it is then filtered and put back again into the same barrel where it is left for seven years. The barrel must be filled to the brim, because there will be no ullage – topping up to compensate for evaporation. After a year or so, the must develops a thin veil (*voile*) of mould which protects it from the air and the colour of the wine deepens to a glowing gold as the slow, gentle oxygenation reduces the level in the barrel by about a quarter. Though entirely dry, the wine has by this time developed a flavour of hazelnuts. It is something like a dry sherry, but lighter even than a montilla.

Plageoles does not make this wine every year: he needs a vintage with fairly high acidity but with very ripe fruit all the same, ideally a hot year when he can pick early. He is not the only producer now making this style of wine, but he is worried that, if it catches the public imagination, growers will be tempted to take short cuts, such as not entirely filling the barrels in the first place. This would accelerate oxygenation, but at unacceptable cost in terms of loss of finesse. Plageoles chooses, incidentally, to declare this wine under the higher appellation Gaillac Premières Côtes, the only example which has come my way. He calls the wine Vin de Voile, which he has registered as his own brand-name.

The mauzac grape is obviously Plageoles' first love: he plans in his retirement to write a book about the history of the various Gaillac grapes, in which you can be quite sure the mauzac will have pride of place. He explained to me that there are several sub-varieties, each of which serves quite a different purpose. The mauzac vert is what he makes his basic dry white from, and it is grown down the road at Roucou-Cantemerle alongside his duras and sauvignon. The mauzac roux, which has a much more browny yellow skin, is used for his sweet wine and his Vin de Voile. This is all grown at Trés Cantous. It is almost unbelievable that the same grapes, from the same vintage, grown in the same place and basically vinified together, can produce two such totally different wines. The sparkling mauzac *nature* is made from two more sub-varieties, the gris and the rose, both grown at Trés Cantous.

But Robert Plageoles is also equally famous for another white wine, this time made from the ondenc grape. Using this rare variety unblended, he has created an extraordinary sweet wine which he calls Vin d'Autan. Autan is the local name for the warm sirocco-like wind which prevails here in the autumn. Plageoles allows the grapes to over-ripen well into the month of November and in this way they dry on the vine. They do not rot because the autan is a dry wind, but the quantity of juice is relatively tiny, reducing the yield by two-thirds. He has managed to get his grapes to the right stage, unbotrytised, every year since 1983 except 1992, when he still managed to make an ondenc *moelleux*, but it was not good enough to earn the Vin d'Autan name. He made it only to keep the name of the grape-variety before the public. 1989 saw a particularly fine Indian summer in Gaillac and the yield from the grapes was as low as 6 hectolitres to the hectare, with a sugar content before fermentation of no less than 26°. The 1995 will be just as good. Plageoles seems to be aiming to outdo some of his charismatic rivals in Jurançon and Madiran. Vin d'Autan, though it does not darken like its Pyrenean cousins, is aromatically complex, loaded with honey and flowers, the texture almost like glycerine, but with just enough citrus at the end to prevent the wine from being over the top. Plageoles describes it as '*à nul autre comparable, il est le vin du vent et de l'esprit'*.

I asked him why he thought the ondenc had all but died out in Gaillac. Anxious not to be without a view, he put forward several possible reasons. It never really made a satisfactory dry wine. Again it is somewhat delicate as a plant, especially liable to oidium: perhaps a sequence of bad winters at some past time had gradually reduced the presence of the vine as the ondenc is particularly susceptible to frost.

In some ways Plageoles can be said to be a heretic, but in others he is strictly purist. For example, he carries over his enthusiasm for varietal wines into his reds as well as his whites. He vinifies a pure duras red, and his gamay is made by traditional methods. His gamay is not a *vin de l'année* at all, just a very good 100% gamay wine. He is somewhat mistrustful of high technology in wine-making: for example, he prefers to do without artificial temperature-control, nor does he have stainless-steel vats. On the other hand he believes in giving his sons their head: he is at pains to point out that they do most of the work, while his daughter-in-law looks after the business side of the enterprise. He has put in the hands of one of his sons the making and the *élevage* of the 100% muscadelle, yes, another unblended *vin doux*, which is given some ageing in wood.

The support which he gets from the family enables him to sit back from time to time and think, deal with his customers and to cement his reputation as the Gaillac-grower best loved by the media. He must be the only wine-maker in the whole of France to have acquired the status of star-*vigneron* without a total commitment to new oak in his *chais*. This is something of a feat at a time when it seems that no one can win medals or competitions without oaking their wines. His reluctance to go overboard about new wood probably stems from his belief that a family vineyard must evolve gradually, and that it is a mistake to throw out the benefits of hundreds of years' experience in favour of what may turn out to be a mere fad. He can trace his ancestors back to the fourteenth century, and the family has been at Trés Cantous for 100 years. He is glad to have learnt so much from his own father, and is equally glad that his sons seem willing to learn so much from him. But he never followed his father slavishly, and he does not expect his sons to be carbon-copies of himself. He claims that, though some of his wines appear to be original, he has not invented anything which is new. This is an uncharacteristically over-modest statement from a man who has been dubbed 'one of the artists of the appellation'.

In between the two Plageoles vineyards is the **Domaine de Bouscaillous (56)**, where there have been three generations of Maurels making wine since the vineyard was planted in 1910. Yvon is the present owner, and he makes a full range of Gaillac. His best red, which he ages in oak for six months, was a prizewinner for the 1989 vintage, and very fine it was too. So is his *classique* red, made from a blend predominantly of syrah with cabernet. I am less taken with his dry white, which is based on len de l'el, but the *vin doux*, exclusively from mauzac, is a really fine example even though sold as non-vintage. He also makes a *vin sec d'autrefois*. One grower told us that Maurel had been the first to revive this traditional curiosity, in which event he deserves more credit than he gets.

We are up on the Premières Côtes now, the vines growing on almost Sussex-like downland, with sweeping contours and long views towards the Tarn valley. If we take the road north-west towards the forest of Grésigne, we pass the **Château de Mayragues (45)** on the left. This belongs to Alan Geddes from Scotland and his French wife Laurence. Alan has retired from international accountancy to try his hand at wine-making. Like many fine houses in the South-West, this building was first transformed into a farm and then abandoned. Of the older parts, there remains a curious five-sided tower. The *encépagement* here is mainly l'en de l'el in the white wine. Alan's sweet wine of 1993 surprised the pundits and himself by taking first prize at the Gaillac fair in 1994. It has the same citrus fruits on the nose as a young Jurançon. In 1995 Alan made a small quantity of ultra-sweet wine from hand-picked, individually-selected grapes, which will be sumptuous.

Crossing the river Vère, follow the little stream up its valley to the village of Campagnac where there are two important vineyards, both of whose wines are readily available in local shops and restaurants. First you reach the **Manoir de l'Emeillé (51)**, which means almond-tree in the local patois. Here Monsieur Poussou has 40 hectares of vines, from seven of which he makes *vin de pays*, and the remaining 33 qualify for full AOC status. There are three reds: the premium wine, called Cuvée Prestige, using braucol and syrah, assisted with some merlot and cabernet; another, called Rouge Tradition, is based on duras, syrah and gamay. Finally there is gamay *primeur*. The dry white wine is from equal parts of len de l'el and sauvignon.

Almost opposite Emeillé, nestling right under the brow of the forest, is the **Domaine de Graddé (50)**, the property of Etienne Coursières. This is the senior of the two vineyards, some of the stock going back seventy years. The red wine is made for keeping, although there is also a *primeur*. The full range of wines includes a white *perlé*, *vin moustillant* and a still sweet white. The soil is more pebbly than across the valley at Emeillé, and the wines have good bite to them.

A property which enjoys a picture-postcard view of Gaillac town is **Mas Pignou (42)**, whose literature promises that the panorama and the wines will ravish you. After a particularly enjoyable tasting, which

merged afternoon into evening, it was moving to watch the twinkling
lights of Gaillac between the rows of vines, while the plants danced and
rustled in the warm autan wind. The 35-hectare vineyard has been in
the Auques family for over a hundred years and they are also helping
out a new neighbour, Nicholas Fraser from Britain, with the vinification of his wine from **Domaine de Perches (43)**. The estate also
includes the Mas de Bonnal, a name which the Auques reserve for their
vins de pays both red and rosé.

Monsieur Auques is jolly and pear-shaped: he somehow makes you
know that you are going to enjoy his wines, even before you have shaken
hands with him. His premium red from Mas Pignou is named Mélanie
after a great-grandmother who was charged with looking after the vines
while the men were away at the front during the First World War. She
acquired quite a taste for running the vineyards, so much so that, when
her husband returned from the front, he found it hard to resume his
position as head of the family. In those days the fortunes of the family
were based on the *vin bourru* so beloved of the Parisians, but nowadays
the Auques concentrate on a conventional range of traditionally-made
wines. A third of the vineyard is given over to the grapes which go into
their *classique*, basically duras and braucol, but with some of the other
varieties too. The Cuvée Mélanie is from 40% braucol and 30% each
merlot and cabernet franc. Mélanie is given up to three weeks' fermentation as opposed to a shorter ten to twelve days for the *classique*. The
prestige wine will last, according to Monsieur Auque, up to ten years.
Of recent vintages, he thought his 1990 had more promise for the future
than the 1989, but he did not mind that I somewhat hesitantly begged
to differ. I gratefully accepted his invitation to go back in, say, five
years' time to resume the debate. I also expressed admiration for his
basic red: although Mélanie had more sophistication, the other wine
had perhaps more typically local character, because of the higher percentage of braucol and duras in it. The range of reds is completed by a
particularly fruity Côtes du Tarn from 3 hectares of duras. The rosé is
from duras, syrah and jurançon noir.

The white wines are, if anything, better even than the reds. The
white *classique* – the Auques make no *perlé* – is half len de l'el and half
sauvignon, and the latter certainly shows through, but not to the point
where it dominates the local len de l'el. It does, however, give the sharp
twist of acidity which is one of the hallmarks of this grape in Gaillac.

The Auques, traditionalists though they are, were the pioneers of
sauvignon in this area. Their dry white is allowed a malolactic fermentation before being given a further year's *élevage* prior to bottling.
Although it can be drunk young, it will keep for up to five years, acquiring considerable body as it ages.

Monsieur Auques also uses his len de l'el to make a delicious, dry
mousseux. The sweet wine is one of the best from the appellation.
Wonderfully honeyed, with aromas of apricots and other exotic fruits, it

rounds off the Pignou range to perfection. Here the mauzac grape comes into its own.

In the same area the Rouquié family own a vineyard called **Mas de Bicary (58)**, and they are quietly making a name for themselves in the region, the 20 hectares of this estate evenly divided between red and white grapes. What I expected to be a short session to buy some of their very good *perlé* turned out to be an extended tasting, which included five vintages of their red wine too. The vinification of the latter is ultra-traditional, with no de-stalking and long *cuvaisons* of up to four weeks. Sometimes the presence of the *rafle* in the must gives the wine a natural taste of wood, but never green and tannic as one might have expected. Of the years 1987 to 1991 inclusive, 1990 stood out as being the biggest wine, most capable of developing really well in bottle. The more recent 1991 was very successful for the vintage. I also tasted the premium wine of 1988, which had a smoky character, with aromas of dried figs and other fruit. Madame Rouquié is a most attentive and instructive tutor and much more will be heard of this exciting property in the years to come. His sweet white is outstanding, with luscious overtones of honey and almonds.

Only just up the road to the north is the **Domaine de la Tronque (49)**, where Claude Leduc is the biological wine-maker of Gaillac par excellence. Conforming to the most rigorous of European regulations, he manages to make a most amazingly good *mousseux brut* which will compare with any others in the appellation. He gives his dry white wine, an intriguing blend of muscadelle and mauzac, a malolactic fermentation, and a long and cold *cuvaison* at no more than 12°. The result is straw-coloured, delicate, pale but surprisingly gutsy.

Among the properties tending to dispense with mauzac for its dry wine is **Château Lastours (16)**, an attractive four-square eighteenth-century manor house in beautiful grounds going down to the banks of the river Tarn. Perhaps the soil here, low-lying and based on gravelly alluvia, is not right for the mauzac grape. Lastours is perhaps best known for its red wine, somewhat in the style of a Médoc, and containing an unusual amount of cabernet sauvignon. The added overtones of braucol give just that element of rusticity to ensure that the individual *goût du terroir* is not entirely lost.

Higher up the hillside, and on the other side of the Route Nationale from Gaillac to Toulouse, is the little village of Saurs. Hidden in the trees is a splendid villa in the Palladian style, just one of a number of châteaux in the area to show an Italian influence and to underline the sometimes Tuscan feel of the Gaillac landscape. **Château de Saurs (15)** is a predominantly red-wine estate, and the château has particularly fine vaulted cellars underneath. Just along the road is the **Domaine Clément Termes (19)**, a large estate with some 60 hectares of vines. The dry white wine here contains an unusually high 80% muscadelle which gives it a floral and spicy character. The red wine, again relying strongly on Bordelais grapes, is not unlike a bourgeois claret in style.

The **Domaine de Mazou (17)**, the neighbouring property on the country road to Rabastens, has been in the Boyals family for five generations, but there has been quite substantial replanting in recent years. Once again the muscadelle is to the fore, contributing to the *blanc perlé* an attractive perfume from the sandy soil in which it thrives. The red wine from this property is very good and often to be found in local restaurants.

Up on the slopes behind Lisle, Christian and Colette Bastide of **Domaine de Long-Pech (23)** have recently started to attract some critical acclaim, especially for their white wines. In addition to their *perlé* and a *classique* white, they also make a white which is 100% sauvignon. Although I have a prejudice against the use of this vine in Gaillac, I concede that this is the exception which proves the rule. This is a really fine white wine, the particular *terroir* mitigating the otherwise steely effect of the grape-variety. This is a round wine with lots of *gras* and real fruit and body.

Their 100% sweet mauzac is especially good also and some of their best grapes are given a few months in new oak. This wine will need several years to show well, but this property is quite capable of competing with the very best of the South-West.

Most of the wine activity in Rabastens is centred round the **Coopérative (B)**, which is on the main road just north of the town. It was started in 1953 and its first vintage was in 1956. After a modest beginning it is now producing as much as its rival at Labastide-de-Lévis, about 80,000 hectolitres a year. It claims to have a quarter of the entire Gaillac market, and 90% of its production is of red wine. This is because of its geographical situation at the extreme southern end of the appellation, where the soil suits the red grape-varieties far better than it does the white. The Cave has its own marketing subsidiary called Cavitarn.

Today the Cave has five hundred members owning between them about 1290 hectares of vines. Paul Espitalié, their young oenologue who gave up so much of his precious lunch-hour to show me round, explained that many growers have less than a hectare of land, polyculture still being the prevalent farming system in the region. Thirty of their members have vines in the Fronton appellation. As will be seen later, the present Fronton area is an amalgamation of the former separate areas of Villaudric and Fronton. At the time of the marriage, the former Cave at Villaudric had fallen on difficult times financially, and the Gaillac Cave at Rabastens took a lease on it to service the rump of the Villaudric *co-opérateurs*. While Rabastens is happy to continue the present service, it is not anxious to extend its Fronton operation, though the wine it makes for its members at Villaudric is fair.

As is to be expected, all kinds of local wine are made at Rabastens. At the lower end of their range are a red and rosé Côtes de Tarn called Henri de Cambournac. There is also a gamay-based *vin de pays*, as well as a complete range of *vins de pays en vrac*. The Gaillacs start with a red *en vrac*, a range of all three colours under the name Olivier de Sérac and a premium range under the name of Marquis d'Oriac. Part of the Oriac red is aged in new oak, and the sample I tasted was rather smothered by the wood: the unoaked version was rather characterful with good rustic qualities. The dry white Oriac is minty in character and could keep a year or two. Again the Cave is experimenting with new wood, and it will be interesting to see how this trial turns out.

The Cave's best wines are perhaps their *blanc perlé*, and their dry sparkler, even though white wines represent only 10% of their production. They are rather proud at having snatched the prize for *perlé* from under the nose of Labastide-de-Lévis! The *perlé* is excellent value for money and one of the best to be found in the region. They used to make the red Château de Brames, but the owner is now taking this on himself. Instead the Cave has recently assumed, on behalf of Yves Stilhart, the making of his wine from the all-red Domaine de Cassagnols at Lisle, which was a prizewinner at the Gaillac fair in 1993. The Cave vinifies and markets separately the wines from ten different private domaines and châteaux, but Cassagnols is the best I have come across.

The terraces where these wines are grown stretch all the way from Rabastens back to Gaillac and there are a number of properties within easy reach of Gaillac itself making excellent wine. One of the most interesting is the **Domaine de la Ramaye (11)** at Ste-Cécile d'Avés. Here Maurice and Michel Issaly, father and son, recall the eccentric traditionalism of Robert Plageoles. The property has come down through Madame Issaly's family, the Toulzes, who made wine here through six generations. Maurice Issaly and his wife come straight from the pages of a Pagnol story – Maurice has the inevitable beret, which is worn permanently indoors and out, his eyes are humorous, twinkling and mischievous. He has not officially retired and doubts whether he will ever do so completely. Madame seems to be a part of the fabric of the place, not surprising since it has been her home all her life and she is one of the best cooks in the region. Their son Michel is, like so many sons of *vignerons* of Maurice's generation, a fully trained oenologist.

A visitor might expect to find tension between the two wine-makers, or at least different points of view, but at Ramaye there is a complete and unanimous devotion to the purest traditions of wine-making in Gaillac. The tasting-room has on its walls pictures of hand-ploughing in the vineyards as recently as 1953. They try to be as *bio* as possible: no animal or artificial fertilisers are used, no insecticides and only weed-killers to the extent that the natural chlorophyll in the plants can absorb the chemicals. All the harvesting is done by hand. The grapes are never de-stalked before the wine is made, and the *cuvaisons* can last for up to thirty days in a good year. Michel told me that, if ever they decide to experiment with de-stalking they will compensate by extending the *cuvaison* to forty days. The accent is on quality and there are no short cuts.

The Issalys never made much red wine until the AOC was granted in 1970: before that, almost all of their production was white, and very little was sold in bottle unless at the request of special local customers. Nowadays they make both red and white, but the policy for both is the same: they are interested only in *vins de garde* from low yields. They have no fixed replanting programme in the vineyards: they simply but ruthlessly eliminate all weak plants to ensure 100% health of all the vines, whose average age is fairly high for the appellation – thirty-five years.

The Issalys' present intention for their red wines is to concentrate on just two: a 100% duras with, for them, a relatively short *cuvaison* of only fourteen days. This will mature earlier than their other red, called Combe d'Avès, from 50% braucol and 50% duras. For this wine there is a rigid selection of only the best grapes, leading to a low yield of only 25 hectolitres to the hectare. The must is vinified for three to four weeks and is returned to the *cuves* to settle and clarify in the cold of winter. In the following spring it is transferred to large old wooden *foudres* where it is matured for two years, with ullage weekly. The wine is fined before bottling but with egg white only. Bottling is carried out by a peripatetic bottling-firm, and Michel can supervise every stage of the process: but he regrets that the plant has built into it a filtration system – he would prefer that the wines were not filtered again before bottling. The wine is then kept in bottle for another year before it is sold. Michel remarked that a wine-maker needed more patience than the bank manager would sometimes allow.

There are three white wines, all of them dry, and all of them with remarkable ageing potential. Les Cavailles Bas is half sauvignon and half len de l'el, the first providing the acidity which the second lacks, but the latter providing the typicity which the former cannot. The most censorious selection of hand-picked grapes gives a yield of only 20 hectolitres to the hectare. The wine is allowed a malolactic fermentation before being aged in wood, one-third of which is new from the nearby forest of Grésigne, the other two-thirds in barrels which have already seen the making of four wines. *Batonnage* (stirring up the lees in the barrel with a stick) is carried out weekly. The wine is fined with gelatine before a final filtering and then bottling. This wine is best drunk three to eight years after the vintage, allowing enough time for the tannins in the wood to resolve themselves.

Of the three white varieties, the mauzac grape ripens last, so picking is later and the yields even lower: just 18 hectolitres to the hectare in a good year like 1995. Only the free-run juices and the first two pressings go into their mauzac wine. The must is fermented in two-year-old barrels for thirteen days at an uncontrolled temperature of 18–23°. There is no racking or aeration of any kind. During the first year, there is twice-weekly *batonnage*, and then for another six months the frequency is halved. The Issalys predict a life of ten years for this wine.

The third white wine from la Ramaye is called *vin de l'oubli* and is after the style of the maderised wines made by Plageoles and Maurel.

(To ease the pain for the customer, it is sold in 50-centilitre bottles.) The wine is made from late-picked mauzac and vinified in small cement *cuves* before being transferred to 600-litre barrels called *demi-muids*. These are filled to the brim and sealed, so as to protract the oxygenation for as long as possible.

The Issalys, like Plageoles, are sad to see that so little modern Gaillac bears any resemblance to pre-war models. Michel said that he has sometimes thought of not bothering with the appellation, and simply producing *vins de table* under the name of the property. He has never done so, because he feels it would be letting down the family traditions, and their vineyards are, after all, in the heart of the very best part of the Gaillac vineyard. He also feels a certain thrill at swimming against the tide in order to keep alive the true typicity of the local wines, as he interprets it. Michel has the burning enthusiasm of so many of the younger generation of wine-makers: but he is able to balance his professional skills nicely with the old ways. He still uses only pure water to clean out his barrels, and he burns the vine-prunings to get rid of the insects and diseases rather than use unnecessary chemicals. One hopes that, with their small-holding, the family's grip on the market is not too precarious to ensure their survival.

Just up the hill from Ramaye is the **Domaine de Canto Perlic (12)**, which has been bought by Alex and Claire Taylor, well known in the English wine-trade, whose principal interest seems to be the making of a *crémant*-style sparkling wine. This is made by the *méthode champenoise* at the Abbaye St Michel in Gaillac town, where there are coopérative facilities for making sparkling wines, saving smaller growers the trouble and expense of arranging for their own storage, *remuage* and *dégorgement*. Taylor calls his wine Cuvée Claire, and it has the typically appley character of the mauzac. There is no *dosage* with sugar.

There is a cluster of very good estates round the tiny village of Boissel, which lies just off to the west of the main road north from Gaillac to Cordes. Just as the ground starts to rise towards the *côteaux*, the gentle gradient allows a good exposure to the sun and the warm autan wind, as well as providing efficient drainage. At the **Château de Tauziès (33)**, the Mouly family, born further north in the Aveyron, moved in during the early sixties and concentrated on making white wines. With the approach of AOC status for the red wines in 1970, they planted an extra 16 hectares with merlot and cabernet sauvignon to add to their holdings of traditional Gaillac grapes. Their red wine is a good keeper, deep in colour and with the expected curranty bouquet.

Only a few metres down the slope towards the town is the **Domaine Barreau (30)** at a property called Trabes de la Chantro. Here Monsieur Barreau makes a very good sweet white wine from a mixture which is very nearly half len de l'el and half mauzac, with just a touch of sauvignon.

Nearby **Château de Candastre (34)** is one of the largest independent Gaillac properties with nearly 100 hectares under vine, most of it AOC. Despite its size, the property limits its range of wines to two whites, one dry and one sweet, and two reds, one light and fruity and the other intended for ageing. The reds seem to me rather dull, but I have always enjoyed the rosé. Candastre has other interests however: it looks after the marketing of a good property at Lisle called Manoir des Augustines, as well as the wines of the Domaine de Pialentou on the left bank just south of the town of Gaillac. They also own a property in Fronton called Château Marguerite.

The red *vin de garde* from the **Château de Rhodes (29)** is well worth looking out for, made as it is from the traditional Gaillac grapes. The vineyards face south-west, which particularly suits the syrah, giving a fat, fleshy character to the wine, as well as its toasted southern bouquet. The white wines come from lower ground where the grapes can ripen more slowly and later into the season.

The small nearby village of Laborie is host to an interesting group of fine wine-makers. The **Domaine des Hourtets (36)** is owned by an Armenian, Edouard Kabakian, whose *blanc sec* is to be found in the UK. He has formed an association with an English dealer which may result in his wines becoming better known on the north side of the Channel. Monsieur Kabakian is at once a fully trained oenologist and a fierce traditionalist, which is a welcome if unusual combination, he relies almost wholly on the country grape-varieties. He will not use Bordelais grapes to make red wine, and he pays only lip service to the merits of the sauvignon grape. His mauzac and len de l'el benefit from a wonderfully sunny exposition, and his white wine is correspondingly classy, fat and rich, though surprisingly dry on the finish. When young, the red wine has a very flowery bouquet, developing a curranty character with age.

Close by, Maryse and Jacques Vayssette had problems with their 1992 vintage, but then who didn't? The sweet wines, still and sparkling, from their **Domaine de Vayssette (35)** have been famous in the region for many years. They always seem to make a wine whose honey is beautifully balanced by acidity: their 1989 is no exception. Already darkening in 1993 it promises well for at least another five years, perhaps more. And neither should their red wine be overlooked: the traditional varieties go to make a thoroughly classic wine – rustic but with layers of interesting flavours.

Another substantial estate further to the east is the **Château Vigné-Lourac (88)** at Senouillac where Monsieur Gayrel has no fewer than 17 hectares of mauzac. He also makes both red and white wines marketed as Château les Méritz, in which he uses len de l'el and muscadelle to balance the mauzac. The red is made from duras and braucol with a touch of syrah.

This area, high up on the Premières Côtes, is home to a number of smaller growers who are making old-fashioned wines, where the essential taste of Gaillac is all-important. For example, Henri Plageoles, a distant cousin of Robert, at the **Mas de Doat (85)** and his neighbour Patrick Raynal at the **Château Raynal (84)** have formed an association, which, while it preserves their individual properties intact and enables them to go on marketing their wines under their own names, also helps them to save on marketing and publicity costs. This is a good way forward for producers who do not have all that many hectares at their disposal. The wines from these two properties are also very good: traditional, rustic, even fairly tough, but essentially what Gaillac should be about, especially at the price level these two growers are able to offer Their partnership is called Côtes de Senouillac.

They have formidable white wine competition from a near-neighbour, Alain Monestié at **Château Moussens (92)**, whose dry white, being from a traditional blend of mauzac and len de l'el, has a singing sappiness as well as fruit, and the balance between acidity and ripeness is well managed. Their rosé is good too, their reds somewhat less impressive apart from their excellent *primeur*.

Domaine de Lacroux (89) is very close by but so different in its style of wine-making. Its dry white, though fruity, is pale and very delicate. So is the rosé, light but lively. Even the *méthode champenoise* is aiming at a somewhat neutral style, made as it is from 100% len de l'el. These wines are somewhat rarefied, elegant but remote from the country spirit of the appellation as a whole. This is more than can be said of Denis and Jean-Marc Balaran, whose wines at the **Domaine d'Escausses (94)** at Ste-Croix, a small village on the very edge of the wine-making area, remain truthful to the *terroir*. The accent here, at the eastern limits of the appellation, is very much on the traditional grapes of the region, and the wine too is typical of Gaillac at its rustic best.

All the properties at this end of the appellation are dwarfed by the **Cave Co-opérative** at Labastide-de-Lévis **(C)**. Created in 1949, its first vintage was in 1951 when it made 13,000 hectolitres for its eighty-one members. Membership has risen to about 350 and production to 100,000 hectolitres. Its large and modern cellars are built at the edge of the plateau, and it is by far the biggest single producer of wine grown on the right bank of the Tarn. With its massive output, nearly a quarter of it AOC, its market-share is about 25% of the whole region.

The flagship wine is its white *perlé*, sold under the frightful, if memorable, name of Gaberlé. This is a blend of 80% mauzac and 20% len de l'el. Though the grapes which go into the making of this wine come from all corners of the area, it has sometimes been one of the best *perlés* on the market. Otherwise the Cave makes a still white which is quite dry, with more than a touch of sauvignon, largely from grapes grown on the lower slopes near Gaillac itself. This wine is as excitingly contemporary as its label. The Cave has also been producing an own-label brand for the English supermarket trade called Domaine de Pradelles. The only sweet wine is a Côtes du Tarn *moelleux*.

The red wines seem on the whole less successful, apart from the curious *vin de pays* made at Cunac, where the co-opérative built a branch in 1956. This is a much lighter wine than mainstream Gaillac, is made for drinking young and can be bought either in bottle or *en vrac*. It is not though a *primeur*. It fills a useful place in the market for those who do not like that sort of wine, but still want something which is easier to drink than a heavyweight red.

A premium red is sold as Cuvée Prestige and is from the traditional duras, braucol and syrah, as is the single-vineyard wine from the Château de Boisse, produced under the direction of the co-opérative. Labastide also make an oaked red called Rive Gauche Prestige, from grapes grown on the left bank of the river, where it is thought that the wines respond more to oaking than those on the north side. This one certainly develops a powerful vanilla nose, characteristic of new wood. There is also a full range of Côtes de Tarn and *vins de pays*, sold either in bottle or *en vrac*. The white Côtes de Tarn has been featured in British supermarkets, where it represents excellent value for money when compared with some other *vins de pays*.

The Labastide co-opérative also owns the vineyards attached to a large château on the left bank of the river called, quite coincidentally, **Château Labistidié (1)**, though not the château itself, which belongs to the association called the Cup-Bearers of France. It specialises in a red *vin de garde*, and a white wine which contains an unusually high proportion of sémillon. The building itself is a splendid one, ideal for formal receptions.

Red wines are much more successful on the left bank than the whites. Indeed some growers here make little or no white wine at all. One well-liked red which is to be found in restaurants in the South-West is that from the **Domaine de Petit Nareye (4)**. The yield from the vines is limited by the relative shallowness of the soil. The premium red is called Renaissance and is generously oaked: the base 80% syrah. The resulting wine, though well made and interesting, is not really like any other Gaillac, and in fact would be hard to pick out as a Gaillac at all. The syrah gives it more of a Languedoc character. The *classique* red is called Les Gravels and to my mind has more of the true Gaillac style.

Also to be noted is the **Domaine de Pialentou (8)**, where Jean-Pierre Ailloud makes his red wine by *vinification permanent*, a method so-called because the crust which normally forms on the top of the must (called in French *le chapeau*) is kept permanently submerged in the must. This is thought to give the wine a particularly good colour and great roundness on the palate. The wine is marketed for Monsieur Aillaud by the owners of Château Candastre.

For those who really like their Gaillac to be rustic, the red wines from Philippe Blanc at **Le Haut des Vergnades (6)** near Cadalen are to be highly recommended for their quality and good value. Made from roughly equal quantities of duras and braucol, they could be hardly more authentic. The braucol almost gives the wine a Marcillac character with the associated flavour of redcurrants and raspberries. The wine can be quite tough two years after the vintage, but the third year can bring it round well.

The third of the growers' co-opératives is to be found here on the left bank. Because only parts of the terrain are suitable for good-quality wine, this is an area where growers cultivate many other crops besides grapes. Vineyards therefore tend to be small and capital investment is hardly tempting to their owners. The co-operative is thus well placed to invest and make improvements in standards of vinification which the farmers could not themselves afford. Hence it is in a position to improve vastly the level of quality of the wines made in this part of the appellation.

The **Cave Co-opérative de Técou (A)** is 7 kilometres south of Gaillac on the way to Graulhet. The president of the co-opérative is himself a *vigneron* from Brens, a small town facing Gaillac across the river. The director, Alain Boutrit, is an oenologist from the Bordelais. 'The wines of the future always have a past,' he says, echoing Oscar Wilde's observation about women. In the vineyards he is concerned to increase quality by clearly defining the different *terroirs*, checking the yields from the vines, the health of the grapes and ensuring they are picked at the right moment of maturity. In the *chais* he employs the most modern equipment and two fellow-oenologists to ensure the best possible vinification. His marketing policy is to concentrate on a clientèle attracted by 'personalised' wines, that is to say designer labels for restaurants etc. This may explain why the wines of Técou are not easy to find on supermarket shelves. They do, however, find their way into some of the best hotels, for example at Cordes.

Computerisation of members' files helps the co-opérative have instant control over the harvesting of the grapes, to separate out the vineyards destined for AOC production, which are then visited to check compliance with the rules and the health of the plants. The fact that the numerous different grape-varieties mature at different times between the end of August and the end of October makes these controls all the easier to police.

Experiments in oaking the red wines were begun in 1986, and have proved encouragingly successful: the resulting prestige wine, called Gaillac Passion, made principally from braucol and merlot, is in great demand and features on the best tables in the region. Next in the pecking order are the red, white and rosé wines called Séduction but Técou also covers the whole Gaillac range.

Técou has a reputation for being the most quality-orientated of the three co-opératives, perhaps because of its relatively small size, which gives an air of greater exclusivity. Its success is all the more deserved because of the generally lower quality of the raw material on the left bank of the river.

It is all too easy to be bewildered by the variety of wines produced at Gaillac. If you go to a château in Bordeaux, you will perhaps be shown the wine of a particular vintage, and, if the property produces white wine too, you might see some of that. In Gaillac, however, when faced by the question of what Monsieur would like to taste, it is difficult to answer.

The recovery of the Gaillac *vignoble* may be too new to say whether this diversity of product is good or bad, either for the producers or for the consumer. One school of thought is that the production of new kinds of Gaillac will expand the market for the growers, instead of sticking to traditional styles of wine. Above all the introduction of grape-varieties which have succeeded elsewhere in France, thereby bringing the flavour of Gaillac into line with other wines, is held to be commercially desirable.

The other argument, which I far prefer, is that the real, perhaps *only*, future for these wines is in preserving regional character. One applauds the wine-makers of Cahors for having excluded the cabernets from their list of permitted grape-varieties, simply because they did not want their wine to become a kind of sub-claret. They had fought the Bordelais long enough for their individuality not to see it lost by becoming another Bordeaux satellite. They see, correctly in my view, that the true individuality of Cahors lies in its devotion to the malbec grape. So it is in Gaillac – whose red wines derive their distinctiveness from the duras and braucol grapes and the white from the mauzac and len de l'el varieties which are nearly unique to Gaillac. I would rather have a glass of real Gaillac than just another glass of good sauvignon.

Could it also be that, by shifting the balance into the production of red wines, which are not always up to the level of the best whites, the local producers are unwise in reversing the decisions to concentrate on white wine production which were taken after the phylloxera? Some will say that that policy was fine as long as there was a market for sweet white wine based on the mauzac grape, but with the swing in taste to a drier style of wine, Gaillac is not really equipped to meet the demand to the required standard. If this is the case they must resist any pressures to phase out the distinctive *perlé*.

Perhaps the multiplicity of wines has in the past been the result of some lack of local cohesion. In other wine-areas some sort of common policy emerged many years ago by consensus if nothing else. In Gaillac this direction has only recently made itself felt. The people now in charge of promotion have really grasped the nettle of finding an image for Gaillac. They need now to establish a wider market, particularly in Paris and the North of France and in overseas countries, in order to provide a wider base for their producers. A business which has an assured market on its doorstep and does not really need to go out into the world to sell its wines is lucky in one way, but it is all to easy for such a perception to lead to complacency and thus decline.

Nevertheless, some of the wines made in Gaillac are quite exceptionally good. A great deal of talent is to be found there. It will be interesting to see whether its fulfilment will be achieved as a result of or in spite of the present diversity of product. Alex Taylor is not alone in believing that Gaillac could today make better wine than Bordeaux, just as it did hundreds of years ago.

PRODUCERS

GAILLAC

Above-average wines are noted in lower case, excellent ones in upper case.

R (r) means red
N (n) means *nouveau* or *primeur*
RO (ro) means rosé
P (p) means *vin blanc perlé*
WD (wd) means dry white (still)
WS (ws) means sweet white (still)
SD (sd) means dry white sparkling
SS (ss) means sweet white sparkling

A. *R* CAVE CO-OPÉRATIVE DE TÉCOU, 81600 Técou Tel:63-33-00-80

B. *P sd* CAVE CO-OPÉRATIVE DE RABASTENS, 81800 Rabastens
   Tel: 63-57-06-64

C. *p WD* CAVE CO-OPÉRATIVE DE LABASTIDE-DE-LÉVIS, 81150
   Labastide-de-Lévis Tel: 63-55-41-83. Also at Sept Fontaines, 8160 Gaillac
   Tel: 63-57-01-30

72. *P wd RO R SD* Albert Ribot, **Le Mas d'Aurel**, 81170 Donnazac
   Tel: 63-56-06-39

5.   Claude Candia, **Domaine de Balagès**, 81150 Lagrave Tel: 63-41-74-48

30. *WS* J.-C. Barreau, **Domaine Barreau** (Trabes de la Chantro), 81600 Boissel,
   Gaillac Tel: 63-57-57-51

73.   Cunnac et fils Tel: 63-56-06-52 **Domaine de Bertrand**, 81170 Donnazac
   Tel: 63-56-09-30

58. *P r* Roger Rouquié et fils, **Mas de Bicary**, 81600 Broze Tel: 63-57-07-93

37.   Jean-Claude Larroque, **Domaine du Bois d'Enguile**, 81600 Laborie,
   Gaillac Tel: 63-57-32-18

*54.   Jacques et Jean Bonnet, **Domaine Bonnet**, St Vincent, 81140 Cahuzac Tel:
   63-33-91-54*

55.   L.Willemborg, **Domaine de Bosc Long**, 81140 Cahuzac Tel: 63-33-94-45

38.   Jacques et Marcel Marty Tel: 63-57-51-66, **Mas Boudac**, 81600 Laborie,
   Gaillac Tel: 63-57-17-68

56. *r ws* Yvon Maurel et fils, **Domaine de Bouscaillous**, 81140 Montels
   Tel: 63-33-18-85

10.   Alain Boullenger, **Castel de Brames Aigues**, 81310 Peyrole
   Tel: 63-57-25-80

62.   Suzanne et Philippe Boissel, **Domaine de Brousse**, 81140 Cahuzac
   Tel: 63-33-90-14

34. *ro* Descombes, **Château de Candastre**, 81600 Boissel, Gaillac Tel: 63-41-70-88

68.   Guy et Brigitte Laurent, **Domaine de Cantalauze**, Lintin, 81140
   Cahuzac Tel: 63-56-07-97

12. *sd* Alexander Taylor, **Domaine de Canto Perlic**, 81600 Gaillac
   Tel: 63-57-18-63

20. *r* Yvan Stilhart, **Domaine de Cassagnols**, 81310 Lisle-Sur-Tarn
   Tel: 63-33-73-80 (bottled by the Rabastens co-opérative)

47.   Patrice Lescarret, **Domaine des Causses-Marines**, 81140 Vieux

48.   C. et M. Jeanjean, **Domaine des Cayrous**, 81140 St. Beauzile
   Tel: 63-33-13-49

22.   Etienne Boyals et fils, **Le Cellier des Augustines**, 10 rue St Louis, 81310
   Lisle-sur-Tarn Tel: 63-33-37-80 (marketed by Château Candastre q.v.)

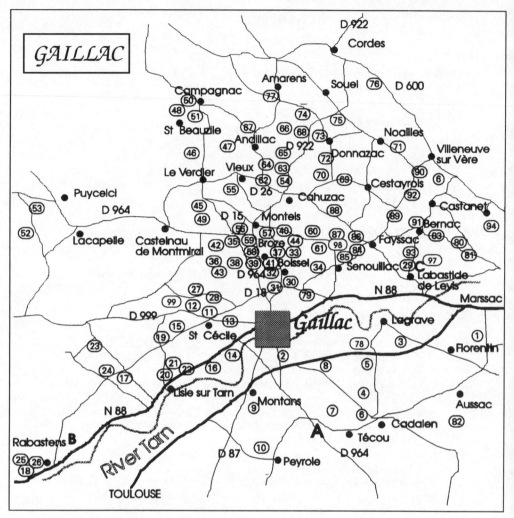

14. J. Chaumet-Lagrange, **Domaine de Chaumet-Lagrange**, Les Fédiès, 81600 Gaillac Tel: 63-57-07-12

63. James Barras, **Domaine Cinq Peyres** (Château Adelaide Martial), 81140 Cahuzac Tel: 63-33-96-18

19. *r* Jean-Paul et François David et fils, **Domaine Clément-Termes**, Les Fortis, 81310 Lisle-sur-Tarn Tel: 63-40-47-80

41. Larroque et fils, **Le Mas des Combes**, Oustry, 81600 Gaillac Tel: 63-57-06-13

66. G. et C. Ramond, **Domaine des Condomines**, 81140 Andillac Tel: 63-33-91-95

97. Bousquet et fils, **Al Courderc**, 81150 Labastide-de-Lévis Tel: 63-55-41-37

9. *n p* J. M. et M. J. Bézios, **La Croix des Marchands**, 81600 Montans Tel: 63-57-19-71

85. *R* Henri Plageoles, **Le Mas de Doat**, 81600 Senouillac Tel: 63-41-78-78

39. M. Cauvin-Geoffroy, **Château Donat**, 81600 Gaillac Tel: 63-57-06-88

60. Jacky Nélain, **Domaine de Durantou**, 81140 Cahuzac Tel: 63-33-90-12

51. *r n* C.-J. Poussou, **Manoir de l'Emeillé**, 81140 Campagnac Tel: 63-33-12-80
26. *C. Hauchard, Château d'Escabes, 81600 Rabastens Tel: 63-33-73-80*
94. *n r* Denis Balaran et fils, **Domaine d'Escausses**, 81150 Ste-Croix
    Tel: 63-56-80-52
82. Jean-Daniel Rouge, **Fargue**, 81600 Aussac Tel: 63-55-48-18
98. Bernard Ferret, **Domaine Ferret**, La Sirventié, 81600 Senovillac
    Tel: 63-41-51-94
59. *ro* Causse et fils, **Domaine de Gayssou**, 81600 Broze Tel: 63-33-18-74
7. Laillier-Bellevret, **Domaine de Gineste**, 81600 Técou Tel: 63-33-03-18
50. Etienne Coursières, **Domaine de Graddé**, 81140 Campagnac
    Tel: 63-33-12-61
86. Yannie et Nelly Lacombe, **Domaine du Grand Chêne**, La Figuérade,
    81600 Senouillac Tel: 63-41-78-40
25. *r* Francis Alquier et fils, **Mas de Grouze**, Grouze, 81800 Rabastens
    Tel: 63-33-80-70
3. Martin et Alain Bounes, **Domaine des Guiraudets**, 81150 Lagrave
    Tel: 63-41-75-09
71. V. Ricardou, **Château les Hauts de Noailles**, 81170 Noailles
    Tel: 63-56-81-83
36. *WD* A. Kabakian, **Domaine des Hourtets**, 81600 Laborie, Gaillac
    Tel: 63-33-19-15
69. Madame Cros et fils, **Domaines Jean Cros**, 81140 Cahuzac Tel: 63-33-92-62
79. Marc **Jeansou**, Route de Viars, 81600 Gaillac Tel: 63-57-11-01
90. *P wd WS Ro R SD SS N* Jean Albert et fils, **Domaine de Labarthe**, 81150
    Castanet Tel: 63-56-80-14
1. Cave de Labastide, **Château de Labastidié**, 81600 Florentin
    Tel: 63-55-41-83
89. *sd* Pierre Derrieux et fils Tel: 63-56-81-10, **Domaine de Lacroux**, 81150
    Cestayrols Tel: 63-56-81-67
21. *Louis Cayre, Lapeyrière, 81310 Lisle-sur-Tarn Tel: 63-33-37-24*
16. *r* J. H. F. de Faramond, **Château de Lastours**, 81310 Lisle-sur-Tarn
    Tel: 63-57-07-09
96. Serge Andrieux, **Château Lavelanet**, 81600 Montans
57. *sd* Mogens Oleson, **Château de Lecusse**, 81600 Broze Tel: 63-33-90-09
23. *p WD WS* Christian Bastide, **Domaine de Long Pêch**, 81310 Lisle-sur-Tarn
    Tel: 63-33-37-22
80. Christian Thomères, **Domaine de la Mailhourie**, 81150 Castelnau-de-
    Lévis Tel: 63-46-03-54
27. Martine Lecomte, **Domaine de Matens**, 81600 Gaillac Tel: 63-57-43-96
45. *WS* Alan etLaurence Geddes, **Château Mayragues**, 81140 Castelnau-
    Montmirail Tel: 63-33-94-08
17. *p r* Boyals et fils, **Domaine de Mazou**, 81310 Lisle-sur-Tarn Tel: 63-33-37-80
99. *ss* EARL Trouche et Fils, **Château Miramond**, Mas de Graves, 81600
    Gaillac Tel: 63-57-14-86
75. *r* Bruno Montels, **Château de Montels** (Domaine de St André) 81170
    Souel Tel: 63-56-01-28
2. *R* Jean-Paul Hirissou, **Domaine du Moulin**, 81600 Brens Tel: 63-57-07-27
92. *WD ro N* Alain Monestié, **Domaine de Moussens**, 81150 Cestayrols
    Tel: 63-56-86-60
67. J. Bros, **Domaine du Palisadou**, 81140 Andillac Tel: 63-33-91-92
74. *R wd* Louis Brun et fils, **Domaine le Payssel**, 81170 Frausseilles
    Tel: 63-56-00-47
43. Nicholas Fraser, **Domaine de Perches**, Laborie, 81600 Gaillac
    Tel: 63-33-16-05

RECOMMENDED WINES ACCORDING TO STYLE

PERLÉ	DRY WHITE	SWEET WHITE	RED
Cave de Rabastens	Dom. de la Ramaye	Dom. de la Ramaye	Cave de Técou
Mas de Bicary	Dom. de Long Pech	Dom. de Vayssette	Dom. du Moulin
Mas d'Aurel	Mas Pignou	Mas Pignou	Dom. des Vergnades
Dom. de Labarthe	Robert Plageoles et fils	Roger Plageoles et fils	Dom. de la Ramaye
Dom de Salmes	Cave de Labastide	Dom. de Labarthe	Mas Pignou
	Dom. des Hourtets	Dom. Barreau	Roger Plageoles et fils
	Dom. de Moussens	Dom. de Long Pech	Mas d'Aurel
		Ch. Mayragues	Dom. le Payssel
			Château Raynal
			Mas de Doat
			Dom. de Labarthe

also:

La Croix des Marchands	Mas d'Aurel	Dom. René Rieux	Ch. Montels
Cave de Labastide	Dom. le Payssel	Dom. Bouscaillous	Dom. de Mazou
Dom. de Mazou	Dom. de Labarthe	Dom. des Terrisses	Dom. Clément Terme
Dom. de Long Pech	Dom. de la Tronque	Terroirs de Lagrave	Dom. Bouscaillous
	Vigné-Laurac		Dom. d'Escausses
	Ch. de Salettes		Mas de Bicary
	Dom. des Terrisses		Dom. de Cassagnols
			Ch. de Lastours
			Ch. de Rhodes
			Terroirs de Lagrave

4. Rotier et fils, **Domaine de Petit Nareye**, 81600 Cadalen Tel: 63-41-75-14

65. H. Marty, **Domaine de Peyres-Combe**, Cinq Peyres, 81140 Cahuzac
Tel: 63-33-92-05

64. V. Bruneau, **Domaine de Peyres-Combes**, La Combe, 81140 Andillac
Tel: 63-33-94-67

8. Jean-Louis Ailloud, **Domaine de Pialentou**, 81600 Brens
Tel: 63-57-17-99

42. R WD WS SD Jacques et Bernard Aucques, **Mas Pignou**, Laborie, 81600
Gaillac Tel: 63-33-18-52

44. R WD WS Robert Plageoles, **Vignobles Robert Plageoles et fils**, 81140
Cahuzac Tel: 63-33-90-40

77. Rolland Mazières, **Château Plantade**, 81170 Amarens Tel: 63-56-08-00

84. Laurent Thomères, **La Raffinié**, 81150 Castelnau-de-Lévis
Tel: 63-57-28-70

11. R WD WS Maurice et Huguette Issaly, **Domaine de la Ramaye**,
Ste-Cécile d'Avès, 81600 Gaillac Tel: 63-57-06-64

84. R Nelly et Patrick Raynal, **Château Raynal**, La Brunerie, 81600 Gaillac
Tel: 63-41-70-02

87. Max Reinbold Tel: 63-41-71-76, **Domaine de Reinbold**, Mauriac, 81600
Senouillac Tel: 63-41-73-32

31. ws SD SS C. A. T. Boissel, **Domaine René Rieux**, 81600 Boissel, Gaillac
Tel: 63-57-29-29

29. r René Assié, **Château de Rhodes**, 81600 Boissel, Gaillac Tel: 63-67-06-02

13. Société Hartfield, **Château Ste-Cécile**, Ste-Cécile d'Avès, 81600 Gaillac
Tel: 63-57-59-57

Rosé	Mousseux DRY	Mousseux SWEET	Nouveau
Dom. de Gayssou	Dom. de la Tronque	Dom. de Labarthe	Dom. de Labarthe
Mas d'Aurel	Mas d'Aurel	Dom. René Rieux	Dom. de Moussens
Dom. de Labarthe	Dom. de Labarthe	Dom. de Vayssette	
	Dom. René Rieux		
	Roger Plageoles		
	Mas Pignou		

also:

Ch. de Candastre	Cave de Rabastens	Dom. des Terrisses	La Croix des Marchands
Dom. de Moussens	Dom. de Lacroux	Ch. Miramond	Dom. d'Escausses
	Dom. de Cantoperlic		Man. de L'Emeillé

61. *wd* L. Willemborg, **Château de Salettes**, 81140 Cahuzac Tel: 63-33-94-45
83. *P* Jean-Paul Pézet, **Domaine de Salmes**, 81150 Bernac Tel: 63-55-42-53
76. Claude Thouy, **Domaine de la Salvetat**, 81170 Livers-Cazelles
    Tel: 63-56-05-06
53. Jacques Oesch, **Domaine la Salvetat**, 81140 Puycelci Tel: 63-33-15-52
70. Michel Vignoles-Marc, **Domaine de Salvy**, Arzac, 81140 Cahuzac
    Tel: 63-33-92-64
15. M. P. Burrus, **Château de Saurs**, 81310 Lisle-sur-Tarn Tel: 63-40-48-32
33. *r* Mouly père et fils, **Château de Tauzies**, 81600 Boissel, Gaillac
    Tel: 63-57-06-06
52. P.-H. Bauser, **Château de Terride,** 81140 Puycelci Tel: 63-33-11-38
    (new owner in 1996?)
28. *ws wd ss* G.A.E.C. Cazottes et fils Tel: 63-57-09-15, **Domaine des Terrisses**,
    81600 Gaillac Tel: 63-57-16-80
78. r ws EARL Terroirs de Lagrave, **Le Terroir de Lagrave**. 81150 Lagrave
    Tel: 63-81-52-20
40. René Teulières, **Domaine Teulières**, 81600 Laborie, Gaillac
    Tel: 63-57-06-82
32. C. Fiault, **Domaine la Tour Boissel**, 81600 Boissel, Gaillac Tel: 63-57-06-05
93. France et Jeffar Nettani, **Château la Tour Plantade**, La Soucarié,
    81150 Labastide-de-Lévis Tel: 63-55-47-43
18. Thierry et Jean-Pierre Pagès, **Cave des Trois Clochers**,
    81310 Lisle-sur-Tarn Tel: 63-40-47-38
46. Monsieur Baron, **Domaine des Trois Moineaux**, 81140 Le Verdier
    Tel: 63-33-93-46

49. *SD wd* Claude Leduc, **Domaine de la Tronque**, 81140 Castelnau
    Tel: 63-33-18-87
24.   Guy et A. M. Golse, **Domaine de Truc**, Trés Cantous, 81310 Lisle-sur-
    Tarn Tel: 63-33-37-50
35. *WS SS* Maryse et Jacques Vayssette, **Domaine de Vayssette**, 86100
    Laborie, Gaillac Tel: 63-57-31-95
6. *R*   J. et P. Blanc, **Domaine des Vergnades**, Haut des Vergnades
    Tel: 63-33-02-02, La Arrayrié, 81600 Cadalen Tel: 63-33-01-70
91.   Werner Schwartz, **Domaine les Vignals**, 81150 Cestayrols Tel: 63-55-41-53
88. *wd* Alain Gayrel-Philippe, **Château Vigné-Laurac**, 81600 Senouillac
    Tel: 63-33-91-16

The Wines of Fronton
and the Toulousain

FRONTON

The river Tarn swings to the north-west after leaving the vineyards of Gaillac. A plateau rises above its left bank to separate it from the river Garonne which it will later join in the plain beyond Montauban. This table-land of flat and rather dull countryside is home to the wines of Fronton and Villaudric, wedded at last after a reluctant courtship and centuries of rivalry. It was an arranged marriage, promoted by the appellation authorities. The wines of both parties now enjoy appellation contrôlée status under the title Côtes du Frontonnais, but the bride and groom, like oil and vinegar, do not mix well, and are entitled to keep their separate identities by adding the suffix Villaudric or Fronton to their official married name.

Large tracts of this countryside, planted with vines as early as the seventh century, were donated in 1122 to the Knights of Saint John of Jerusalem, known also as the Knights Templar, whose principal concern was the safety of the traditional Christian sites and relics in the Holy Land. From their frequent journeys to the Middle East, they brought back to Fronton a particular grape-variety, which they had discovered on the island of Cyprus, where it is still grown to this day. Called négrette, because of its dark skin and the deep colour of its juice, it is, after nearly 900 years, still the predominant variety in the wines of Fronton, to which it lends a unique character.

According to the local historian, Adrien Escudier, in 1904 there were 8000 hectares under vine in the Fronton-Villaudric area. Today the area has shrunk to under 2000 hectares. The 1904 figure must have included substantial plantations of inferior stocks, cultivated after the phylloxera in an effort to keep production levels up. Among these were varieties which have now altogether disappeared, including jacquez, herbemont, yorck and the foxy othello. In the middle of the last century, there were to be found alongside the négrette a huge list of ancillary *cépages*, including the white mauzac and folle blanche, called locally chalosse, as well as a red mauzac and the red mérille. Later and more important varieties have included the two cabernets, gamay, syrah and malbec, here sometimes called bordelais.

But it is the négrette grape on which the reputation and originality of Fronton is founded. The bunches of fruit are small and compact, and the grapes are perfectly round. It is particularly suited to the very poor soil of the region, for in richer ground it would be too rampant and it likes, too, the hotter climate of this southern situation. Its skin is thin, so it is vulnerable to frosts and diseases, as well as disliking humidity. The dry autan wind suits it admirably. Though the juice is dark, it is low in acidity and lacks backbone: but it is rich in the taste of ripe red fruits, ideal for a quick-maturing wine. Sometimes it is spicy, even peppery, and some commentators detect a note of liquorice. This style, lighter than many in the South-West, has enabled growers to secure a particular niche in the bars and restaurants of nearby Toulouse, where it occupies something of the same place as Beaujolais in Lyon. Toulouse has been the principal buyer of Fronton for nearly two centuries, since the decline in the river-trade with Bordeaux and the demise of the port of Montauban.

To make up for the lack of acidity in the grape, growers blend it with the sturdier cabernets, syrah and gamay, and sometimes with a little malbec. The rules of the present appellation require the négrette to be blended with at least 30% but no more than 50% of these supporting varieties, of which the cabernets must not exceed 20%. In practice some producers regard this as a blueprint for their vineyards but not necessarily every one of their Fronton wines: some like to make a wine which is more or less 100% négrette, using up the other varieties in different *assemblages* of AOC wine, or in *vins de pays*.

The two towns of Fronton and Villaudric are at the geographical heart of the appellation. There are two quite distinct types of soil – a reddish crumbly stone, sometimes called *rouget* and a light clay soil which has broken down into an almost sandy consistency – and everywhere a great deal of pebble, making the land fit for very little else except the growing of vines. Underpinning this inhospitable terrain is a base of iron and quartz, which give the wines their fullness and bouquet, as well as a pleasantly almondy bitterness on the after-taste.

The diminution in the size of the vineyard in the last hundred years is partly due to the persistence of diseases such as black rot, mildew, oidium and the phylloxera; partly also to the failure of the hybrids planted in their wake. As serious as any of these was the disastrous spring frost of 1956 which obliged some growers to start all over again. Nevertheless, enthusiasts for the cause had secured the grant of VDQS status for the Villaudric vineyards in 1945 and Fronton two years later, and the **Cave Co-opérative** of Fronton **(11)** was created in 1946. Its first vintage in 1947 yielded a total of 11,200 hectolitres from 170 growers, which implies an average holding of less than 1¹/₂ hectares each. Since then production has quadrupled and the wine-making capacity multiplied by ten, so there is plenty of room for expansion. Today the Cave accounts for about two-thirds of all the Fronton made. In addition to its appellation wines, it makes twice as much again of *vin de pays du comté tolosan.*

In the early days of VDQS, Villaudric too had its own cave co-opérative. When full AOC status was granted for the combined vineyards in 1975 there was no real need for two co-opératives and the one at Villaudric, the smaller of the two, started to decline as the Fronton Cave gradually recruited Villaudric growers. Eventually in 1987 the Villaudric Cave folded and the Gaillac Cave at Rabastens (q.v.) took on the lease of the building to serve the few members who did not want to transfer to Fronton. There is still a great deal of partisan feeling between the two towns, reflecting a long history of rivalry. In the Religious Wars, Villaudric was Catholic and Fronton Protestant: nowadays the separatism is reflected in less violent ways, for example by the retention of the Burgundy-shaped bottle by some Villaudric growers, to distance them from their rivals in Fronton.

The growers in the two rival areas still claim a distinctive character for their wines. Villaudric, perhaps because traditionally they never destalked their wines, claim a firmer structure and more finesse, while Fronton boast a greater fruitiness and more alcohol. It is likely that the variation in style depends not so much on whether they come from one town or the other, but on the particular soil and *encépagement* of each vineyard.

The Fronton Cave is on the northern outskirts of Fronton itself. Its director is Jack Verdier, who is proud of his English Christian-name (given to him to commemorate the arrival of an English officer called Jack, by parachute in the middle of the night, in the family garden in Bordeaux during the war). Monsieur Verdier considers himself extremely fortunate to have trained as an oenologist in Bordeaux under the great Emile Peynaud. He joined the Fronton Cave in 1990.

Monsieur Verdier is responsible for two-thirds of all Fronton made, so he must observe the rules strictly – there is no question of being able to slip into his AOC range a wine which is 100% négrette. Such a wine must, strictly speaking, be sold only as a *vin de pays.* Verdier says that, at the end of the day, the label may not matter too much, because there is little price differential between the AOC and the *vins de pays*: it is more a question of the permitted yield from the vines – 50 and 80 hectolitres to the hectare respectively. It was interesting, though, to taste the Cave's 100% négrette, one of a range of varietal wines produced by them as *vins de pays.* It was not as dark as expected, but it was bright and clear and well presented. It began better than it finished, with a fresh, fruity nose and more red fruits on the palate. It lacked structure, follow-through, and, characteristically of the grape, acidity. A year after the vintage it was temptingly drinkable all the same.

The AOC range starts with a basic red and rosé, presented simply as Carte Blanche, or, more expensively, as Cuvée Olympique. Only the packaging is different, to commemorate the fact that the Cave's Fronton has twice been chosen as 'house-wine' to the Olympic Games. The next level of quality is their market-leading Comte de Négret, which is made from grapes grown by the most competent of their members with the best parcels of land. Such growers can produce wines which are better even than the single-domaine wines which the Cave makes for seven private owners. This wine clearly demonstrated the extra weight and structure to be gained from blending the wine from négrette with those from other grapes.

The Cave also makes two oaked reds: the first, which is usually given rather less wood than the other, is called Fronton Vanel and is made for the famous restaurant of that name in Toulouse. The style of the wine is light and very commercial. The top of the range Haut-Capitole, aged in new wood for nine months – '*Comme un bébé*,' said Jack Verdier – brings into question maturing a wine based on négrette in new casks, a problem which cropped up again and again on visits to many other Fronton producers.

Of the seven single domaines for which the Cave is responsible, they list only two on their price-list. The one which I have tasted is called Domaine Marcelot, or Château Marcelot as its label proclaims. This had a very intense, fruity bouquet. It finished a bit short, but a little more ageing was needed than the two years which it had had when tasted.

As well as the Fronton and Gaillac Caves, there are just over forty private producers of Côtes du Frontonnais: three times as many, according to one of them, as there were in 1983. Many must be hoping to emulate the success of Patrick Germain, who has created from a wilderness of scrub and brambles a vineyard which today extends to 115 hectares. His **Château Bellevue-la-Forêt (5)** is the largest vineyard in the South-West.

In 1974 Patrick gave up attempts to stay on in Algeria and Morocco and with the benefit of his experience as a wine-maker in North Africa, his purchase of 25 hectares of land at Fronton coincided with the grant of AOC in 1975. There was absolutely nothing on the land, not even the most modest of houses. While his first grapes were maturing, he built, with the aid of Emile Peynaud, the present *cave de vinification* and as recently as 1990 he added the underground *chais d'élevage* to house his new oak barrels.

The present estate was assembled piece by piece, and today there are about 60 hectares of négrette, 17 of cabernet franc, 13 of cabernet sauvignon, 17 of syrah and 8 of gamay noir *à jus blanc*. Twenty-two per cent of the production is in rosé, of which there are two kinds: the first is from 70% négrette and 15% each syrah and gamay; the second is pure négrette. The rest of the wine from this property is red, for Patrick Germain makes no white *vin de pays*.

There are two real red Frontons. The first is entirely copy-book, with its 50% négrette, a 25% mixture of the two cabernets, and the rest in syrah and gamay. The different grapes are vinified separately at temperatures between 24 and 28° according to the character of the year and the frequency of *remontage* will vary correspondingly. After the *assemblage*, the wine gets a sudden short sharp attack of the cold at minus 4° to prevent the formation of bitartrate of potassium crystals, which do not affect the wine but are said to put off consumers. The wine is matured in its *cuves* for four or five months before filtration and bottling. Patrick Germain recommends a coolish 14° as the best drinking temperature. This is a fine, peppery, spicy wine with a long smoky finish, and it keeps well. It is the wine you are most likely to find representing Fronton in the United Kingdom.

The second red is pure négrette and is called, perhaps a little preciously, Ce Vin, Une Idée d'André Daguin, the famous Gascon restaurateur from Auch. The grapes come from two distinct types of terrain, the first stony, producing fruit which calls for a high vinification temperature to extract the tannins and colour; the second sand and pebbles, the grapes from which are vinified at a lower temperature of 20–24° so as to develop the fruitiness, suppleness and finesse in the wine. The final blend is matured for eight months and is intended to be drunk cool but not chilled – cellar temperature would be ideal. This is a really lovely, fresh and fruity wine: better than the pure négrette from the cave co-opérative, because it has some weight and structure as well as fresh fruit, and I noticed no lack of acidity or tannins.

In many walks of life, the successful attract gibes and snide remarks from those lower down the ladder of achievement. In Patrick Germain's case, however, every Fronton grower I talked to went out of his way to praise what Patrick has done for the appellation, and to pay tribute to the standards of his wine-making. In turn he has a very healthy respect for what some of his colleagues are doing, especially for François Daubert, whose vineyard called **Domaine de Joliet (27)** is just the other side of the motorway from Bellevue-la-Forêt. Monsieur Daubert moved in after the creation of the appellation in 1978 and bought this 20-hectare property, all of which is on the sandier type of soil but with quite a lot of iron close to the surface. To start with he found the négrette grape difficult to handle: it was liable to rot and was what winemakers call *fragile*. In 1984 he sought the advice of an oenologist who advised him to pull most of it up and plant something else. His instinct told him that this was bad advice: the négrette had flourished in Fronton for eight hundred years and other growers seemed to manage with it. François Daubert went to the other extreme and started to experiment with making a 100% négrette wine, which he sold *en vrac* as *vin de pays*. The medals started rolling in, so he began bottling it for serious sale in 1986. It had a big success at Vinexpo, the important biennial Bordeaux wine fair, and François settled down to an *assemblage* of 90% négrette and 10% syrah. If the press and his customers were ecstatic, then his own conscience was appeased.

Today François Daubert makes this wine almost entirely from négrette, with a cuvaison of ten days at a relatively low temperature of 25° or so. The wine is supple and easy to drink, at its best one or two years after the harvest. Forbidden by the rules to proclaim its *encépage-ment* on the label, François Daubert does the next best thing by putting a picture of a bunch of négrette grapes in a small white square in the centre of the label on a dark green and gold background, so that the grapes and the legend 'la négrette' shine from the bottle like a beacon.

Inventive wine-makers seem often to have a streak of poetic fantasy about them: François Daubert reminded me a little of Robert Plageoles in Gaillac, because he believes firmly in the importance of the wine-maker behind the wine. 'A good vigneron,' he said, 'should be like a good conductor, extracting the maximum from his "players", but never imposing himself on the composer's raw material.'

Daubert also makes a conventional Fronton: it is very good, needing about four or five years to show to its best. But his négrette is so out-standing that I think it is almost a waste of the négrette grape to cover up its freshness with the usual cocktail of supporting varieties. I have often thought that the people responsible for drawing up the rules of the appellations in South-West France should have insisted on more rather than less of the traditional grape-varieties of each region.

The Domaine de Joliet also produces a rosé, made by *saignage* from the négrette, but Daubert's second original creation is his 100% mauzac *doux*, which he is obliged to sell as *vin de pays*, because there is no such thing today as white Fronton. His first effort in this direction was in 1990 from 2 hectares of grapes. The following year he made next to none, and in 1992 he was obliged to pick the grapes a great deal earlier than he would have wished. Even so, the wine had the typical apple-and-pears aroma of the mauzac, with considerable richness and the flavours of quinces and honey. It is rather elegantly sweet, neither vul-gar nor powerful, but quite individual. Grapes from vines about thirty-five years old are used for this wine, vines which were already at Joliet when Daubert arrived in 1978 from the West Indies. They are allowed to over-ripen on the vine, and are lightly pressed before fermentation at a low temperature of 10–15°: in a good year the *cuvaison* will be a little over three weeks before a short *élevage*, leading to early bottling. The wine is not intended for keeping, and is at its best within two years from the harvest, while it is still fresh.

Claude Vigouroux is another grower to make a *vin doux*, this time from sémillon grapes at the northern end of the appellation, where there is more clay in the soil than further south. Claude bought **Domaine Baudare (3)** in 1964, though his father had been established in the region as a grower for many years. At the beginning only 1 hec-tare was planted with vines, rather miserable ones at that; 5 other hectares contained some superannuated fruit trees. Claude pulled down the weakling trees and gradually expanded the property to its present 25 hectares. Nowadays the family grows nothing but vines, except for a few sunflowers on a small patch down by the stream which is too damp for grapes. The vineyard is one continuous plantation which makes for homogeneity in the wine as well as ease of cultivation.

Claude's son is often on hand to welcome visitors. Like many of his generation, he has been formally trained in oenology. This has given him a sophistication and polish which might have surprised his grandfather, as well as the know-how to compete in modern markets. He explained that the family had only 40% of their vineyard planted with négrette. This meant that only another 40%, consisting of other grapevarieties, could go to make an AOC wine, otherwise the négrette proportion would fall below the statutory 50%. So the remainder, especially syrah and gamay, goes to make a *vin de pays* which they sell as Domaine de Baudare: their AOC red is sold as Château Baudare. For the latter, the grapes are hand-sorted on their arrival at the *chais* and they are given a slightly longer fermentation at a higher temperature before being matured in large new *foudres*. Because these containers have a lower proportion of wood to wine than the more usual 225-litre *barriques*, the taste of the oak is gentle, and three years are enough for this wine to become fully mature, with plenty of soft red fruits and a spicy finish.

The Baudare range is completed by a rosé made from tannat and cabernet franc, and a dry white made exclusively from sauvignon. For the latter the grapes are given a *macération pelliculaire* of up to two days, which is unusually long. After the juice has been drawn off the. *bourbe*, it is kept at a low temperature for a few days, during the last two of which the yeasts are added so that they can settle before vinification is allowed to begin. The fermentation is maintained at 18° by means of refrigerated plates submerged in the *cuves*.

Because the vineyards in Fronton are relatively flat, picking is done nearly everywhere by machine – the Vigouroux share one with three other local growers. No less than 80% of their wine is exported, a remarkable achievement: some goes to Taiwan and Korea. Of the rest, some is sold *en négoce* through their namesakes in Cahors as well as *en vrac* at the door. Their customers tend to be upset if they find supermarkets selling wine more cheaply than the price they have paid elsewhere, so sales to *les grandes surfaces* are under the label Domaine de la Viguerie. There is also a prejudice in France that, if you market wine through supermarkets, you devalue its image.

The Vigouroux are long-time friends of the Ferrans, who own an estate called **Château Cahuzac (9)** 2 or 3 miles away from them in the small hamlet called Peyronnets. Claude Ferran is another who is taking up sweet wine, in his case an experimental muscat not yet being marketed. Claude claims that his family are the oldest wine-makers in Fronton: they can trace back to one Guillaume Cahuzac who, in 1776, bought a parcel of land which was in due course to form the nucleus of the present vineyard. The Ferran-Cahuzac family has been there ever since. After the phylloxera and the 1956 frosts, they took the opportunity to improve the *encépagement* of the vineyard on each occasion.

Claude's mother is of Venetian origin, her family having fled Fascist Italy in the 1920s: in those days refugees were allowed into France only to work on the land, and a large number settled in the Frontonnais where they did a great deal to bring new life to a derelict region. Much of the land was in the ownership of big estates, with tenants who couldn't be bothered to do much even to maintain standards in the vineyards. Nowadays conditions have changed: Claude says that today it is almost obligatory to study oenology before you can take on even the smallest vineyard.

Claude himself trained as an agricultural engineer at Ste-Livrade-sur-Lot and at first intended to become an arboriculturist, not a winemaker. But when Fronton got its AOC his father persuaded him to return to the family vineyard, where prospects looked a lot brighter than they had for years. They expanded the vineyard still further to its present 43 hectares, large for the area though less than half the size of Bellevue-la-Forêt. To provide room to store the wine, particularly with a view to increasing the proportion sold in bottle, additional *chais* were built in 1985 which have nearly doubled the capacity. They now have room to store 6000 hectolitres, roughly four times their present bottled production. In addition to the family, they have three permanent staff in the vineyards.

Claude Ferran's present range of wines is fairly simple, despite the size of the vineyard. There is a rosé made from 85% négrette and 15% gamay, which is *saigné* from the first of his reds, called *vin de printemps*. It also bears the name Peyronnets, and so far no one has seemed to mind that the négrette content is way over the top. Also called Le Peyronnets is another wine, high in négrette (70%), with 15% each of gamay and syrah. The gamay is replaced by cabernet sauvignon in another wine which is one of only two of the reds to bear the Château Cahuzac name: the other is their top-of-the-range red where the négrette is reduced to 50% and the balance is made up equally from syrah and cabernet sauvignon. The red wines have a good deep colour, deep ruby or garnet, with a generous bouquet of soft fruits, including prunes, with suggestions of tobacco and pepper. The flavour lingers well in the mouth, and with age the wines develop aromas of autumn leaves, and of fruits pickled in brandy. The wines of this property have an agreeably rustic quality.

Another good wine-maker at this northern end of Fronton is Guy Pérez at the **Domaine de Callory (10)**. The property is in his wife's family, the Montels. Madame works in the local pharmacy, and her father was mayor of the local commune, so the family has interests outside the vineyards. Madame told me that her great-grandfather made wine here, then there was a gap of one generation before her father took the vineyards on, and it was he who, after the 1956 frosts, dug them all up and replanted them. Today they have 27 hectares on the typical poor sandy *boulbènes* (decomposed clay) of this part of the appellation. Her husband looks after the vines and the wine-making, while she deals with the business side when she is not at the pharmacy. They have a teenage son, but, after three poor vintages in a row, he seems to have lost interest, temporarily at least, in becoming a *vigneron*. The parents are not optimistic that he will change his mind, because they think the outlook for small growers is bleak. In Fronton they do not have the benefit of a big name like Bordeaux, where the dealers have slashed their prices for the lesser growths to such an extent that it is impossible to compete. Supermarkets had been offering six free bottles of Bordeaux to customers who bought a full dozen. Where did this leave people like them? Madame believes that many are now taking the EC bribe to dig up their vines and change to other crops which carry a subsidy.

The operation in this vineyard is traditional, and they believe in long *cuvaisons*. They pick by machine: Madame Pérez says the modern style of machine is so selective and gentle that her husband does not need to de-stalk the grapes. She also prefers machines because temporary labour at harvest-time is unreliable, and she recalled how, when the Gulf War broke out just at the time the vines were getting their winter-pruning, two Moroccans walked out on her to go and fight.

About 40% of the production at Callory is *vin de pays*, and very good it is in its class: it is made from syrah, cabernet sauvignon and merlot. The wine is fresh, aromatic, supple and well balanced. The AOC red, of which they make only one style, does of course have its statutory pro-portion of négrette and a bit more besides, the supporting varieties being cabernet and syrah only. After the wine has been made in concrete and the malolactic fermentation is over, it is transferred to enormous old *foudres* where it matures for eighteen months before being bottled. Madame Perez showed me one which contained 402 hectolitres, quite the largest I have ever seen in the South-West.

An interesting grower new to the market is Louis Duplan, who bot-tled his own **Domaine de la Bruyère** for the first time in 1993, and started winning medals straight away. Though easy to drink young, the wine has good structure and could last four or five years. The rosé is delicious too.

In an appellation where the best wines tend to be light, fruity and early to mature, it is surprising to come across Frédéric Ribes, who believes firmly that he can preserve the typicity of the négrette grape, while making a better-structured wine that will last longer without risk of oxidisation. But then Frédéric is a close friend of Patrick Ducournau whom we shall meet in the Madiran, the land of tough tannic wines fit only for the d'Artagnans of this world. In fact it was Patrick who strongly recommended that I should visit **Château du Roc (40)**, where the Ribes family live, just south of the town of Fronton.

Frédéric and his brother took over this 13-hectare vineyard from their father when he retired in 1988. The sons had already made some experiments in wine-making on their own, before persuading their father to leave the co-opérative and to give them the chance to see what they could do. Their father agreed because it was the easiest way of continuing the family farm. The grapes here are picked by machine, but Frédéric gives them a rigorous selection before the best are tipped, a hod at a time, into small concrete *cuves*, without de-stalking or crushing or any pump. The négrette is vinified for seventeen days, and the syrah and cabernet are given three weeks. A year after the vintage the 1991 négrette was black, ripe and deep, with considerable body and substance. A year later, what Frédéric called the exuberance of the négrette had mellowed and he found on the nose a whiff of tar.

After *assemblage*, the Ribes' wines are very complex, and they make you realise how similar the aromas from the négrette and syrah are when the grapes are vinified this way. The 1992 one year on was incredibly dark, but absolutely bright, and the nose was highly spiced as well as fruity, with characteristic hints of liquorice. The highly personal expression of the négrette grape has led one commentator to compare Ribes' results to those of Alain Brumont with the tannat grape in Madiran.

Since the father retired, the family has acquired a further 5 hectares of vines. The mix of grapes is almost standard, though they have only a little gamay: it is not their style. They think so little of it that they forgot to pick the 0.2 of a hectare of it which they had bought a few months previously. The plan is to replant it with négrette. Fréderic told me that the farm is now a monoculture – except for a few sheep which he keeps, because he loves a gigot of lamb for Sunday lunch. The property is very simple, giving little idea of the quality of the wines made within. The buildings are long and low, covered by an old pantile roof scorched by the heat of the sun. The walls are built partly of the rose-pink flat Toulouse brick; and partly of a kind of compacted mud which insulates the maturing wine well from changes in temperature.

The Ribes do not believe in weeding between the vine-rows: the grass limits the yield, as well as making it easier to drive picking-machines up and down. The Ribes have their own which is of the more modern gentle kind which does not beat the vines into lifelessness as it picks the grapes. Frédéric did, however, confess to me that, if the weather was good, he rather enjoyed doing a bit of hand-picking himself.

For quick turnover, the Ribes turn 15–20% of their crop into rosé which is *saigné* from 60% négrette and 20% each syrah and cabernet sauvignon. Frédéric gives it only four hours with the skins before he draws off the pale pink juices. He bottles the wine in February to preserve its early freshness, and accepts that, by the end of its first summer, it is past its best and starts to darken in colour too.

Frédéric makes two kinds of red wine: one is a 70% négrette for early drinking. He says he likes this wine to taste after two years as if it was four or five years old. But his heart is in his bigger, more 'serious' red wine which is only 40% négrette and 30% each cabernet sauvignon and syrah. *Remontage* takes place daily, and the *chapeau* (the crust which forms on the top of the wine as the carbonic gas forces the solids in the wine to the surface) is also broken up and re-submerged every day. The object is to give the wine as much chance as possible to absorb the tannins and other extract from the solids. This wine is given nine months or so in oak casks, one-quarter of which are renewed each year. Two years after the harvest the wooded 1991 was still very tannic, and will need some time to come round, but probably less than the 1992 which I tasted from the wood. It was surprisingly powerful and concentrated for the year: the Ribes had been lucky to harvest their négrette before the rains.

Just round the corner from Le Roc is the **Château de Ferran (23)**, a building in the Empire style. Here Jean Gélis has taken over from his uncle Jean René Vidal, who was in lonely charge when I visited him n 1993. Jean has a 24-hectare vineyard of which 19 are currently producing: the rest are planted with young vines. After the 1956 frosts Vidal joined the co-opérative, but left it in 1985 because he missed the contact with his customers. It was also more profitable for him to make and bottle his own wine than simply sell the grapes to the Cave.

When Fronton was granted its AOC, he grubbed up a lot of the old grape-varieties, but he kept some mérille and malbec which he still uses for his red AOC, and he still has some cinsault and mauzac, though he uses neither of them in the wines he sells. He told me that it was common in the old days to blend a little mauzac with the négrette, because it gave the spark of acidity which the négrette was otherwise lacking. This is curious because, in Gaillac, mauzac is known for its weakness in acidity.

The vineyard and the wines which it produces are dominated quite properly by the négrette, which makes up 60% of the total. It gives particularly good fruit to his rosé, which also features the taste of *bonbons anglais* so popular with the French. The red wine is given only a moderate length of time in a variety of different *cuves*: Monsieur Vidal preferred his old cement ones to the rest. The processes are not sophisticated, temperatures are controlled simply by removing wine from warm containers into cold ones, and he found this sufficient. He matured his wine for up to a year once the malolactic fermentation is over and he did not believe in new wood for Fronton: '*La négrette n'est pas son truc*,' he says.

The red wine of this property may well be found in the United Kingdom as 30% of production is exported, most of which comes to England. He regularly wins stars in the *Guide Hachette*, which is both authoritative and influential.

On the western edge of the appellation, **Château Flotis (24)** is calling out for the same loving care to be exercised on its buildings as the Küntz family have lavished on its vineyards. Roger Küntz's ancestors came from Alsace and wine-making has been in their blood for hundreds of

years – some of their forebears were *vignerons* in the Loire. Roger himself served in the French army for years, latterly in North Africa. After
many years in the desert he felt he needed the green French countryside,
and arrived on the doorsteps of a branch of Crédit Agricole in Gascony,
'*un Colonel en retraite*', looking to borrow some money to buy a farm in
Tursan, which happened to have a few vines. He joined the local cave
co-opérative and started to learn how to grow grapes.

His son Philippe, meanwhile, was training to be a vet. His enduring
love of horses is reflected in their present stud of fifty fine animals, but
he switched his training to general agriculture. Father and son gradually began to feel that what they wanted above all else was to be able to
make and bottle their own wines, as well as growing the grapes which
went into them. But the prospects for a private wine-maker in Tursan
were not easy, because the local Cave had a near-monopoly on production. Roger decided to look further afield, until he found and bought
Château Flotis in Fronton in 1973, just before the AOC was granted.

The property has a long history, going back to the *ancien régime*, but
it had fallen on bad times, having belonged to an advocate from
Toulouse who is remembered more for his love of the good life than his
skill in the court-room. The Küntz had little in the way of capital, so
what money they had they spent on the vineyards and the *chais*. At first
it was an uphill struggle: it was six years before their first vintage in
1979, only one year after the début of Bellevue-la-Forêt. Philippe literally hawked the wines of Flotis round in vans, but at least this produced
an immediate cash return, better than trading with some of the restaurants who were very slow to pay their bills (and still are). The problem
was that the price per litre was not enough to service their capital
investment. Hence the decision to market in bottle which gave a much
better return. At that time very few other private growers were doing
anything except selling *en vrac*.

Today there are 35 hectares of vines at Flotis. The vineyard is on the
highest ground, the rest in the appellation, the ascent very gradual on
all sides except the west, where the terrain plunges steeply into the valley of the Garonne at the village of Castelnau d'Estrefonds. Half of the
terrain is of the sandy *boulbène* type on the very highest ground, a red
pebble-mixed sandstone. The first is said to give the wine its fullness
and roundness, the second its finesse, fruit and elegance. The *encépagement* recalls that of Monsieur Vidal – 60% négrette, still some malbec
and mérille, leaving space for less cabernet and syrah than usual.

Their mainstream red wine is half négrette, with a quarter each of
cabernet sauvignon and syrah. The grapes are picked by machine and
vinified – stalks, pips and all – for eight to ten days. The bouquet is
flowery: in the mouth the wine is spicy and very easy to drink, the finish persistent. Roger Küntz surprised me by saying that it was perfect
with fish, with exotic cuisines and with desserts based on chocolate.
This was one of the more extravagant claims I have heard on behalf of
Fronton, but Roger Küntz is an extravagant sort of character. To listen

to him is like hearing a recording of General de Gaulle's favourite speeches. At least he is easy to follow.

Philippe is more restrained and handles the business and marketing side of the enterprise. He is also the moving spirit behind a recently begun trade *en négoce*. His list includes wines from neighbouring appellations such as Gaillac, Cahors, Madiran and Côtes de Gascogne, all under his own labels.

Philippe Küntz believes that Fronton is popular in Toulouse not just because it is the local wine, but because it goes particularly well with the outdoor lifestyle of that city. The customers of the open-air bars and cafés take well to a wine which is easy but not flabby, clean but not watery. In this respect Fronton is fortunate that the wines made by its neighbouring rivals are not nearly so easy to drink. Madiran, for example, is better suited to the damp winters of Gascony than the hot sunshine of Toulouse.

Philippe described to me the lighter style of red which he makes for early drinking. It is similar in character to the more or less pure négrette wines which we have already met. It is called *vin de printemps* and is marketed, as its name suggests, during the spring and early summer following the vintage. There are also two small *cuvées*, one from old vines and which includes the rustic mérille and malbec, the other called Carmantran Rouge. Carmantran is the name of the neighbouring property where the family lives. There is also an attractive rosé.

This is a very serious as well as a commercially important vineyard. Father and son feel proud that students from Toulouse University, who would formerly go to Cahors or to Fitou to do their field-studies, now come to Château Flotis. The vinification is a model of control and strictness. Supermarket representatives will not allow otherwise: today the official analysts come three times a week to check the health of the evolving musts. Flotis has won so many prizes and medals that they have stopped entering for them. It is only one-third the size of Bellevue-la-Forêt but has done very well to become just about as well known as its larger rival.

VILLAUDRIC

It is time now to cross over into Villaudric, home of one of the doyens of the combined appellation. Monsieur **Urbain Blancal**, whose domaine **(44)** bears his name, cedes seniority to only one other, Pierre

Arbeau, who has now retired as the patron of Château Coutinel and Château St Louis. Like the Küntz, the Arbeaus have a substantial business as *négociants*, and we have already come across them handling some of the red wines of Domaines Jean Cros at Gaillac.

Monsieur Blancal has never harboured ambitions on the scale of the Arbeau family. He has been content to nurture his 17 hectares just outside Villaudric in the most traditional way possible. His son has a top job in agricultural administration, and the father no doubt wonders whether the wine-making at home will stop when he retires, for he has no one else to take it on. A visit to Domaine Urbain Blancal is a joy because Monsieur has a lovely mischievous twinkle, the cheeks of a cherub, and is quicker with the repartee than many colleagues ten years his junior; and that is saying something in this part of France.

It is hard to know which is the more surprising – the cosseted comfort of the family home, or the structured chaos of the *chais*. The open outbuildings attached to the latter are garnished with an incredible variety of old bottles, implements and barrel-hoops of every size and in a more or less advanced state of rust. In his cellars, Monsieur Blancal has a magnificent collection of old *foudres*: on their cross-bands repose the samples which the law obliges him to have on hand in case the official analysts pay a visit. Monsieur Blancal is so well known that they never seem to come, so treasures dating back to the 1960s stand there accumulating dust until the neck-labels are barely discernible among the cobwebs.

I was rebuked by Monsieur Blancal for describing his methods as 'traditional', a word which, at least in the French, had a pejorative ring. He preferred *'classique'*. He does not believe in de-stalking his grapes, but he gives them only a short *cuvaison* of four or five days: the different varieties are vinified separately, 50% négrette, 14% cabernet franc, 8% syrah, the remainder being made up from cinsault, mérille and gamay. Some of his vines are more than sixty-five years old. He ages his wines in his old *foudres*, of course: the gentle and gradual oxygenation through the medium of old wood is incomparable, he says. He likes to see the malolactic fermentation finished and the wine clarified before the real winter cold arrives, so that he does not have to heat up the wine to finish its vinification. The big old barrels apparently do not need much attention, provided you do not let them dry out, another reason for getting the wine into them early, and they must be full for at least nine months of the year.

Monsieur Blancal is a proud Villaudricois. He says that the people of Villaudric are truly Toulousain, while the inhabitants of Fronton really belong to Montauban, and he has retained the traditional Burgundy-shaped bottle which was once generally used in Villaudric. So has Baron François de Driesen, whose **Château la Colombière (14)** is within walking distance. Fronton and Villaudric had been merged into one appellation before he arrived in 1983, but that in no way diminishes his partisanship. He maintains that the wines of Villaudric have more structure and age better than those of Fronton, which is why he is not interested in making a wine that is 100% négrette. He says that in Villaudric such a wine would not be capable of ageing, but the difference is remarkable when you add even a touch of, say, cabernet to the négrette.

The Driesen family had been *vignerons* in Provence for many years, so I asked the baron what had brought him to Villaudric. He replied that prices had been cheap in Villaudric when he was looking round for a vineyard of his own; he had wanted to be near a big city with excellent communications, and he already knew Toulouse well. La Colombière had belonged to the Church until the time of the Revolution – there was once an important foundation called the Abbey of Dorade at Villaudric, and La Colombière was the private home of the abbey's bailiff. The house no doubt derives its name from the imposing dovecot which is its most noticeable feature. There are 25 hectares of vines of which 20 are now producing from a soil which the Baron described as typically Villaudric: masses of round flinty pebbles, which reflect the heat of the sun upwards on to the maturing fruit. He has 60% négrette, 25% in the two cabernets, 15% gamay and a little syrah, malbec and jurançon, the last-named of which he uses for a *vin de pays*.

Monsieur le Baron is unique in the Fronton area: he is the only private grower to make his wines by *macération carbonique*. He chose to adopt this technique because the négrette grape has a thin skin like the gamay, and thus responds well to maceration without pressing. This method requires a low yield of high quality grapes which are picked by hand, then everything goes into the *cuves* with no preliminary crushing or de-stalking. The wine is allowed to make itself, without any pressing or handling, under a layer of carbonic gas. The Baron proves by his results that this technique is not limited to the production of quick-maturing fruity wines for early drinking, as in Gaillac *primeurs* for example, because his wines keep well after a long *élevage* of up to twenty-four months, according to the style of the wine. The wines are fined but not filtered before bottling. The Baron's Frontons remain aromatic and supple, but have some weight too.

There are three red wines from La Colombière. The first, which you might imagine – quite wrongly – to be top of the range is called Réserve du Baron: it is at least 75% négrette, and like the others of its kind, it is meant for early drinking at cellar temperature. Nevertheless it spends two winters on its lees. Paler than many Frontons, it has a real *goût du terroir*, which gives it more authenticity than some of its more ambitious older brothers. The next red, called simply Château la Colombière, is cherry-coloured and shot with darker hues. The complex bouquet carries plenty of fresh red fruits which fill the mouth, but the wine remains supple and the tannins are smooth. The finish is aromatic and develops well with age. The hint of vanilla comes not from ageing in wood, but from a slight taste of the stalks which went into the must. The Baron thinks that his 1990, which in Fronton as everywhere else was a wonderful year, will peak about 1996.

The top-of-the-range red is called Baron de D, and is made from grapes grown on the best parcels of land. It has only 50% négrette, the balance being almost all cabernet, with just a little gamay. This wine acquires considerable depth with age, but the underlying structure remains light. Of his red wine production this represents about 20%, the rest being more or less equally divided between the other two *cuvées*. The Baron recommends that all his red wines should be allowed to rest for a month after travelling, and should be opened two hours before they are to be drunk.

Monsieur le Baron also makes a pink wine, which he calls *gris* rather than rosé: it is so pale that the authorities did not want to pass it as an AOC Fronton at all, but they were finally persuaded by its quality. Since all the red wines are made by *macération carbonique*, the rosé cannot be drawn off it in the usual way. Instead it is made by direct pressing without any maceration from an *encépagement* headed by 60% gamay. The only colour it takes on is that which is given out by the skins and pips during the actual pressing: it is almost a white wine made from red-wine grapes. It has no great bouquet, but in the mouth develops surprising length.

Château La Palme (35) would be by far the largest vineyard in Fronton if all its 200 hectares were given over to the vine, but the Ethuin family have 110 hectares of maize and are also the second or third biggest growers of *haricots verts* in France. These activities leave a mere 35 hectares for the grape. Many Fronton vineyards describe themselves as châteaux, usually without any justification. La Palme is, however, a real château, a handsome rectangular building on two storeys approached by a ceremonial staircase. Beneath there is a cellar the length of the building, which Madame Ethuin is planning to convert into a tasting- and sales-room. It links two huge outbuildings which flank the château, one of which contains the *chais*.

The property dates back to about 1800 and was formerly in the ownership of the Lignères family, one of whose scions became Mayor of Toulouse. At the beginning of this century there were about 100 hectares of vines, worked by twelve pairs of oxen, and the château was the hub of a small hamlet which has entirely disappeared. It even had its own baker. After the disasters of the second half of the nineteenth century, its importance gradually declined: the vineyards were not replanted and when Madame Ethuin's parents bought it in 1962, there were no vines left. The last had been wiped out by the frosts of 1956.

Nevertheless the property had enjoyed a distinguished wine-history: it was the first property from the Haute-Garonne to win the coveted Grand Prix d'Honneur in 1835, and it also took the gold medal at the Toulouse exhibition in 1892. Thus the Ethuin family, who arrived from Lille in search of a more agreeable climate than that of the industrial north, had every right to be optimistic about rebuilding the vineyards. But they soon found that theirs were on lower ground than most in the area, and that there is a great deal more clay than usual under the light *boulbènes*, so the vines can flood quite easily. Sometimes machines cannot be used for picking. It is, in fact, surprising that wines can be made here at all, let alone ones of such good quality. They are fruity but less structured than many, so Madame Ethuin wisely concentrates on producing a style which is easy to drink and which matures early: in 1993 she made her first venture into a 100% négrette wine.

The *encépagement* of the vineyard is standard for Fronton. All her grapes are de-stalked and crushed conventionally before vinification. The *cuvaison* is relatively short, only five or six days. Madame Ethuin has all manner of *cuves*, and has no particular preference for one kind over another. Her mainstream red represents 90% of her production, from a 50% négrette base. It has a very fragrant bouquet, a lovely brightness in the glass and the freshness and vivacity which the short fermentation brings to it. The négrette flavour is quite pronounced and makes this wine highly typical of the appellation, for all its lightweight style. Madame also makes a rosé, *saigné* from the red: half négrette, half cabernet franc. This, too, is excellent, quite one of the best in the region with plenty of fruit and mercifully no *bonbons anglais*.

Madame Ethuin said quite frankly that both the *encépagement* and the terrain at Fronton were wrong for new wood, but to swim with the tide she has had a go, and makes about 5000 bottles of a special *cuvée*. I agree with her private judgement in this respect.

La Palme sells mainly to *les grandes surfaces*, and makes no attempt to hide its commercial face. The property is rather off the beaten track and obviously cannot rely on sales at the door like smaller, better placed vineyards. For example **Domaine Caze (12)** is not only in the town of Villaudric itself, but its front door opens directly off the main street. You walk straight from the pavement into the *chais*. Opposite you, a huge pair of barn-doors lead into a yard to which the grapes are brought at vintage-time from the vineyards beyond. On your right, a ramp without steps leads down to the wine-making area, a large V-shaped building whose form is dictated by the geography of the village streets. This *chais* feels like the the prow of some huge galleon, though its rows of splendid old *foudres* were never meant to contain rum!

This atmospheric property is built of the pretty flat pink bricks of Toulouse, interlarded with the kind of rounded pebbles and flints to be found in the vineyards of Villaudric. It belongs to Maurice Rougevin-Baville who serves in the French air-force. His young daughter Martine is in charge of the 12 hectares of vines and the making of the wine from the grapes which they grow there. In the past the family has always relied on employees to deal with the wine-making, and Martine says she is the first member of the family to take it on. She has four sisters but none of them was interested, so she went off to study oenology at Montpellier and, later, Toulouse.

For all her state-of-the-art training, Martine is not following fashion. Her wines are resolutely old-fashioned although she shares a picking machine with some other growers. From a traditional *encépagement*, she goes in for long *cuvaisons* at a temperature of 30° in the old barrels or, if need be, some cement *cuves*. The barrels are over one hundred years old, and come in all shapes and sizes. The largest of them contains 113 hectolitres. The *remontage* is still carried out partly by hand and there is no *pigeage* – the breaking up of the *chapeau*. The wine is matured in the *foudres* for up to eighteen months before it is fined and bottled.

Martine's first vintage, 1990, is half négrette and half cabernet sauvignon. For a Fronton it is very big indeed, with red fruits and even figs prominent on the palate, and a deliciously persistent liquorice finish. The unresolved tannins suggested a long life ahead with little risk of the fruit drying out. This wine manages to combine a good négrette character with an old-fashioned structure. The 1993 is also excellent.

Another grower who achieves a similar style of wine, though by more usual methods, is Marc Pénévayre. He and his father Louis have a property called **Château Plaisance (38)**, with *chais* in the middle of the village of Vacquiers in the south-east corner of the appellation. Their house, too, opens on to the main street, but the vineyards are in scattered parcels a mile or two up the road towards Fronton.

After the end of his training, Marc took a job heading up a wine-research establishment near Saumur in the valley of the Loire, but he always intended to come back to the family vineyard. He was in no hurry, until one day a neighbour of his father's announced that if the Pénévayres didn't want to rent his 8 hectares of vines, he would dig them up. Marc was back in a flash. He was in time to anticipate the restrictions on new planting, and took advantage of the chance to create 3 more hectares of vineyard. Today they have a total of 20, and their home and *chais* date back to the eighteenth century.

The Pénévayres have the standard mix of grapes in their vineyards, all of which are picked by machine. There is a group of twenty growers who share the use of two machines: I asked Marc whether this caused many arguments. He smiled and said that they had all learnt the art of diplomacy rather fast. They do not de-stalk their grapes, but on the other hand they do not go in for long *cuvaisons*: a mere six days for the gamay, eight or nine for the négrette, and a bit longer for the cabernets and syrah.

Marc told me that they have about 1000 private customers, not all of whom like the same style of wine. He therefore does not necessarily bottle all his wine at the same time. Like Gilbert Geoffroy, whom we shall meet in the Côtes de Duras (page 193), he may do up to three separate *mises en bouteilles*, say in April, June and August following the vintage. Although Marc likes his wines to be well structured, he does not see why they should not be ready, say, three or four years after the vintage. However big they may be, he says, they must be easy to drink.

Marc is experimenting with a little wine in new wood, and he calls this special *cuvée* Thibault de Plaisance after his young son. In good years he also makes a little rosé and a white *vin de pays* from the standard Bordeaux varieties.

The wines of Château Plaisance are among the best. The mainstream red has a brilliant ruby colour: the nose recalls prunes and the finish is spicy. The wooded version was well made, but I was not persuaded that the oak did anything worthwhile for the wine. All the same, Marc Pénévayre has to be on anyone's short-list of Villaudric growers.

Richard Mayor is the only absentee-proprietor I know of in Villaudric or Fronton. This may be what is behind my reservations over the operations at **Château Montauriol (35)**. Here the *chais* is billed as '*Le plus Bordelais de l'appellation*', which indicates at once the style of the property. It was bought by Mayor, a successful Swiss property-developer, as recently as 1987, and he must have spent all his fortune on it. It is even harder to be critical, because 5 of the 48 hectares are devoted to experimental clonal development for the benefit of the cave co-opérative. He has engaged a highly talented wine-maker from his own country; he has, as may be imagined, a lively marketing and development department; and he has installed the most modern plant imaginable. In spite of and perhaps because of all this, I cannot bring myself to admire the wines. The media writers, those who award the medals and prizes, and those who worship at the shrine of new oak, all think that Richard Mayor and his team can do no wrong, and perhaps I am just being perverse in disagreeing with them.

The welcome you get from Jean-Claude Vuichard, the wine-maker, and Michel Gache, who is in charge of marketing, could not be warmer. I decided to overlook the fact that the publicity hand-outs contain virtually no hard facts about the vineyards or the wine-making, and to concentrate on the generous offerings which were poured into my glass. First came a white *vin de pays* sold under the brand-name Peyroutet, an agreeable if unremarkable start to the tasting. The 1990 rosé which followed, though past its best, was interesting because it was made with 100% négrette and had been left to undergo a malolactic fermentation. There was still plenty of fruit on the palate.

The red 1990, from which the rosé had been *saigné*, was very dark and smoky, light in texture and not likely to improve. The 1991, made from the usual Fronton *assemblage*, had little individuality; and the older 1989, which had been partly matured in new wood and partly in old *foudres*, was so like a claret that nobody would have guessed it was a Fronton: 'Le plus Bordelais' indeed. The oaked version of the same wine was so tough and tannic that it may never come round before the fruit goes.

What really put me off was a new line called Réserve du Grand Veneur (The Master of Hounds), whose bottle bears a label made of real leather: it is offered at twice the price of any of their other wines. Apart from the vulgarity of the presentation, the wine is as tough as old boots. Surely any Fronton after four years ought to hold out some prospect of maturing during one's lifetime?

The treat of the visit was a 1987 red. This was quite stylish, and seemed to me to have a good dose of malbec. When I told Jean-Claude Vuichard that I liked this, it was as if I had said I liked wine-gums: I got the impression that they had outgrown such unsophisticated delights.

The problem with Montauriol is that, despite all the talent and the money, one looks in vain for a house-style or a sense of direction. It is hard to distil from the glossy literature what they are aiming to achieve, particularly when the labels do not correspond with the descriptions of the wines. For example, there are two different labels for an apparently identical red, and none at all for the rosé.

The UK importers of Château Montauriol described Fronton in 1987, the year of Richard Mayor's purchase, as being 'as fashionable as flared trousers'. That is not exactly fair to the likes of Patrick Germain and the Küntz family, but it remains true that, of all the major appellations in the South-West, Fronton is still the Cinderella beyond its region of production. The citizens of Toulouse have discovered that there are other wines than Fronton in the world, so the growers need additional markets. There is no reason why they should not succeed: Fronton's generally lighter style, and its aptitude to accompany a wide variety of foods, to say nothing of its excellent value for money, should ensure it a bright future once the present glut of poor vintages is out of the way. Producers would do well to concentrate on the expression of the négrette grape, and neither drown it with other varieties nor be too heavy-handed with new oak. The promising vintage of 1995 may prove an upturn.

Much more to my taste is the property just down the road from Montauriol, **Château de Peyreaux (46)**, where Madame Vovette Linant de Bellefonds proudly continues the wine-making traditions which she evolved with her grandfather Maurice. This distinguished family was for many years an essential pillar of the Franco-Egyptian world: Maurice, a distinguished lawyer, was adviser to the French Viceroy in Cairo and later to Premier Léon Blum on Middle Eastern affairs. He retired to the Frontonnais, where he bought Peyreaux in the early 1930s. He had no wine-making experience and his 30 hectares of vineyards went at first into the making of fairly ordinary wine. But, when the spring frosts of 1956 virtually destroyed the vineyard, he and his granddaughter decided to replant it with quality grapes and to make real wine in the old-fashioned way. They soon made an enviable reputation for quality production in an area which was then little-known outside Toulouse. Maurice lived to the ripe old age of 102 and died as recently as 1982, leaving Vovette to take on the responsibilities. Even when he was ninety-six, Maurice was still driving a car and taking an active interest in the vineyards.

Today there are two wines: an AOC Fronton of high quality in which there are no additives allowed, and for which only the wines from the vats are used, no *vin de presse* at all; and a *vin de pays* called Vin d'Antan, which uses all manner of rustic grape-varieties, including the despised aramon, two different gamays, mérille and jurançon noir. As so often happens in this book, one arrives at the end of the section with the wheel turned full circle – with wines made in the old-fashioned way, owing little to modern technology, and well able to hold their own with the best.

VIN DE PAYS DU COMTÉ TOLOSAN

Many Fronton producers make wines which they cannot declare under the appellation: for example, they may be made from red grape-varieties which are not authorised, while white wine is not covered by the appellation at all. In either case the growers are obliged to de-classify their wines and market them as *vins de pays du comté tolosan*, 'tolosan' being the dialect equivalent of 'Toulousain'. In the middle ages, the Comté Tolosan was a considerable power: its Counts were nearly as important as the kings of France themselves. It is from the Counts of Toulouse that the painter Toulouse-Lautrec was descended.

Today the *vins de pays du comté tolosan* come from parts of Tarn-et-Garonne which are not included in any other classified wine-making area. Tarn-et-Garonne is a département created at the time of the Revolution, and something of a ragbag of bits and pieces of the *ancien régime* which did not fit into the new pattern. As a result it includes parts of Quercy and the Agenais, both having different local characters, climates and terrains, as well as their own *vins de pays*. There are two other self-sufficient *vins de pays*, those of St Sardos and the Côteaux et Terrasses de Montauban as well as a small VDQS area centred on the small town of La Ville-Dieu-du-Temple, whose wine comes from vineyards on the almost imperceptible slopes of the land enclosed by the converging Tarn and Garonne rivers.

Outside the Frontonnais, you will almost certainly not be able to find any private grower making *comté tolosan*, and the rest of the production is exclusively in the hands of the cave co-opérative at La Ville-Dieu-du-Temple, which also handles a large part of the crop of Côteaux de Quercy and nearly all of the Montauban *vin de pays*. Its raison d'être was, however, the small area of VDQS round La Ville-Dieu itself.

LAVILLEDIEU-DU-TEMPLE

With the perverted logic beloved of French bureaucracy, the name of the appellation is written as Lavilledieu, all one word, as it has been written for centuries. It seems, however, that there are a number of towns bearing this name in different parts of France, so the authorities decided to rewrite this town's name so that it is spelt in three words instead of one. The spelling of the appellation has not, however, changed with it.

The Cave was originally built in 1949 for the growers of La Ville-Dieu and its neighbouring communes. The moving spirit was a local grower named Monsieur Faust, who was its first president and who worked hard to obtain VDQS status in 1952.

The vineyards date back to ancient times and were among those to be developed by the Knights Templar, who took a grant of lands in the region at the same time as they acquired tracts of Fronton. After the frosts of 1956 the VDQS almost disappeared – there was even a period when no wine was declared under it at all. The huge new Cave had lost its original purpose, so it took in wines from the *vins de pays* areas. In more recent times the little vineyard of Lavilledieu has re-established itself, though for most of the farmers the vine remains a relatively small part of their operation, about 5% of the local revenue. The Cave has over 600 members of whom about 250 are home-based Lavilledieu growers.

With the Cave's own VDQS and the three *vins de pays*, each made from different grape-varieties, the vintage-time at La Ville-Dieu is highly complicated, since every grape-variety is vinified separately. *Cuvaison* periods can vary from four days for the gamay to fifteen for the cabernets and tannat. Again the same varieties from different *terroirs* may ripen at quite different times: for example, the gamay from the *causses* will be at least a week later than the same wine from the plains. For these reasons, the reception of the grapes at the Cave can last for a whole month.

VDQS Lavilledieu represents about 12% of the Cave's output, and remains its best wine. The appellation is confined to red and rosé wines from thirteen communes. Its proximity to Fronton explains its 10% négrette: there is 25% each of gamay, syrah and cabernet franc and 15% tannat. The wine has good depth, and no grape-variety is allowed to dominate, so its character is hard to define, but it is agreeably rounded and soft, though with good body and balance. I was surprised how gentle and unaggressive the oaked version of this wine was, but Jean-Pierre Bénassac, the director of the Cave since 1972, thought he had overdone the new wood. I can only think that he has not been to Montauriol. His superior wine is called Cuvée des Capitouls, named after a group of producers of gourmet delights at nearby Castelsarrasin.

The Côteaux de Quercy was quite clearly the best of the *vins de pays* from this Cave. The flavour of the malbec grape shows through well. Merlot and tannat, the other Cahors varieties, also go into this wine, but there is some cabernet and gamay too, though no syrah which does not like the chalky soil of the *terroir*.

The *comté tolosan* wines come from such a disparate area that they are made on a varietal basis. The syrah from the Cave is a chewy sort of wine, but I like the cabernet better for its good fruit. I was disappointed by the Cave's Côteaux et Terrasses de Montauban. Perhaps the 1992 vintage I tasted accounted for the sourness of the wine, but that cannot be the whole story, because there are private producers of this *vin de pays* who made a really attractive version in that rain-soaked year.

VIN DE PAYS DES CÔTEAUX ET TERRASSES DE MONTAUBAN

It was Aline Romain, who has only recently handed over her **Domaine de Montels (2)** to her two sons Philippe and Thierry, who was largely responsible for the creation of this new *vin de pays*. Montels is not far from the small town of Albias, a little way north-east of Montauban up the Route Nationale 20. In 1973 Aline and her husband Raymond moved in after a dramatic and turbulent life. Aline was born and bred in Algeria, where she had at first wanted to become an English teacher, but she soon switched to training as a statistician, and got a job with a foundation researching tuberculosis. She met her husband-to-be and they decided to start farming. They came to metropolitan France and bought a farm in the Ardennes where they made a good living for thirteen years. But while they had been prospecting in France, their travels had taken them to Montauban where they had fallen in love with the southern sunshine and the temperament that goes with it. They also shared the appetite of the local residents for good food and wine. They decided to move there and found Montels.

Almost immediately Raymond died, leaving Aline alone to bring up her two sons, then aged thirteen and ten. Instead of developing Montels as a general farm, like those of her neighbours, she decided to turn it into a vineyard. She went to study oenology at Montauban, Toulouse and finally Bordeaux, while at the same time setting about the replacement of the poor hybrid vines on the farm with noble varieties. Today they have gamay, syrah, jurançon, cabernet, tannat and merlot. Her aim was to make a vineyard worthy of domaine-bottling, something which was at that time unheard of in Albias, although there had been a vineyard of sorts at Domaine de Montels for hundreds of years.

To justify domaine-bottling, she needed to be able to call her wine something better than *vin de table*. She applied to be incorporated within the Fronton AOC area, but in retrospect she is not surprised they would not have her, because Albias is a fair way from the Fronton vineyards. Similarly she was not allowed to join the Côteaux de Quercy, because the *terroir* there is quite different, being predominantly chalky. It was all too much for the bureaucrats to try to accommodate just one grower, and a woman at that.

There was only one solution: to create her own appellation. She chivvied some local growers into clubbing together, and between them they gave birth to the *vin de pays des Côteaux et Terrasses de Montauban*. Nowadays Aline and three others are the only producers who do not belong to the co-opérative at La Ville-Dieu, but Aline heads the Groupement des Producteurs, which now numbers about forty growers. The independents, with a grant from the city of Montauban, have produced their own common label, featuring a drawing by Ingres, Montauban's most famous son.

At Montels there are 25 hectares of vines from which they make two reds. One of these is given some time in new oak and is a tough and tannic affair made from half cabernet franc and half tannat. Though I like its unusually herby nose, I preferred the unoaked red made from a less formidable formula of 50% syrah, and 25% each cabernet franc and gamay. This wine has a much more delicate blend of fruits and can be drunk much younger. There is also a little rosé made from half gamay and half jurançon. Philippe gave me a bottle of some experimental dry white made from jurançon *à jus blanc*, which was lovely, and they have now started to sell it commercially.

Philippe and Thierry would like to increase the percentage of wine sold in bottle, because this would raise the image of the property: meanwhile quite a lot of their sales are *en vrac*, and Philippe is an indefatigable presence at markets and fairs up and down the country, where he has built up a faithful and enthusiastic clientèle.

I asked Aline Romain about the prospects for the 1993 vintage, as the rain-clouds gathered overhead and the picking-machines stood idle in the vineyards. She replied, 'We don't have bad years: it's just that some are better than others.' Thus spoke a real trouper not to be daunted by yet another harvest in the mud. Philippe was all smiles when I asked him about his 1995.

When I left Montels she waved me in the direction of the **Domaine du Cayrou (4)**, another independent vineyard in the hands of a family called Brunet, but when I got there they were still busy picking in the vineyards. Their 1993 doubtless turned out better than their 1992, which they had to de-classify because of the terrible weather at vintage-time.

At the **Domaine de Puyseguère (3)** Michel Cerles was lucky to have got all his grapes in. He was happy to take a break from a rigorous *triage* of his table grapes, muscat de Hambourg, which were undergoing a process of the most thorough scrutiny before being dispatched in the direction of Paris.

Michel is interested only in producing the best he can from the means at his disposal, which is why he has dug up his fruit trees: there is no money to be had from them except on the mass-market, which does not interest him. The family had always had a few vines, even at Conques from whence they came, and from where Michel's grandfather sold his surplus wine to the cafés and bars of Decazeville. They moved to Montauban in 1938 at a time when the *bassin houillier* was already in decline.

The property used to be called Pinceguerre, but Michel Cerles is a gentle person and objected to such a bellicose name. He tries to be as biological as possible in his wine-growing: no chemicals are allowed near the grapes after June except for the ecologically acceptable Bordeaux Mixture and he picks by hand whenever possible. The family used to take on forty pickers and make a real fête of the *vendange*, but nowadays they make do with as many friends and family as they can persuade to help.

Michel has 5 hectares of red grapes currently producing, and 2 more of white grapes. He plans to make from these both a dry wine and a *moelleux*. For his red wines, he has the standard mix of cabernets, merlot, gamay and tannat. He de-stalks all of them and they get a relatively long *cuvaison* of fifteen days, some of the wine in stainless steel which he prefers, the rest in old cement *cuves* which have been in the family a long time. The wine is matured until the May following the vintage, to enable the *cuves* to be cleaned and made ready for the ensuing harvest. The wine is fined with bentonite, but not filtered. About 2000 bottles are made, the rest being sold *en vrac*, all to locals who inevitably leave him with no stock to keep until it is really mature. His wine needs more than a bare year – it was beautifully bright and a dark garnet colour, there were bitter cherries on a most attractive nose, a lot of fruit in the mouth, but there were still tannins unresolved, which was hardly surprising in the light of the fifteen-day *cuvaison*.

It was obvious to me why Aline Romain had decided not to throw in her lot with the co-opérative, but I was rather surprised by Michel Cerles' indignation when I put that question to him. He compared selling your grapes to the Cave with putting your children *en pension*. It was refreshing to find such devotion, but I keep my fingers crossed that Michel's small vineyard will yield a decent living, as well as decent wines, on the slim margins he is obliged to accept in local conditions.

Perhaps all the local growers will benefit from a recent joint venture, involving the independent growers and the co-opérative at La Ville-Dieu-du-Temple. The purpose is to put the wines of Montauban on the map by linking the *vin de pays* with the town and its famous son Ingres. Under the slogan 'Now Montauban has its own wine', they should be able to seize their own share of the local market. The co-opérative will select thirty or so of its best growers for the promotion. The town of Montauban itself claims one-third of the local vineyard, which extends to 295 hectares divided between eighty-four growers in all, including the three independents. It is encouraging to see such collaboration between the co-operative and the independent sectors: many other appellations could well copy the example of Montauban.

VIN DE PAYS DE ST SARDOS

The amorphous area of Tarn-et-Garonne contains one final *vin de pays*: that which is based on about 180 hectares of land belonging to members of the cave co-opérative of St Sardos. About 120 hectares are currently planted with vines, an unusual combination of syrah, cabernet franc and tannat.

St Sardos is a tiny village in the sparsely populated area on the left bank of the Garonne called the Lomagne. It is a great area for the cultivation of garlic. We are almost into Gascony, but the character of wine and country are more typical of the Garonne valley, and the mix of grape-varieties is not wholly Gascon either.

The soil is in part a chalky clay, what the French call *argilo-calcaire*, otherwise the kind of decomposed clay which has broken up into a fine almost sandy texture like the *boulbènes* of Fronton, and elsewhere there are plenty of small stones called *graves*. The wine made here enjoyed a good local reputation back in the fifties, sold mostly *en vrac* and to locals at the door to accompany a good *magret de canard*. A disproportionately large Cave, capable of vinifying 45,000 hectolitres of wine, was built in 1957, so at that time there must have been plenty of optimism. By the middle of the next decade, the Cave had 700 members, a rather more impressive figure than the total of their holdings of vines which was only 400 hectares (an average of little over half a hectare each). This is another area of polyculture, and in recent years one has seen crazes for maize, sunflowers, millet and all manner of crops succeed each other as the fashions of agricultural politics have waxed and waned. The farmers have been encouraged by rapid advances in irrigation technology, and the grants available for its installation, in an area where droughts in summer are the rule rather than the exception. The cultivation of cereals, and of fruit and vegetables too, became more profitable than that of grapes. Growers began to dig up their vines, a process which continued for twenty years until by 1988 the once important vineyard had nearly disappeared.

Enter Jean-Claude Delpech who, with a few other enthusiasts, set about reversing the trend. They have so far had a very good result, production having reached half the volume of wine made in the heady days when the Cave was built. The vines which have been replanted are all noble varieties, capable of better things than a mere *vin de pays*. As a result an application has been made for VDQS status, and, if the patience and zeal of today's growers is anything to go by, they will get it.

They make a dry and a sweet white wine as well as a *mousseux* by the champagne method, but it is the red wines on which the reputation of St Sardos rests. The everyday red has a little gamay as well as abouriou in it, but is nevertheless based on the three varieties mentioned above. The superior red called Gilles de Morban has only the syrah, cabernet franc and tannat. There is a rosé, *saigné* from the same grapes, called Domaine la Gravette. These three wines are excellent value and may be found in restaurants in the region as well as the local shops. They are well worth looking out for. There is also a rosé from black muscat.

In a slightly different class are two wines from single properties which the Cave vinifies for the owners. That from the Domaine du Tucayne keeps to the basic *encépagement*, but it is given ageing in new wood for about nine months, after a maceration of eight to ten days at a high temperature of 30–32°. This will peak after five years in a good cellar.

The grapes for this wine are picked by hand, as are those from the other single domaine, called de Cadis. The vines are grown in a particularly pebbly soil, with a perfect south to south-west exposition. Yields are kept to below 40 hectolitres to the hectare, and the grapes are exclusively syrah (60%) and tannat (40%). This is a big fleshy wine, made at a temperature which can be as high as a dangerous 35°. This is essentially a wine for keeping, though it is not given any ageing in oak.

The Cave at St Sardos is definitely one to watch, and should have a bright future under its dynamic management.

HAUTE-GARONNE: DOMAINE DE RIBONNET

Strategically placed astride the river Garonne, Toulouse was an important embarkation point for the wines of the upper valley of the river in the days when Bordeaux needed them for blending. Since the phylloxera, the vineyards of the Haute-Garonne, which at one time were substantial, as were those of the Ariège, have dwindled in importance. Today they are just a part of the polycultural pattern of the regional agriculture. Production is entrusted to local co-opératives, which make wine for sale at the door to local residents. It does not rise above *vin de table* quality. The Caves at Escalquens, just off the motorway to Narbonne, and at Longages and Bérat in the Garonne valley itself on the road to Tarbes, are examples of this kind of production. Otherwise no wine of any importance is being made south of Toulouse today.

Except, that is, at the extraordinary pioneering vineyards of the **Domaine de Ribonnet** (Tel: 61-08-71-02) near Beaumont-sur-Lèze, half an hour's drive out of the city. The domaine is a rather unlikely château, dating back to the fifteenth century but modernised at the beginning of the twentieth, built high on a ridge which separates the Garonne from its little tributary, the Lèze. The château is at the heart of a huge estate which includes 32 hectares of vines. In the early 1900s it was bought by a local worthy called Clément Ader, a pioneer-aviator and a celebrated engineer. He restored it and developed the vineyards which had been wiped out by the phylloxera. The grape-varieties which he planted were in no way special, but the wine must have been made in considerable quantities, because the old *chais* houses a dozen or so concrete tanks of 500 hectolitres each, which were installed at about the time of the First World War. Around 6000 hectolitres represented about three years' production, none of which was bottled at the property: it was all traded *en négoce*. The capacity to hold such quantities of wine would have enabled Monsieur Ader to play the market, without being at the mercy of the dealers.

In 1923, Domaine de Ribonnet passed into the hands of a Belgian textile family, but, with the gradual replacement of wool by plastics in the 1960s, the owners fell on lean times and the domaine went into decline, the vineyards with it. A Monsieur Gerber, a rich Swiss businessman, bought it in 1975 but died soon afterwards, leaving the property in the hands of his young son Christian, who owns it to this day. Little by little Christian has replanted the vineyards, and his first vintage was in 1982, a highly propitious year in which to make a début.

Christian Gerber is modernising the *chais* gradually. He has left the old Ader cement *cuves* because the cost of demolishing them would outweigh the benefit of the space liberated, but they are no longer used. Sadly the old collection of *foudres* has gone: all that is left are traces of the railway system which engineer Ader invented to move them about the *chais*. Gerber has created 2800 hectolitres of *cuverie* in stainless steel as well as 300 *barriques* in new and nearly new oak for ageing his wines.

Gerber is following the varietal path, that is to say making wines grown from a single unblended grape-variety. In an area which has no tradition of its own, and thus no local character to preserve, this is an exciting way of exploring the possibilities, even if it involves much trial and error. Gerber has been able to show that, on his particular soils, he is able to make a first-class wine from an enormous range of grape-varieties. You name it and he grows it. A tour round his *chais* might yield the following delights:

- a blend of chasselas and sylvaner (with a wonderful banana nose);
- a sauvignon, rich fruity, exotic and full;
- a pinot grigio;
- an aligoté, already showing quality while still fermenting;
- chardonnay from two cuves; one big and lime-juicy, and another from young vines;
- a pinot noir 1992, still in cask, with a lot of concentrated ripe fruit, from a small parcel of land called Taberly;
- a marsanne 1991, still in the wood in which it was made, dark and almost sweet with the taste of the oak. Late-picked and bizarre;
- another marsanne, this time 1990, in bottle, more conventional but very distinguished;
- a 50/50 merlot/cabernet sauvignon blend from 1992, thinnish because of the year. (It seems that, in a bad year, the more noble the grape the more likely it is to disappoint);
- a cabernet franc 1992 from old vines;
- an assemblage from a little vineyard called Cabirol. Twenty of Gerber's friends each put up 3000 francs which guarantees them between 400 and 600 bottles a year for twenty years: after that, all rights revert to Gerber, who sadly told me that I was too late to join this privileged club. The blend is 25% each cabernet franc, cabernet sauvignon, merlot and 12$\frac{1}{2}$% each malbec and tannat. A tough, rustic wine, much up my street;
- a sémillon which was still working; lovely wild flowers and grape-fruit on the nose;
- various *cuves* of the two cabernets, merlot and syrah.

Christian Gerber's latest experiments are with viognier and chenin blanc, neither of which is yet producing.

After such an experience, he took me to his office with picture windows over the vineyards to the Pyrenees. The views are just as beautiful as his publicity suggests, particularly in the evening light. The tasting continued in his family kitchen where he opened bottles from the domestic supply. The final treat was a 1982 cabernet franc: the nose had some vegetal character, but the style was elegant and soft, classic and gentle. Gerber said that, in his view, as his wines age, they pass through a 'Bordeaux' stage into an 'Italian' one, in terms of structure, tannin and acidity.

Christian Gerber comes from an obviously rich background: no one could have recreated such a property and its vineyards without substantial resources. But he is being careful not to over-extend himself, or to be too extravagant, as his concern over Ader's *cuves* shows. He trained with Jean-Claude Vuichard, the wine-maker at Château

Montauriol in Fronton, and indeed Jean-Claude started as wine-maker at Ribonnet (together they found Richard Mayor his vineyard).

Strictly speaking the property is in no known area of appellation, which gives Christian Gerber a freedom which he would not enjoy in, say, Fronton. It is relatively easy for him, as a grower who has rapidly acquired a mega-star reputation for quality wine, to get whatever *dérogations* may be needed from the authorities to do what he wants, because his wines are not in competition with the ordinary table wines of the local growers. In an area of AOC, where other growers too would be aiming at the quality end of the market, he would have a much more uphill task with both bureaucracy and the competition.

I asked him how he managed to go on planting in the face of the present ban. He said that there were growers who were prepared to sell existing vineyards to him at a price which would compensate them for forgoing the *prime* which the EC was willing to give them if they dug up their grapes. Gerber is then allowed to dig them up himself and replant with his own chosen varieties without offending the authorities.

Ribonnet is a vineyard unique in the South-West. In any other hands it might just become a rich man's toy, but Gerber knows how to make really good wines and his appetite for experiment is as insatiable as it is irresistible to the wine-lover. His reputation as one of the best wine-makers of the Midi-Pyrenees is based on professional merit: there is nothing of the hobby-farmer about him. His wines may be bought (with others) at his own retail shop at 53 Rue de la Concorde, Toulouse.

PRODUCERS

Côtes du Frontonnais

An asterisk denotes properties making good wine typical of the appellation.

1. Pierre Salesses, **Château d'Aubuisson**, 31340 Vacquiers Tel: 61-84-93-36
2. Joseph Ferrero, **Château Barrès**, 82370 Labastide-St Pierre Tel: 63-64-05-12
3. *Claude Vigouroux, **Château Baudare**, 82370 Labastide-St Pierre Tel: 63-30-51-33
4. •Monsieur M. Bonhomme, **Château Bel Air**, 31620 Fronton Tel: 61-82-45-75
5. *Patrick Germain, **Château Bellevue-la-Forêt**, 31620 Fronton Tel: 61-82-43-21
6. Robert Trégan, **Domaine Bois d'Huguet**, 82370 Campsas Tel: 63-64-02-31
7. Pierre Selle, **Château Bouissel**, 82370 Campsas Tel: 63-30-10-49
8. Monsieurs Ph. et A. Selle, **Château Boujac**, 82370 Campsas Tel: 63-30-10-80
47 Louis Duplan, **Domaine de la Bruyère**, 82370 Labastide-St-Pierre Tel: 63-30-51-75
9. *Claude Ferran, **Château Cahuzac**, 82170 Fabas Tel: 63-64-10-18
10. *Monsieurs Pérez et Montels, **Domaine Callory**, 82370 Labastide-St Pierre Tel: 63-30-50-30
11. *CAVE CO-OPÉRATIVE, 31620 Fronton Tel: 61-82-41-27: Château Caudeval; Château Cransac; Château Majorel; Domaine Jouaninels; *Domaine Marcelot; Domaine Ramoundade; Domaine Roussel
12. *Monsieur Rougevin-Baville, **Domaine Caze**, 31620 Villaudric Tel: 61-82-92-70
13. Muzart Frères, **Château Clos Mignon**, 31620 Villeneuve-les-Bouloc Tel: 61-82-10-89
14. *Baron François de Driesen, **Chatêau la Colombière**, 31620 Villaudric Tel: 61-82-44-05
15. Denis Bocquier, **Château la Coutelière**, 31340 Vilemur-sur-Tarn Tel: 61-82-14-97
16. Madame Manoelle Arbeau, **Château Coutinel**, 82370 Labastide-St Pierre Tel: 63-64-01-80
17. Gilbert Bocquet, **Domaine de la Crabière**, 82370 Campsas Tel: 63-64-05-72
18. André Déjean, **Domaine Croix Peyrat**, 82370 Campsas Tel: 63-30-65-58
19. Monsieurs Dauban, **Château Dauban**, 31620 Fronton Tel: 61-82-45-43
20. •André Abart, **Château Devès**, 31620 Castelnau d'Estrefonds Tel: 61-35-14-97
21. *GROUPE VILLAUDRIC, 33 Route d'Albi Tel: 63-33-73-80; Domaine des Cabannes 81800 Rabastens; Domaine de Dispan; Domaine des Terres Blanches
22. Robert Béringuier, **Domaine de Faouquet**, 31620 Bouloc Tel: 61-82-06-66
23. *Jean Gélis, **Château Ferran**, 31620 Fronton Tel: 61-82-39-23
24. *Küntz père et fils, **Château Flotis**, 31620 Castelnau d'Estrefonds Tel: 61-82-10-03
25. Monsieur Foncelle-le-Chevillier, **Domaine de la Foncelière**, 31620 Bouloc Tel: 61-82-12-31
26. Madame M. H. Faggion, **Domaine de Galitran**, 31620 Villeneuve-les-Bouloc Tel: 61-82-07-28
27. *François Daubert, **Domaine de Joliet**, 31620 Fronton Tel: 61-82-46-02
39 **Château Lacour-Carré** see Domaine Raimon Jouan
28. Serge Galvani, **Château Lafon de Bangi**, 31620 Bouloc Tel: 61-82-04-27
29. Pierre Lescure, **Château Las Places**, 82370 Labastide-St Pierre Tel: 63-30-51-27

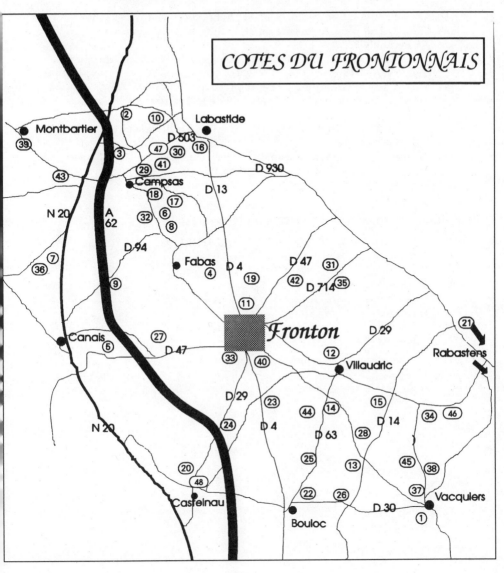

30. Madame Campillo-Perry, **Château Laurou**, 31620 Fronton Tel: 61-82-40-88
31. Jean Marie Cardetti, **Domaine de Lescure**, 82370 Labastide-St Pierre
    Tel: 63-30-55-45
32. Savin-M. Descombes, **Château Marguerite**, 82370 Campsas Tel: 63-64-08-21
33. Jean-Louis Delmas, **Domaine de Matabiau,** 31620 Fronton Tel: 61-82-96-01
34. Richard Mayor, **Château Montauriol**, 31340 Villematier Tel: 61-35-30-58
35. *Madame Martine Ethuin, **Château La Palme**, 31340 Villemur-sur-Tarn
    Tel: 61-09-02-82
36. Société Lacaze, **Domaine du Parc**, 82170 Dieupentale Tel: 63-02-532-38
37. *Marc Pénévayre, **Château Plaisance**, 31340 Vacquiers Tel: 61-84-97-41
38. François Prat, **Domaine des Pradelles**, 31340 Vacquiers Tel: 61-84-97-36
39. Catherine et Eric Lacour, **Domaine Raimon Jouan**, 82700 Montbartier

40. *Famille Ribes, **Château le Roc**, 31620 Fronton Tel: 61-82-93-90
48 Philippe Laduguie, **Domaine de St. Guilhem**, 31620 Castelnau d'Estrefonds Tel: 61-82-12-09
41. SCEA Château St Louis, **Château St Louis**, 82370 Labastide-St. Pierre Tel: 63-30-52-15
42. Michel Lugou, **Domaine de Tembouret**, 31620 Fronton Tel: 61-82-40-4
43. Monsieur Gaillard et Weber, **Domaine de la Tisarne**, 82370 Campsas Tel: 63-64-02-75
44. *Urbain Blancal, **Domaine Urbain Blancal**, 31620 Villaudric Tel: 61-82-44-09
45. Amédée Virac, **Château Virac**, 31340 Vacquiers Tel: 61-84-97-82
46. *Vovette Linant de Bellefonds, **Château Peyreaux**, 31340 Villematier Tel: 61-84-36-48

Vins des Côteaux et Terrasses de Montauban

1. CAVE CO-OPÉRATIVE DE LA VILLE-DIEU-DU-TEMPLE, 82290 La Ville-Dieu-du-Temple Tel: 63-31-60-05
2. Philippe et Thierry Romain, **Domaine de Montels**, 82350 Albias Tel: 63-31-02-82
3. Michel Cerles, **Domaine de Puyseguère**, St Martial, 82000 Montauban Tel: 63-03-11-57
4. Maurice Brunet, **Domaine du Cayrou**, Léojac, 82000 Montauban Tel: 63-64-57-12

The Wines of the Dordogne: Bergerac

Like the Lot and the Tarn, the river Dordogne rises in the mountains of central France. Its descent from its craterous source in the Auvergne is more rapid than theirs, its gorges shorter in length but steeper, and frequently dammed by hydro-electric projects which generate much of the power used in the South-West. It is not until the valley begins to widen out near Argentat that its course becomes more peaceful, assuming the majestic tranquillity which endears itself so much to travellers and holiday-makers. Here the adjoining hillsides begin to show signs of the cultivation of the vine, for example the Côteaux de Glanes already described (page 69).

Today the wines of the Dordogne mean, for all practical purposes, the wines of the Bergeracois: in the rest of the valley and the modern département of Dordogne wine-making has virtually died out except for small quantities by the local farmers for home-consumption. Sadly, the Livran family whose Domaine de Vignaud de Léparon at St Michel l'Ecluse is just within the département have given up. There are also a few scattered co-opératives of small growers making modest *vins de table*. But where are the vineyards of Brantôme nostalgically described in La Mazille's *La Bonne Cuisine du Périgord*, or the wines of Périgueux itself? He writes:

> Round Périgueux, along the hillsides, the small farmers make a white wine with such a perfumed bouquet, at the same time so unctuous and vigorous, that one is astonished at the way in which it is so modestly kept on the back shelf of the cupboard, when it can easily challenge the best-known growths of Bordeaux and elsewhere; its only fault, which explains all, is that too little is made for it to become better known . . . unfortunately, the rarity of such bottles keeps them a secret and people who have been able to taste them are privileged indeed.

Would that I were one of the few, though La Mazille was writing in the 1920s, when there may have been a few surviving vines from the pre-phylloxera era.

The Périgord was able to boast an honourable roll-call of wines before the destruction of its vineyards by that plague. In the region south of Sarlat, the hillsides of Gaumiers, Florimont and Daglan, overlooking the little river Céou, yielded wines which could reputedly compare in terms of bouquet with the best of Cahors. Zette Guinadeau-Franc in her evocative book on the gastronomy of the region recalls how, as a child, she would be given some of her Uncle Alfred's wine which was so old that it had paled to the colour of onion skin. It was usually a bit dried out and often smelled of the cork, but Uncle Alfred, announcing solemnly its vintage-year which was always well before the end of the last century, would hold the containing bottle in a firm grip while he chipped off the red wax with his wooden hammer:

> His eyes would moisten, and his voice would become tender as a lover's, his heart broken by the death of his old vines. Uncle, your wine had neither perfume nor quality, but we all used to raise our glasses and admire through the crystal its colour of dried petals. We inhaled the scents of the past with a renewed sense of nostalgia. Uncle, why did you not have the courage to replant our land with vines grafted on to American stock? The dead plants on our hillsides, with their twisted and blackened stumps, all reproach you for having abandoned them. Our passion for our land and our love of its wine should have given you the necessary courage.

So it was that, within the space of a few years, there disappeared for ever the best growths of the Périgord, whose vineyards had once covered 200 square miles.

The vines of Domme, Coste Calve, St Cyprien, Bézenac and Saint-Vincent at one time shared with forests of truffle-oaks dry chalky slopes which produced vintages of quality. There was also fierce local pride in the wines of Chancelade, Bourdeille, St-Pantalys, Brantôme and Montpon, which were put into large wooden barrels and loaded on to flat-bottomed barges coming from the Auvergne down the Dordogne. At Castelnaud they were joined by those from the valley of the Céou. Downstream the river Vézère brought the harvest from the hills of the Corrèze. The boats carried stakes and stave-wood, and on the return journey took on hoop-wood for making barrels and casks already filled with the good wine of the Périgord which would bring a little sunshine to grey Auvergnat farms.

Meanwhile the descent of the river was slow, disrupted by the tolls of Bergerac, where land-owners on either side of the river exacted tribute and often forbade passage altogether if their own wines had not already gone downstream. Libourne had St-Emilion to defend, protecting its famous growths with new fines: it was good luck if they did not send the Périgord barrels back upstream. Boatmen and cargo had to pay another duty when they reached Lormont, where the monks sold them a laurel branch which, on presentation at Bordeaux, entitled them to unload on the Quai des Chartrons.

Nowadays the upstream farmer scarcely makes wine any more, except for his own table. He has experimented with high-yielding American hybrids, rarely grafted with French vines. The young of the family have left home, he is often on his own, his back tired of carrying the sulphur spray up the steep slopes. Nevertheless, even today it is a point of honour for the peasant-grower to make his wine carefully. The old farmers have a respectful pride in their own wines, even if these are a bit rough and low in alcohol. Moreover the vintage is a time for celebration.

Zette Guinadeau-Franc describes the traditional wine-harvest in this way:

> In small family vineyards the habit has survived of neighbours all helping each other with the *vendange*, on the understanding that the service would be reciprocated all round. It is an occasion for getting together and gossiping, tongues being sometimes as sharply pointed as the *sécateurs*. You have to stand up straight from time to time to rest the back and there is no question of being paid piece-rates. There is a break at mid-day, where the last spoonfuls of soup are laced with red wine and there is meat to eat in honour of the pickers: pot-au-feu, chicken, roasts of pork, some vegetables, dishes filled with waffles and dried fruits bought in the local town, bananas and oranges. No plums or nuts because you saw those every day. All this food is well washed down with wine while family news is exchanged, something which people have little time for during the fine weather. The men share their own gripes, usually politics and prices, but always remember to compliment the women of the house on the quality of the food. Happily tiny vineyards like these will never feel the need to pick by machine.

The destruction of the Dordogne vines by the phylloxera was total. In other wine-growing areas of the South-West I have sometimes found pockets of pre-phylloxera vines but in the Dordogne valley I have not found one grower who boasts any vines as old as this. The upstream farmers did not replant their vineyards on anything like the pre-phylloxera scale. The same factors applied in the Dordogne as in the valley of the Lot: the general poverty of the population which prevented the purchase of new American *porte-greffes*; the lack of alternative possible crops which obliged whole families to leave the area; the loss of life in two world wars; and the intervening world recession of the 1930s.

In the lower reaches of the valley, there is a sharp contrast as you arrive in the canton of Bergerac. Here the countryside is much richer, and the farmers have always been more prosperous: other crops can be more easily cultivated, and the landholdings have always been in larger units. But there are other factors that have governed the entire re-creation of this *vignoble* which are buried deep in history.

In 1255 Bergerac undertook allegiance to the English Crown. In return, Henry III granted Bergerac a semi-autonomous jurisdiction so long as it remained loyal. Apart from the difficulty of governing such a large empire as the English Crown then enjoyed in France, Henry saw that a special relationship with Bergerac might open up trading advantages in the county of Guyenne. Bergerac won important privileges: the right to tax the wines of the *haut-pays* if the river were chosen as the means of their transport, as well as the right to ban the entry of all wines other than its own into the city. More important, however, was the exemption from the *grand privilège* enjoyed by Bordeaux, which meant that Bergerac, alone among the wines of the interior, had free right of access to the ocean. Until the end of the Hundred Years' War, when the English were expelled from South-West France, Bergerac was able to develop and enjoy special links with its English and North European markets. Even after the return of Bergerac to the French Crown in 1450, exemption from the *grand privilège* remained intact. Indeed François I confirmed Bergerac's special position in 1520.

The long struggles of the war had effectively split Périgord into two halves: in the north Périgueux aligned itself with France, while in the south Bergerac chose allegiance with England. Even after the peace, this division was to be re-opened by the Wars of Religion which the Reformation brought in its wake. The north was Catholic, while Bergerac was almost entirely Huguenot. We may be surprised even today by the ferocity of these religious struggles but we have to remember that, for the Bergeracois, Protestantism was no milk-and-water English type of revolt. To them it meant all-out Calvinism. The town of Ste-Foy-La-Grande was referred to as the Geneva of France.

It was natural for the Bergeracois to expand their trading links with Protestant Holland where they had already started to develop markets. This link was to be strengthened even further by the disastrous revocation by Louis XIV of the Edict of Nantes, ending the religious toleration which Henri IV had given the Huguenots in 1598. Following the restoration of Catholicism as the sole and official religion of all France, there was a mass exodus of population, many of the Bergeracois naturally seeking refuge with their sympathetic clients in Holland, rather than emigrating to England or the New World as so many other Huguenots did. These expatriate Bergeracois were ideally placed to foster and strengthen the trading links with their native town.

It was the Dutch connection too which saved Bergerac from the consequences of abolition of its trading privileges during the Revolution, because, in its golden age of trade with Holland, Bergerac had developed such strong markets that it scarcely felt the new competition from other wines of the *haut-pays*. It had also started to develop the concept of single-domaine wines, after the Bordeaux pattern. So there emerged a hierarchy of quality with the brands of the vineyard-owners stamped on the bottom of the barrels and sometimes too the precise name of the area from which they originated. These wines were referred to as *marques hollandaises*, an expression still current today. For many of today's winemakers in Bergerac, Holland remains the most valuable export-market. Just as the British have remained loyal to claret for hundreds of years, so the Dutch have remained faithful to Bergerac, despite changing fashions in wine – the switch from white to red and from sweet to dry.

Before the phylloxera, Bergerac made a certain amount of red wine, mostly on the right (north) bank, but by far the greater production was white, made from grapes grown on both sides of the river. The wines of the left (south) bank were generally regarded as better, and they were almost without exception sweet. The Dutch called them the Madeiras of the Périgord.

The wines from the right bank were used entirely for blending, and were exported as such, even losing their Bergerac name at the hands of the dealers. Because these wines fetched much less money than the left-bank dessert wines, the right bank was not immediately replanted after the phylloxera. The continuing Dutch market for sweet wines gave every inducement to replant the quality vineyards of the left bank.

Monsieur Amaury de Madaillan, the owner of Château Perrou, which, with its 75 hectares of vines under cultivation, is one of the largest of present-day Bergerac properties, gives a fascinating account of how the Bergerac vineyards were reborn. He should know as well as anyone, because his family is one of the oldest in the southern Périgord. His crumblingly elegant property dates from the seventeenth century, and enjoys magnificent views from its terrace looking down into the river valley. His Uncle François is said to have had the largest *chais* in the region, but nowadays the family have stopped making their own wine and sell their crop to the co-opérative at Le Fleix.

According to Monsieur de Madaillan, there were twice as many vines in the Bergerac vineyards before the phylloxera as there are today, but the yield was much lower; in 1837 it was as little as 9 hectolitres to the hectare. The vines were planted at random and not in rows. The vine-yards were on the hillsides – there were none in the plain, where the farms were all rented out by the land-owners. The death from phyllox-era was a slow one – it took about twenty years between 1876 and 1896 for the vineyard to be entirely wiped out. The right bank was allowed to revert to woodland, while the left initially developed polyculture as a way of survival.

The first phase of restructuring came with the replanting of grafted vines. In those days, oxen were used in the vineyards. Larger and stronger beasts were required to work on the higher sloping ground where the best vines grew, so the vines there had to be planted further apart lower down the hillsides. Here the gradients were less steep, so smaller oxen were strong enough. Paradoxically, the better vineyards were less densely planted than the more ordinary ones, the opposite of modern viticultural practice. The growers developed a kind of double-yoke which enabled the oxen to work in pairs on either side of the vine-rows. The height of the yoke, which would normally be between 1 metre 10 centimetres and 1 metre 15 centimetres, dictated the height of the stakes supporting the plants, and thus the height of the growth of the vines. It is not hard to see where the design of modern harvesting machines originated. With the coming of tractors after the Second World War, the rows of vines became more widely separated, up to 4 metres apart, because nobody had foreseen the modern kind of mini-tractor which can work in relatively small corridors between the vines.

It was about this time, too, that a dry style of white Bergerac began to emerge to meet the changing taste in white wines. Monsieur de Madaillan was not the only grower I spoke to who thought that the switch to a drier palate was a direct consequence of a change in dietary habits. When people did not get enough to eat, or perhaps in times of war or enemy occupation, they needed a lot more sugar, and this was provided usefully by sweet wines. These also accompanied better the richer and fattier style of cooking from past times. Today, when people need less energy, they have lighter food, for which drier wines are usually thought to be more appropriate.

Monsieur de Madaillan does not regret that a lot of people see Bergerac as a satellite of Bordeaux, an image which many of the younger growers are trying to change. He explained that, with the end of the river traffic, it was inevitable that Bergerac should become more closely linked with Bordeaux, because of its international importance and its fast road and rail links to all parts of Europe. He is not worried that Bordeaux might actually swallow up Bergerac: Bordeaux has enough problems selling its own wines, without taking on the burden of an expanded vineyard.

Wine-makers who seek to assert the independence of Bergerac cannot escape the fact that the vineyards are a natural eastward extension of those of Bordeaux. The vines of Montravel on the right bank rub shoulders with those of the Côtes de Castillon which themselves adjoin St Emilion without a break. The structure of the soil is also a continuation of that which underlies the red wines of St Emilion and Castillon, so it is not surprising that the red wines of Bergerac grown on that side of the river have a natural kinship with those of their more famous Bordelais neighbours. It is not until you reach Pécharmant, at the very eastern end of the Bergeracois, that a particular kind of pebbly-sandy soil with a touch of iron below gives an individual *goût du terroir* to the red wine. On the left bank, the Bordeaux district of Entre-Deux-Mers adjoins Saussignac without a break, and Monbazillac in turn adjoins Saussignac.

The kinship with Bordeaux is accentuated by the use of the same grape-varieties in both areas. The only physical distinction is political: the Bordeaux vineyards are in the département of the Gironde, while the Bergerac vineyards are almost all in the département of Dordogne. If it were not for this artificial boundary, might the two areas have merged? Could not the inner appellations of Bergerac, such as Monbazillac and Pécharmant, survive alongside the inner appellations of Bordeaux such as Sauternes and St Emilion?

The total output of the Bergerac region has varied enormously. In 1835, when the yield per hectare was but a quarter of what it is today, the average production was about 140,000 hectolitres. Following the post-phylloxera replanting, it rose to about 800,000 at the turn of the twentieth century, and today it is only a little over half that figure. This reflects the drop in production of *vins de table*, though not in quality wines, whose production has remained constant through the century. The present extent of the Bergerac vineyard is approximately 11,000 hectares.

The creation of areas of appellation contrôlée for Bergerac began in 1936 with the grant of the basic Bergerac appellations. For the red wines, there were two, Bergerac and Côtes de Bergerac: the difference is not in the altitude or geographical position of the vineyards, but the alcoholic strength of the wines. The Côtes wine can generally be expected to be superior to a wine of the basic Bergerac name. For the white wines, there are three appellations, which also depend on alcoholic strength and sweetness. First, there is Bergerac Sec, which must have a minimum of 10° and a maximum of 13° alcohol and no more than 4 grams of unfermented sugar per litre. Next in line comes Côtes de Bergerac where the alcohol range is 11–13° and the wine may retain more sugar. Finally there is Côtes de Bergerac Moelleux where the respective figures for alcohol and sugar are higher still. The maximum yield per hectare is 50 hectolitres, which is often exceeded in plentiful years. Excessive yield is less detrimental to dry white wines than to red wines or the sweeter whites.

The difficulties of nomenclature are further complicated by the existence of inner appellations within the Bergerac area. With the exception of Pécharmant, they are all for white wines only. First and most famously there is Monbazillac, grown on the slopes rising out of the valley opposite the town of Bergerac. These wines are exclusively sweet – ultra-sweet in fact – and are required to contain a potential of at least 13° alcohol. In practice, and in good years, it is quite usual for the best wines to achieve 14° alcohol, and to contain 4° of residual sugar, a formula often spoken of as '14 + 4'. Production is limited to 40 hectolitres per hectare, but, as we shall see, the best wines are made from much smaller yields.

Adjoining Monbazillac to the west is the little known area of Saussignac, which was granted AOC status as recently as 1982. In practice most of the wines of this area are sold under the general Bergerac titles, although there is a small production of *vins liquoreux* after the style of Monbazillac, which local growers are keen to develop under the Saussignac name.

On the right bank, and immediately adjoining the Bordelais, is the area called Montravel which enjoys the benefit of three appellations of its own. Again these wines are marketed more and more under one or other of the basic Bergerac appellations, the Montravel name being reserved for the better growths. Basic Montravel is dry and akin to Bergerac Sec. Côtes de Montravel is *moelleux* in style, though the tendency is to ferment out the sugar fairly fully, producing wines which are no more than *demi-sec*. Haut Montravel is a fully sweet wine, now rather rare, and like Saussignac models itself on Monbazillac. Its production is limited to five communes. Declaration under the Montravel name has fallen by two-thirds over the last thirty-five years, largely because of the tendency to replant white vines with red ones, and the red wines do not enjoy the Montravel appellation.

The fourth of the inner white wine appellations is Rosette, from vineyards immediately to the north of the town of Bergerac. These wines are *moelleux*, but most of the growers entitled to use the Rosette name market their wines simply as Bergerac.

Finally, there is the red Pécharmant appellation, exclusive to about 260 hectares of vines grown on the hillsides east of Bergerac on the right bank. No white wine can be sold as Pécharmant, and few producers in practice grow any white grapes except for their own consumption.

I make no apology for concentrating on these inner appellations of Bergerac, because it is they which more often assert an individual style. At the end of the chapter there is however a list of the largest growers of basic Bergerac, who do not declare under the inner appellations.

MONBAZILLAC

This is undoubtedly the most famous wine grown in the département, as well as one of the oldest of the Dordogne vineyards. Nowadays it covers about 2500 hectares and produces annually some 50,000 hectolitres, rather over 10% of the total AOC production of the Bergeracois. (These figures can vary widely from year to year.) Monbazillac is always a very sweet wine: there is no such thing as a dry Monbazillac. Like Sauternes, it is based on the sémillon grape with minority support from muscadelle and/or sauvignon.

The way to the vineyards lies due south of the town of Bergerac. As you begin to leave the valley, the ground starts to rise in shelves, the rich fertile soil of the plain giving way alternately to layers of sandstone, then chalky clay. The hill of Monbazillac itself appears like a green-striped curtain in front of you, and, beyond it, the landscape changes to one of gently rolling hills. It is on the north-facing slopes of the Monbazillac hill that many of the best growths are made. This exposition brings the danger of frosts in spring, but it is also largely responsible for the unique character of the wine. The climate is temperate, so that in the autumn the lie of the land causes the formation of morning mists which are slow to clear, because the sun does not reach the grapes until it is high in the sky. Only after midday does the warm October weather draw the moisture first southward up the slope of the land and then into the atmosphere, dispelling the mist which in the meantime has produced a microscopic fungoid growth. This is called *botrytis cinerea* or 'noble rot', which shrivels the skins of the grapes and causes the juice inside to evaporate. The reduced volume of liquid is correspondingly more concentrated in sugar. This is the same phenomenon which occurs in the wines of the Sauternais, but nowhere else in the

South-West, even where the making of sweet white wines is a speciality. To extract the maximum natural sweetness from the grapes, the pickers go over the plants several times instead of picking all the grapes at one go. The idea is that every grape should be gathered at maximum ripeness. In the South-West this is called *tries successives*.

Before the Revolution, when honey was the usual source of sugar, the cultivation of bees was forbidden in the Bergerac vineyards, in order to prevent over-chaptalisation. Chaptalisation is the term, named after the French chemist Chaptal, for the addition of sugar to the fermenting must of the wine. Growers were not tempted to add to the efforts of nature by artificial means: for them the effects of botrytis were sufficient without extra sugar.

But the Dutch insisted on a regular supply of Monbazillac, year in and year out, whether or not the vintage conditions were favourable to its making, and it was these ultra-sweet wines which formed the backbone of the trade with Holland. As a nation, the Dutch in those days must have had a very sweet tooth indeed, because they asked for added sugar to be included: sometimes, when the wine reached them they even added *eau-de-vie* as well! Sugaring of the wine came to be abused by unscrupulous producers: it was a cheap and easy substitute for *tries successives* and was a false substitute for botrytis in bad years when the fungus refused to appear.

Especially after the Second World War, the standards of wine-making in Monbazillac fell sharply and badly affected the reputation of the wine. In 1939 a bottle of Monbazillac fetched the same as a bottle of Sauternes (not Yquem of course), but during the fifties and sixties it sold for only a quarter of the price of its rivals. Monbazillac still had its devotees, but the wine tended to be bought as an apéritif and at a much reduced price. Bernard Ginestet has likened the wine at that period to an ageing actress – still much talked about, but no longer able to hold the front of the stage. Certainly the Monbazillac growers had not only lowered the quality standards but had lost their foothold in the marketplace. The image of the wine of Monbazillac had slipped. Nevertheless the potential for quality has always been there, and there was never any question of going over to the exclusive production of dry white wine or red wines. Other areas of Bergerac have done this, but have had a job to compete, and today sell for a third of the price of good Monbazillac.

For there has been a revival in the demand for Monbazillac and in the quality of its production in recent years. This mirrors a similar situation in Jurançon, and is a combination of a slight swing of the pendulum towards sweeter wine in the 1980s and the emergence of a new generation of producers who see the future for their vineyards in the development of maximum individual character (what they call *typicité*) in their wines: the true *goût du terroir*. Take Dominique Vidal for example, who makes the wine at the pioneering property **La Borderie (22)**, just round the corner from the co-opérative. His mother's family has for many generations owned the **Château Treuil-de-Nailhac**, for

which Dominique makes the wine at La Borderie, where it is also bottled. His mother's grandfather was a pioneer in his own way too, for he
was among the first to market his wine in bottle rather than in cask.
Treuil-de-Nailhac is on the top of the Monbazillac hill, just round the
series of bends which take the road south to Eymet.

On his father's side, the Vidal family are relative newcomers to the
Bergeracois: they come from the Midi, and Dominique has the passionate intensity and total dedication you might expect from his origins.
The two properties give Dominique the foundations which he needs to
experiment in new techniques to improve quality. He even makes red
wine for a neighbour at Château Fonrousse, on whom he frankly tries
out his experiments.

Of the 60 hectares currently under vine at the two family properties,
15 are given over to red Côtes de Bergerac, some of which is given ageing in new wood. Both versions from the 1990 vintage were rich and
fruity, and quite forward, somewhat reminiscent of a good Pécharmant.
The wood was not at all prominent on the special *cuvée*, and
Dominique explained that for him the question of wood was one of balance, whether you used new or old wood, or a mixture of the two. He is
obviously fascinated by *élevage* in wood: a feature of the *chais* at La
Borderie is the wonderful collection of huge old barrels which are still
in use, while in the adjoining buildings are the new oak *barriques* from
the famous Tonnellerie Radoux. Dominique is convinced that you have
to examine every new barrel very carefully, particularly for smell – if
there is a dry and dusty odour to the wood, that is how the wine will
turn out.

In an average year, one-third of his white wines will be dry, the
remainder sweet. In 1991 he had to de-classify part of his Monbazillac
production, and in 1992 he felt obliged to sell all of it off as Bergerac
Moelleux. At the moment he is making two kinds of dry wine, which
has to be sold as Bergerac and not Monbazillac: one is from sauvignon
sometimes with some sémillon, the other is from 100% muscadelle.

But, as always in Monbazillac, one comes for the sweet wines. It was
fascinating to compare the styles of the two Borderie properties. The
Treuil-de-Nailhac has a pronounced muscat character, and Dominique
Vidal says that this is due to the high proportion of muscadelle grapes
at that property. Vidal believes that it is the muscadelle which gives
Monbazillac its particular style and differentiates it from Sauternes.
The wines at Treuil-de-Nailhac seem more forward on the whole than
at La Borderie where the pronounced features are citrus and exotic
fruits such as mangoes on the bouquet. 1990 and 1991 were quite
exceptionally rich, the wines reaching 14 + 7 and 14 + 10 respectively.
Some of the Borderie Monbazillac is given oak-ageing, and these wines
are surprisingly delicate, because of the tact with which Dominique
Vidal handles his wood.

One of his projects for the future is to convert an old outbuilding into
a cold-room for experimental treatment of white grapes. Techniques of

gradual degradation of the grapes at low temperatures will extend the field of *macération pelliculaire*: he will also be able to use the room for stopping the fermentation of the sweet wines, and for anti-tartaric refrigeration before bottling. He has already installed three fine wooden barrels which he has acquired from Michel Roches at Domaine du Haut-Pécharmant, from whom, incidentally, he buys Pécharmant wine which he markets under the brand-name Lentilhac.

One unexpected feature of this innovative wine-maker is that he does not vinify his grape-varieties separately. This is also the case at the adjoining properties of **Château de la Haute-Brie et du Caillou (29)** and **Château Poulvère (34)**, at least in years where the grapes are really healthy. Very confusingly, these vineyards belong to the family of Jean Borderie, who has no connection whatever with the property next door bearing his name. Jean himself is now seventy-four and still is sole owner of La Haute-Brie which covers 17 hectares, while just down the road Poulvère, with its 64 hectares, is spread among the family. Jean used to be merely the manager and part-owner, but his family were able to buy out the other shares in 1977, an arrangement which has done much to simplify the problems of inheritance affecting the two properties.

As well as these 81 hectares in Monbazillac, Jean owns 6 hectares of Pécharmant, which is vinified at Poulvère, as is the wine from La Haute-Brie. But the wines are otherwise separately matured and marketed. The Pécharmant is sold under the name Les Grangettes and is priced with the best. The red, rosé and dry white wines from the two Monbazillac properties are sold under the name of Domaine des Barses, leaving the titles of the two Monbazillac estates to be used exclusively for Monbazillac wine.

The vineyards were almost entirely wiped out by the disastrous frosts of 1956, although there are still a few plants which derive from an earlier replanting in the 1920s, when Jean was a boy. His family have a long history in the region: his grandfather was a professional fisher of salmon from the Dordogne; his father was going to be a priest, but the vocation faltered and instead he took a job and married the boss's daughter. The family has not looked back since. They have a quite specific replanting programme – 2 hectares are replaced every year to keep the vineyard young and to stop the yield falling away too much. Jean thinks that there is not as much replanting in Monbazillac as there ought to be, and it is an ageing wine-area. The grapes from old vines, of course, give the better wine, but no plant is immortal.

Since 1992 you cannot benefit from the appellation Monbazillac if you pick by machine. Jean sees the point of this, but thinks it is a pity that he cannot harvest mechanically the sauvignon for his Monbazillac, because he likes to leave these early maturing grapes on the vine as long as he dares, and there are advantages in being able to harvest in a hurry if the rain-clouds start to gather.

The Borderies make what I call a modern-style Monbazillac. They do not aim for the last ounce of sugar in the juice. They are quite happy if only 60% of the grapes develop botrytis, because the remaining unaffected grapes give a fresher fruitier character and prevent the wine becoming too heavy. This policy also enables them to produce a more consistent style of wine year on year, a factor which is particularly appreciated by the high proportion of trade buyers. Around 70% of the wines from these two properties are sold *en négoce*. Half the Monbazillac is sold *en vrac*: some goes to a Bordeaux *courtier* and the rest they sell off as best they can to regular private clients and restaurants. Wine from a total of 87 hectares takes quite a bit of marketing.

The sweet-wine *encépagement* is normal for Monbazillac, with a good 25% muscadelle. The juice from the grapes is drawn off the *bourbe* at low temperatures and is then vinified in enamelled steel or cement for a minimum of fifteen days, more in good years. The fermentation is stopped by refrigeration. The wines are kept in the *cuves* for eighteen months before they are bottled. The Borderies believe neither in new nor old wood.

Jean Borderie was keeping his fingers crossed for the 1995 vintage. He could not remember having sprayed so much in his life as he had done in 1992–94, at least fourteen times in 1993 compared with an average of nine. He calls mildew 'the cancer of the vine' and extra spraying makes the cost of production considerably higher and does nothing for the quality of the wine. At least he hopes that his vintage will prove better than his prunes. He has extensive orchards of plum-trees as well as vines, and the harvesting of the plums gives work to the vineyard-workers while the grapes are ripening.

It is only a short step from each of the above properties to the **Cave Co-opérative de Monbazillac (19)**, an unmistakable building on the west side of the road from Bergerac to Eymet. In its day, the Cave was one of the pioneers in the revival of Monbazillac, and today, under the direction of Jacques Blaquière, claims half the total production. The visiting traveller may wonder how it is that this establishment can discharge that function. Its large, impressive retail shop is devoted to the sale of the more expensive of the Cave's wines, the odd bottle of single-malt whisky, tins of *foie gras* and other up-market products. You will look in vain for a barrel from which you can fill up your cubitainers; the accent is on the top-of-the range wines such as the wooded *liquoureux* from the Château de Monbazillac itself, probably the most expensive wine of the appellation. Where else does a co-opérative sell wine at a price higher than that fetched by the most prestigious private growers?

It is only fair to add that the Cave also sells wines which it makes for other properties in the region. Notably it manages the production of Château Septy, an old-established estate which was one of the thirty-two *marques hollandaises* and which has been turned into a joint venture between members of the Cave and outside enthusiasts. It is said that the situation of Château Septy, on the lower slopes of the Monbazillac hill, is so favourable that often the harvest is finished there before the grapes at Château Monbazillac are ripe.

Jacques Blaquière also makes the wine for Château Le Haut Poulvère (no connection with the Château Poulvère already discussed) and Château Monrepos, and all these wines are sold at prices barely more than half that of Château Monbazillac. Apart from the sweet wines they also make Pécharmant for Château Renaudie, one of the best properties in that appellation, and red Bergerac for Château La Brie (again no connection with La Haute-Brie). La Brie is interesting because it, too, was one of the famous thirty-two *marques hollandaises*: today it houses the local agricultural college where young growers can come and study the latest techniques. Former students include Colette Bourgès, whom we shall presently meet in the context of Rosette. The Cave has taken advantage of its managership of La Brie to create an experimental vineyard for the development of new improved clones of sémillon, sauvignon and muscadelle, the classic white grapes of the region.

The Cave has also forged a special relationship with peripatetic wine-maker Hugh Ryman and his English associates. The Ryman family can claim a special distinction in the area because it was Hugh's father Henry who bought the Château La Jaubertie at Colombier in 1973 and played a large part in developing the demand for dry white Bergerac. Under Hugh's supervision and with his staff, the Cave makes dry white Bergerac for three estates: the Domaine de la Croix, a 27-hectare property at Issigeac belonging to a Monsieur de Conti, the Domaine Grand Pouget and Château Haut-Peygonthier which has 35 hectares. The sémillon grapes from these properties are used to make a blended dry wine. The sauvignon grapes from Grand Pouget make a characteristic wine with what Ryman calls 'zippy herbaceous exotic fruit flavours'. Under his direction, the Cave also makes Monbazillac from the harvest at Château des Hébras for Eric de Bazin. These wines are marketed by Ryman under his own label and are widely available in the United Kingdom. We shall come across more Ryman wines later in the Côtes de Duras and the Marmandais.

The Cave is not without its critics: some think it spends too much on its image and its shop-window; others are said to be unhappy about the Japanese management techniques which are being foisted upon members. It is easy to understand the reaction of country-growers, some of whom have been making wine all their lives, to being told how to plant and grow their vines. Some of the private producers are upset by what they see as aggressive marketing: one complained bitterly to me that the Cave had, without any consultation, started to sell a blended Monbazillac under the same name as his own property, which is one of the most respected locally.

However, the co-opérative has undoubtedly done a great deal to help revive the standards of Monbazillac. Perhaps its most famous public role is as owner of the beautiful Château de Monbazillac, which dominates the Dordogne valley for many miles. As well as making good wine, it receives over 40,000 visitors a year to its sixteenth-century interior. It houses some of the most highly polished antique furniture I have ever seen, as well as some priceless manuscripts of Erasmus and other sixteenth- and seventeenth-century Protestant literature, the property once having been the stronghold of the most fanatical Protestants of the area. Also very much worth seeing is the well-displayed wine museum. A mid-morning tour of the château, followed by a tasting and a picnic in the cool woods to the south is a very pleasant way to spend a hot day.

By mid-afternoon you may be ready to head west and follow the Monbazillac ridge to **Château de Theulet (36)**, which has been in the family of Serge Alard and his son Pierre for many generations (Pierre says he thinks he is the sixth). This property is another of the *marques hollandaises*. Pierre told us that, after the revocation of the Edict of Nantes, the then owner founded a *maison de commerce* in Holland to foster the trade in Bergerac wine. Féret, whose commentary on the wines of Bergerac published in 1903 is still much sought after and respected, rated the wines of Theulet particularly highly, even though, after the phylloxera, the vineyard had been replanted largely with red wine grapes. Pierre explained that with the sugar shortage in the First World War, there was a sudden demand for Monbazillac to satisfy a craving for something sweet, so a lot of replanting was carried out, this time with the traditional white varieties.

At Theulet itself all but 7 of the 32 hectares are now planted with white grapes – 80% sémillon, 12% muscadelle and 8% sauvignon. Pierre Alard aims to make as much Monbazillac as possible, because it fetches a much better price, and it is the *vin du terroir*. But he will always make a little dry white, and in some years he has to if the conditions are not right for Monbazillac. For example, if October is wet, botrytis will not form and the grapes will start to rot before they have developed enough sugar, so he is thrown back on to the making of a dry wine. The dominance of the sémillon in the *encépagement* gives his *sec* an unusual richness and fullness – what the French call *gras* – which distinguishes it from wines with a bigger sauvignon content.

It is still the Monbazillac which is the basis of Theulet's reputation, and his is one of the best. There are two *cuvées*, of which one is matured partly in stainless steel and partly in new wood. The other is made entirely in steel. The prestige wine can start with up to 25° sugar, so the Alards are not afraid to make a rich and traditional Monbazillac, redeemed from excess by a lovely twist of acidity right in the middle of the palate.

The red wines are made largely from grapes grown at two other properties which the Alards formerly rented but have probably bought by now: Château la Calevie at Pomport and part of Château Rauly at Monbazillac. These wines are also excellent and are keepers. They are totally de-stalked before a long fermentation of three weeks at 30–32° with *remontage* twice a day. The best *cuves* are put into new barrels after the malolactic fermentation, and one-third of the barrels are replaced each year. As may be expected, these wines have splendid structure and the wood does not seem to dominate. The wines of Château Theulet are usually available from quality merchants in the United Kingdom.

Another vineyard which is close by to Theulet, and which was also much admired by Féret, is **Château le Fagé (44)**. Again, like Theulet, it has been in the same family for many generations and the wine, too, is well known in the UK. François Gérardin must be immensely proud of what is one of the most beautifully situated of all the Bergerac estates: crowned by a long low chartreuse-style building complete with classical triangular pediment, the vines start at the top of the Monbazillac ridge where the sauvignon and muscadelle are planted. It is these grapes which give finesse and suavity to the wine. Planted in vertical rows in the direction of the slope, the sémillon grape takes over on the lower ground, where grape-variety and soil combine to give the maximum sugar and structure to the wines. A feature of the property is the excellent natural drainage: even in the wettest weather the water runs away quickly. The Cave where the wine is made has been built at the bottom of the slope, so that the grapes can all be taken downhill instead of up the steep gradients to the château.

The vineyard dates back to before the Revolution, but at the time Féret was writing it was mostly planted, like nearby Theulet, with red grapes. In modern times it was François Gérardin's grandfather, Albert Géraud, who built the reputation of the wine, largely by promoting it himself at country fairs. Even in those days it was one of the more expensive *crus*. He became mayor of the local village of Pomport and a much respected member of the community, but he never recovered from the death of his son who had been a prisoner for five years during the Second World War. When he retired he handed the vineyard over to his son-in-law, Maurice Gérardin, François' father. François took over the running of the vineyard in 1983.

Though the property is famous largely for its Monbazillac, François describes the making of that style of wine as like 'taking your cheque-book to the casino'. If your luck is in, you can make a great wine, but more often than not the result is less spectacular: some years are catastrophic. Modern techniques can nowadays ensure that there is some future for most wines even in poor years, but in Monbazillac you are almost totally at the mercy of the weather. This was why François decided to diversify into making dry white wine, rosé and Côtes de Bergerac red. His aim is to produce the best range of wines overall. Modestly he does not claim to make the best of any single style, but he is proud that his total output, judged as a whole, is second to none. It is noticeable that, in Monbazillac in particular, many growers make a marvellous sweet wine but do not always take the same trouble with the other wines of the Bergerac appellations, if they make them at all.

François philosophically assumes that each year, with his white grapes, he is going to make nothing but a dry wine. If the conditions are right for Monbazillac, that is a bonus. He is unable to be precise about the *encé-pagement* of his vineyard, because many of the grapes go back to the post-phylloxera planting when the vines were planted at random and not in rows, but he thinks he may have as much as 90% sémillon. Even in a good Monbazillac year, he does not wait for all his grapes to botrytise: like Jean Borderie he believes that if some grapes in a bunch remain unaffected by the rot, the resulting wine is that much fresher and fruitier. François Gérardin is therefore making a 'modern' Monbazillac, less honeyed than some, but elegant and with plenty of acidity to prevent the taste cloying. 'When the wine is young,' he says, 'you can separate out in your mouth the alcohol, the botrytis and the fruit: when these have all merged to produce one indivisible flavour, the wine is mature.' Because of the small percentages of sauvignon and muscadelle, the Monbazillac grapes are all vinified together in enamelled cement. He thinks this is the only really neutral material. The fermentation can last for up to ten weeks and the wine is not bottled until 2½ years after the vintage.

If the style of the wine is to be dry, the grapes are given skin-contact for a few hours and fermented at no more than 16–18°.

About a quarter of the production at Le Fagé is red Côtes de Bergerac, from a high 90% of ultra-ripe merlot, with only a little cabernet franc and malbec. Gérardin is not keen on stainless steel except for the initial stages of production and as soon as fermentation starts he prefers fibre-glass for his red wine. The *élevage* is for eighteen months, the resulting wines being fruity and attractive when young, then closing up rather like Bordeaux before blossoming out again after a few years in bottle.

François completes his range with a pale rosé, one of the best in the region, made from equal amounts of the two cabernets. Over half of his output is exported: the balance is either sold in bottle to private clients in France, or *en vrac* to the trade if he does not think any particular wine is up to standard.

Not all the best vines look down on the valley of the river Dordogne. Just over the top of the ridge behind Le Fagé is the large domaine of **Château Bélingard (51)**. The Bosredon family and their ancestors the Clauzels have owned this estate for many hundreds of years: the Bosredons themselves go back to the tenth century. The beloved grandmother of Laurent, the present Comte, died only a few years ago just short of her one hundred and third birthday, relishing daily the old vintages of Bélingard such as 1959 and 1948. Laurent acknowledges that she is still the presiding genius of the vineyard, and names his best *cuvées* after her in homage.

Laurent did not set out to be a wine-maker at all, having trained in marketing, acquiring skills which no doubt stand him in good stead today. He arrived at Bélingard with his charming wife Sylvie in 1981, 'like a man from Mars who knew nothing about wine'. He went straightaway to Bordeaux where he trained in oenology and came under the influence of Denis Dubourdieu, one of the pioneers of *macération pelliculaire* and other modern techniques. He was fortunate that his first vintage at Bélingard was the fabulous 1982. Laurent de Bosredon decided immediately to abandon the path of making wines which are just easy to drink, and to concentrate on quality and the maximum expression of the *terroir*.

There has always been a high proportion of red wine made at Bélingard: the reliable Féret reports that at the turn of the century there was twice as much red as white. Laurent de Bosredon does not ignore the present tendency in Bergerac towards the production of red rather than white wines, even though his heart is really in the production of Monbazillac. He is set upon retrieving what he fears is a lost tradition of real Monbazillac-making; he doubts whether many modern Monbazillacs will last as long as those which his grandmother so dearly loved.

The château has some 85 hectares under vine, though 25 of them are some distance away near Monestier and so do not qualify for the Monbazillac appellation. The property itself looks west down the valley towards the hills of Castillon, where General Talbot met his death on the battlefield at the close of the Hundred Years' War. In the immediate foreground there used to be, in the middle ages, a château from which local barons launched an attack on the city of Bergerac, one of the first engagements of that war. Bélingard is the only place in France from which you can see simultaneously the starting point and finishing post of that marathon. You might say that it took a hundred years to make a net advance of some thirty miles.

The 60 hectares of vines which you can see from the terrace at Bélingard are exceptionally pleasing to the eye. As is usual in the district the vines are planted in the direction of the fall of the land, but here the folds of the hills produce an endlessly fascinating pattern of cultivation, the various parcels divided by alley-ways of grass. The effect is of an abstract monochrome study in green. You can sit, and no doubt Grandmother did, for hours on end enjoying the interplay of the sunlight on the different angles and shades in the vine-rows.

In Celtic Bélingard means 'the stone of Bélin', the sun-god of the Celts. On a hilltop nearby is the small tumulus called Moncuq which means 'the hill of twilight'. The druids were once very important in this district – it is said that, long before the Romans planted their vineyards in France, they had a technique for making a ritual wine based on the juice of the wild vine and honey. It was forbidden to all but the priests to make or drink this in their own homes: the hoi-polloi were untruthfully told it was made from mistletoe. At Bélingard the Bosredons have unearthed a druidical sacrificial chair in a wonderful state of preservation, which was used for human sacrifices to Bélin, so they have some claim to being the owners of the oldest vineyard in France.

The policy of Bélingard is to make as much Monbazillac as the vintage conditions will allow. With a yield which they strictly limit to a maximum of 20 hectolitres to the hectare, sometimes as little as 10, and with never more than 30 hectares of vines yielding grapes suitable for Monbazillac wine, the production is relatively tiny for such a large property, usually about 350 hectolitres. The *encépagement* is 80% sémillon and 10% each sauvignon and muscadelle. Usually two different *cuvées* are made, the first in a lighter fruitier style, for which the harvesting is done bunches at a time so that some of the grapes will not have been attacked by botrytis. The fermentation in fibre-glass is stopped when the wine has attained about 13° alcohol, and the wine is matured in *cuves* for six months before being transferred to old barrels. These hold 600 litres each and are called *demi-muids*: the wine is left here for twelve to eighteen months before fining and bottling. Laurent de Bosredon described the style of this wine as a compromise between the *gras* of Sauternes and the finesse of a sweet Loire.

For the prestige *cuvée*, which is named in honour of grandmother Blanche de Bosredon, the grapes are individually picked only when they have been thoroughly attacked by the noble rot. This requires several *tries successives* and implies draconian selection of fruit and a tiny yield. It is not surprising that this wine is sold at double the price of the basic *cuvée*. The wine is fermented in new wood, and is then matured also in new wood for up to 20 months, with regular ullage and racking. It is fined with egg white before being bottled. Tasted after only six months in bottle, and thus at a time when there was still infinite possibility of development, I still found this wine to be more in the 'modern' style than its vinification and *élevage* might suggest. The balance between sweetness and acidity is superb. Great years such as 1990 and 1995 will last for decades.

Of their other Bergerac wines, there are two dry whites, one fermented and matured in new wood and the other, which I preferred, vinified traditionally, although the oaked wine would be good with spicy fish dishes. Each is 50% sémillon, with the unoaked wine having 15% muscadelle to balance the 35% sauvignon. The oaked wine is 50% sauvignon, and there is no muscadelle.

Under the name of Abbaye Saint-Mayme, another property on the estate, they make a *moelleux* from 100% sémillon which they are targeting at the English taste. Sylvie de Bosredon almost apologised for this wine, and I was able to tell her without embarrassment that it was not to the taste of this Englishman. She smiled sympathetically. The wine was light, with a hint of sweetness, very much in the modern style of off-dry table-wine which the French are beginning to take to with their meals.

Again with the red wines I preferred the unoaked version to the wooded one, which I found rather lacking in weight. The unoaked wine was very attractive with a deep cherry colour – probably needing five years from the vintage to show its best. It is unashamedly easy to drink, and would be a good wine for entertaining. Maybe the oaked wine, too, needs more time to benefit from its rather complicated vinification and *élevage*. It comes from old vines, half of them merlot, the other half cabernet sauvignon. The fermentation may be as long as twenty-four days, and once the malolactic fermentation is finished the wine is transferred to *barriques*, 10% of which are new, 70% have already had one wine made in them, and the remainder two wines. The wine stays in the barrels for fifteen months with quarterly racking.

Laurent de Bosredon's business training is perhaps behind his extraordinary success in exporting his wines – more than 80% of his total production is sold in this way. Here he is mirrored by another ex-businessman, Jacques Blais, a graduate of the Paris Ecole Supérieure de Commerce, and an enthusiastic cellist in what little spare time he has. Blais owns a relatively small property of some 9 hectares called **Château Haut-Bernasse (24)**, which he bought in 1977. Though largely devoted to the production of Bergerac Sec, Monsieur Blais is keen, when conditions permit, to make about 50 hectolitres of high quality Monbazillac. He aims to combine the essential qualities of the *terroir* with the opportunities of modern technology. Thus he has always banned weedkillers from the vineyards and picked his grapes by hand, even before this became obligatory under new rules made in 1992 for Monbazillac (though not for other Bergerac appellations). His nods in the direction of progress include experimentation with a new way of growing the vines in the shape of a lyre (*en lyre*) as recommended by the National Agricultural Research Institute in Bordeaux. He also gives his Monbazillac two years in wood before bottling. Nearly all his dry white wine is exported and about half his Monbazillac, though his red sells better at home.

Jean-Pierre Martrenchard has 7 hectares of vines at Monbazillac, but another 63 distributed over other parts of the Bergerac area and into the Côtes du Duras at Loubès-Bernac. His home and *chais* are the **Château le Mayne (66)** near Sigoulès. The Monbazillac is his flagship because it seems that the rest of his production is given over to the making of wines for early consumption: good quality but easy drinking. Less than a year after the vintage his red Bergerac already shows very well with a mature colour, hazelnuts and plums in the bouquet and an attractive open-air style. It would indeed make a good barbecue or picnic wine, though that sounds unintentionally patronising. It is not surprising that he has no difficulty selling this style of wine to supermarkets, which are among his best clients. He used to be very keen on knocking on people's doors and ringing the bells of the local restaurants, but he does less of this nowadays, since his wines have become well established and popular.

He has no fewer than 50 hectares of Bergerac vineyard which does not qualify as Monbazillac, and it is of course from there that he derives the grapes for his very commercial red wines, and his dry white Bergerac too. There are two kinds of this: a pure sauvignon wine and another which has the usual mix of Bergerac grapes but with more sauvignon than most.

Martrenchard's grandfather was a policeman, and it was his father who got the bug for wine-making. Jean-Pierre himself went to Blanquefort agricultural college and by 1986 he had become sufficiently established to win a hotly contested election for presidency of the Syndicat des Vins de la Région de Bergerac. He has a staff of fifteen to help him run his business-like and impressively modern *chais*.

In contrast to his mainstream operation, which is highly commercial, there is no trouble or expense spared on his 7 hectares of Monbazillac grapes. Jean-Pierre is convinced that in the larger wine-areas such as Bordeaux the notion of appellation will soon cease to have any importance: he believes that the future is with the smaller regions. Each property furthermore has its own character in his eyes, and the wine-maker's job is to extract the maximum advantage from his particular corner of the appellation. From his own vineyard he judges that he can make a wine more floral than Sauternes, which he therefore does not try to copy. He agrees with the lighter more fruity approach of the 'modern' Monbazillac makers, bottling his wines at something like 13 + 3. He is somewhat shy about discussing his techniques, and the sales literature does not indicate what may be the difference between his two *cuvées* of Monbazillac. All that can be said is that one is more rich and honeyed than the other.

There is nothing 'modern' about the Monbazillac which emerges from the cellars of Gilles Cros at **Clos Fontindoule (38)**, which is tucked away in a small valley just south of the Monbazillac ridge. It would be hard to imagine a more archetypal *vin liquoreux* than the deep golden-amber liquid which pours so generously from his pipette as he proudly displays his 1988 and 1976 vintages. Yes, these were the wines which he was offering for sale in the summer of 1993. The former was not yet all in bottle and even the 1976 had not been bottled for long – there were still some casks awaiting his attention.

Every great appellation seems to have its old ultra-traditional wine-maker, what the French often call the *personnage de l'appellation*. In Monbazillac this has to be Gilles Cros, whose family have made wine at Fontindoule since the time of Napoléon III. The name of the property derives partly from the large fountain hewn out of the rock which goes back to Celtic times: *'doule'* is said by Monsieur Cros to be a word for the kind of large cylindrical open *cuve*, of which he still has several examples dotted around his farm. Perhaps farm is not quite the right word, because he has no other crops: just a few cows to make the manure for the vineyards. No weedkillers or artificial fertilisers are ever allowed near the place.

His methods are of the simplest. The *encépagement* is traditional: 70% sémillon, 20% muscadelle and 10% sauvignon. The grapes are encouraged to grow as near to the ground as possible so as to maximise the chances of noble rot. He usually contents himself with only two *tries*. The harvesting has always been done by hand: Gilles Cros believes that those who harvest by machine always pick too early, so he is pleased that they have been outlawed now for Monbazillac, though this has pushed up the price of the average bottle considerably.

He has indulged in the luxury of an electronically controlled press, which saves him labour-costs, but otherwise the vinification operation is of the most basic, limited to the time-worn operations of racking, fining and filtering. No question of any new oak, but after about two years in the cement *cuves*, which themselves date back to before the Second World War, the wine is put into huge old barrels until he is minded to bottle the wine, never less than three years later. The design of his labels has remained unchanged since 1934, when the family started bottling its own wines.

His customers seem to consist exclusively of loyal private buyers and famous restaurants all over France and Switzerland. He does not let his wine anywhere near shops, though in years when he is not pleased with his output he may sell some *en vrac*.

A visit to taste Gilles Cros' wines is an occasion never to be forgotten. You will be treated to a variety of reminiscences: perhaps also to a commentary on modern morals or wine-making techniques. It is hard to know which of the latter he abominates the more. The young come in for a share of his criticism. 'When the apples need picking, they grow too high: the strawberries are too low, and, as for the grapes, that's much too much like hard work. *La philosophie de la vigne n'est pas la sienne.*' He is, however, obviously a much respected character himself for he was mayor of Monbazillac for some while. He told me how one day he received a phone call and a mysterious voice said, '*Vous allez recevoir une autorité: la Reine-Mère d'Angleterre.*' '*J'ai répondu: aucun problème.*' He said she was absolutely charming, which of course came as no surprise; moreover she seemed to enjoy her visit to Monbazillac as much as he did, and that too seems quite likely.

Gilles Cros will take you to his tasting-room-cum-office which is in an outhouse also housing some of his venerable barrels. You will be given an *incassable*, one of those unbreakable glass coffee-cups, themselves the shape of half a barrel, and into this humble receptacle will be poured Monsieur Cros' best wines. The shock of their quality is with me still: the 1988 was nectar enough, but the 1976 was, and will be for many years, fantastic. There are no apologies here to modern taste: Monsieur Cros obviously believes in playing the Monbazillac card for all it is worth. The most astonishing wine of all, though, was the 1990 which he said was the finest he had ever made. The grapes were brought in at 28°: the texture of this young wine in the mouth was quite extraordinary, viscous almost to the point of being oily, incredibly rich in sugar and alcohol, not yet married to the incredible fruit which was the characteristic of that great year. This wine will not be bottled until 1996 at the earliest.

Gilles Cros is no longer a young man but he has no thought of retiring, at least not until his 1990 is safely in bottle. He has a son who works the vineyards with him who will take over in due course. It will be very good news for all Monbazillac lovers if the son continues the traditions of his father and is able to maintain the enormously high quality of the wines of Fontindoule.

SAUSSIGNAC

The vineyards of Saussignac link Monbazillac to the east with Entre-deux-Mers to the west without a break. Saussignac is the most recent (1982) of the Bergerac inner appellations, but has remained small, even

though it covers five communes: Saussignac, Razac-de-Saussignac, Gageac, Monestier and Rouillac. The annual production averages less than 1000 hectolitres.

The name Saussignac may be applied only to a *vin moelleux*, required to reach 12° alcohol and to have at least 18 grams per litre of residual sugar. There is also an upper limit on the sugar content, which strictly means that the wine is not supposed to be *liquoreux* in the Monbazillac sense, though a handful of producers are experimenting on those lines under a special dispensation from the authorities.

Dry white wines and all red wines from the area must be declared as Bergerac. Because the rules for sweet Saussignac and Bergerac are broadly similar, a great deal of sweet white which is made within the appellation is declared as Bergerac Moelleux and not Saussignac. Many growers have not been persuaded to take the risk of applying a little-known name to an already familiar style of wine.

There are only a dozen or so growers who today declare Saussignac as such. Now that Monsieur Amaury de Madaillan has joined the Le Fleix co-opérative, **Château Court-les-Mûts (3)** is the largest independent Saussignac vineyard by far, and one of the best in Bergerac. Pierre-Jean Sadoux has expanded the property from 23 to 56 hectares, largely by planting sauvignon to make a dry white wine, and even here the annual production of sweet Saussignac barely reaches 100 hectolitres, even in a good year. Nevertheless much of the credit for the establishment of the appellation must go to him; he was the first president of the Saussignac *syndicat* of growers.

Court-les-Mûts enjoyed a fine reputation in Féret's day, and he wrote that the property had shown singular resistance to the phylloxera. In fact at the beginning of this century, it was still entirely planted with 40 hectares of ungrafted vines. When Monsieur Sadoux's father bought it on his return from Algeria in 1960, it was in a run-down state, but now it is one of the show-places of the area, a point of reference for all Bergerac-fans, including those who like their red wines gently oaked.

Sadoux Senior started with only 14 hectares, and the present vineyard has been assembled patiently over thirty years. Pierre-Jean, his son, is a highly qualified oenologist and has been a consultant to local growers. In 1986 he was joined by another oenologist, Henry Mondié. Stainless-steel *cuves* were installed, and new oak experimented with.

The small amount of Saussignac *moelleux* is made entirely from sémillon grapes and vinified at 20°. It has an underlying almondy flavour, and with age develops hints of apricot, walnuts and honey. Monsieur Sadoux also makes a little sparkling wine by the *méthode champenoise*. It is mostly from ugni blanc, the Armagnac grape.

Some of the most interesting local growers are those who are making a *liquoreux* from botrytised grapes in the style of Monbazillac. Gérard Cuisset at **Château les Miaudoux (9)** first tried this in 1990 and made a truly magnificent wine. Sadly there is none left because Cuisset undersold it: discerning enthusiasts realised they were on to a good thing and snapped up the stock. After that wonderful vintage, Gérard was able to make only eleven *barriques* in 1991 and six in 1992. He managed only one *trie* in 1992, because the rains came to ruin the remaining grapes. In poor years like that, he is lucky to achieve a yield of 5 hectolitres to the hectare. In 1992 it took fifteen people three days to pick the grapes for his 6 *barriques* (fewer than two thousand bottles), so the resulting wine has to be fairly expensive. I asked Gérard what he lived on, and he reminded me that he had 18 hectares of vines overall, so he is able to make a fair quantity of red and dry white wine as well as his beloved *liquoreux*. He also has 8 hectares of plum-trees from which he makes prunes.

For the sweet wine, Gérard Cuisset presses the grapes direct into his oak *barriques*. The barrels he bought for his first effort in 1990 were used again for the 1991 and 1992. Being an optimist, he has bought a few new casks for his 1993, but he may well have put them aside for his 1994 or even his 1995, which will no doubt be very fine. The wine is fermented at low temperature for about a month, until it has developed about 14° alcohol which Gérard regards as an optimum. His problem is with the residual sugar, because the rules of the appellation allow only 3.5°, whereas he has about 7°, even in a bad year like 1992. There is no difficulty as long as he gets clearance from the authorities in advance, but that is no way to make wine in the long term. It also upsets other local growers who are keeping to the rule-book.

There are two English growers at Saussignac making wine like Gérard Cuisset. More correctly, one and a half, because Richard Doughty is half-English, half-French. He trained as a geologist and spent some years in different parts of the world applying his acquired skills before deciding that he did not find them entirely fulfilling. So he went to La Tour Blanche which, as well as being a famous Sauternes château is also the only specialist training-ground for would-be makers of *vins liquoreux*. There Richard was lucky enough to find an inspirational teacher, who persuaded him that he must become a wine-maker. Richard could not afford to buy in Bordeaux, so he looked around and decided that Bergerac was being undersold, under-exploited and might just suit his pocket as well as his new-found training. He bought his Saussignac vineyard, which he has re-named **Domaine de Richard (11)**, in 1988.

He got off to a disastrous start. In his first vintage, 1989, there was a violent hailstorm on 8 July which destroyed three-quarters of his crop. The vines, however, staged a recovery and were rich in sugar, so he decided to make all his wine that year in the sweet Saussignac style.

Since then he has made a little dry wine, and has 5 hectares of red wine grapes, but the bulk of his energies and enthusiasm go into his *liquoreux*. He disagrees with the idea that you set out to make a dry wine, and then, if conditions permit, switch into sweet wine. He holds that you have to make this decision in advance and gamble on the weather. It is a question of regular and rigorous pruning, and *vendanges vertes*: the picking in July of enough unripe grapes to ensure that those remaining can develop the required concentration and sugar. You will be too late to do all this if you wait to see what the autumn weather is like. On the other hand, if it lets you down, you end up with a lot of very expensively made dry white Bergerac.

Richard Doughty was quite pleased with his first sweet wine in 1989, but it was nothing like as good as his 1990. Even so, he hands the prize for that year to Gérard Cuisset, about whose 1990 he waxes ecstatically. On the other hand he thought that his own 1991 was every bit as good as Gérard's, even though it did not have the depth of the earlier and greater year.

Richard strikes one as a particularly British kind of eccentric. It is easy to imagine him as a model-railway buff or as a radio ham, and he could be both. He has total dedication. Probably he does not suffer fools or ignorant customers gladly, but his single-minded vision should enable him to profit from the new identity of Saussignac which he is a part of creating. It is a high-risk business: if the likes of Cuisset and he are to succeed they need to expand production to make the product better known, and with the current ban on new planting, that would mean uprooting existing vines, and turning from the production of bread-and-butter red and dry whites into the chancy business of gambling on the noble rot. Perhaps 1995 will recoup the lost bets on 1992, 1993 and 1994

Doughty is generous as well as determined. He has helped an English newcomer who has just bought a few hectares nearby: Patricia Atkinson at **Clos d'Yvigne (12)** is now making good wines of all styles, after setbacks which would have defeated most people. Perhaps, though, in the long run the success or otherwise of these pioneers may depend on whether they are able to secure a second appellation – Premières Côtes de Saussignac – so as to dispense with dependence on the goodwill of the authorities in giving annual *dérogations*. Richard Doughty and his friends give the lie to the views of those who, only a few years ago, were inclined to write off Saussignac as an appellation without a future. The new Saussignac producers have youth and time on their side, as well as talent and boundless enthusiasm: but there is still a long way to go.

ROSETTE

Rosette and Cinderella: two charming names to describe the tiniest of the Bergerac appellations. Rosette is a wine to be drunk young, before it becomes an ugly sister. It is medium-sweet and packs more punch than the purity of its name might suggest, at least 13° alcohol. But it is not rosé, and therein lies the confusion which may have bedevilled its success. The wine does not have, nor did it ever have, a pinkish character. It is called Rosette because that is the name of a tiny village, hidden away in the gentle hills behind Bergerac. Here, shielding the town from the north, is an amphitheatre of vineyards which were once the centre of Bergerac production.

Today nearly all the wines hereabouts are sold as Bergerac, and yet the wines of Rosette have a character which sets them apart. Madame Colette Bourgès is one of only six regular makers of wine declared under this almost forgotten appellation. She has her home and 6 acres of Pécharmant vines in the suburbs of the town of Bergerac, but, over to the west of the town, past the back of the railway station and up into the hills, she has 2 hectares of sémillon, from which she makes Rosette. The vineyards were replanted by her great-grandfather after the phylloxera, but because her own father did not enjoy good health he had to cut back on his activities, and it was the Rosette vineyards that had to go. Colette took over the family properties in 1985, and at once set about serious studies at the Lycée Agricole at Monbazillac. She decided that, when conditions permitted, she would re-create her lost Rosette vineyards. Today she calls the wine **Clos Romain (1)**, after her son.

The vines straddle the crest of a hill which has more clay in its soil than her other vineyards at Pécharmant. The land will one day be planted with nothing but sémillon, when Colette gets round to digging up some old red wine grape-varieties from which she makes a little red Bergerac for sale *en négoce*.

Colette Bourgès does not wait for botrytis, but she does pick her sémillon as late as the weather allows. The grapes are given a cold fermentation, and when the alcohol gets to about 13$\frac{1}{2}$° she stops it. I think she slightly overdid the sulphur in her first vintages, and the later years I tasted showed no trace of it. The wine looks innocuous enough, very pale in colour and fresh and summery on the nose. It is *moelleux* rather than sweet, very refreshing and perfect as an apéritif wine, but you will not need too much of it. Colette cannot understand why those local growers who are allowed to do not sell their wine as Rosette, for she believes it was the forerunner of Monbazillac. After the Hundred Years' War, the monks of the region became tax-exiles when the French Crown exacted heavy dues from the Church to rebuild the French state. They moved to the Protestant south bank and took their wine-making skills with them, and Monbazillac has never looked back. After driving me to see her Rosette vines, Colette kindly piloted me to the vineyards of her friends and fellow Rosette-producers, the brothers Bernad at the **Château Puypézat-Rosette (2)**. I was relieved that Colette led the way, because Puypézat is really in the back of beyond, lost among the woods, even though these hills are gradually being swallowed up by the builders of suburban *pavillons* for the bourgeois of Bergerac.

Jean-Jacques and Jean-Pierre Bernad are twins: the one outward-going, business-like and straight-to-the-point; the other calm and quiet. But their partnership works well if the wine from their 11 hectares of Rosette is anything to go by. They, together with Colette, are responsible for over half of the modern production of Rosette. This may not be much in total terms, but it does explain their command of this very special, almost private production.

Their father bought this estate after leaving Algeria in 1961, but it is his two sons who deserve the credit for having put Rosette back on the map. In 1981 no grower declared any wine at all under the Rosette appellation, but the following year the Bernads did, rather to the consternation of the wine authorities who were reluctant to accept a declaration from only one grower. The hint was dropped that they had better persuade some others to join them, so they got together with Colette Bourgès and between them saved the appellation from extinction. Jean-Jacques thinks that his neighbours are crazy to spurn their very own appellation but he is the first to admit that it is no skin off his nose. '*Ils resteront dans les mêmes sabots,*' he says of them. The Bernads insist on authenticity: no machines are allowed in the vineyards, all fertiliser is organic and weedkillers are banned. They are covert biological growers in fact. They also spurn the modern light-weight glass bottles, preferring the more expensive old-fashioned thick dark green ones. Their vinification is traditional, they use neither new nor old wood and the wine is bottled six months after the vintage. They surprised me by disclaiming the use of caramel for colouring, as if I might have thought that they would stoop so low. The implication was that others were not so fussy.

Unlike Colette Bourgès, they add a little muscadelle to their Rosette, but will not hear of using sauvignon, again implying that others may do so. It is not illegal, just not authentic. Their wine is deeper in colour than Colette's, but Jean-Jacques said that it held its colour well with age.

Rosette is more than a curiosity. It has a character of wild flowers and fresh hay which you do not always find in other Bergerac *moelleux*. It would be a great pity if Rosette got submerged in the larger Bergerac appellation, and I hope that its six evangelists will persuade others to help them spread the word.

MONTRAVEL

The appellation Montravel covers fifteen communes on the right bank of the Dordogne. They lie to the north of the main road, which runs westward along the valley from Ste-Foy-la-Grande to Castillon-la-Bataille. Montravel is divided into two mutually exclusive sub-areas, each of which is entitled to use the Montravel name, but they may not use the name of each other. One of these, called Haut-Montravel, occupies the hilly ground in parts of five communes, at Nastringues, Fougueyrolles and the higher areas of Port Ste-Foy, St-Antoine-de-Breuilh and Vélines. The other area, Côtes de Montravel, envelops

Haut-Montravel and extends into the hinterland to include Bonneville, Lamothe-Montravel, Montcart, Montpeyrou, Montazeau, Ponchapt, St-Michel-Montaigne, St Vivien and part of St Méard-de-Gurçon.

Each of these three appellations is restricted to white wine, so if you make wine in Montravel life is complicated. Your red wine can only be labelled Bergerac or Côtes de Bergerac; you may call your dry white wine Montravel Sec or Bergerac Sec according to choice, the technical requirements being for all practical purposes the same. But if you make sweet wine, you must declare it under the rules of either Côtes de Montravel or Haut-Montravel (depending which area your vines are in), otherwise the wine must be sold as Bergerac Moelleux.

Côtes de Montravel is a medium white wine. Though properly called a *moelleux*, it is not as sweet as most wines of that style. Haut-Montravel on the other hand is a fully *liquoreux* wine after the style of Monbazillac and the new sweet Saussignacs. Bergerac Moelleux is therefore not always an appropriate label for either of the Montravel sweet wines.

It is no surprise, therefore, that many growers have decided to avoid the complications of the appellation rules, and, in the interests of more effective marketing, limited themselves to the simple Bergerac titles. Even so, any wine bearing the Montravel name, in whatever style, is likely to be better than its Bergerac counterpart, because the producers who use the inner appellation tend to apply it to their better *cuvées*. Dry Montravel often has a crispness that is sometimes lacking in the general run of dry Bergerac, and growers do not adopt the inner appellations unless confident that they can justify the implied superiority. Thus, in bad years, a grower who would normally declare his wine as Montravel is more likely to declare under Bergerac instead.

Much of the wine in the Montravel area is red, selling as Bergerac. This was not always so: historically the reputation of Montravel rested on its sweet wines. As in Bergerac generally, the years following the Second World War saw a rapid growth in red wine production, and an equally marked switch away from the sweeter style of white towards dry wine. The relative productions of the immediate post-war years compared with those of modern times illustrate this vividly:

	1946/8	1991
Montravel	22,400 hl	17,000
Côtes de Montravel	34,330	2,942
Haut-Montravel	20,665	630

Much of the apparent drop in total production is accounted for by the switch to red Bergerac and the use of the Bergerac name for the white wines, but the collapse of the demand for the sweeter Montravels is dramatic.

Monbazillac has already been through this patch and come out the other side. Perhaps Montravel has just turned the corner too. Certainly there are some devoted enthusiasts who are anxious to restore it to its former glory. Jean-Claude Banizette at **Domaine de Libarde (15)**, for example, still has bottles of the 1947 vintage to serve as a model of what Haut-Montravel ought to be, even if the ancestral 1929 is now no longer more than a folk-memory: for that is how long these old wines last. His family made their first vintage in the village of Nastringues in 1903 and Jean-Claude takes a pride in the part he has played in reviving the old traditions. For four years he was president of the Syndicat Viticole de Montravel, and was active in persuading a number of local growers to exchange some of their land with each other in order to rationalise their holdings. The effect of the inheritance laws is all too often to divide up vineyards into ever smaller and smaller parcels which make for inefficient working, as well as for lack of homogeneity in the style of the finished wine. It therefore makes sense for owners to swap parcels of vineyard with each other so as to produce larger single units, *dans un seul tenant* as they say.

Jean-Claude says that his *liquoreux* represents about a third of his output. It is also, in a good year, nearly one-half of all the Haut-Montravel made. In poor years, such as 1992, it does not aspire to being a real *vin doux*, only reaching 12° or so of alcohol, but his 1989 for example, which was his first effort in this style, is really rich. His experience tells him that after about four years these wines stop developing, but take off again into a ripe old age after a few years' rest. His 1989 is waking up: the residual wood still shows, giving the wine a bouquet reminiscent of antique furniture, but this will go as the oak does its work, and in due course the wine will be very fine indeed.

While he waits for these sweet wines to develop, Jean-Claude Banizette has to live, and so he makes a Montravel Sec as well as red Bergerac, and very good they both are. The white is unusually floral and crisp. He once experimented with *macération pelliculaire*, but his Belgian customers complained that the wine had lost its character, so he stopped doing it. Unusually he also vinifies the grape-varieties together, like some of the Monbazillac growers.

Jean-Claude has as a friend the *maître de chais* at Château Filhol in the Sauternes, who is able to supply him with second-hand barrels which he uses for his red wine: in good years he likes to give his Bergerac a six-month stint in wood which has already seen two wines. Otherwise he believes in only partial *égrappage* and as long a vinification as possible according to the vintage. Accordingly his red wines have real structure, and take longer to come round than the average Bergerac.

Jean-Claude Banizette's successor as president of the local *syndicat* is an oenologist called Daniel Hecquet, a well-known personality on the Bergerac scene. With impeccable academic credentials, he spent some time at Château Yquem before getting a job with the Chamber of Agriculture in the Loire valley. But his family came from Montravel, owning two vineyards today called **Château Calabre** and **Château Puy-Servain (7)**. He was therefore glad to come south again and become a consultant oenologist to a number of Bordeaux producers, then being offered the job of resident oenologist with the Comité Interprofessionel des Vignerons de la Région de Bergerac. In addition he is also retained as an adviser by about twenty local growers.

This was how he became associated with Guy-Jean Kreusch, a Luxembourger, who was looking to buy a vineyard in Pécharmant. Hecquet advised him on his choice of property, and since then they have become associated in a joint venture on the top of the downs at Montravel, where they have created a vineyard called **Domaine de Krevel (5)**. The name is an amalgam of 'Kreusch' and 'Montravel', and the wine is all *sec*. They started with 2 hectares in 1987, but it has now grown to 8, with 5000 plants per hectare 1¹/₂ metres apart. The yield is scrupulously controlled in plentiful years with *vendanges vertes*, and in August the surplus leaves are stripped to ensure maximum ripeness of the grapes. Picking is by hand, and sometimes there are two *tries*, which is unusual in the making of dry white wine. The grapes are rigorously sorted and de-stalked before a partial *macération pelliculaire* of the sauvignon and muscadelle grapes. The wine is fermented in new wood, of which a quarter is replaced each year. It stays in barrel for nine or ten months with frequent *batonnage*. Daniel Hecquet says this wine will keep for some years and is best appreciated without food. I tasted the 1991 and the 1992 both from the wood: I preferred the latter, even though it was a more difficult year, but both were wonderfully fruity and aromatic. The wood, though, was powerful, and it would have been interesting to taste an unoaked version of the same wine. Monsieur Hecquet might have thought such an idea heretical.

The wines which Daniel Hecquet markets as Château Calabre are unwooded, while those labelled from Château Puy-Servain are oaked. Of the former the dry white was indeed very dry, while its oaked counterpart had a great deal more body and *gras*. The wooded *liquoreux* from 1992 (13.5 + 6.5) is going to be very fine one day, and is a worthy ambassador for those trying to revive this style of wine. It is a pity that there were only fourteen casks of it made. The wooded red from 1991 was, however, disappointing, and I doubt whether it is ever going to come right. It was good, though, to taste the unoaked Calabre 1986, which was agreeably mature. In fact Hecquet apologised for its age: he seemed amazed when I told him that I had not yet even thought of looking at any of my 1986 claret. He appears to have no time for older wines, like many other growers who spend most of their lives in the company of very new wine.

Daniel Hecquet is at the forefront of a move to alter the rules for the Montravel appellation. The idea is to have three grades of white wine – *sec*, *moelleux* and *doux* – replacing the three existing appellations. At the same time, he would like to see created new appellations for red and rosé Montravel with the same legal requirements as red and pink Bergerac. The natural consequence of this would seem to be to encourage producers to abandon the Bergerac appellation altogether and develop a sharper image for Montravel. This is not a theme which is developed in the *syndicat*'s proposal to the authorities, but the concept would seem logical in view of the geographical position which Montravel enjoys, sandwiched between Bordeaux and Bergerac, while not quite having the style of either.

At **Château Laroque (32)**, in the hills above St-Antoine-de-Breuilh, the La Bardonnie family are the only fully biological wine-growers in Montravel that I have came across. At Libarde they use no chemicals at all except for Bordeaux Mixture and sulphur, both of which are accepted by biological practitioners as natural. They would prefer to tackle mildew with doses of sea-salt, but accept that salt does not do much for the implements. They would also like to avoid spraying the vines to avoid killing the ladybirds which are so effective in dealing with the red spiders. The La Bardonnies keep their own live-stock to provide the manure, which is the only fertiliser they permit and no weedkillers of any kind are used.

The Laroque vineyards were much more extensive at the time Féret was writing than today's 8 hectares, of which only $1^1/_2$ are given over to white grapes. During the intervening years the family were members of the Montravel co-opérative for forty-three years, but they left in 1987 because of their biological convictions. They like to make a sweet Haut-Montravel whenever the vintage conditions permit, but in bad years, there is just not enough sugar in the grapes, so they make a Montravel Sec which is flowery and delicate. Their 1991 *liquoreux* was properly honeyed and very elegant. They have no difficulty in selling their production to local buyers and to shops specialising in biological produce.

I make no apology for dwelling on the sweetest of the Montravel wines, because the other styles are available all over the Bergerac area. However, mention must be made of distinguished producers of the *moelleux* Côtes de Montravel style. Madame Cécile Mahler-Besse, for example, is not only part-owner of Château Palmer in Margaux, but also owns the **Château de Montaigne (19)** in Montravel. Though geographically precluded from making Haut-Montravel, the family is making an excellent white wine at the sweeter end of the range under the Côtes appellation. The château is also known to countless visitors as the home of the French philosopher of the same name.

Jean Itey de Peironnin is another grower whose property, the attractive eighteenth-century **Château La Raye (31)** at Vélines, has been in the family for centuries: here again the speciality is a Côtes de Montravel, although the red Bergerac too has won prizes. Jean-Marie Bertrand, who has two nearby properties – **Domaine de Golse** and **Château la Cabanelle (6)** – which have come to him from different sides of his family, also likes to make a sweeter style of wine when the year is right, but the production is small though excellent. Jean-Yves Reynou is another whose vines at **Domaine de Perreau (22)** are divided into two parcels: he makes a very high quality sweet wine from grapes grown at the top of his vineyard at Marot, where there are so many pebbles that only the vine will grow.

These growers on the Côtes also make excellent dry Montravel, but there are plenty whose only white is dry, though they make red Bergerac too. M. le Comte de Peyrelongue has 48 hectares at Fougueyrolles where the family used to make a sweet wine of high reputation, but the style is now dry to meet the market's demands. The wines from his **Château Péchaurieux (14)** are largely sold *en vrac*, but those which are bottled for sale under the château-label are excellent.

One of the largest of the Montravel properties is the **Domaine de Gouyat (2)**, where the Dubard brothers make wonderful red Bergerac (including an oaked version sold under the name of Château Laulerie), as well as a dry Montravel of good quality. Another wine of great repute is **Château de Masburel (10)** at Fougueyrolles, where Roland Barthoux, who bought it in 1979 at the age of only twenty-four, goes from strength to strength. Jacques Dubernet at the **Château des Berneries (13)** hedges his bets between Bergerac and Montravel Sec, with a large proportion (45%) of sauvignon in his vineyard, like the Guillemer brothers at **Château de Bloy (29)**, where the Montravel Sec is made entirely from sauvignon. Although sold as Bergerac *moelleux* and not as Côtes de Montravel, they make 100 hectolitres a year of sweeter wine as well as the rest of their range, which includes both qualities of red Bergerac.

Any complications surrounding the various appellations applicable to the wines of Montravel may perhaps be best resolved by a glance at the lists of growers on pages 182–4.

PÉCHARMANT

Xavier de Saint-Exupéry, the wine-maker at **Château de Tiregand (14)**, told me that the wines from Pécharmant had not always been exclusively red: his great-grandfather, the Comte de Panouse, who was famous among other things for having built the railway from Paris to Orléans, was already winning medals for the wine of Tiregand in 1894, but in those days much of the vineyard was given over to the making of Rosette. By 1956, the vineyard was making only white wine, from vines produced at Château Yquem, the Countess of Saint-Exupéry being related to the Lur-Saluces family, the owners of that property.

In Féret's day, the wines of Tiregand were made partly from vines grown on the high ground close to the present château and partly in a vineyard called La Terrasse. Féret said that the latter was the finest of all the Dordogne vineyards.

It is the red wines of Pécharmant which are famous today. The growers make almost no white wine to sell in any quantity, although at Tiregand they make a little in order to 'introduce' the red wines at tastings and on formal occasions. It can be called only Bergerac Sec – there is no such thing as white Pécharmant. The modern appellation is confined to red wine. It goes back to 1946, although growers had been using the name Pécharmant for years as a means of denoting a superior grade of Bergerac. Today, perhaps because of the ease of communication with the rest of France, and because the vineyards are within such easy reach of the centre of Bergerac, many Pécharmant vineyards belong to newcomers to the region: businessmen who want a change of enterprise, local professional people who would like to identify themselves more closely with their *terroir*, or even wine-lovers from abroad anxious to try their hands at producing as well as consuming.

All of this must make the Saint-Exupérys, with their long tradition in the region, smile. One wonders whether they welcome this diverse competition, or whether they are perhaps nervous of it. Perhaps both, because it no doubt serves to concentrate their minds wonderfully and to make sure that they stay at the front of the field. Nothing is harder in any competition than leading from the front. For the Saint-Exupérys it must be harder than most, for they have the prestige of one of France's leading families and the beauty of an incomparable estate to uphold.

The *chais* at Tiregand are all that are left, apart from the bread-oven, of the 'old' château, a building which is some distance away from the present family home. The cellars are themselves a beautiful building, worth a visit on their own account, set in the middle of the elegant Tiregand park, which houses some magnificent rare centenarian trees. At one end of the *chais* is a window which was once a doorway giving access to and from the 'old' château. The wines of Tiregand can always be tasted here during normal visiting hours, and you can also buy some of Madame's delicious pâtés to take away with a bottle for your picnic. Her *foie gras* is worthy of the château's best wine.

After the 1956 frosts, the family had to make a fundamental choice: either to sell their grapes to the co-opérative in Bergerac from then onwards, or to invest the large sums required to reconstitute the vineyard. Only 4 hectares of vines had survived, and in 1961 the château was producing only 117 hectolitres of wine. Possibly because Xavier de Saint-Exupéry had already decided to train as an agricultural engineer and take a course in oenology at Bordeaux, the family chose the path of replanting; but this time, because Pécharmant had by then its own appellation, entirely in red wine grapes.

There are now 31 hectares in production, which makes Tiregand the largest as well as the oldest-established and best-known Pécharmant producer. Because of Xavier's training in agriculture, the château takes particular care of the soil: no artificial fertilisers are used, only the manure from their own animals, and every few years the ground is analysed and if necessary a corrective manuring is carried out to ensure perfect balance.

The vineyard is planted with 50% merlot, 25% cabernet franc and 25% cabernet sauvignon, a normal *encépagement* for Pécharmant as well as Bergerac generally. From the younger grapes, only recently replanted on the old Terrasse site so highly praised by Féret, they make a wine which is called Clos de la Montalbanie, lightish in weight and not for long keeping. As early as three years after the vintage it can start to take on a little orange colour and a hint of farmyard on the nose, but the wine is very agreeable and easy to drink.

For the main château-wine the grapes are entirely de-stalked and given a long *cuvaison* of three weeks or so, the merlot perhaps a little less than the cabernets. Xavier favours enamelled stainless steel, because it can be used for maturing the wine as well as making it. He is short of space in the *chais*, so he will gradually replace the few fibre-glass *cuves* which are not dual-purpose.

The wine is very lightly oaked: the best *cuves* only are matured in new casks, of which one-sixth are replaced every year. The barrels come from various makers, because, as Xavier says, you average out eccentricities of cooperage that way. The wines of Tiregand are for keeping, although some say that they mature more quickly than they used to. One wonders whether this is because of or in spite of the new wood.

The Pécharmant appellation covers the communes of Lembras, Creysse, St-Sauveur and the town of Bergerac itself. Colette Bourgès, our Rosette-maker, has a magnificent panoramic view of the whole town from the top of her 6-hectare vineyard, just up the hill from the industrial estate. It is called **Clos les Côtes (3)** and is planted with the standard *encépagement* enriched with a little malbec. The slopes are steep enough to need terracing, so Madame Bourgès weeds each row only in alternate years, to allow the soil a chance to compact itself without disturbance. This helps to prevent erosion and firms up the ground to allow small tractors to pass between the rows of vines. Machine-picking would be possible, but she prefers to pick by hand.

The exposition is magnificent, due south, looking over to the hill of Monbazillac, so the sun can reach every bunch of grapes without Colette having to strip away any of the leaves. She does not de-stalk her grapes, and she gives each variety a separate three-week *cuvaison*. It is surprising that her wine is as round and soft as it is, by no means aggressively tannic. She does not believe in new wood – just a year's *élevage* in enamelled concrete before bottling. Her 1990 won a gold medal in Paris in 1992: it is a very handsome wine to look at, deepish in colour but entirely bright. The nose is rich with blackcurrants and prunes, the flavour deep with fruit and the finish long.

A little further along the ridge, but still within walking-distance of the centre of town (just) is the vineyard called **La Métairie (10)**, roughly the same size as Mme Bourgès'. The brain behind this vineyard is the Man from Montravel, Daniel Hecquet; the money behind it that of Guy-Jean Kreusch and a few other enlightened investors determined to practise traditional methods of wine-making. They bought the estate on Hecquet's recommendation in 1984 and started with only 3¹/₂ hectares, planted with the usual mix of grapes. Since then they have planted 3 more hectares entirely with merlot at a density of no less than 6500 plants to the hectare, in rows 1.5 metres apart. From these young grapes they make a wine which is entitled to appellation, but which is called Puy de Grave. Time will tell whether Hecquet recommends the absorption of this new parcel into the mainstream wine. If he does, the resulting wine will be 80% merlot, unusually high for the area, unless the vineyard decides to produce two or more *cuvées*.

Wine-making at La Métairie is traditional. All picking is done by hand, the grapes are all de-stalked and they are vinified for up to four weeks. The *élevage*, however, is more modern. Hecquet is, as noted at his own property in Montravel, an enthusiast for new wood, this time barrels that have already been used to make one wine. The grapes are totally de-stalked and the alcoholic fermentation is anything up to four weeks. The wine spends one year in barrel after the malolactic fermentation is over.

The wine from the older vines is one of the very best of all Pécharmants, some say the best of all. Three years after the vintage, I found little trace of oak left in the 1990, though it will not be at its best until 1998 or so. It was loaded with fruit, cherries and plums dominating both bouquet and flavour. This is a very big wine, with a steely structure typical of the appellation at its best.

Not all the Pécharmant vineyards are in a suburban location. **Château Champarel (9)** is relatively remote, almost at the end of a country road leading over the top of the hills into the next valley, the Caudau. The 6¹/₂ hectares belong to Madame Françoise Bouché who is married to a Bergerac dentist. Her decision to become a *vigneronne* was taken entirely on impulse – she had always loved wine, but had no family tradition in it and so is largely self-taught. Madame Bouché wisely started out as a member of the co-opérative when she bought Champarel in 1970, but left it in 1974 to pursue what she saw as the only way forward. She modestly says that any improvements she has made have been as a result of her own experience, for which she has paid. She criticises colleagues for their reluctance to change their ways.

Madame Bouché has no plans to expand her vineyard, even if she was allowed to plant more vines, which at present she is not. She believes that 6¹/₂ hectares is as much as she can manage without losing the total control which she insists on having over the operation. Her dentist-husband helps when he can: when he puts away his drill for the weekend, it is only to pick up his pruning-knife. They employ a permanent vineyard worker so as to enable them to concentrate on the vinification and the *élevage*.

The Bouchés are builders as well as wine-makers. After creating for themselves out of the old farm-buildings a lovely home in the Périgord style, they have constructed a huge underground *chais* below the vineyard, which is on higher ground up the hillside. When I told her it reminded me of Château Ausone in St Emilion, she smiled ruefully and said that at Ausone the cellars were natural, whereas at Champarel they had cost a great deal of money.

Her vineyard is half merlot and half cabernet sauvignon. The vinification is not unusual, but the wine is given a year in wood, one-third of which is renewed every year. In difficult years, she shortens the period in oak. For example, it was not evident in her 1991 two years after the vintage: the wine, though perfumed and with good acidity, is not surprisingly less attractive than her 1990, which was a deep garnet colour, with a spicy bouquet, excellent attack and plenty of body. The finish was already long, and in a few years this wine will be outstanding. Her 1989 was every bit as good, which is unusual because most Bergerac-growers I have met rate their 1990 superior. 1992 was generally a poor year, but Champarel turned in a very good wine.

On the other side of the small country-road from Champarel is the much larger **Domaine du Haut-Pécharmant (11)**, belonging to the Roches family. With its 23 hectares this vineyard is second in size only to Tiregand. Michel Roches used to be a tobacco-grower, but in 1982 came back home to help his mother who had been nursing the family vineyards since the death of her husband in 1973. She had started to concentrate on the sale of wine in bottle; today nearly all the wine from Haut-Pécharmant is sold in this way. Since his return, Michel has launched a programme which has included the building of a new *chais* and the purchase of new oak casks. Roches is bent on experiment: he has tried for example a special Cuvée Veuve Roches from 70% cabernet franc, perhaps inspired by Daniel Hecquet, his consultant oenologist. Haut-Pécharmant has to be on anyone's short-list for this appellation. Some of its wine is bottled and sold by Château La Borderie in Monbazillac under the name Lentilhac, as already noted on page 151.

Through the woods and down the hill to the north you come to the **Domaine des Bertranoux (7)**, the passion of Guy Pécou who is the main Ford dealer in Bergerac. '*Chez moi*,' he says, '*le garage c'est le fils, le vignoble c'est la fille*,' for he and his wife have no children. He adds that for him the vineyard is a leisure-substitute since he believes neither in holidays nor television. Pécou bought Bertranoux in 1973 and was determined that he was going to make one of the best of all Pécharmants. Sheer quality of product was the only way in which other growers would take a man from the motor-trade seriously. He prides himself on his attention to detail – for example he prefers to have short corks, spending the money saved on the best quality material. He uses the old-fashioned heavy glass bottles in preference to the modern lightweight ones. His stainless-steel *cuves* were specially made to fit the low ceilings of his *chais*. His oak *barriques* are new every year, and he does not hesitate to de-classify his wine, as he did partly in 1991, if it is not up to standard. Strict control of the yield from the vines by *vendanges vertes*, harvesting by hand, long *cuvaisons* and more than a year's *élevage* in wood are matters of course. It is small wonder that the resulting wine is the most expensive of the Pécharmants which I managed to price. Pécou's 1990 is a wonderfully deep old-fashioned wine, with aromas of truffle and the farmyard. It promises to be a long keeper and has a class about it which reminds you of a Bordeaux *cru classé*, but 45 francs a bottle ex-cellars is not exactly giving the wine away.

Madame Best at **Château de Biran (15)** is more modest in her ambitions, but no less successful in her achievement. Her property is at the eastern-most extremity of the appellation, on the high ground between the villages of Creysse and Mouleydier. She and her husband, now retired from an important job with L'Oréal, the cosmetics business, bought Le Biran in 1970. Originally built as a chartreuse-style single-storey country home, it had been added to at the turn of the century, and Madame Best is pleased that the virginia creeper has covered up some of the less attractive features of the new extension. This is a manageable and welcoming country home – with 10 hectares of vines. From the terrace behind the house the views are magnificent towards the south.

The once-flourishing vineyard had fallen into neglect in the hands of previous owners, but Madame Best set about replanting it in 1976, though it was not until 1990 that she made her first wine for sale to the public. The grape-varieties divide 40% merlot, 30% each of the cabernets. Madame Best says she may plant a little malbec later. There are three quite distinct *clos*, each of which is named after one of her children, Grégoire, Roxanne and Damien.

François is her full-time wine-maker, virtually 100% green in his attitude to weedkillers, fertilisers and the use of chemicals generally. Above all he will not hear of machine-picking. The vinification is traditional, with total *égrappage*, two to three weeks' vinification in stainless steel: the *élevage* though is in new wood, one-half to one-third of which is renewed every year: most of the barrels come from Séguin-Moreau in Cognac.

Madame Best's business connections no doubt helped her to an introduction to the London market, as well as to prestigious outlets in Paris. Other customers include distinguished restaurateurs and private buyers. All her wine is sold in bottle. She had already sold out her 1990 when I visited her, but her 1991 was close to be being mature, pale at the rim of the glass. The nose was smoky with hints of liquorice, and on the palate the touch of iron which underpins the soil of this area was beautifully balanced by prunes and caramel. This is obviously a vineyard to watch, catching up fast on the best of the established properties. Proof lies in the quality of the notoriously wet 1992 vintage.

The great characteristic of Pécharmant is that there seem to be no second-rate wines made there, so any kind of selection becomes difficult, even invidious. Pécharmant clearly has a head-start in front of all other Bergerac reds, and it seems that those who are now making the finest examples are set to keep things that way.

Finally a brief word about the co-opératives which I have not so far specifically commented on: they form an important part of the total Bergerac production.

The Cave called Producta is a marketing rather than wine-making organisation. Unidor is not a producer either: it is the co-opératives' own co-opérative, handling all the bottling of Bergerac co-opérative wines. The only other Cave on the left bank of the river, apart from the

Cave at Monbazillac, is the **Cave de Sigoulès (11)**. Sigoulès is a small country town just outside the Monbazillac appellation. At a recent count there were over three hundred members, many making wine outside the inner appellation areas and thus entitled only to call their produce Bergerac. The main production at Sigoulès is therefore Bergerac Sec and Bergerac Rouge, with a good deal of Bergerac Moelleux as well.

Founded in 1938, it can today hold 10,000 hectolitres of wine in stock while the total annual production is nearly 30,000 hectolitres. In addition to the AOC wines of Bergerac they also make a fair quantity of *Vin de pays de la Dordogne*, being either de-classified Bergerac or wine which does not for one reason or another qualify for AOC, for example if it is made from grape-varieties which are not permitted for the appellation. The equipment is of the latest, including rotating *cuves* for the red wines and efficient temperature control to ensure a slow fermentation of the white. The present director is Philippe Deschard whose aim is to establish a separate identity for Bergerac and to free it from its Bordeaux strings. In winemaking terms this means producing a range of wines which are less tannic, quicker-maturing and more supple than traditional Bergerac, including a dozen or so wines from individual properties. The Cave at Sigoulès is today the biggest single producer of wines in the Bergerac region, and has a dominant position in the market for the basic Bergerac appellations.

Linked with the Cave at Sigoulès is the co-opérative at Montravel which produces and markets a very varied range of wines: its members come from properties of every description within the equally varied Montravel area. There are two red Bergeracs, the better of which is called Haut-Branac: there is also a Montravel *sec* but perhaps most interesting is the Côtes de Montravel marketed as Moulin de Sindi.

Rather better wine is made at the Cave at **Le Fleix (4)**, though it is smaller. Mention has already been made of the fact that Amaury de Madaillan at Château Perrou now sends all his grapes to Le Fleix, and this must represent a sizeable proportion of the Cave's turnover because Monsieur de Madaillan owns or farms no fewer than 100 hectares. Starting in 1940 as an organisation dedicated mainly to making ordinary wine from grapes no longer entitled to appellation, the Cave has pursued a policy of insisting only on the best raw materials.

In the north-western corner of the appellation are the **Cave du Vignoble Gursonnais** (B) and the much smaller **Cave des Deux Vignobles** (A). These deal exclusively in the basic levels of Bergerac production in these outlying areas. Much more interesting is the **Cave Co-opérative de Bergerac (1)** itself: apart from Bergerac Sec and Rouge, this Cave is responsible for no fewer than 2000 hectolitres of Pécharmant annually, just about a quarter of the total production (see Pécharmant).

There follow details of growers making wines within the inner appellations, most of whom also make basic red and dry white Bergerac. This chapter concludes with a list of the largest growers who do not make anything except either or both of these, and whose wines are likely to be found in shops or restaurants locally.

PRODUCERS

Monbazillac

20 *CAVE CO-OPERATIVE DE MONBAZILLAC, 24240 Monbazillac. Tel: 53-57-06-38.

11. *CAVE DE SIGOULES, 24240 Sigoulès. Tel: 53-58-40-18.

7. CAVE PRODUCTA, BP 193, 24100 St. Laurent-les-Vignes. Tel: 53-57-40-44.

17. *Christian Roche, **L'Ancienne Cure**, 24560 Colombier. Tel: 53-58-27-90.

41. Christian Monbouché et Michel Simon, **Domaine de la Barde-Haute**, 24240 Rouffignac-de-Sigoulès. Tel: 53-58-43-19 See also **Château des Saurtes**

55. *Gérard Alexis, **Château Barouillet**, 24240 Pomport. Tel: 53-58-42-20.

21. *M. et Mme Labasse-Gazzini, **Château le Barradis**, 24240é Monbazillac. Tel ; 53-58-30-01. (Biological producer).

68. M. et Mme Dornic, **Château Barrière**, 24240 Pomport. Tel: 53-58-43-91.

51.**Comte Laurent de Bosredon, **Château de Belingard-Chayne**, 24240 Pomport. Tel: 53-58-28-03.

19. *Gérard Lajonie, **Château Bellevue**, 24240 Monbazillac. Tel: 53-57-17-96.

66. *Michel Royère-Blanchard, **Clos Bellevue**, 24240 Flaujac. Tel: 53-58-40-23.

13. Marléne et Alain Mayet, **Le Bois de Pourquié**, 24560 Conne-de-Labarde. Tel: 53-58-30-61.

22. *Armand Vidal, **Château la Borderie**, 24240 Monbazillac. Tel: 53-57-00-36.

108. M. Bourdil, **Château de Bouan**, 24520 St. Nexans. Tel: 53-58-32-82.

52. Maxime Dumonteil, **Domaine de Boyer**, 24240 Pomport. Tel: 53-58-43-90.

109. M. Geneste, **Les Brandines**, 24520 St. Nexans. Tel: 53-58-31-65.

2. Jacky Mélet, **Clos des Cabannes**, 24100 St. Laurent-les- Vignes. Tel: 53-57-35-53.

28. Paul Yourassovski, **Domaine de Cabaroque**, 24240 Monbazaillac. Tel: 53-58-34-48.

43. Madame Lacoste, **Château Caillavel**, 24240 Pomport. Tel: 53-58-43-30.

42. Pierre Eymery, **Château le Caillou**, 24240 Rouffignac-de- Sigoulès. Tel: 53-58-43-03/

110. Dominique Jourdas, **Domaine les Cailloux**, 24240 Pomport Tel: 53-27-86-26.

69. Jacques Couture, **Clos du Casse de la Croux**, 24240 Monbazillac. Tel: 53-58-33-73.

70. Jean-Pierre Turquaud, **Clos le Casteleau**, 24240 Colombier. Tel: 53-58-34-39.

56. Denis Dupas, **Domaine de Chantalouette**, 24240 Pomport. Tel: 53-58-42-36.

71. Mme Lucie Beigner, **Château le Chrisly**, 24240 Pomport. Tel: 53-58-42-35.

63. Franz Rudolf Neufling, **Le Clou**, 24240 Pomport. Tel: 53-24-02-21.

65. Gilbert Jean-Régis, **Château Combe des Bois**, see Ch. de Peytirat no. 65.

72 Robert Alexis, **Domaine de Combet**, 24240 Monbazillac. Tel: 53-58-34-21.

8. Eliane Bataille, **Domaine de Conty**, 24100 Bergerac. Tel: 53-57-30-61.

73. Bernard Sergenton, **Domaine des Doris**, 24100 St. Laurent - des-Vignes. Tel: 53-57-47-28.

44. *François Gérardin, **Château le Fagé**, 24240 Pomport. Tel: 53-55-62-25.

74. Serge Lagarde, **Domaine de Foncalpre**, 24240 Pomport. Tel: 53-55-42-32.

75. Dominique Tremblet, **Château la Foncalpre**, 24100 St. Laurent-des-Vignes. Tel: 53-57-32-38.

76. Paul Chassagne, **Clos la Fonnestalve**, 24240 Pomport. Tel: 53-55-62-25.

38. *Gilles Cros, **Clos Fontindoule**, 24240 Monbazillac. Tel: 53-58-30-36.

45. *Christiane Alary, **Château Fontpudière**, 24240 Pomport. Tel: 53-57-47-27.

77. M.P.Violet Quemin, **Château de la Fonvieille**, 24240 Monbazillac. Tel: 53-58-30-07.

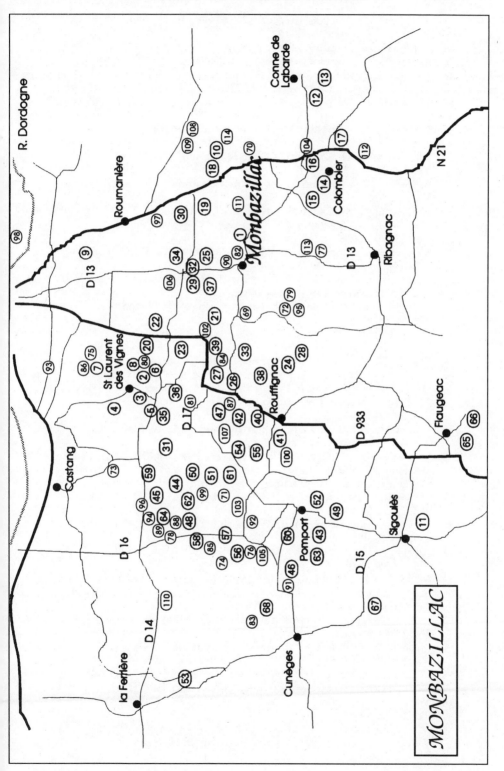

26. Michèle et Jean-Claude Barès, **Clos les Forêts,** Bouffevent, 24240 Monbazillac. Tel: 53-58-37-32.
54. Nadine Fauche, **Gaffou**, 24240 Pomport. Tel: 53-58-42-17.
78. Pierre Vignet, **Château la Gamade**, 24240 Pomport. Tel: 53-58-42-40.
46. *Georges Pelletant, **Château la Gironie**, 24240 Pomport. Tel: 53-58-42-09.
47. *Albert Monbouché, **Château Grand Chemin Bélingard**, 24240 Pomport. Tel: 53-58-30-57.
35. **Château Grand Conseil**, see Domaine de Theulet et Marsalet, no. 35.
 5 P. et J-P. Nadal, **Château Grand Marsalet**, 24100 St-Laurent-les-Vignes. Tel: 53-57-30-59
79. *Thierry Despres, **Château la Grande Maison**, 24240 Monbazillac. Tel: 53-58-26-17.
80. A. Cathal et Fils, **Domaine des Grands Champs**, 24100 St.Laurent-les-Vignes. Tel: 53-57-42-57.
57. R. Castaing et fils, **La Grange Neuve**, 24240 Pomport. Tel: 53-58-42-23.
24. *Jacques Blais, **Château Haut-Bernasse**, 24240 Monbazillac. Tel: 53-58-36-22.
29. *Jean Borderie,**Domaine de la Haute-Brie et du Caillou**, 24240 Monbazillac. Tel: 53-58-30-25.
39. Serge et Jean-Claude Géraud, C**hâteau Haute-Fonrousse**, 24240 Monbazillac. Tel: 53-58-30-28.
85. GAEC Durand, **Château Haut Malveyrein**, 24240 Pomport. Tel: 53-58-39-45.
90. Alain Sergenton, **Domaine Haut-Montlong**, 24240 Pomport. Tel: 53-58-81-60.
59. Eric de Bazin, **Château des Hébras**, 24240 Pomport. Tel: 53-63-44-40. (made under Hugh Ryman's supervision at the Monbazillac Co-opérative).
14. Hugh Ryman, **Château la Jaubertie**, 24560 Colombier. Tel ; 53-58-32-11.
81. Michel Monbouché, **Château Ladesvignes,** 24240 Pomport. Tel: 53-58-30-67.
82. Jean et Albert Camus, **Domaine de la Lande**, 24240 Monbazillac. Tel: 53-58-30-45.
83. Thierry Baudry, **Château Larchère**, 24240 Pomport.Tel: 53-58-25-84.
 1. Jean-LouisConstant, **Château Lavaud,** 24560 Colombier. (Sold from Domaine Constant 24680 Lamonzie St. Martin). Tel: 53-55-62-25.
27. *Christian et Patrick Chabrol, **Château Malfourat**, 24240 Monbazillac. Tel: 53-58-33-10.
86. Jean Chaussade, **Domaine de la Marche**, 24100 Saint Laurent-les-Vignes. Tel: 53-57-30-91+.
114. Alain et Christophe Geneste, **Château les Marnières**, 24520 St. Nexans Tel: 53-58-31-65
111. M. Jestin, **Château la Maroutie**, 24240 Monbazillac. Tel: 53-24-52-78.
84. Christian Verdier, **Château Moulin de Malfourat**, 24240 Monbazillac. Tel: 53-58-34-30.
87. Philippe Couture, **Domaine Maye de Bouye**, 24240 Rouffignac-de-Sigoulès. Tel: 53-58-36-76.
67. *Jean-Paul Martrenchard, **Château le Mayne**, 24240 Sigoulès. Tel: 53-58-40-01.
112. M. Roche, **Domaine de Mazière**, 24560 Bouniaugues. Tel: 53-58-23-57.
60. Domaine Pierre Missègue, **Bertrand**, 24240 Pomport. Tel: 53-58-43-97.
12. Solange Borderie, **Domaine les Monderys**, 24.560 Conne de Labarde. Tel: 53-58-34-63.
88. M. et Mme Lambert, **Domaine Monlong**, 24240 Pomport. Tel: 53-58-44-10.
89. Vincent Rousserie, **Vignobles de Montlong**, 24240 Pomport. Tel: 53-58-80-29.

68. Castaing père et fils, **Domaine du Moulin**, 24240 Cunège. Tel: 53-58-41-20.
62. *Claude Larrue, **Moulin de Sanxet**, 24240 Pomport. Tel:53-58-30-79.
95. Jacky Pruvost, **Moulin des Pezauds**, 24240 Monbazillac, Tel: 53-58-34-77.
90. SCEA Poujol, **Château les Moulinières**, 24240 Monbazillac.
    Tel: 53-58-33-49.
91. J.J. Daillat, **Château les Olivoux**, 24240 Pomport. Tel: 53-58-41-94.
92. M. Tricou et fils, **Château Pech La Calevie**, 24240 Pomport.
    Tel: 53-58-43-46.
58. René Labaye, **Le Pécoula**, 24240 Pomport. Tel: 53-58-41-89.
25. C. Loisy, **Château Péroudier**, 24240 Monbazillac. Tel: 53-58-30-04.
 3. Pierre Cathal, **Clos le Petit Marsalet**, 24100 St. Laurent- les-Vignes.
    Tel: 53-57-53-36.
30. Famille Gineste, **Domaine du Petit Paris**, 24240 Monbazillac.
    Tel: 53-58-30-41.
93. Claude Arfel, **Clos du Petit Poncet**, 24100 St.M Laurent- les-Vignes.
    Tel: 53-57-01-86.
107. Jean-Pierre Uzès, **Domaine de Peyrecagne**, 24240 Pomport.
    Tel: 53-58-28-52.
 6. Jean-Pierre Mayet, **La Peyrette**, 24100 St. Laurent-des-Vignes.
    Tel: 53-27-12-99.
94. M. et Mme Todoverto, **Domaine de Peyronnette**, 24240 Pomport.
    Tel: 53-24-00-83.
65. Jean-Régis Guibert, **Château de Peytirat**, 24240 Flaugeac. Tel: 53-58-45-08.
96. Mme Daniel, **Castel la Pèze**, 24240 Pomport. Tel: 53-57-46-30.
23. Georges Beaudouin, **Château Pintoucat**, 24240 Monbazillac.
    Tel: 53-57-00-84.
18. *Jacques de Meslon, **Château de Planques**, 24560 Colombier.
    Tel: 53-58-30-18.
 4. Maurice Chevalier, **Domaine de Poncet**, 24100 St. Laurent-les-Vignes
    Tel: 53-57-30-98.
34. *Jean et Francis Borderie, **Château Poulvère**, 24240 Monbazillac
    Tel: 53-58-30-25.
31. Pierre Borderie, **Le Rauly**, 24240 Monbazillac. Tel: 53-57-67-45.
15. *Jean Revol, **Château la Rayre**, 24560 Colombier. Tel: 53-58-32-17.
97. Janine Pecher, **Domaine des Reclauds**, 24240 Monbazillac. Tel: 53-58-23-55.
48. Jean Gouy, **Château le Reyssec**, 24240 Pomport. Tel: 53-58-42-08.
49. Laurent Grima, **Château Roc de Caillevel**, 24240 Pomport.
    Tel: 53-38-84-61.
64. Nady Reiser, **Domaine de la Roquerie**, 24240 Pomport. Tel: 53-57-45-35.
98. Yvette Lacroix, **Château la Rouquette**, 24100 Bergerac. Tel: 53-57-64-49.
99. Nicole Guilhon, **Château St. Mayme**, 24240 Pomport. Tel: 53-57-05-20.
100. Michel Simon, **Château les Saintes**, 24240 Rouffignac-de-Sigoulès.
    Tel: 53-58-46-83.
101. SARL Vignobles Rocher Cap de Rive, **Domaine de la Salagre**,
    24240 Pomport. Tel: 53-24-01-29.
50. *Bertrand de Passemar, C**hâteau de Sanxet**, 24240 Pomport.
    Tel: 53-58-37-46.
40. Christian Beigner, **Clos la Selmonie**, 24240 Rouffignac-de-Sigoulès.
    Tel: 53-58-43-40.
113. M. Carrère, **Château de Thénoux**, 24240 Monbazillac. Tel: 53-58-38-53.
36. *Pierre Alard, **Château de Theulet**, 24240 Monbazillac. Tel: 53-57-30-43.
35. *René Monbouché, **Domaine de Theulet et Marsalet**, also Château Grand
    Conseil, 24240 Monbazillac. Tel: 53-57-94-36.
37. *Jean-Pierre Monbouché, **Château de Thibaut**, 24240 Monbazillac.
    Tel: 53-58-38-01.

102. *M. et Mme Bilancini, **Château Tirecul-la-Gravière**, 24240 Monbazillac. Tel: 53-57-44-75.
103. Michel Lagrange, **Château Tout Vent**, 24240 Pomport. Tel: 53-58-42-24.
22. *Armand Vidal, **Château Treuilh-de-Nailhac**, see 20. La Borderie.
10. *Alain Geneste, **Domaine de Troubat**, 24520 St. Nexans. Tel: 53-58-31-65.*
32. Yves Feytout, **La Truffière Tirecul**, 24240 Monbazillac. Tel: 53-58-30-23.
16. Lucien Roux, **Domaine de la Verdaugie**, 245460 Colombier. Tel: 53-63-65-00.
104. Roland Pasquet, **Château le Vieux Colombier**, 24560 Colombier. Tel: 53-24-31-98.
105. Dominique Vilate, **Château Vieux Malveyrien**, 24240 Pomport. Tel: 53-58-42-29.
33. Liliane Gagnard, **Château Vieux Touron**,24240 Monbazillac. Tel: 53-58-21-16
106. Edgard Gouy, **Château Vignal la Brie**, 24240 Monbazillac. Tel: 53-24-51-18.

SAUSSIGNAC

13. SCEA du **Château Baudry la Tour**, also Château La Tour, 24240 Monestier. Tel: 53-61-17-71. White moelleux for supermarkets sold as Clos Monestier
6. Jean-Paul Rigal, **Domaine du Cantonnet**, 24240 Razac- de- Saussignac. Tel: 53-27-88-63.
4. *Jacques et Jean-LucLescure, **Le Castellat**, 24240 Razac-de-Saussignac. Tel: 53-27-08-83.
14. Ginette Biaussat, **Château les Cavailles**, 24240 Saussignac. Tel: 53-27-92-28.
15. Pierre Carle, **Château le Chabrier**, 24240 Razac-de-Saussignac. Tel: 53-27-92-73.
3. *Pierre Jean Sadoux, **Château Court-les-Mûts**, 24240 Razac-de-Saussignac. Tel: 53-27-92-17.
16. M. et Mme Brouilleaud, **Clos la Croix Blanche**, 24240 Monestier. Tel: 53-58-45-82.
17. **Famille Cuisset, **Château les Eyssards**, 24240 Monestier. Tel: 53-58-45-48.
23. Bernard Rigal, **Domaine des Frétillères**, 24240 Razac-de-Saussignac. Tel: 53-27-89-61 and 53-27-92-69
8. Serge Géraud, **Château desGanfard**, 24240 Saussignac. Tel: 53-27-87-52.
18. Mme Francine Festal, **Clos des Ganfards**, 24240 Saussignac. Tel: 53-27-81-04.
10. Gilbert Caille, **Domaine les Grimoux**, 24240 Saussignac.Tel: 53-27-87-52.
5. Sylvie et Claude Sergenton, **Domaine de Lacombe**, 24240 Razac-de-Saussignac. Tel: 53-27-86-51.
19. Denis Guibert, **Château Mayne du Bost**, 24240 Monestier. Tel: 53-58-81-20.
9. *Gérard Cuisset, **Château les Miaudoux**, 24240 Saussignac. Tel: 53-27-92-31.
20. Thierry Daulhiac, **Château le Payral**, 24240 Razac-de-Sausignac. Tel: 53-22-38-07.
21. Francis et Serge Pialat, **Domaine des Picots**, 24240 Razac-de-Saussignac. Tel: 53-27-93-37.
22. Jonathan Alexander, **Domaine du Pigeonnier**, 24240 Monestier. Tel: 53-58-49-57.
2. Jean Gazziola, **Les Plaguettes**, 24240 Saussignac. Tel: 53-27-93-17.
1. Daniel Richard, **La Prade**, 24240 Saussignac. Tel: 53-27-93-34.
11. *Richard Doughty, **Domaine de Richard**, La Croix-Blanche, 24240 Monestier. Tel: 53-58-48-94.
7. SCEA de Touraille, **Domaine de Touraille**, 24240 Razac-de-Saussignac. Tel: 53-27-80-01.

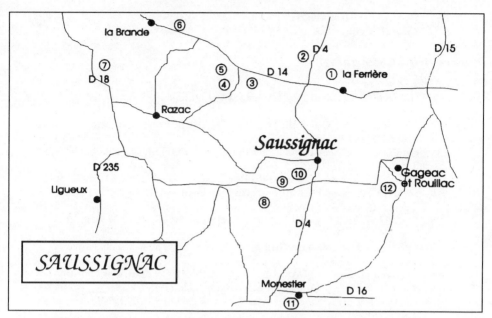

SAUSSIGNAC

12. *Patricia Atkinson, **Clos d'Yvigne**, Le Bourg, 24240 Gageac et Rouillac.
Tel: 53-22-94-30.

HAUT-MONTRAVEL

Sweet White
9. CAVE CO-OPÉRATIVE DE PORT STE-FOY, 78 Route de Bordeaux,
33220 Port Ste-Foy Tel: 52-24-75-63.
34. Jean Marceteau, **Domaine de Bien Assis**, 24230 St. Antoine de Breuilh,
Tel: 53-24-80-00 (formerly Le Rival)
35. *D. et C Feytout, **Château de Bondieu**, 24230 St. Antoine-de-Breilh
Tel: 53-58-30-83
12. Paul et Gyl Marty, **Domaine de Conterie**, 33220 Fougueyrolles
Tel: 53-24-77-66
13. SCEA du Vignoble des Berneries, **Château des Crumes**,33220
Fougueyrolles Tel: 53-24-78-18. Dry white sold as Château des Berneries.
36. Jean-Paul Gérome, **Château Haut-Poncet**, 24230 Vélines Tel: 53-27-55-63
32. *Jacques Faurichon de la Bardonnie, **Château Laroque**, 24130 St. Antoine-
de-Breuilh Tel: 53-24-81-43
15. *Jean-Claude Banizette, **Domaine de Libarde**, 24230 Nastringues
Tel: 53-24-77-72
10. *Roland Barthoux, **Château de Masburel**, 33220 Fougueyrolles
Tel: 53-24-77-73
37. Francis Lagarde, **Domaine de Mayat**, 33220 Fougueyrolles
Tel: 53-24-84-42 and 53-24-77-59
38. *M. et Mme Deffarge, **Château Moulin Caresse**, 24230 St. Antoine-de-
Breilh Tel: 53-27-55-58
39. La Famille Favreau, **Domaine de la Nougarède**, 24130 Le Fleix
Tel: 53-24-70-06
7. *Daniel Hecquet, **Puy-Servain-Calabre**, 33320 Port Ste-Foy-et-Ponchapt
Tel: 53-24-77-27 (see also Montavel Sec, 5 Domaine Krevel)
Le Rival see Domaine de Bien Assis

11. *Christian et Jean-Marie Valette, **GAEC de Roque-Peyre**, 33220 Fougueyrolles Tel: 53-24-77-98

Cotes de Montravel

Medium white
  4. CAVE CO-OPERATIVE DU FLEIX, Le Fleix,24130 La Force Tel: 53-24-64-32
24. CAVE CO-OPERATIVE DE MONTRAVEL, 24230 Lamothe-Montravel Tel: 53-58-62-25
33. CAVE CO-OPERATIVE ST. VIVIEN ET BONNEVILLE, 24230 Vélines Tel: 53-27-52-22
29. Frères Guillermier, **Château du Bloy**, 24230 Bonneville, Tel: 58-27-50-59
40. Mme Brigitte Fried, **Château Dame de Fonroque**, 24230 Montcaret Tel: 53-58-65-83
28. M.et Mme Claude Ledemé, **Domaine du Denoix**, 24230 Montcaret Tel: 53-58-61-08
  6. *Bertrand, **Domaine de Golse**, 33220 Port Ste-Foye-et- Ponchapt Tel: 53-57-47-79
21. Jean-Bernard Basset, **Domaine de Gourgueil, Château des Chaumes Perdus**, 24230 St. Michel-de-Montaigne Tel: 53-58-64-53
41. Richard Lacombe, **Domaine des Illarets**, 24230 St. Michel-de-Montaigne Tel: 63-58-52-49
42. Chavant Père et Fils, **Domaine des Jolis Bois**, 33220 Ste-Foy Tel: 53-24-77-07
19. *Mme Mahler-Besse, **Château de Montaigne**, 24230 St. Michel-de-Montaigne Tel: 53-58-60-54
20. Jean-François Ley, **Château Moulin de Bel Air**, 24230 St. Michel-de-Montaigne Tel: 53-58-63-29
43. SARL Moro Diffusion, **Château Pagnon**, 24230 Vélines Tel: 53-27-10-72
22. *Jean-Yves Reynou, **Domaine de Perreau**, 24230 St. Michel-de-Montaigne Tel: &53-58-67-31 (red Bergerac sold as Château Marot)
  3. **Philippe et Marianne Mallaod, **Château Pique Sègue**, 33220 Ponchapt Tel: 57-46-01-34
31. *Itey de Peironnin, **Château la Raye**, 24230 Vélines Tel: 53-27-50-14
  8. *Jean Rebeyrolle, **Château la Ressaudie**, 33320 Port Ste-Foy Tel: 53-24-71-48
16. André Peytureau, Château de Ségur, 24230 Montazeau Tel: 53-27-51-89
23. GFA Ley et Fils, **Château des Templiers**, 24230 St. Michel-de-Montaigne Tel: 53-58-63-29
26. Philippe Poivey, **Château le Tour Montbrun**, Bonneville, 24230 Montcaret Tel: 53-58-66-93

Montravel

Blanc sec only
25. Bernard Gachet, **Château Bellevue**, 24230 Lamothe-Montravel Tel: 53-58-60-88
44. Frères de Pillot, **Château Berjon**, 24320 St. Antoine-de-Breilh Tel: 53-58-59-20
13. ***Château des Berneries** (see Haut-Montravel, Château des Crumes)
45. Comte Gilles de Nazelle, **Châteaux Bonnières et Brésirou**, 33220 Fougueyrolles Tel: 53-61-27-69
46. Robert Descoins, **Château Brunet-Charpentière**, 24230 Montazeau Tel: 53-27-54-71

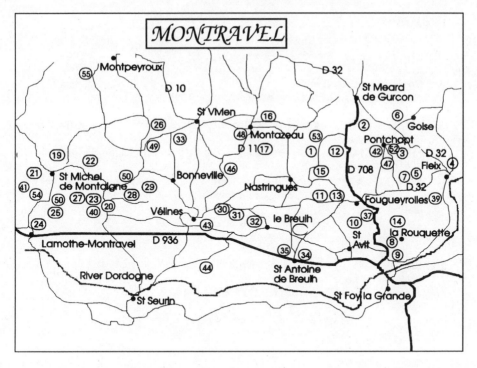

47. GFA Devigne, **Château la Cabanelle**, 33220 Ponchapt Tel: 53-24-80-08
1. Pierre Santénéro, **Château la Croix Laulerie**, 24610 St. Meard-de-Gurçon
   Tel: 53-82-40-45
17. Pierre Santénéro, **Château la Font du Parc**, La Font du Parc,
   24230 Montazeau Tel: 53-62-40-45
2. *Dubard Frères et Soeur, **Domaine de Gouyat** (also Château Laulerie),
   24610 St. Méard-de-Gurçon Tel: 53-82-48-31
48. Messieurs P. et J. Joyeux, **Château Les Grimards,** 24230 Montazeau
   Tel: 53-63-09-83
49. M. Loubery et fils, **Château Haut Maine**, 24230 Bonneville Tel: 53-27-50-61
5. *Daniel Hecquet, **Domaine de Krével**, Calabre, 33220 Port Ste Foy-
   Ponchapt Tel: 53-24-77-27
50. M. et Mme Verseau, **Château Lespinassat**, 24230 Montcaret
   Tel: 53-58-34-23
27. Patrick Pouget, **Château Moulin de Bouty**, 24230 Montcaret Tel: 53-58-
   66-13
51. Jean-Yves Moyrand, **Château Moulin de Garreau**, 24230 Lamothe-
   Montravel Tel: 53-58-69-33
14. *Comte de Peyrelongue, **Château Péchaurieux**, 33220 Fougueyrolles
   Tel: 53-24-71-50 (also Château Briat Bellevue)
52. Yves-Eric Sahut, **Château de Ponchapt**, 33,220 Port Ste-Foy Tel: 53-24-76-91
53. *Vignoble Barde, **Château le Raz**, 24610 St. Méard-de-Gurçon
   Tel: 53-82-48-41
54. Messieurs M. et Y. Boyer, **Domaine de la Roche-Marot**, 24230 Lamothe-
   Montravel Tel: 53-58-52-05
55. Patrick Violleau, **Tertre des Moulins de la Garde**, 24610 Montpeyroux
   Tel: 53-80-77-55

PÉCHARMANT

1. *CAVE CO-OPERATIVE DE BERGERAC, 72 Boulevard de l"Entrepôt, 24100 Bergerac Tel: 53-57-˜16-27
2. Monsieur Vénèque, **Domaine Brisseau Belloc**, made at the Bergerac Co-0pérative, see 1. above
7. *Guy Pécou, **Domaine des Bertranoux**, 24100 Creysse Tel: 53-22-46-29
15. *Mme Arlette Best, **Château de Biran**, 24100 St. Sauveur de Bergerac Tel 53-23-20-47
9. *Françoise Bouché, **Château Champarel**, Pécharmant, 24100 Bergerac Tel: 53-57-34-76
4. Michel Roches, **Château Cifar**, see Domaine du Haut-Pécharmant 11. below
6. B. Durand de Corbiac, **Château de Corbiac**, 24100 Bergerac Tel: 53-57-20-75
16. Gérard Lacroix, **Les Costes**, 24100 BergeracTel: 53-27-32-42
3. *Colette Bourgès, **Clos les Côtes**, Les Costes, 24100 Bergerac Tel: 53-57-59-89
20. M.H.de Labatut, **Château les Farcy** made by Roches at Domaine du Haut-Pécharmant no. 11 q.v
14. Francis Romain, **Domaine les Galinoux**, 24100 Bergerac Tel: 53-57-97-88
5. Georges Baudry, **Domaine du Grand Jaure**, 24100 Lembras Tel: 53-57-35-65
10. *Guy-Jean Kreusch, **La Métairie en Pécharmant**, 24100 Bergerac Tel: 53-24-12-21
12. *Gilbert Dusseau , **Chartreuse de Peyrelevade** Tel: 53-57-33-30 and **Château Malbernat** Tel: 53-57-44-27 both 24100 Bergerac
11. *Michel Roches, **Clos Peyrelevade** Tel: 53-57-44-27, **Domaine du Haut-Pécharmant** and **Château Cifar**, both Tel: 53-57-29-50 and Tel: 53-57-29-50 all at 24100 Bergerac
21. G. Morand-Monteil, **Château Terre Vieille** (Domaine de Grateloup) , 24520 St. Sauveur Tel: 53-57-35-07
22. B. et D. Fauconnier, **Château de Tilleraie**, Pécharmant, 24100 Bergerac Tel: 53-57-86-42
14. *La Comtesse de Saint-Exupéry, **Château de Tiregand**, 24100 Creysse Tel: 53-23-21-08
8. *André Coll, **Domaine de Toutifaut**, 24100 Creysse Tel: 53-63-40-73

MONBAZILLAC-BASED PRODUCERS WHO ALSO MAKE PÉCHARMANT

a). CAVE CO-OPERATIVE DE MONBAZILLAC, Chiateau de Monbazillac BP2, 24240 Monbazillac Tel: 53-57-06-38 sold as Château Renaudie
b). J.R.Guibert, at Château Peytirat, 24240 Flaugeac Tel: 53-58-45-08 sold as Domaine de la Curguétère
c). Jean Borderie, Domaine de la Haute-Brie et du Caillou, 24240 Monbazilac Tel: 53-58-30-25 (sold as Les Grangettes)
d.) Yves Feytout at La Truffière, 24240 Monbazillac Tel: 53-58-30-23
e). *Paul Pomar, SCEA Pomar-Lagarde,St.Christophe, 24100 Bergerac Tel: 53-57-71-62
f). *Christian Roche at L'Ancienne Cure, 24560 Colombier Tel: 53-58-27-90
g). *Dominique Vidal =at Ch. La Borderie, 24240 Monbazillac, Tel: 53-57-00-36 sold as Pécharmant Lentilhac and made at Domaine du Haut-Pecharmant (no. 11 q.v.)

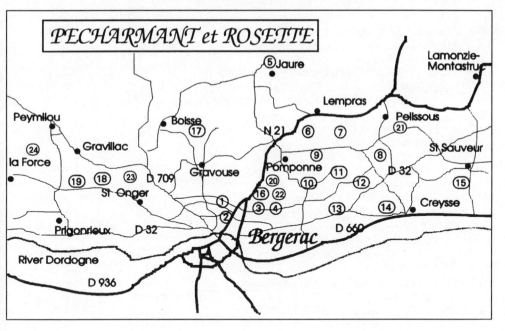

ROSETTE

23. *Nicolas Eckert, **Domaine de la Cardinolle**, 24130 Prigonrieux
Tel: 51-63-28-77 (red Bergerac sold as Château Gravillac)
18. François Eckert, **Château Combrillac**, 24130 Prigonrieux Tel: 53-24-69-83
3. *Colette Bourgès**, sold as **Clos Romain**, made at Clos les Côtes,
Les Costes, 24100 Bergerac Tel: 53-57-59-89 (q.v.)
19. Odile Brichèse, **Domaine de Coutancie**, Coutancie, 24130 Prigonrieux
Tel: 53-58-01-85
17. *Bernad Frères, **Château Puypezat Rosette** 24100 Bergerac
Tel: 53-57-27-69
24. Philippe Prévot, **Château de Spinguelèbre**, 24130 Prigonrieux
Tel: 53-58-85-29

SELECTED PRODUCERS OF RED AND WHITE BERGERAC AOC

Producer	Red	White	Tel
Patrick Bertrandie, **Dom. des Auvergnats**, 24240 Monestier	✓		53-58-80-52
M. Gaulhiac, **Ch. les Bardoulets**, 62 ave. du Périgord, Bardoulets, 33220 Port Ste-Foy	✓	✓	57-46-32-00
Vignobles Barriat, Etrenville, 24560 Issigeac	✓	✓	53-58-71-60
J-Marie Teillet, **Dom. de Beauregard** 24610 Villefranche-de-Lonchat		✓	53-80-76-34
J-Claude Argivier, **Clos de Brugère**, 24270 St. Rémy-sur-Lidoire	✓		53-80-40-04
J-Louis Piazzéta, **Les Brandeaux**, Puyguilhem, 24240 Thénac	✓	✓	53-58-41-50
Denis et Anne Goyon, **Ch. Caillevet**, 24240 Thénac	✓	✓	53-58-80-71

Producer	Red	White	Tel
Jean-Paul Migot, **Dom. de Capulle**, 24240 Thénac	✓	✓	53-58-42-67
*Jean-Louis Constant, **Dom. Constant**, 24680 Lamonzie St. Martin	✓	✓	53-24-07-08
Daniel et NicoleReynou, **Ch. la Croix de Vedelle** 24610 Villefranche-de-Longchat	✓	✓	53-80-77-51
Marcel Murer, **Dom. de Fraysse**, 24500 Eymet	✓	✓	53-23-81-38
SCEA LA Gr.Pleyssade, **Ch. La Grande Pleyssade**, 24240 Mescoulès	✓	✓	53-24-05-81
M. et Mme Barse, **Dom. les Graves**, 24240 Gageac-Rouillac	✓	✓	53-24-01-11
*Cathérine et Guy Cuisset, **Ch. Grinou**, Route de Grinou , 24240 Monestier	✓	✓	53-58-46-63
Mme MoniqueCollot, **Ch. Haut-Puy-Grénier** 24610 Villefranche-de-Longchat	✓	✓	53-81-38-89
De la Verrie, **Ch. Jeambrun**, 24240 Gageac-Rouillac	✓	✓	53-27-92-92
M. et Mme Duhazé, **Dom. de Maison Neuve**, 24520 St. Nexans	✓	✓	53-57-20-28
*M.et Mme Biau, **Ch. de la Mallevieille** 24120 Monfaucon	✓	✓	53-24-64-66
Michel Roche, **Dom. de Mazière**, 57 24560 Bouniaugues	✓		✗3-58-23-
J. et A. Lajonie, **Ch. Les Merles**, Tuilière, 24520 Mouleydier	✓	✓	53-57-17-96
M. Rousserie, **Vignoble de Monlong**, 24240 Pomport	✓	✓	53-58-80-29
~Mme Rouillon, **Ch. Moulin de Montarut** 24610 Villefranche-de-Longchat	✓		53-80-77-47
M. et Mme Fournier, **Ch. la Moulière**, 24240 Gageac-et-Rouillac	✓	✓	53-84-12-18
*SA Panisseau, **Ch. de Panisseau**, 24240 Thénac	✓	✓	53-58-40-03
Paul Dessales, **Dom. de Planquetorte**, Planquetorte, 24100 Bergerac	✓	✓	53-57-00-15
*Albert Cuisset, **Dom. Pourcaud**, 24240 Monestier	✓	✓	53-58-44-36
Michel Prouillac, **M.Prouillac**, 24240 Sigoulès	✓	✓	53-58-40-92
Jean-Pierre Roulet, **Ch. Repenty**, (also Dom.du Grand Vignal) 24240 Monestier	✓	✓	53-58-41-96
AudieLandat et fils , **Dom. du Siorac**, 24500 St. Aubinde Cadalech (also leads small groupement of verjuice producers)	✓	✓	53-24-50-76
*C.Lavergne, **La Tour de Grangemont** 24560 St. Aubin de Lanquais	✓	✓	53-24-31-50
SCEA de Conti, **La Tour des Gendres**, 24240 Ribagnac (also Dom. Moulin des Dames)	✓	✓	53-57-12-43
*Jean-MarieHure, **Ch. Tourmentine**, 24240 Monestier	✓	✓	53-58-41-41
Mmes Dupré, **Ch. Le Trouillet**, 24240 Gageac-Rouillac	✓	✓	53-27-83-77
*GAEC Fourtout et fils, **Clos des Verdots**, 24500 Conne de Labarde (also **Ch. la Tour des Verdots**)	✓	✓	53-58-34-31
Serge Lagarde, **Dom.de Vigneaud**, 24240 Monestier	✓	✓	53-58-80-54

The Wines of the Middle Garonne: Côtes de Duras, Marmande, Buzet, Brulhois and the Agenais

LES CÔTES DE DURAS

The vineyards south of Saussignac, sandwiched between the southern-most part of the Bergeracois and the Bordeaux district of Entre-Deux-Mers, are called Côtes de Duras after the small country town of that name, overlooking the valley of the river Dropt (pronounced 'Drow'). The town of Duras has a historical and political importance far in excess of its size. Since the middle ages it has been the site of a fortified castle, at the centre of most of the struggles which have characterised French political history in the South-West up to the Revolution.

The Lords of Duras were ennobled to the status of duke by Louis XIV. They usually supported revolt and protest, but always succeeded in coming out on top, even though they had the habit of backing the losing side. In the Hundred Years' War they sided with the English Crown; in the religious wars of the Reformation they were Protestant for as long as it suited them; in the struggles of the Fronde they were on the side of the rebels, and when the going got rough for them with their local subjects, they took refuge with their political protectors in Bordeaux and at the English Court. Yet they managed always to make their peace with the rulers of France until, with the coming of the First Republic, they were swept away by the revolutionary tide, their château sacked and their influence smashed.

The ducal line died out in the nineteenth century, remembered by few and loved by none: they had been cruel overlords, exacting from their subjects every feudal due in the book. In particular the vineyards of the area were all held in tenancy from the duke, who had the right to make and process his own wines before anyone else was allowed to make theirs, ensuring him an unfair advantage in the markets downstream. Growers were also obliged to take a substantial part of their crop to the château by way of tribute. Under the *ancien régime*, there was no yeoman tradition of wine-making, as in the Bergeracois. The Comté of Duras was ruled as a strict feudal serfdom.

Today it is hard for those visiting this apparently drowsy corner of the Lot-et-Garonne to imagine the effects of one armed struggle after another down the centuries, or the disastrous consequences of the plagues which followed in their wake. No sooner were the vineyards of Duras replanted during the brief intervals of peace and some sort of normal life established for the peasantry than another war broke out, the vineyards were pillaged and the entire local community wiped out by disease, the vines with them. Sometimes it was necessary to encourage mass-immigration in order to re-stock the local population. It is not surprising that the community took their chance in 1789 with the more extremist elements: the first Republican government in Paris sent a Monsieur Lakanal, a native of Toulouse, to expunge as far as possible all traces of the old nobility in Duras. Lakanal even required the residents to dismantle some of the fortifications and towers of the old château. The government had plans, at first eagerly supported by the locals, to make the river navigable for wine-traffic, but Lakanal refused to pay the locals for their work, saying that they had already made enough money from looting the château and selling off its contents.

This was no doubt true, but as an argument for non-payment it did not appeal to the worthy revolutionaries of Duras, who felt they had a perfect right to take whatever remained of the wicked duke's assets. So they sent Monsieur Lakanal back to Paris with a flea in his ear. To this day the decapitated towers of the ruined château bear witness to the uncompleted efforts of this maladroit politician.

The immediate result of the Revolution was that the former ducal vineyards were offered for sale. The only people who had enough money to buy them, even at the knockdown prices ruling at the time, were the local artisans and small-time professionals who had feathered their nests very nicely in the wake of the chaos caused by the Revolution. So the vineyards of the region came into the ownership of the nouveaux-riches and those peasant-growers who had managed to keep a little gold hidden under their mattresses.

This historical background explains why most of the vineyards of Duras are today small and scattered. It also explains why 46% of the current production is in the hands of the co-opératives.

The feudal system had at least given the residents of Duras some cohesion. The Revolution destroyed it, and ever since Duras has suffered a crisis of identity. Politically and agriculturally it has little to bind it to the Bergeracois, and even less to Bordeaux: the separation from the latter was established once and for all by the inclusion of Duras in the département of the Lot-et-Garonne, rather than with Bordeaux in the département of the Gironde. Its farming is geared to the production of maize, sunflowers and prunes, emphasising its links with Agen rather than Bergerac or Bordeaux, but its wines, made as they are from the same grape-varieties as both of its larger neighbours, struggled after the phylloxera to achieve either a reputation of their own or a market.

Yet the vineyards of Duras have a long and honourable history. Given the seal of approval by at least one pope – no matter that he was the uncle of the ruling lord of Duras at the time – the wines of the Côtes de Duras were admired by the English during their occupation of the region and by François I who called them 'nectar'. One achievement at least of the dukes of Duras was to use their political influence abroad as well as at home, to spread the fame of Duras wine to the courts of eighteenth-century Europe.

In a way it is not surprising that Duras was one of the first (as early as 1937) of the wine-growing regions to benefit from the grant of AOC status. But appellation contrôlée is more concerned with reputation and authenticity than character. It is here that the problems of Duras have lain, and it has taken forty years or so for the local growers to establish their own niche in the market-place.

They have been both helped and hindered by using the same grape-varieties as Bordeaux: merlot and the two cabernets for their red wines and sémillon, sauvignon and muscadelle for their whites. While they have sometimes been able to undercut their Bordelais neighbours, whose prices have often risen in unjustified proportion to the quality of their wines, the Duraquois have found it hard to establish a style which sets them aside either from Bordeaux or Bergerac. In one breath they sigh for the right to call their wines Bordeaux, but at the same time relish their independence and the struggle to find their own *typicité*.

Nowhere is this dichotomy better illustrated than by the existence of two co-opératives. One is just outside the town of Duras itself in the Lot-et-Garonne: the other is over the border into the Gironde at Landerrouat.

The **Cave de Landerrouat (A)** has approximately the same number of members making Duras as Bordeaux wine. Many members enjoy both appellations because they have vineyards in both départements. The vinification and *élevage* is the same for both wines, but the Duras *encépagement* may have rather more merlot in it. The Landerrouat Cave was the first of the two, its founder Monsieur Bireaud, whose family is still making Duras wine today, having been the *locomotive* of the appellation back in 1937.

There is nothing much between the two Caves in size: Landerrouat has about eighty-four members making 25,000 hectolitres between them, while the **Cave Berticot (B)** at Duras had eighty-six members in 1992, making 27,000 hectolitres. I asked the directors of each Cave why they didn't join forces, but got no satisfactory answer. Apart from the obvious difficulties in trying to engineer mergers of such enterprises, the real answer may lie in a different approach to wine-making and marketing. At Landerrouat, they aim very much at the large buyers, the supermarkets: they do not seem to want to attract small buyers. Thus, they will make up blends of wines to suit the requirements of large clients, who often send their own staff to supervise the *assemblage* of 'their' wines. The accent is on finding a market for whatever the members produce.

Berticot, on the other hand, sees the best way of developing its members' interests as asserting an individual character for the appellation. Berticot has a much more retail-orientated approach, having a large and attractive shop which accounts for over 25% of its sales. Although Berticot is the junior of the two Caves, having started only in 1965, Landerrouat is taking no chances: it is just finishing the construction of a large new *chais* in the post-modernist style, which will be exclusively devoted to their Duras members. Berticot is retaliating, if that is the right word, with new underground storage facilities which will allow it enough space to expand for the foreseeable future. I asked the president, Monsieur Goubier, why the Cave was called Berticot. He said that Berticot was the name of a former well-known local resident, a barrister. The wines are variously called Comte de Berticot and Duc de Berticot, but Monsieur Goubier said that Berticot was in real life no more than a plain mister: the titles Comte and Duc were invented by the Cave to denote grades of quality, mirroring the rise of the lords of Duras.

Monsieur Goubier is president of Cave Berticot, his father having joined it in 1969. In those early days the members felt they needed a Cave which looked exclusively after the Duras growers, especially those who were trying to mark out a future for dry white sauvignon wines (today a third of the wine vinified at Berticot is sauvignon). Despite the progress made in recent years by red Duras, the accent is still on white wines at Berticot. All their grapes are de-stalked, and all the white grapes are given a *macération pelliculaire* for six to twelve hours. After two pressings in their ultra-modern pneumatic presses, the varieties are vinified separately. All manner of different *cuves* are used, but each is temperature-controlled.

Despite the accent on dry sauvignon, I was more interested in the Berticot *moelleux*. I doubted the wisdom or necessity of oaking the sauvignon, but the *moelleux* had undoubtedly benefited from its three months in new wood. The 1992 from a light year was rather delicate in the style of a Rosette, but the 1990 was altogether deeper with an exotic perfume of melons and peaches. Monsieur Goubier said they are waiting for the right year to experiment with over-ripe grapes. This will be interesting, because there are as yet only two private producers in Duras making that style of wine. Perhaps 1995 will have fitted the bill.

I was less happy with the Berticot reds: they make a 100% hand-picked merlot by *macération carbonique* for drinking within the year.

What I was hoping to find was a good basic unoaked red of premium grade, but there seems to be a hole in the range. The reds which Monsieur Goubier kindly showed me were all oaked, and to my taste rather too much so. I am sorry if this will upset Michel Rolland, the wine-maker at Le Bon Pasteur in Pomerol, whom the Berticot Cave has engaged to supervise the *élevage* of their wines in wood. But Duras is not Pomerol and I wonder whether there is enough fruit in the local wine to justify the twelve to eighteen months which some of it spends in *barriques*.

Hugh Ryman has expanded his interests from the Bergeracois into Duras. His wine-makers have vinified the wine for two members of the Berticot co-opérative, the owners of Domaine de Colombet and Domaine de Malardeau. The latter is a 13-hectare estate, where Ryman's team are in charge of making what he calls a lively, fruity and well-balanced wine from 90% sauvignon and 10% sémillon. Ryman has built an extraordinary career and international reputation for wine-making, without, until very recently, owning any vineyards or his own wine-making plant. Having acquired in Australia a first-class training in the making of modern wines, especially dry white wines, he is able to put his expertise at the disposal of growers seeking to increase the quality of their wines and thus their place in the market. He is also able to find growers all over the world who are able and willing, under his supervision, to make wines to suit the requirements and price-ranges ordained by supermarkets, by whom Ryman is retained as a consultant. The resulting wines are always well made, even if they do have an international rather than local style. Duras, which has such a difficulty in establishing a character of its own in the shadow of Bordeaux, is an ideal field for Ryman's type of operation.

All the Berticot wines, including Ryman's, have deservedly won a good slot in the overseas market: over 40% of them are exported, and there is no difficulty in obtaining them in the UK. What impressed me most about the Cave was that it is manifestly run for the benefit of its members: all too often it seems co-opératives are run in spite of them.

There are about 300 growers in Duras, of whom over one-half are members of one of the co-opératives. Of the remainder, fewer than fifty represent a core of quality production, making, bottling and marketing their own wines. A bearded Burgundian, Gilbert Geoffroy, the owner of **Domaine de Laulan (20)** has developed a *syndicat* of private growers to raise the standards of production.

Some Duras wine-makers have roots in the region which go down a long way, but Gilbert Geoffroy proves that you do not have to be a native Duraquois in order to produce first-class wine. A fellow-grower, and one of the best at that, has dubbed him '*le cerveau de l'appellation*' ('the brain behind Duras'). Gilbert's family come from near Chablis. He trained as a farmer, not a wine-maker, because as a young man he wanted to go with all his best friends to study general agriculture at Montpellier, rather than viticulture on his own nearer home. Only later in life did he come back to wine, though his earlier training has not been wasted.

The Domaine de Laulan is to the east of the town of Duras, high on the top of a hill. This is the edge of the plateau which starts to drop into the valley, where the river forms the southern boundary of the appellation. Gilbert bought Naulan in the early seventies. There were then only 10 hectares under vine, all planted with old sémillon and muscadelle. As there were no red grapes, and Gilbert is not keen on the semi-sweet style of *moelleux* for which the vines he found there would have been useful, he put in hand a total replanting of the vineyard. He now has 19 hectares, more or less equally divided between red and white grapes. He insists on the best possible equipment, and his buildings include a temperature-controlled *chais d'élevage*, the only one of its kind in the appellation outside the co-opératives.

The only white grape which he has is sauvignon: he saw from the beginning that this was where the commercial future of white Duras lay. He makes two *cuvées*: the basic one is not given a *macération pelliculaire* for he believes that unless you intend to mature the wine in new wood, which he does with his special *cuvée*, a preliminary cold maceration destroys the freshness of the wine: it becomes heavy and develops potassium salts. The wooded wine, however, is given this skin-contact, then fermented and matured for six months in barrels which have already seen the making of one wine. This special sauvignon is named Emile Chariot after Gilbert's maternal grandfather.

These wines are among the best in the style which has made for Duras its modern reputation. It was interesting to compare the two in the same vintage. The mainstream wine had a good elderflower nose, typical of the grape, but at the same time with more fruit than one finds in some examples. The finish was long and opulent. Gilbert recommends it with asparagus or with charcuterie and, of course, fish, but only when the wine is mature: he thinks it needs two years. Although I had had reservations about the Berticot oaked sauvignon, I had none at all about Gilbert Geoffroy's: it was even finer and deeper in fruit than his mainstream wine, with suggestions of pineapple. The wood, nevertheless, is prominent, but more on the palate than the nose.

The *encépagement* of red grapes is conventional except that he has 5% in malbec, which he thinks gives a little rusticity to his wines. Harvesting is by machine because the terrain is relatively easy. The grapes are all de-stalked, and the inferior bunches are rejected by hand before the good ones go into the press. The different varieties are vinified separately in a variety of *cuves* at temperatures controlled by an *échangeur*. This is a kind of pump which extracts juice from the *cuve* and freezes it before returning it to the rest of the must. The *cuvaison* is relatively short, only about ten days. When I raised my eyebrows at this, Gilbert said he was not trying to make a Médoc: he felt he could give the vines maximum expression while preserving a certain lightness and elegance of fruit. This certainly shows in the main *cuvée*, whose malolactic fermentation he hopes to see finished by December in the year of the vintage, before the wine is returned to the *cuves* for maturing. He does not bottle all his wine at once. Some is drawn off as early as June following the vintage to make about 10,000 bottles for clients who like a lighter style of wine. He may bottle some more in the autumn of the same year and the remainder in the month of May, eighteen months after the vintage.

He reserves some of his best *cuves* for a special wine, one-third of which is given a year in new wood. This is awarded the premium name of Duc de Laulan. Sometimes Gilbert adds to it a little of the *vin de presse* which he has matured separately and kept by for the purpose. I have tasted two vintages of this wine: the 1989 was, in Gilbert's own words, rather arid in style, the fruit masked by tannins which he felt were by no means certain to resolve themselves. The 1990 was much better. The bouquet was still waiting to develop and somewhat discreet, but the wine was full of fruit and beginning to blend nicely with the oak.

Gilbert also offered me two vintages of the mainstream red. The 1992 must have been one of his *primeur* bottlings because my visit was during the summer following the vintage, and the wine was already in bottle. It was made from grapes picked before the rain, so the merlot, the first variety to ripen, dominated the wine, which was agreeably chewy in texture with a fresh, cherry flavour, light in body and easy, very more-ish. The 1990, being from a much better year, may have had longer in barrel, because it was still dark and meaty on the nose, leathery almost. It reminded me of a St Emilion in character. This was a big wine which would keep well.

For quick turnover, and to offer as a prelude to visitors' tastings, Gilbert Geoffroy makes a little rosé, *saigné* off his red wine. This means that a short while after the red grapes start to give colour to the red must, some of the juice is drawn off so that fermentation can continue without the colour darkening any further. Gilbert's rosé has wild strawberries on the bouquet and in the mouth, and a surprisingly long finish. He also makes a *méthode champenoise* from his black grapes, and you can round off a tasting with an *eau-de-vie* made from kiwis! Mention should be made of a range of second wines which Gilbert sells as Domaine des Arnauds.

Like so many growers in the South-West, Gilbert has a large band of loyal private customers to whom he either sells at the door or by mail-order. He also supplies restaurants through a wholesaler, thereby cutting out the problem of slow payers and even bad debts for which restaurants are notorious among *vignerons*. He has also been exporting about 40% of his output, but is finding the going tough in the international recession: it is good news that he has reorganised his representation in the UK after his previous importers fell victim to recession. His wines are commercially attractive, and should appeal to a wide public as well as more critical enthusiasts.

A grower who seems to spend more of his time on the road than in his vineyard is Guy Pauvert. This is surprising because he has no fewer than 64 hectares of vines at his **Domaine Amblard (33)** near St Sernin-de-Duras. By doing the rounds of the local markets and fairs in the summer he has built up a database of more than 6000 private customers. After the *vendange*, he sends mail-shots off to them and, in November and December, takes to the road with a container-lorry full of his wines to deliver to his clients personally. He unloads some into a small van before making his calls: a huge lorry might frighten the customers rather than encourage them. In this way he likes to feel that he maintains personal contact with them. He must be right because they go on giving him repeat orders. At Easter he goes through the same process all over again, but this time with his Belgian customers who make up a large part of his goodwill. Travelling thus, he sells about 80% of his output; the remaining 20% is exported through more conventional channels.

Meanwhile nothing is skimped back at the vineyard, where the highest standards are strictly maintained. Guy Pauvert is making some of the best Duras on the market and he has a staff of ten to help him. This is a far cry from his grandfather's day, when the farm was devoted to polyculture. Even when Guy was a boy, his father had only 5 hectares of vines and the wine was sold off *en vrac* to *négociants* who came and collected it. Guy has expanded the vineyard to its present size by reclaiming land devoted to other crops and by discreet purchases when adjoining land became available. He has also developed a policy of selling his wine only in bottle.

Guy regrets having planted out his new vines before the modern fashion for high-density planting became general. He compensates by allowing his vines to produce a lot of growth and by not weeding between the rows, which are 3 metres apart. The plants themselves are immaculately kept, surplus leaves being stripped away regularly during the ripening season to allow the sun to get to the bunches of grapes as much as possible.

Sauvignon represents two-thirds of the white grapes, the remainder being sémillon and muscadelle. It is noteworthy that in Duras the *encépagement* for the dry wines is generally higher in sauvignon than in Bergerac, perhaps because Duras is a younger vineyard. If the market for dry white wine persists, we will see the Bergerac growers switch more and more into sauvignon too.

Guy Pauvert is not dogmatic about *macération pelliculaire*. If the grapes are totally healthy when they are brought in, he may do it. He does, however, keep the juice for a week at 7° before fermentation, which is otherwise conventional. He does not use new wood because, he says, his clients in general do not like the results.

Despite the size of his vineyard, which is the largest in Duras, Guy Pauvert does not complicate his life by proliferating different *cuvées*. He has just two white wines, one dry and the other *moelleux*. The sauvignon-orientated *sec* is prettily pale and flowery, but not lacking in individuality. Sometimes it is marketed as Domaine La Croix-Haute. The *moelleux* is excellent, packed with wonderful fruit and all sorts of exotic flavours, but never overpowering: a delicious apéritif wine. It is hard to understand why this style of wine is declining in popularity, but Guy's production figures speak for themselves and reflect similar trends already noted in Bergerac. It seems that taste is polarising between the very dry and the very sweet.

The red wine from Amblard is made from equal quantities of merlot and each of the two cabernets. *Egrappage* is total and the *cuvaison* is long, between three and four weeks according to the season, the cabernets being generally given longer than the merlot. The varieties are vinified separately in enamelled concrete: Guy sends them to his underground *chais* for their malolactic fermentation, because during the early winter this space has retained something of its summer warmth. For the winter season proper, the wines are brought back to the surface, because Guy believes that a cold winter will help to clarify them. When the weather starts to get warm again, the wine goes back below ground until it is ready for bottling just before the next vintage. In Guy's view, there is no particular merit in constant temperatures at least until the wine is in bottle. His 1990, three years after the vintage, was fully ready, despite its long vinification. It was full of fruit and very easy to drink, not at all heavy and everything which a good country red wine should be. The 1994 and 1995 will be worthy follow-ups.

The Blancheton brothers have one important advantage over most of their fellow-growers: they enjoy a prime site just outside the town of Duras on the road leading into it from the north and so have an ideal pitch for capturing the passing-by trade. Patrick is the wine-maker and his brother Francis is in charge of the business side. Their father Claude has officially retired, but like all retired *vignerons* he is always available to advise the younger generation. He is also in charge of entertaining the customers.

The tasting-room where Claude will dispense to you the Blancheton wines is all that is left of an ancient *chais*. The building formed the heart of an enormous vineyard on this site, shown clearly on archival maps of the area. The property is called **Château La Moulière (6)** and is named after a Monsieur Lamolhière who became the feudal tenant of it from the dukes of Duras at the end of the sixteenth century. Lamolhière was not a native of Duras, but part of one of the waves of immigration into the area. The family died out in 1687 when the last of the line was sent to the galleys for his Protestant beliefs. The property, with its extensive vineyards, reverted to the dukes who re-let it to one of their local trustworthy friends: it must have been an important estate, because it was allowed to fly an oriflamme, a privilege granted to only a handful of houses in the area.

Like Lamolhière, Claude Blancheton too is a relative newcomer to Duras. When he moved in from the Gironde and bought the château in the 1950s, there were only 6 hectares of vines surviving. By 1982 these had grown to 16 and today there are 26, divided equally between the production of grapes for red and white wines.

Although the Blanchetons have roughly equal quantities of the three basic red grape-varieties, Patrick is nervous about relying too much on cabernet sauvignon because it is liable to the disease called eutypiose. This is widespread further north, and there is not yet any known antidote or cure. They have also grubbed up their few malbec grapes: Patrick says that the plant is unpredictable and its yield varies too much from one year to the next. He follows the general pattern of making a mainstream conventional red, and another which is given some ageing in wood, in his case in barrels which are renewed one-third each year. The 1990 versions of both wines won gold medals in Bordeaux. Patrick tends to keep the *cuvaison* just short of three weeks as he thinks that anything longer tends to make the wine too tannic and astringent. Though he has both enamelled concrete and stainless steel, he prefers concrete for his reds because it is less susceptible to variations in temperature. This is particularly important to him because he likes to ferment the red at as a high a temperature as he dares, about 34°. The wines are not filtered until after the malolactic fermentation is finished, but rackings are frequent and the wine is fined with egg white before bottling.

As well as 9 hectares of sauvignon the Blanchetons have 2¹/₂ of sémillon and 1¹/₂ of muscadelle, but Patrick explained that he does not make an old-fashioned half-sweet *moelleux*, because it is difficult to market. He agreed with me that this was a pity, because it is the style of white wine which always used to be made in Duras before the fashion for sauvignon: it was what the local bars sold in the pre-Pastis age, and what in those days you offered to casual visitors.

Patrick is not short of takers for his dry sauvignon, a Paris gold medal winner against stiff local competition. But his real love is his first and so far only *liquoreux* which he made for the first time in 1990. Although botrytis does not apparently reach Duras, he was able to harvest his grapes that year with 25° of natural sugar, and like his colleagues in Saussignac he needed a dispensation from the wine authorities to call this extraordinary effort a Duras *moelleux*. I was not surprised to learn that he had been to oenology college with Pascal Labasse who is doing much the same kind of thing in Jurançon, as we shall see. Patrick's *liquoreux* is not mentioned on the price-list of Château La Moulière: the figure of 90 francs a bottle would look rather strange alongside the more modest prices which Francis is asking for the other wines of this excellent property. Since Patrick only made eight *barriques* of the golden nectar, maybe he does not want to sell it at all. Duras wine of this style is very rare: in fact Patrick thought there was only one other grower making it, Monsieur Bireaud at the Domaine du Vieux Bourg.

If there is nobody at home when you call at the Château La Moulière, the family has a shop in the main square of Duras where you can buy their wine and also other vinous and gastronomic goodies. It is called

Chai et Rasade. I will leave readers to work out for themselves Francis'
little joke.

Another young grower, Michel Fonvielhe, could not be more different from Patrick Blancheton if he tried. Patrick is jovial with a short
black crew-cut and the kind of shape which no doubt earned him an
important place on the rugby field a few years back. Michel Fonvielhe
is quiet and modest, but obviously burns with no less intensity. His
family can claim over two hundred years as Duraquois, and they have a
row of centenarian sémillon vines among the 19 hectares that are currently planted with grapes at their **Domaine de Durand (19)**. Michel
took over from his father in 1985 but is still under forty: he has in the
meantime done much to enhance the reputation of the vineyard, having
won numerous medals, the national award for young wine-maker and
substantial acclaim from all sections of the national and regional press.

Michel has an unusually high 35% cabernet franc in his red grape
encépagement, completed with 40% merlot and 25% cabernet sauvignon.
He makes just one red wine which is given a long maceration, all the
varieties being vinified together. Selected *cuves* are given ageing in
wood, but he does not want the wood to dominate. He believes in flexibility and trusts to his instincts in matters like de-stalking, where his
decision will depend on the health of the grapes and the character of the
vintage. The *élevage* is long, as much as two years, so this is obviously
not a wine for early drinking. He also makes a rosé by *saignage* from it.

The white wine *encépagement* at Domaine de Durand is not quite
conventional: there is only 25% sauvignon, the balance being made up
with 30% sémillon, 30% muscadelle and as much as 15% ugni blanc and
colombard, a reminder that Gascony is not far away to the south.
Michel uses his sauvignon and a touch of the muscadelle for his dry
white wine which has excellent fruit and style: the 1992 I tried was a little *perlé*, but none the worse for that. The remainder of his white grapes
go into his *moelleux*, which he too finds trouble in marketing. Some of it
he sells *en vrac*. I found his 1987 excellently balanced with a refreshing
bouquet of citrus fruits and good acidity to match the underlying honey
on the palate.

Despite his natural quietness and modesty, Michel Fonvielhe is no
slouch when it comes to marketing, having a place on the wine-lists of
many of the most prestigious restaurants of the South-West: Trama at
Puymirol, Vanel in Toulouse, Madame Gracia at Poudenas, Lebrun at
Pujols, and so on. He has built an eye-catching tasting- and sales-room
so that passers-by on their way through to Agen may be tempted to try
his wines. Ideally he would like to get his whole operation under one
roof, but his expansion has been piece-meal and it would be expensive
as well as difficult to start building from scratch again. He thinks that
continued press and media attention are valuable to him because the
problem with Duras in his eyes is that it has no urban centre to act as a
magnet of interest. It is certainly in the middle of nowhere, but I
pointed out to him that for the visitor that was part of its charm. Michel

is full of optimism: Duras is still an underused and underplanted appellation, and he, too, may one day start making a wine from *vendanges tardives*.

Although the largest Duras vineyard is Guy Pauvert's at Domaine
Amblard, **Château La Grave-Béchade (10)** stands out as being the
only real château, in the architectural sense of the word, making wine
under the appellation. It is only a few kilometres to the west of the town
of Duras, just below the small village of Baleyssagues. Béchade has
always been a common name hereabouts, representing a dynasty of
once-peasant farmers who were already numerous before the
Revolution. Some of them made good as a result of that upheaval, and
the present château bearing the Béchade name is what we would call a
Victorian country house with the addition of imitation pepper-pot
turrets and other decoration of the period. It was built in 1860 by a local
dignitary called Abdon Béchade, whose name and mustachioed medal-
lion is today carried by the best red wine of the property. The château
stands in the middle of a large estate, with exceptionally fine outbuildings. It was bought in 1963 by the present owner, Daniel Amar, on his
return from North Africa, and he has spared no expense in creating a
modern vineyard of 58 hectares, converting the outbuildings into a
first-class series of *chais*, including a large reception-hall which is used
for banquets and local functions. Monsieur Amar also owns a property
called Château Le Mayne in the Gironde, where he makes wine under
the Bordeaux Supérieur appellation: in addition he has a wine-whole-
saling business, dealing in the finest growths of Bordeaux and
Burgundy. It is easy to see that this is a totally different kind of operation from those of all the other private growers in Duras.

The creation of the vineyard and the equipment of the converted
buildings was in 1976 entrusted to Daniel Bensoussan, who is also the
oenologist in charge of production. He has installed every kind of modern aid to wine-making: each *cuve* has independent temperature control
with an electronic master-switchboard, such as is used in only the
largest plants; two huge stainless-steel tanks for freezing the sauvignon
before bottling so as to prevent the formation of crystals in bottle; the
cuves are used for nothing else. There is sterilised bottling of course:
you name it and Grave-Béchade has it.

It was a relief to find that the wines were up to the standard of this
equipment, undoubtedly some of the best Duras currently being made.
A fifth of the vineyard is given over to sauvignon grapes: there are no
other white ones. The vinification is conventional and the resulting
wine has agreeably greenish tinges, with delicate fruit on the palate.
The bouquet develops with age and the wine acquires a soft roundness
in the bottle – Monsieur Bensoussan recommends it with fresh goats'
cheese.

The other 80% of the Béchade grapes are red, in the normal ratio
40: 30: 30. Some rosé is made, and the bulk of the red comes in three
grades, the top two of which are from grapes picked by hand, and the

Abdon Béchade premium wine is aged in oak. The basic red has more merlot in it than the others, where the cabernets are correspondingly more dominant. It can be drunk young, to accompany charcuterie and roast meats, but it develops with age and the increasing depth and character of the wine would be good with game and strong cheeses. Perhaps because of the house-connections with neighbouring Bordeaux, the two premium reds have some affinity with claret and would show to good advantage with many *crus bourgeois* of the Gironde. Perhaps also because of the links with other wine-areas, Monsieur Bensoussan tends to make you feel that La Grave-Béchade exists in a vacuum in Duras – that as well as being the best Duras it is the *only* one, as if the artisan growers who make up the backbone of the appellation do not exist.

It was therefore something of a pleasure to remember that there were plenty more real country wine-makers to visit. Lucien Salesse has officially retired at the **Domaine de Ferrant (39)**, but as mayor of the commune of Esclottes and President of the local Duras Confrérie, he will have plenty to keep him out of mischief. He hopes that his son will carry on the traditions of four generations in the making of wine and the conversion of plums into prunes. Monsieur Salesse was not the only wine-maker to tell us that in Duras some of the best wine comes from vineyards which are immediately next to the plum orchards, of which he has 15 hectares: nearly as many as he has under vine.

His 20 hectares of grapes are divided roughly two-thirds red and one-third white. He makes two white wines: a *sec* exclusively from sauvignon which has a pronounced elderflower and gooseberry character when young, but which develops fruitiness and good body with age. He also makes a *moelleux* from sémillon with a little sauvignon to give it a point of acidity. Monsieur Salesse said he was too old to start experimenting with *macération pelliculaire* or with new wood, although he had no doubt that his son might have a go with both. The vinification is therefore simple and old-fashioned, though the temperatures are strictly kept to about 18°. The dry sauvignon wine is bottled as soon as possible, but the *moelleux* usually waits until just before the following vintage. I was lucky to be offered a tasting of his 1986 *moelleux*, made before he dug up his muscadelle grapes which gave the wine a pronounced almondy character. The 1992 was more 'modern' in style, with the sauvignon influence stronger than in the older wine.

Monsieur Salesse told me that in former times before any red wine was grown seriously in Duras and before the vogue for sauvignon, it was not true that a *moelleux* wine was all you drank and with every course of a meal. Even those who made this style of wine for resale also had a few hybrid red grapes from which they made a table wine for everyday consumption. If they didn't, they would buy some *en vrac* from a neighbour.

Today, red Duras can be made only from the noble grape-varieties. Monsieur Salesse grows only a little cabernet franc nowadays, mostly to make a rosé for summer drinking. He is gradually simplifying his vineyard, concentrating on merlot and cabernet sauvignon, which he has in roughly equal quantities. Harvesting is by machine which he owns jointly with another grower. All the grapes are de-stalked before the different varieties are vinified separately for between ten and fifteen days. Some of the wine he bottles promptly like Gilbert Geoffroy, the rest remains in vat for one year. His customers include a number of restaurants in Toulouse, as well as private buyers for his bottled wine: he sells some off through the trade *en vrac*. One of his wines used to be available in the UK under the name of Château de Gourdon, but I believe he has discontinued this as a separate brand. Today he just concentrates on the one red, which is deep in colour and has a great deal of merlot fruitiness. I find, though, that his white wines have generally more finesse.

Lucien Salesse's father used also to own what is now the adjoining vineyard of **Château Bellevue Haut-Roc (38)**. In the late 1940s he employed a young Italian refugee from the Mussolini regime, who had fled to a country which also made wine and where he hoped the sun would shine almost as strongly. It was not long before Salesse Senior offered Monsieur Rossetto the tenancy of the adjoining farm on the profit-sharing system called *métairie*. Nearly twenty years later, in 1968, both men died suddenly. Rossetto's son, Bruno, took over the *métairie*, while the Salesse estate was divided equally between the young Lucien, who took the Domaine de Ferrant, and his sister, who took over Bellevue and became Rossetto's landlord. Later in 1979, Bruno Rossetto was able to buy his freehold from the Salesse daughter. So today Lucien Salesse and Bruno Rossetto are neighbours and fellow-producers of Duras and prunes.

Bruno remembers replanting the vineyard at Bellevue Haut-Roc twice: once when he was a boy after his father took over the property, and again when he bought the freehold in 1979. Even at that stage there were still a lot of hybrid grapes which were not allowed under appellation rules, so Rossetto was ruthless in weeding them out and replanting with merlot and cabernet. Nowadays the 10-hectare vineyard is divided equally between red and white grapes.

Rossetto is short and dark like a Gascon, but with blue eyes and a transalpine smile. He also has the independence of his adopted country. As a tenant who has enfranchised himself, he does not like being told by the authorities what he can do. For example, he accepts intellectually the need for a uniform starting date for the *vendange*, but would like to think that the rules don't apply to him. He follows his own whim on matters such as the length of fermentation – sometimes he admits to getting it wrong, but claims that is his right as a private grower. Some years it may be ten days, others three weeks. '*Je vinifie avec le nez,*' he says. He has a consultant oenologist, whose advice he respects but often does not follow.

In his father's day, all the wine from Bellevue Haut-Roc was white: it was also *moelleux*. Like other growers Rossetto is finding it difficult to market this traditional style of wine, so he concentrates on a dry white, though he still has as many sémillon vines as sauvignon. He has a little ugni blanc, too, which is still allowed as a supporting variety in small quantities. His 1992 was very pale and had a delicate and typical sauvignon bouquet, but in the mouth the fruit was surprisingly big: Bruno thought he could detect bananas. The finish was long, and though bone-dry had more than a suggestion of honey. This was one of the best sauvignons I came across in Duras or anywhere else. For his red wines he has a little malbec, otherwise equal quantities of merlot and the two cabernets. He makes them in concrete, though he has a little plastic for *élevage*. He is against the use of new wood for either his reds or whites.

At the other end of the appellation, almost into Saussignac, another highly individualist grower is causing a stir among Duras-fanciers. In 1989 Monica Buggin sold **Château Lafon (21)** in the small village of Loubès-Bernac to Pascal Gitton, a bearded wine-grower from Sancerre, where he has a famous and substantial vineyard. For Pascal, therefore, Château Lafon is a *vignoble secondaire*. He was attracted to Duras by the challenge of making wine in an old-established AOC area which had not caught the public imagination in the way it should have done. He has set out to do everything his own way, regardless of expense, which is something he could not have contemplated except on the back of an already established business.

Pascal maintains that his village was the cradle of the Duras vineyard. Gallo-Roman coins have been found nearby and there are remains of a Merovingian chapel. History also relates that Norman monks made wine here for several centuries, their tombs having recently been discovered in the district. After the wars of religion, the fanatically Huguenot mistress of the fortress of Théobon decided to annex the vineyard of Loubès-Bernac and had the Norman prior murdered. Because of her religious connections she was able to develop trading links with the Dutch, as the Huguenots of Bergerac had done, and the vineyard thrived on it for more than a century and a half. The daughters of the house of Théobon took pot luck at the court of Louis XIV, where one became his mistress and one the mistress of another courtier. When Louis tired of Lydia, both ladies returned to their native Duras, where Lydia shut herself up in Théobon and her sister withdrew to what is now Château Lafon. At the time of the Revolution, the mayor of Loubès, a left-wing *avocat*, ordered Théobon to be partially dismantled, but he did acquire Château Lafon for himself where wine-making somehow survived all the national upheavals and has continued to the present day.

The property is at just about the highest point of the Lot-et-Garonne and enjoys day-long sunshine. The soil is particularly chalky, more so than lower down in Duras: Pascal Gitton thinks this may explain why the wines of Loubès-Bernac tend to generate more alcohol than other Duras. He has 12 hectares, from 5 of which he makes red wine and white from the rest. Although he makes a pure sauvignon wine, most of his white grapes are sémillon, which form the basis of a dry wine and also a *moelleux*. The dry sémillon is particularly good, with a combination of honey, herbs and fresh hay on both the nose and palate. I liked it rather better than the sauvignon, though you have to be careful what you say about the sauvignon grape to a man from Sancerre.

Because he has a lot of malbec vines, the red wines from Lafon tend to be somewhat confusing, depending on the *assemblages* which Pascal fancies to make from one year to the next. In 1990, for example, he made a wine from 100% merlot, which seemed to me dull compared with his blended wine of the same year from 25% malbec, 50% cabernet sauvignon and only 25% merlot – no cabernet franc. This was quite astonishingly good with a real *goût du terroir*. He gave us tastings from the wood of a young 1992 merlot, as well as a blend from 1991 which was 65% malbec and which surprisingly tasted nothing like a Cahors.

Pascal is not, of course, able to spend all of his time at Château Lafon, but he does try to get there for all the important events in the wine-calendar. When he is away, his predecessor, Madame Buggin, is on hand to keep a watchful eye on the vineyard, but Pascal's arrival is the signal for a great bustle of activity. He maintains an almost perpetual open house, with friends, buyers, bottlers and *négociants* coming and going, sometimes without warning and often a day or so late. What might seem to be total disorder in any other enterprise may just be a facet of Pascal Gitton's restless personality. As a relative new boy in Duras, he needs to experiment, and his natural curiosity may well lead him in directions where he will be able to establish a distinctive house-style. However that may not be what he wants; perhaps he just wishes to relax from making Sancerre and do as he likes in his holiday-vineyard. Why not?

CÔTES DU MARMANDAIS

The small town of Ste-Bazeille sits astride the Route Nationale 113 from Agen to Bordeaux. It is not in the least remarkable except for the volume of traffic which thunders down its main street, but its mayor is a very important man. **Fernand Lagaüzère (4)** is both the president of the *syndicat* of the Vins des Côtes du Marmandais and a private producer of the wine in his own right. The combined burdens of his various offices oblige him to leave the wine-making to his son and today the family make wine mostly for themselves, friends and customers of long-standing. I asked him whether there were any other independent growers making Marmandais wine and he mentioned his neighbour **Monsieur Simonnet (5)**. They both have vineyards at Rizens on the edge of the town, but he suggested that I concentrated on the two caves co-opératives which dominate local production: **Les Vignerons de Beaupuy (2)** on the right bank of the Garonne, and its rival, **La Cave de Cocumont (3)** on the left bank. The interests of the two are well served by the independence and integrity of Monsieur Lagaüzère, who

is more than able to ensure fair play between them. He opens ceremonial functions at both, particularly at the time of the harvest. He
describes the bustle of activity at that time as 'a real ballet of tractors'.

I was surprised that Monsieur Lagaüzère did not mention Pierre and
Christian Boissonneau, whom I discovered to have 6¹/₂ hectares of vines
in the Marmande appellation. Perhaps this was because their large
domaine, Château de la Vieille Tour at St Michel-de-Lapujade, is just
over the border into the département of the Gironde. Most of its production is of wine which enjoys the benefit of the Bordeaux Supérieur
appellation. All the same, Pierre Boissoneau is proud of his Marmande
wine. He by no means treats it as a sideline, even though his Bordeaux
production is six times as big.

The Boissonneau-Bordeaux and the Boissonneau-Marmande vineyards are separated by a little stream which is the boundary between the
two appellations. The château has been in the family since 1839, but
Pierre pointed out that this meant little when related to the history of
the tiny village of Lorette close by, whose diminutive church was built
by Eleanor of Aquitaine at the end of the twelfth century. In the middle
of his complex of farm-buildings stands a *pigeonnier*, an outstanding
feature which is pictured on some of his labels, and which used to serve
the whole of the local population.

Monsieur Boissonneau explained to us how the wines of Marmande
had made the transition from VDQS status to AOC in 1990. The wine-
authorities had made it a condition that growers should have at least
25% of their land planted with one or more varieties particular to the
South-West of France: syrah, malbec and fer servadou which are
already familiar, and more especially a variety which crops up only as a
rarity elsewhere but is the hallmark of Marmande, abouriou. The powers that be were anxious that Marmande should be able to distinguish
itself from its neighbours, Duras to the north and Buzet to the south.
Boissonneau anticipated the new rules by planting no less than 45% of
his Marmande vineyard with the local varieties. Now that the new vines
are mature, they dominate the resulting wine through their typical rustic qualities. Boissonneau's Marmandais is no Bordeaux lookalike. It is
more individual and original than any of the wines I later tasted from
either of the co-opératives. Both Beaupuy and Cocumont have been
slower to follow the thinking behind the new rules, towards which they
display nothing like the enthusiasm of Monsieur Boissoneau.

The Marmande wine from Vieille Tour is called **Domaine des
Géais (1)**, to differentiate it from the Bordeaux wines which the estate
makes. Sometimes it is to be found in shops as Domaine de St Martin,
but there is no difference between the contents of the bottles despite the
labelling. This is another case of a wine-maker being anxious not to
devalue his goodwill on the shelves of the supermarkets. The production is sophisticated, enjoying the benefit of the most modern plant.
The short *cuvaison* of only five or six days is by no means surprising
in the Marmandais, where the aim is to produce a fruity rather than

a long-lasting wine. Boissonneau vinifies some of his many grape-varieties together, for example the merlot and the abouriou which ripen early and at the same time, then the syrah and fer servadou, and finally the two cabernets. Boissonneau uses no wood and leaves the wine in the *cuves* until it is bottled just before the following vintage.

Although the Boissonneaus export as much as 70% of their production, their Marmande seems to be little known in the UK, which is a pity, since the wines of both the co-opératives are represented here from time to time. Beaupuy was formed in 1948 and is the senior; Cocumont followed later in 1957. Monsieur Bonnet, the oenologist at Beaupuy, believes that his members have a higher proportion of abouriou than the growers on the left bank, whom he says rely more on malbec for their quota of 'rustic' grapes. Before the emergence of the Beaupuy Cave, abouriou had almost died out in the Marmandais, according to Bonnet. It is called locally *gamay de beaujolais*, which is confusing on two counts: it has nothing at all to do with the real gamay grape, which is the essential grape of Beaujolais. Furthermore the real gamay is also a permitted supporting variety in Marmandais. Bonnet said that abouriou was valuable because of the fruit and colour it gives to the wine, as well as its local character.

The soil round Beaupuy on the right bank is largely *argilo-calcaire*, chalk mixed with some clay, whereas on the left bank at Cocumont it is sandier, more like the Gascon *terroir* which it adjoins. According to Monsieur Bonnet right-bank wines tend to mature more slowly. No doubt this has encouraged Beaupuy to age some of its best *cuves* in new wood, but I wonder whether this will turn out to justify the investment or the extra price to the consumer. There are two such wines being made at the moment. Each has 25% abouriou: the one called Richard Premier is completed by 45% cabernet sauvignon and 30% merlot; the other is 75% cabernet sauvignon and is called Beaupuy Prestige. The former is less woody, because the barrels used are not quite new, but three years after the vintage none of the elements had really started to come together. The Beaupuy Prestige was a better wine, though more heavily oaked. It had good style and balance with plenty of prunes in the fruit, but it will need a long time to come round.

The mainstream wines of the Cave come in two ranges: first a group called Tradition, which bear names such as Le Cloître, L'Authentique, Le Vieux Manoir and Clos de Brézet. These are not single-domaine wines, even if the last-named suggests it is a second wine of the Domaine de Brézet mentioned below. The vinification of these wines is very similar, only the *encépagements* seeming to differ, ringing the changes between the supporting 'rustic' grapes. Of the 'Bordeaux' varieties merlot seems to take precedence over the others except in Clos de Brézet. L'Authentique is made from grapes coming exclusively from the commune of Marmande itself. Le Cloître was the wine I liked the best of all those I tasted at Beaupuy, apart from the single-property wines. It was also very nearly their cheapest. The more ambitious version, called Cloître d'Or, was big and clumsy by comparison, the 20% syrah content giving it quite a chocolatey taste. Perhaps it needed time, but I found it thin and rather sour, with some suggestions of drains on the nose.

The Beaupuy co-opérative also makes and bottles wines from a number of single domaines, of which I tasted first Domaine de Lescour. The 1988 was just starting to brown after five years, but it was still dark, plummy and truffly. La Renardière, of which the 1990 still needed time, was also deep purple, with a woodland undergrowth smell on the nose, toasty and tannic: Domaine de Brézet, for my money the best by far, was well balanced with good fruit and just the right amount of rusticity to differentiate it from its Bordeaux-satellite neighbours. Finally there are a number of short-fermentation wines – quickies – of which the less said the better. They are marketed under the name Marmandelle.

The Beaupuy co-opérative has obviously done a lot in the last twelve years or so to face up to the competition from Cocumont across the river. In terms of capital investment it has a new reception area for the grapes, a new shop and tasting-area, a new bottling plant and packaging warehouse. It has also brought its marketing and presentation bang up to date. It may, however, be trying to do too much. I find the sheer range of its products confusing and the standards vary a good deal. The best wines are good, but there are some which I would want to eliminate if I were in charge.

The regime at Cocumont across the river is very different: there are far fewer wines, although the total production of AOC Marmandais is over twice as large as at Beaupuy. Jean-Marie Mourguet was in his last year as director at Cocumont when he invited me to spend a few hours with him. I would not have been surprised if he had asked me to come some other day, because at the time the Cave was in the process of taking delivery of two enormous stainless-steel *cuves*. The traffic had been held up for miles around by a cohort of gesticulating gendarmes, who seemed far more agitated than Monsieur Mourguet, who was taking the event in his stride. The entire staff of the Cave had their heads out of the windows to watch the arrival of these two monsters, which reclined horizontally on the biggest trailers I have ever seen. *Convoi exceptionnel* indeed.

Monsieur Mourguet exudes a passionate enthusiasm: at seven o'clock in the evening he would have taken me on a tour of the vineyards if I had not been frightened of losing booked hotel accommodation an hour's drive away. It was a pity to have to refuse this offer, because a stroll through the vines often tells one more than a tour of the *chais*: one *cuve* is much like another, but no two vineyards are ever quite the same. From the windows of the Cave's offices he expounded on the topography of the left bank, comparing it with the very different layout across the Garonne at Beaupuy. At Cocumont a shelf rises out of the valley, rather as at Monbazillac, to create a plateau about 100 feet above the level of the river. Then come the rolling hills, the *côteaux*, on a ridge of which the Cave stood. The views all round were magnificent. I asked Monsieur Mourguet whether he thought it was right to build such a utilitarian building as his Cave so close to the Romanesque church just behind it: he said that, even if the Church in the middle ages had known a thing or two about picking a good site, that did not give them exclusivity. The pretty church features on the labels of one of the Cave's prestige wines.

Cocumont differs from Beaupuy in that it has members with vines in the Gironde – thus, like the Boissoneaus, they make Bordeaux as well as Marmande. This has produced tensions over the years between Cocumont and the wine-authorities. Many of the Cocumont growers, who can get more money for wine bearing the Bordeaux name, did not see why they should have to dig up a quarter of their Marmandais vines to comply with the new rules. This may explain why the abouriou grape is not grown nearly so much on the left bank as it is on the right. Before 1789, Marmande was even sold as Bordeaux, but the First Republic put a stop to this, another achievement of the hapless Monsieur Lakanal.

Jean-Marie Mourguet is very conscious of the deep divide in the appellation caused by the wide Garonne which flows through its middle. The split is accentuated by the ban on planting grapes between the Garonne and the Canal du Midi, which runs parallel to the river but a few kilometres to the south. The land between the two waterways is almost certain to flood after heavy rain. The river, too, is largely responsible for the need to have two co-opératives. It would not have been feasible to expect growers on one bank to have to deliver their wines to a Cave on the bank opposite, if only because the one bridge in the region at Marmande is an impossible bottle-neck at all times. However, if the Marmandais could have made do with one co-opérative, it might, through being able to speak with one voice, have obtained its right to appellation contrôlée many years earlier than it did.

The Cave at Cocumont has one of the most fully automated winemaking plants in the South-West. Jean-Marie was proud of the fact that, once the grapes are in after the *vendange*, there is no grape-juice or human being to be seen among the *cuves*. Everything is operated electronically and by remote control. He denies that this imposes any restraints on the wine-maker: decisions are made solely on the basis of tastings carried out daily during the vinification and at frequent intervals during the *élevage*. Jean-Marie is also fully in favour of picking-machines which are used by all his members. He particularly likes the newer kind, which manages to weave between the rows of vines, selecting only the ripe bunches, rather than battering away at whole plants. He says that if the vines are properly looked after and the bunches correctly exposed to the machine, the latter can do a better job than the hand-picker, leaving the unripe grapes on the vine and taking only the minimum of leaf and stalk with the ripe ones.

But for all his new technology, Jean-Marie, contemplating his retirement, admitted to being a bundle of contradictions which he had not fully resolved for himself. He is at heart a country wine-maker, which is where he started life. He has a friend living down the road, a Monsieur Dumas, who is said still to have some *liquoreux* wines *derrière les fagots* going back to 1914: not for sale, of course. (As at Duras, this was the style of wine which used to be made locally until the Second World War.) At the Cave Jean-Marie has made a feature of a fascinating museum of old viticultural implements. There is also a display of fishing-nets and wood-cutters' tools to remind visitors that the vineyards represent a halfway-house between two quite different cultures: that of the Garonne valley and that of the forests of the Landes not far away to the south.

Both the co-opératives make rosé and white wine, but only in small quantities compared with the production of red. At Cocumont there are two basic red wines: a light one called Floriade, vinified at low temperatures and based on the early ripening merlot and abouriou. Jean-Marie Mourguet describes this as a fun-wine for drinking among friends, lightly chilled. His red called Tradition is aptly named: altogether more serious, it is made conventionally with a fermentation of eight to twelve days at a more normal temperature of 28–30°. The *encépagement* is 75% from merlot and the two cabernets, the remaining 25% being made up of abouriou, malbec, fer servadou, gamay and syrah: a cocktail representing all the grapes which are allowed to go into Côtes du Marmandais. The result is delicious, declared to be better than the Cave's Bordeaux by all around me when I tasted it. Cocumont produces one other non-oaked red, a single-domaine wine which they make and bottle for Jean-André Lafitte at Château La Bastide. There are also three oaked wines, the vinification and *élevage* of which appear to be identical: the difference lies in the *terroirs* from which the grapes for each come. I do not believe that the oaking of these wines does any more for them than it does at Beaupuy: the local character, the *goût du terroir*, is eliminated.

A Cocumont wine available in the UK is that which Hugh Ryman's team used to make at the Cave de Cocumont for Robert Schult, the owner of the substantial **Château de Beaulieu**, a couple of miles up the road from the co-opérative. Schult has now gone fully independent and is making a rather distinctive oaked red wine based on the two cabernet grapes. It will be interesting to see whether, as the appellation develops, more growers such as he will want to go their own way and break away from the co-opératives. Obviously their problem at the moment is the world recession and the glut of wine following four abundant but unexciting vintages. However good the local co-opératives may be, the competition from a few independent producers could do much to accentuate the distinctive character of the Marmandais wines.

Comparison between the two Caves is hard because Cocumont spills over into Bordeaux. Jean-Marie Mourguet told me that, at Cocumont, they have 330 members, of whom 250 or so declare under the Marmandais AOC from 950 hectares of vines. This suggests an average holding of nearly 4 hectares each. (These figures do not include the production of *vin de table* or *vin de pays de l'Agenais*.) At Beaupuy there are 280 members with a total of 650 hectares, and 60% of their production ranks for AOC. The rest is either *vin de table* or *vin de pays*. The latter can be very good indeed, usually based on the bouchalès grape which gives a really plummy rustic character to the wine. The right-bank landholdings tend to be smaller and the production of non-AOC wine bigger than on the left bank, even after making allowance for the left-bank vines which are over the boundary into Bordeaux.

The less complicated the wines of Marmandais, the better they are. The reds, which are simply made and old-fashioned, are delicious with a very special character that tends to get lost through over-sophistication, particularly through the use of oak. If the growers take advantage of the abouriou grape, they ought to be able to find an expanding place in the market, provided they keep the style of their wine young, fruity and easy to drink.

CÔTES DE BUZET

The spread of viticulture from Narbonne to Bordeaux under the Romans passed through what is now the Côtes de Buzet, an area which lies on the slopes of the left bank of the Garonne between Agen and Marmande. Excavations a little further into the hinterland at Mézin and Moncrabeau have thrown up pruning-knives from the ancient world, which have proved that there were wine-growers at work here in the second century AD.

As elsewhere in Aquitaine, the growing of grapes played an important part in the polycultural system of farming. In peasant homes, the making of wine served two functions: provision for the family, and the making of a little extra which brought in cash to pay for those few commodities not produced by the farm. You also had to keep the tax-collector at bay, whether he was the feudal bailiff under the *ancien régime*, or *le fisc* as he is called nowadays. The accent was on quantity, rather than quality. Until the nineteenth century home-consumption absorbed half the local production, every adult drinking on average 200 litres a year, or, in modern terms, three-quarters of a bottle a day. Since women in those days drank little or no wine the men never went thirsty. It was a point of honour for every farm of good standing to produce a respectable wine for its own table.

Buzet was, however, near enough to Bordeaux to become an important source of supply for the dealers there. The farmers of Buzet gradually expanded their vineyards to make far more wine than they needed at home and Buzet slowly became absorbed into the Bordeaux system, its wines sold both to and as Bordeaux. The period following the Revolution saw the beginning of a switch from the production of *vins ordinaires* to better quality wines, to meet the demands of an expanding market. As with other areas of the *haut-pays*, the middle of the nineteenth century was a golden age, brutally cut short by the diseases which hit all the vineyards of the South-West, principally of course the phylloxera.

When eventually the growers of Buzet chose the path of grafting on to immune American rootstocks, they decided to propagate the malbec, bouchalès and mérille grapes at first. Gradually the two cabernets were encouraged in order to approximate the Buzet wines more to those of the rest of Bordeaux. Ironically it was the determination of growers all over France to stamp out fraud and bad practice in the vineyards and the *chais* which caused a further unforeseen crisis for Buzet – in 1911 it was decreed that no wines outside the département of the Gironde might be sold under the name Bordeaux.

Disinherited and nameless, Buzet entered into a long period of agony. Its rebirth was late, painful and beset with false starts. A handful of local activists worked hard to obtain VDQS status in 1953, but even this did not on its own provide the necessary impetus. It was the creation in 1955 of the cave co-opérative – **Les Vignerons Réunis des Côtes de Buzet (1)** – which was to mark the start of recovery.

The period in the wilderness had resulted in bastardisation of the vines: the first imperative was to restore the quality of the stock, particularly by encouraging the adoption of the merlot grape. Specialist help from outside made it possible to identify which types of soil would best suit the three important grape-varieties: the poor and porous flinty pebbles for the cabernet sauvignon, the softer, lighter, more sandy, pebbly soil for the cabernet franc, and the heavier clay-like textures for the merlot. The secret of the success of the Buzet co-opérative today lies in its early identification of the different types of soil within the appellation.

This concentration on quality production has had spectacular results. When the Cave was founded, the production of *vin de table* represented 92% of the total output, 10,800 hectolitres of it: by 1982 75% of the production was of appellation wine, with only 25% *vin de table*, the total having risen to some 72,000 hectolitres. In the intervening period the unremitting hard work and sacrifices of the growers had resulted in full AOC recognition in 1973. The vineyards now stretch from the edge of the forest of the Landes in the west nearly to Agen in the east. To the north they are bounded by the river Garonne, and in the south they look down from the hills into Gascony.

The co-opérative has 250 or so members making wine from 1600 hectares, an average of just over 6 hectares each (higher than the average for most co-opératives). The Cave is responsible for the production of 85% of the total output of Buzet AOC. A notable feature is the concentration on the use of new wood for ageing the wines: only 30% of the production escapes the attention of their resident *tonnelier*, Yves St Martin. Buzet is the only co-opérative in the South-West to have a barrel-maker as a permanent member of staff – every year Yves makes up to 800 new *barriques*, the wooden casks which hold 225 litres or so of wine. There are 4000 of them altogether in the Buzet *chais d'élevage*, which means that 20% are renewed each year. The wood comes mainly from the forests of the Tronçais in Central France. Fortunately for the Cave, Yves has a son who has studied at the cooperage school in Beaune, and who will take his place in due course at Buzet. Visitors to the Cave can ask to see the barrel-making in progress, and, whether or not you like your wine to taste of new oak, the process is a fascinating one.

Yves says that the wood has to be stored out of doors for at least two years to make it resistant to all kinds of weather. He will show you how the staves – *douelles* – have to be cut so as to fit together when the fire is applied to them: the subtle angles are obtained by the use of a wooden set, a rather unsquare square. The staves have to be dampened to stop them catching fire. The furnace is made from off-cuts of the same wood; this is apparently vital to the quality of the ultimate barrel. While still hot the wood is bent over a sort of model barrel, and the staves are then brought together at the base before the bands are put in place. In the old days these used to be made of willow or other pliable wood, but nowadays they are made of iron.

I asked Yves what he thought of the idea of avoiding the costly replacement of whole barrels by simply renewing the flat, uncurved ends every year instead of the whole barrel with its expensively moulded staves every few years. This is what the innovative Patrick Ducournau does in Madiran, as we shall see. Yves St Martin was dubious, but then any barrel-maker would be, wouldn't he? Every *barrique* costs about £300, but this is only the beginning of the expense to the wine-maker. There is the cost of the space which these casks occupy in the cellar and the labour-costs inherent in maturing the wine in single barrels rather than cement tanks – every barrel needs individual attention from the point of view of *soutirage* and ullage. It takes the same length of time to check and remedy the state of health of a 100-hectolitre *cuve* as it does the condition of a 2.25 hectolitre *barrique*. All the same, it seems that those who oak their wines in new wood are more than able to pass on the additional overheads to the consumer, who has

quickly become accustomed to the idea that an oaked wine carries a large premium.

This Cave is one of the most go-ahead in the South-West. It also enjoys one of the best reputations. The plant is ultra-modern: it is copiously staffed with more than seventy employees and the working environment is highly agreeable. No expense has been spared on the conditions of work, and the office block makes this retired London lawyer green with envy. Monsieur Champemont, the director, explained to me that they have a satellite Cave at Espiens where members can bring their wines to be pressed. It has no front-of-house facilities, but serves as a useful means of quick delivery for some of the members who have properties in the distant corners of this rambling appellation. It presses about one-third of the total production, and serves the same purpose as the satellite Gaillac Cave of Labastide-de-Lévis at Cordes.

The Cave produces a variety of styles of wine, of which 95% is red. Small amounts of rosé and white wine complement the range, but it is the red wines for which the area is best known. The white and pink wines, though well made, have little individuality and could just as well come from any of the Bordeaux satellites. The red wines do, however, have a distinctive character: some call it a taste of prunes, attributing it to the fact that the local fruit orchards of Lot-et-Garonne produce more prunes than any other area in Europe. This explanation conveniently avoids the fact that the plum-trees from which the prunes derive are not grown on the left bank of the river at all, because the soil is too stoney and the trees fall over all too easily in the wind. However it is true that Buzet wines do enjoy, for whatever reason, a particularly deep, fruity, southern character which can, in the hands of a winemaker who wants to preserve the typicity of his wine, set it aside from the wines of nearby regions. They are also usually darker and fruitier than the wines of the other Bordeaux satellites.

There are three main ranges of red wine made at the Cave. In rising order of price and quality they are called Tradition (sometimes available in the UK as Cuvée Henri IV), Carte d'Or and Baron d'Ardeuil. The new wood is handed down like children's clothes from the best to the cheapest: otherwise they all have a similar *encépagement*: 50% merlot and 25% each of the cabernets. Even the Tradition is given ten to fifteen days' vinification. The Carte d'Or comes from a lighter soil and vines which are on average twelve years old, while the Baron comes from much older vines and the grapes are hand-selected before vinification. Their stay in new wood is fifteen months or so. Monsieur Champemont thinks that the Baron is at its best after eight to ten years, the others after five to eight years. The wine is named after a local aristocrat, whose wife was for some years more than a secretary to Napoléon, who consoled her long-suffering husband with a barony.

There is also a range of all three colours in bottles which look hand-painted and have no paper-labels: *serrigraphié* is the French term for this style of presentation which is more appropriate to perfumes than wines. The intention is obviously to reflect the style of the product: wines of short maceration for early drinking. The red in particular is quite attractive, fruity and quaffable, but it lacks any distinguishing character.

The mainstream rosé is made from a blend of merlot and cabernet franc and should be drunk cold and young: it has a redcurrant colour, darker than some pink wines, and fermentation at low temperature ensures its freshness. The white wine is based on sémillon with a little sauvignon and muscadelle: only three-parts dry, it has undertones of honey and acacia blossoms as well as citrus fruits.

Buzet has taken the lead in establishing a portfolio of single domaines for which they make and bottle the wine either at the individual properties or at the cave co-opérative itself. By far the best of these is the wine which comes from the Château de Gueyze, a pretty building in a rather isolated location half an hour's drive east of the co-opérative. It is scarcely lived in and is fortunately undergoing renovation; there are no wine-making facilities, but there are 80 hectares or so of vines in lovely rolling countryside. The land is on high ground and consists of rather meagre *graves*; the exposition towards the south-west and west is splendid. The wine has an exceptionally firm structure, with good tannins and considerable elegance. Its long ageing in oak means that it is a wine for keeping, and the makers say it needs ten or even fifteen years to show its best. By then it should have developed a gamey nose, and a flavour of ripe strawberries. There is a second wine from this property called Tuque de Gueyze, which has a higher merlot content and thus matures sooner: it is softer and has a slight bitterness about it which is not at all unattractive. At least until recently it has avoided the attention of the *tonnelier*.

Other domaine-clients of the co-opérative are Padère, which used to be independent, Bouchet and Balesté, this last producing a well-rounded rather light wine, maturing earlier than some other Buzets. It sometimes has a Graves-like character with a mushroomy nose. Then there is Larché which has been taken up by supermarkets in England. Others include the unfortunately named Château de Piis, Château Bougigues and Château du Tauzia. Monsieur Champemont claims that all these châteaux are vinified separately because they display different facets of the *terroir*, but even so this co-opérative is not trying hard enough to get away from underneath the skirts of Bordeaux. The strategy seems to be to copy the wines of the Gironde rather than to produce wine with a distinctive character. There is, however, no denying the commercial success of the operation, the quality of its production, or the benefits which it secures for its members. But for wines with an identifiable local message, one has to look elsewhere.

As far as I know, there are only eight independent Buzet producers. There is also the cave co-opérative at Goulens in the adjoining area of Côtes de Brulhois which has members with vines in the Buzet appellation area.

A private grower whose wines I have enjoyed over a ten-year period is Jacques Thérasse who has now handed over to his son Bernard the 20-hectare vineyard called **Château Sauvagnères (7)**. This is tucked away in rolling downland country near the small town of Ste-Colombe-en-Brulhois towards the eastern end of the appellation. 'Château' is a bit of a misnomer, because there is no house as such here at all: just a modern farm building containing the usual range of wine-making facilities, built in a fold of the hills which divide the Garonne valley from Gascony.

The family is Belgian: Bernard's father had a *négociant* friend at Libourne in the Gironde who tempted him into trying to find a small vineyard in the Bordelais. The prices were in Jacques Thérasse's view astronomic, so he shelved the idea until by accident he found these 20 hectares in Buzet on the market. He bought the land in the 1970s and planted it with the typical Buzet mix of 40% merlot, 30% cabernet sauvignon and 30% cabernet franc. He also included a small parcel of sauvignon to make some white wine with. Bernard told me that his father built the *chais* himself.

A comparison between the wines made in 1989 and in the following year illustrated a change in policy. It was not just that 1989 was a tougher, more traditional style of vintage than 1990 – Bernard had deliberately switched to a more fruity and supple style of wine intended for quicker maturity. He had shortened the *cuvaison* to between twelve and fifteen days from an old-fashioned twenty-one days which he had given the 1989. He justified this on the grounds that the softer style was more in keeping with modern tastes, and in this respect he is no doubt right. But I could not help feeling that, excellently made though the 1990 was, it had lost the sense of *terroir* which I liked so much in his much more classic 1989. There were, in fact, two 1989s because in that year he made his first and only experiment with new wood. The oaked wine was still dark and dense in 1993: the black wine of Buzet? There was a bouquet of beeswax with some vanilla, but not too much. The assault on the palate was overpowering: the fruit and acidity were well balanced but the tannins were still aggressive. The wine needed at least another two years before it even started to soften. Bernard has decided to have no more truck with new barrels: he says that all oaked wines tend to turn out much the same, a comment which is beginning to sound less and less daring than it did a few years ago.

Even his unwooded 1989 could do with more time. It had a gamey bouquet, with some leather, what the Bordelais call 'horses' saddles': I thought it had class and would back it against the odds to beat the more obviously charming 1990, which was dark too but with much more forward fruit. The later wine was just about drinkable three years after the vintage, which is what Bernard obviously wants. Even so it will last well and could now be showing itself off at its best.

In years when Bernard Thérasse has more merlot than usual, he makes an *assemblage* which uses up this surplus, calling it Domaine des Jonquilles. It used to be available in the United Kingdom, and was said to be rather like a good Pomerol. Nowadays wine under the same name is sometimes to be found in French supermarkets, but is more likely to be Bernard's mainstream wine in disguise.

Bernard also opened his sauvignon from two vintages. The 1990 was obviously mature, and, though it was bone-dry, it had developed hints of exotic fruits and even honey. The 1992 was fresher, of course, with the characteristic gooseberry taste of the grape, but which I had generally found lacking in wines made from it in Aquitaine. At this latitude, the sauvignon gives a much richer style of wine than in, say, the Loire.

Buzet seems to be an appellation which has attracted a variety of immigrants from all parts of France and beyond: in fact none of the local growers I met had been born or bred in the Lot-et-Garonne. Across the hillside from Bernard Thérasse his friend Daniel Tissot, with whom he shares a harvesting-machine, boasts an ancestry in the Jura where for generations his family had been *vignerons* near the town of Arbois. His vineyard, called **Domaine du Pech (8)** is a mirror–image of Bernard Thérasse's, with just a little parcel of grapes for white wine. He gives his sauvignon grapes twelve hours' skin-contact before vinification in fibreglass. He also makes a little rosé, *saigné* from his cabernet grapes. The main production, though, is red from the same *encépagement* as Bernard's. After total *égrappage*, the grapes are vinified for up to three weeks in stainless steel. His first vintage was in 1980, since when he has won twenty-five medals. He started to experiment with new wood in 1991, but only for part of his crop, and then only if the barrels had already been used for making one wine. The rest of his red wine is matured in wonderful old oak *foudres*, the only ones of their kind which I saw in Buzet. His 1991 is barely ready after 5 years.

Tissot's wines are very good indeed. He explained that his vineyards were on much higher ground than most other growers', so he had not suffered too much from the frosts in 1991. Even so it was not surprising that his 1990 shone above the wine of the following year, though both were excellent. They were round and fruity with a particularly good attack, a feature which I had found over the brow of the hill at Sauvagnères. The tannins were not too aggressive either, despite the relatively long fermentation. Daniel Tissot exports not only to obvious markets such as the UK, Holland and Belgium but has loyal customers in Central Africa too.

It is the marketing which is the principal worry of Patrice Sterlin, who bought the large estate called **Château de Frandat (4)** just east of Nérac in 1980. Of the 60 hectares, 27 are given over to vines, 3 of which are devoted to grapes for the making of Armagnac and Floc de Gascogne; they are in the Armagnac appellation area as well as Buzet. Patrice was trained as an agricultural engineer so he enjoys growing his fruit and cereals as well as his vines. This château is a real one, or almost: it is more in the style of a manor house with a tiled eighteenth-century tower, though most of the building goes back much further than that – the vineyard dates from the time of Napoléon. Patrice Sterlin bought it from a member of the co-opérative, who passed on to him the fag-end of a contract which had nine years still to run. The year of its expiry, 1989, was traumatic in two ways: the vintage was destroyed by hail, but more important in the longer term was his decision to leave the co-opérative. He had perfectly good plant rotting in his *chais*, which he was not allowed, as a *co-opérateur*, to use for wine-making, although his agricultural training was making him itch to have a go.

His first year as an independent producer was 1990 and he was lucky to have such a wonderful vintage with which to launch himself. With advice from oenologists, he made two *cuvées* of red wine, one with new wood, the other without. Though he believes in total *égrappage*, he also believes in a long fermentation of three weeks when conditions allow. Some of the best parcels of land are picked separately for independent vinification. Even though he uses new wood, it is not all that new, since it will already have had one wine made in it: the effect of oak in his wine is very gentle.

The wine made in new wood is called Cuvée du Majorat, a term which denotes a soldier who gave special service to Napoléon on the battlefield and received an extra pension and medal in recognition. Patrice said that one of his ancestors was a *majorat*, who had been particularly valiant at the Battle of the Nile against the English, though he believes some of his forebears were of Anglo-Saxon origin. The 1990 Cuvée du Majorat will prove to be a Buzet of real class and originality when the oak has done its work. Even the unwooded wine of 1990 was very big with a cherry and prune style to it. By comparison the 1991 was more obvious, but even so the wine is good for a vintage which had been decimated by spring frosts.

Even more difficult was 1992, but Patrice Sterlin's wine was amazingly big and impressive. Perhaps his training in agriculture had taught him how to keep his plants healthy through a wet autumn, and free of rot through the almost continuous rain which plagued the harvest. It was something of a miracle that his grapes could be harvested as late as they were, healthy and full of fruit.

To enable him to concentrate on the marketing of his wine, Patrice Sterlin has just taken on a full-time wine-maker, Marc Quéatinier, who was for some years associated with Clos Triguedina at Cahors. Each obviously recognises the talents of the other in fields where they clearly overlap, and each goes out of the way to give the other due credit for his contribution to the finished wine.

For the future, Monsieur Quéatinier will get on with the wine-making, while Patrice Sterlin will develop the business side. He has already identified areas of France where he thinks he can create interest: Paris, the North and Alsace, in particular. Elsewhere in France he will work through agents. He is also keen to develop relationships in the United Kingdom, where he already has a foothold.

The small amount of white wine from this property is made, unusually, from 100% sémillon. It reminded me rather of Gitton's white Duras, with its aromas of hayfields, herbs and honey: some acacia too. Patrice Sterlin has some sauvignon coming on which will soon be mature enough for wine-making. He makes a rosé too, entirely from his cabernet franc grapes. There is nothing insipid about this pink wine: it manages to pack an unusual amount of the soft red fruits which one associates with the grape-variety. It is, however, the sheer quality of his big sturdy red wines which stays in the memory the result of a well-balanced contribution between the new and the traditional, between a true *goût du terroir* and a wine which should do well in the market-place.

In an appellation where native Gascons seem thin on the ground, Jean Ryckmann seems more Gascon than D'Artagnan himself, though his family was Flemish, coming from Hazebrouk. His father, who was wounded at Verdun in the First World War, and family settled in France in 1937, but when the North was invaded in 1940 they moved south to Buzet. When the South in turn was occupied, Jean fled to the woods where he learnt to live on nettles and anything else that came to hand.

Jean Ryckmann has had many trades in his time. He once had a garage in the local village, but when his father died he decided to take on the vineyard at the family property called Versailles. The authorities would not let him call his wine Château de Versailles for fear there might be some confusion, so Jean settled for the slightly more humble **Domaine de Versailles (6)**. Though clearly sign-posted, Jean's vineyard is in the back of beyond, north of the village of Montagnac-sur-Auvignon. The house is of the simple country style with a magnificent, welcoming kitchen. The chimney-piece is decorated with a mixture of pious pictures and hunting-gear, and doubtless the cauldron in the fireplace contained some delicious soup. The long kitchen table, with the traditional deep drawer in one end to contain the family bread supply, was covered with a typically practical oil-cloth, and on one side of the room the old stone sink drained through a hole cut into the thick walls into the garden outside.

The living conditions are simple, and the wine-making is to match. Jean Ryckmann doesn't worry about *égrappage* any more since the machine, which was second-hand anyway when he bought it, broke down in 1979 and he has not bothered to replace it. He vinifies all his grapes together, though one year he did make a separate *cuvée* of merlot, because it had matured much too soon for the cabernets. He explained that, in the old days, the different varieties were all planted together in the vineyards and never in separate parcels, so naturally they all went into the *cuves* together. '*Les anciens n'étaient pas plus fous que nous,*' he said. He prefers cement to stainless steel, which he claims is carcinogenic and not always as stainless as it is made out to be: he has a friend whose steel *cuve* rusted through a combination of acidity in the wine and sulphur. (One couldn't help wondering what the wine itself had been like.) Jean likes long *cuvaisons* in principle, but insists that each year has to be assessed when the time comes. He prefers to rely on his instincts and not be dogmatic.

He has 8 hectares of vines, 4 of which he rents out to a neighbour's daughter, with whom he is on more than merely commercial terms. On her 4 hectares she makes wine which she sells *en vrac*, but always as Domaine de Versailles. On his, Jean makes just one *cuvée* of red wine from roughly equal quantites of merlot and the two cabernets. He told me that, when his family showed no interest in the property or in developing its vineyard, he dug up all the old vines, which included many varieties no longer tolerated in the appellation, and replanted with the *cépages nobles*. His first harvest was supposed to have been in 1977, but it was ruined by hail. The experience was almost repeated in 1978, but he managed to make a little wine that year, which was very good indeed although he had to wait until midsummer the following year before he could induce the malolactic fermentation.

I expected Jean's wines to be honest country bottles, probably a bit rough and rustic. When he opened them, however, I was amazed and delighted. They were all highly sophisticated and of the best quality, despite the simple conditions in which they had been produced. His 1987, a generally poor vintage, had lovely ripe fruit and real character despite the rain in which it was picked. The 1986 was much firmer, though lightish in colour; the balance was most attractive and the wine was *à point* in the summer of 1993. The 1985 was even better, highly perfumed and very fine: it was just beginning to blossom. In the mouth it was quite chewy and it obviously has a long future.

I asked Jean Ryckmann his views on the use of new oak, having already anticipated his reply because quite clearly there was no sign of it in any of the wines we had tasted. He himself dislikes it; he says that country people think it makes the wine indigestible. On the other hand he says there is nothing like a barrel which has already seen five or six wines made or stored in it. He also hates the use of chemicals: he insists that wine should be as natural as possible. Once you start adding to it, you might just as well be making Coca-Cola. He is, however, in favour of harvesting-machines because, he says, you sometimes have only a week to pick and if you let the grapes get too ripe they are fit only for jam.

Jean clearly loves his *métier*, but he obviously has problems with marketing his wine. He admitted being curious to see how Patrice Sterlin was going to get on with his. All Jean's vintages from 1988 onwards were still in the *cuves* in 1993, though they will be none the worse for that in due course. He sells a little to *négociants* and mostly to private buyers. He is wary about restaurants: they are bad payers and he also says they rarely have any idea how to handle wine properly. He once had a friend to stay who lives in the Champagne area, and thought to take him out to a local restaurant, quite an up-market one. As a gesture of politeness to his guest he ordered a bottle of champagne wine, and was surprised to see the waitress arrive at the table carrying it tucked under her arm like a hot-water bottle. She explained she was warming it a little because it had only just come out of the freezer.

It is hard to say why Jean Ryckmann does not have better luck with his sales. He shrugs off the quality of his product modestly: in the past, he says, any wine which was sold in bottle was regarded as a *vin vieux*. But his prices are as reasonable as the wine is good. I asked him why the independent producers of Buzet did not form their own association like they have done in Duras: he said that there were always personality problems when so few people were involved, and they had all acquired the Gascon spirit of independence even if they were not native Gascons.

It is easy to forget that although Buzet is connected through its wine-history with Bordeaux, it has one foot firmly in Gascony, and that some of its more southerly producers make Armagnac and Floc de Gascogne as well as Buzet. **Château de Pierron (3)**, on the very outskirts of Nérac, is one such, a reminder that the town of Nérac was once the palatial seat of Henry IV when he was still prince of Navarre. The wine of Pierron is very dark, like a Cahors to look at: it has a characteristically blackcurrant nose and in the mouth there is a lot of fruit. I have, however, found it a bit loose-knit, lacking in acidity and good tannins, even in a year such as 1990 when one would have expected evidence of a capacity to age. On the other hand it is a good country-style Buzet, ready three or four years after the vintage.

Another producer facing towards Gascony rather than Bordeaux is Thierry Schellens who owns the **Domaine de Tourné (5)** near Calignac, just east up the hill from Patrice Sterlin. The wines from Tourné have won many medals in their time and they age well. The 1986, for example, seven years after the vintage, was only just beginning to show a bit of orange in the glass, the colour still basically a bright garnet. The nose betrayed some signs of age, a bit dusty and flinty and the style was generally dry, but there was a deal of merlot showing through in the fruit, rather like a mature St Emilion. This wine has class and deserves its reputation. It has been taken up by the négociant Georges Vigouroux of Cahors fame.

I doubt whether there is any private producer in Buzet who is making anything other than very good wine. Madame Sainrat-Comblong at **Château la Hitte (2)** is at the centre of the appellation, close to the town of Lavardac, and her wines tend to be dark like Pierron, the colour of ripe blackberries rather than purple. The flavour is very reminiscent of cherries, with some prunes and blackcurrants. The texture is roughish and rather rustic in a most agreeable way.

It often happens that, in areas where a cave co-opérative dominates the production, the private producers outside it feel that they do not get a fair crack of the whip. One of them, for example, told us that when he was invited to submit samples of his wine for assessment by the panel of the influential *Guide Hachette*, he was advised to leave them with the local Cave for onward dispatch with all the other wines of the appellation. The samples must have got lost because they never reached the tasting panel. Again, the president of a powerful co-opérative will almost inevitably also be the president of any *syndicat* supposed to represent all the producers in the appellation: not unnaturally he tends to look at the problems of the area through the Cave's spectacles. A private grower may well feel that his president is not representing him properly while he is wearing a co-opérative hat. Suggestions from independents can get passed to the Cave's executives and not always followed up because there may be no benefit in them for the Cave. Again a grower who happens to have vines from which he is able to make brandy as well as wine may be told he cannot continue his membership of his co-opérative if he makes it as a private sideline.

I hope that the intrepid *vigneron*, who has vines very near to the cave co-opérative in Buzet itself and who is trying to set himself up as an independent producer, will not suffer through living in the jaws of the dragon. Bigger men than he have had cause to complain. For example, the **Cave Co-opérative at Goulens (9)** in the adjoining Côtes de Brulhois has eight members who also have vines in Buzet. Brulhois is very bitter about the fact that one year, when the wine was already made, Buzet refused to authorise the use of the AOC label because, it said, the wine had not been made within the appellation area. In previous years there had been no problem and in the year in question there had been no suggestion until well after the vintage that the seal of approval would be withheld. Brulhois, out of what one can only assume was sheer cussedness, promptly built a special *chais* to vinify the wines of its Buzet-growers at Montagnac-sur-Auvignon, so thwarting the efforts of Buzet to poach the eight *vignerons* in question.

Such squalid tales do little to enhance the reputation of the Buzet Cave which is doing too good a job to need to stoop to strong-arm tactics of this sort. It has recreated the reputation of the region single-handed and the image of Buzet is probably higher today than any other of the Bordeaux satellites. It ought not only to tolerate competition from other growers in the appellation, but welcome it.

CÔTES DU BRULHOIS

The countryside facing Agen on the left bank of the Garonne, together with some of the country to the east of the town on the right bank, is called the Brulhois. Nobody can be sure how it got this name: some say it derives from the word *brûler*, meaning to burn, a reference to the ancient tradition of distilling wine through 'burning'; others to the colour of the wines themselves, which were often called 'black' like Cahors. The most likely theory is that Brulhois was the name of a feudal lord, traces of whose family have been lost in the murk of medieval history and the smoke of later revolutions. The vineyards of the Côtes du Brulhois, which immediately adjoin those of Buzet to their west, were certainly being cultivated as such in the latter years of the Roman occupation, so that they figure among the oldest in France.

Today they straddle the boundary between two modern départements. In the Lot-et-Garonne, which also includes most of Duras, Marmande and the whole of Buzet, the wine-making takes place at the **Cave Co-opérative de Goulens-en-Brulhois (1)**, near the small town of Layrac just south of Agen. In the Tarn-et-Garonne to the east, the base of most of the production is the **Cave Co-opérative de Donzac (2)**, just across the river from Valence d'Agenais.

The wines of the area were well known in the Middle Ages and were exported in quantity. In 1306/7 no less than 48,000 hectolitres went down the river to run the gauntlet of Bordeaux. This is more than four times the total modern production of VDQS Brulhois. Records of the seventeenth century tell of the efforts of local producers to prevent their wines being defrauded by others. No doubt there was fierce local competition from the once-extensive vineyards of Moissac, just upstream on the right bank. These have today disappeared, having in post-phylloxera times been replanted entirely with the famous Chasselas table-grapes, themselves entitled to AOC Moissac in their own right. Just by the bridge over the river at La Magistère there are still the slipways going down to the water's edge, from which wine-casks were loaded into the flat-bottomed boats as at Douelle on the Lot.

The decline of wine-making in the Agenais – for it was by that name that the district was known until the invention of the modern départements at the time of the Revolution – followed the same pattern as in Buzet and Marmande, except that the wines of Agen/Brulhois had never been part of the Bordeaux vineyard. As at Buzet, the reconstruction in the trade of local wines was given a kick-start by the creation of the co-opérative at Goulens in 1957. It began with humble *vins de table* made from any grapes which their 50 members happened to have in their vineyards, many inferior hybrids from the immediate post-phylloxera period. Today, apart from a little white, there is no *vin de table*, just *vin de pays de l'Agenais* and Côtes du Brulhois VDQS.

The Cave has 250 members with a total of only 110 hectares, because this is an area where nearly all the peasant farmers still practise polyculture. The membership has even dropped in recent years because of new rules which prevent growers from making both VDQS and lower-quality wines from the same vineyard. Although the *vin de pays* can be made from a wide range of grapes, including many old-fashioned ones such as alicante, jurançon, corapu and mérille, many farmers have even more rustic ones which they are not willing to dig up just for the sake of making a few hectolitres of slightly higher-grade wine.

Monsieur Sentex, the present director of the Cave at Goulens, explained to me that the Côtes du Brulhois VDQS wines, which received their eventual recognition in 1984, are allowed to contain tannat, cot and fer servadou in addition to the classic merlot and cabernets. This, he believes, gives them their specific *goût du terroir* and distinguishes them from their Buzet neighbours. Certainly the taste is very characterful, even if the bouquet is not especially original. Four years after the vintage the 1989 was light, fully mature and most agreeable with charcuterie and cheese. Apart from the white *vin de table* and a little sparkling wine, all the wines of this Cave are red or rosé. They are extremely good value: the *vin de pays* will not set you back more than 10 francs a bottle, nor the Brulhois more than 13. There are two red Brulhois VDQS wines, the better *cuvée* being called La Cuvée des Anciens Prieurés and selling for about 15 francs in 1993. The Buzet wine sells at about the same price as at the Buzet Cave.

The Cave's eight members with vines in Buzet make 550 hectolitres between them, which suggests a total holding of no more than 11 hectares, and yet they have their own branch at Montagnac. Once bottled, the wine is stored at Goulens and distributed from there. It will be remembered that the Cave also vinifies the wine from Thézac-Perricard described in the chapter on Cahors. Maurice Calmette does not advertise this fact on his Vin du Tsar label, but the business must be welcome to Monsieur Sentex, representing as it does a bonus of nearly half as much again over what his own members make.

There are no private producers of Côtes du Brulhois in the Lot-et-Garonne, but in the Tarn-et-Garonne to the east there are four in addition to the co-opérative at Donzac. René Frémont at **Cavaille Haut (5)**, near Castelsagrat in the hills on the right bank of the river, hails from Normandy. He has only just over 1 hectare of vines, and he sells all his wine back home. Just to the south Catherine Orliac is the owner of the attractive **Château de la Bastide (4)** at Clermont-Soubiran, perched in the hills above Valence with marvellous views south to Gascony. Her wine is often to be found in local restaurants.

Jean Hébrard and his father Jacques say that, apart from a neighbour, Monsieur Val, who has a small vineyard called **Vignes de la Pujade (6)** and who sells a little Brulhois *en vrac*, they are the only private left-bank producers. Their *chais* is a little way down the road from the Donzac co-opérative, which they have not joined because they had always had their own *cuves* and equipment. Most of the wine which the Hébrards make is sold as *vin de pays de l'Agenais*, and contains some abouriou and syrah. The remainder, which is VDQS Brulhois, is made from 50% cabernet, largely the franc, 30% merlot, 10% tannat and 5% each of malbec and fer servadou. The property is called **Domaine de Coujétou-Peyret (3)**; Peyret is the name of the hamlet and Coujétou the name of a property which they own some 8 kilometres away, and which they have added to Peyret to personalise the wines a little.

The Hébrards have 2¹/₂ hectares of Chasselas table-grapes in addition to nearly 16 hectares of wine-grapes. They have, too, an extensive orchard of cherries, but apart from their various fruits, they have no other kind of farming. The local soil is light and sandy, but with layers of red sandstone beneath which give the wine a firm structure, and the vineyards have a good south-facing position. Jean, who is largely taking over from his father, picks the grapes by machine and they are all de-stalked before vinification for between one and two weeks according to variety and vintage. He also makes a little rosé which is *saigné* from the cabernet franc vats. The *vin de presse* is sometimes used to beef up the *vin de pays*, but it is not used in the VDQS Brulhois, the best *cuves* of which spend a year in fibre-glass before being bottled: otherwise Jean likes to bottle the rest of his wine within the year to make space in his crowded *chais* for the next vintage. His wine is bottled by a peripatetic bottling-plant, because he does not have space for his own.

The Hébrard wines are very good indeed: they have a fruity rusticity and a fair amount of tannin which make them a good accompaniment to country cooking. The same qualities, while much appreciated in the area of production, may make the wines difficult for the Hébrards to sell in the wider market, where the fashion is for the soft and supple. It is the local grape-varieties which no doubt give the Coujétou-Peyret wines their originality. It makes you realise that, as you travel inland up the Garonne valley, the influence of the Bordeaux character diminishes slowly but surely.

VINS DE PAYS DE L'AGENAIS

As well as in the areas already described, the title Agenais is used to denote a recognised *vin de pays* made almost anywhere within the département of Lot-et-Garonne, of which Agen is the county-town. The range of permitted grape-varieties is wider than it is in the appellation areas, encompassing most of the old grapes associated with the South-West. Yield is limited to 70 hectolitres to the hectare, and the overall yield, including *vins de table* from any vineyard making *vin de pays*, must not exceed 100.

Though thinly populated, the Agenais is a big area including many changes in soil and climate, so the style of wine sold as *vin de pays* can vary considerably. Generally the red wines are dark and purplish in colour, with good extract: they often feature a strong redcurrant and raspberry taste, especially if made from the bouchalès grape. For example, the red *vin de pays* from the Marmande co-opérative at Beaupuy shares this characteristic with a good privately produced version from the south-west corner of the département at Sos on the edge of the Landes forest: it is called **Domaine de Campet (10)** and is often to be found in restaurants in the region of Nérac.

Not far from Sos is the diminutive **Cave Co-opérative du Mézinais (9)**, named after the small town of Mézin, almost over the borders into the Gers. Its backers hoped that the Cave would be allowed to use the appellation Côtes de Gascogne, but political geography and the rigidity of the bureaucrats won the day once more. This is rather a pity because the production is basically white and the wines taste just like the wines from Gascony to the south, in no way like the Bordeaux-style whites of the rest of the appellation. Monsieur Mario Verzéni, who started this venture and is its *locomotive* today, says that he tried in vain to compromise with a new *vin de pays d'Albret*, but the authorities wouldn't have that either. It would have been highly appropriate: the family name of Henry IV is much used in the area, commemorating the memory of this most popular of French kings in this corner of France.

Monsieur Verzéni set up this wine co-opérative in 1984 in parallel with the general agricultural co-opérative which he was already running in the area. At the beginning there were just fourteen members making 2800 hectolitres of wine. Progress has been modest in terms of membership: there are now twenty-four, but the production has trebled, and Verzéni hopes to see it top 1 million litres by 1996. Although only two members have more than 20 hectares of vines, the average is a reasonable 5$\frac{1}{2}$ hectares. The Cave restricts its membership to the canton of Mézin and a few adjoining communes, and it is almost within shouting distance of Madame Garcia's famous restaurant La Belle Gasconne at Poudénas just down the road.

Conversion from *vin de table* status to *vin de pays* gave the members quite a fright, but the need to dig up a quantity of unauthorised vine-stocks was mitigated by financial support from the state during the transitional period. Today they have only ugni blanc, colombard and gros manseng. It will be seen later that these are the grapes typical of the white wines of the Côtes de Gascogne, which have achieved such popularity in recent years. The style is hardly Agenais at all and nor are the grape-varieties used on the permitted list for the Agenais *vin de pays*. Monsieur Verzéni says that they may try making some red wines too, if and when the ban on new planting is removed.

His one concern is to maintain and improve standards: I had the feeling that there may be one or two maverick members who might tend to backslide in this respect. For example, the Cave has, as a matter of policy, decided to own its own harvesting-machine. This is not simply made available to members as and when they need it: the Cave sends it out to members' vineyards, and it does the harvesting under strict supervision. The Cave is also responsible for getting the picked grapes back to the *chais* for processing. Good production is rewarded by higher prices to the producers: good wine will be paid for at double the price of poor, and in extreme cases the grapes will be rejected altogether if they do not come up to a minimum standard. If a member does not attain a reasonable quality level for three consequent years, he is asked to leave.

The vinification is quite sophisticated for such a small Cave, with three days' refrigerated filtration, separately pressed *jus de bourbe* and a further period at cold temperatures before the fermentation is allowed to start. Most of the wine is sold to the trade *en vrac*, although about 7000 bottles are produced per year.

The operation at Mézin is at the opposite end of the spectrum from, say, the Cave at Buzet, where the rows of gleaming stainless-steel tanks and the 4000 new oak *barriques* contrast strangely with just two sheds and some *cuves* at the side of the road near Mézin. One of the sheds was converted instantly on my arrival into a *salle d'accueil* by simply dusting down a picnic table and two chairs. Monsieur Verzéni is rather too modest when he concedes that '*Ce n'est pas le meilleur vin du monde, mais ce n'est pas le pire*,' because his exiled Côtes de Gascogne-style wine is both good and good value.

A red wine lighter in style than many Agen reds is made at the **Cave Co-opérative des Sept Monts (8)** at Monflanquin in the northern part of the county. The character is reflected to some extent in the wines of Thézac-Perricard already met. The designation of the Agenais seems on the whole to be rather ill co-ordinated, so that, for example, there is no single *syndicat* or other organisation to promote the wines or to give information about producers. The list below is therefore bound to be incomplete. Readers should not hesitate, if they see a sign by the road-side indicating a *vin de pays de l'Agenais* for sale, to call and taste. They could be in for a pleasant surprise.

PRODUCERS

Côtes de Duras

A.   CAVE DE LANDERROUAT, Les Peyrières, 33790 Landerrouat
Tel: 56-61-40-57

B.   * CAVE BERTICOT, 47120 Duras Tel: 53-83-75-47

Private growers (postcodes 47120 unless otherwise stated)

5.   Francis Blanchard, **Domaine des Allégrets**, Villeneuve-de-Duras
Tel: 53-94-74-56

33. *Guy Pauvert, **Domaine Amblard**, St Sernin-de-Duras Tel: 53-94-77-92

34. Denis Pénicaud, **Domaine des Argiles**, St Astier-de-Duras Tel: 53-94-73-91

*31. Simone Mondin, **Domaine du Barrail**, St Sernin-de-Duras Tel: 53-94-77-72*

38. *Bruno Rossetto, **Château Bellevue Haut-Roc**, Esclottes Tel: 53-83-78-11

29. Dominique Manfe, **Domaine les Bertins**, St Astier-de-Duras
Tel: 53-94-77-34

3.   Martin Agostini, **Le Bourg**, Loubès-Bernac Tel: 53-94-77-17

37. Michel Prévot, **Domaine Las Bruges Maumichau**, Monteton
Tel: 53-20-44-51

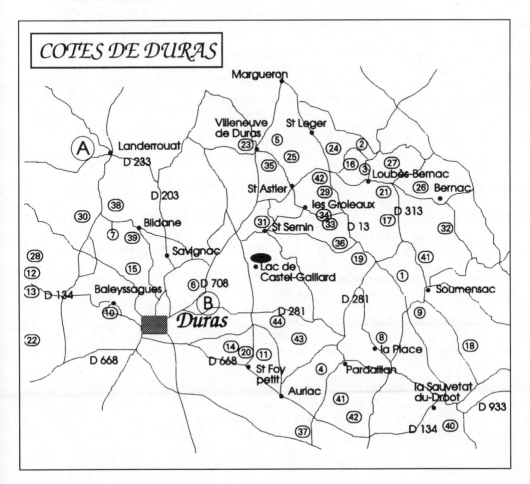

17. *M. H. Dupont*, **Clos du Cadaret**, *Loubès-Bernac Tel: 53-94-77-20*
40. Jacques Testet, **Domaine du Chauffour**, St Pardoux Isaac Tel: 53-93-85-46
30. Alain Mariotto, **Domaine de la Chêneraie**, Esclottes Tel: 56-61-34-73
28. *Régis Lusoli, **Domaine des Cours**, Ste-Colombe-de-Duras
    Tel: 53-83-74-35
25. François Joussiaume, **Château Lou Cramay**, Villeneuve-de-Duras
    Tel: 53-94-78-52
19. *Michel Fonvielhe, **Domaine de Durand**, St Jean-de-Duras
    Tel: 53-89-02-23
18. Jean-Michel Esclavard, **Domaine d'Eybro** , Soumensac Tel: 53-89-01-81
13. Gérard Dalla-Longa, **Vignoble de Faurie**, 33790 Dieulivol Tel: 56-61-67-19
39. *Lucien Salesse, **Domaine de Ferrant**, Esclottes Tel: 53-83-73-46
36. Jean-Luc Prévot, **Domaine La Fond du Loup**, St Jean-de-Duras
    Tel: 53-89-02-59
26. *Jean Lagroye, **Domaine de la Fonlongue**, Loubès-Bernac
    Tel: 53-94-78-54
23. Andrew Gordon, **Le Grand Mayne**, Villeneuve-de-Duras Tel: 53-94-74-17
41. Serge Teyssandier, **Domaine du Grand Truchasson**, St Jean-de-Duras
    Tel: 53-89-01-13
12. Bernard Dalla-Longa, **Château Graneraux**, 33790 Dieulivol
    Tel: 56-61-85-56
10. *Daniel Amar, **Château la Grave-Béchade**, Baleyssagues Tel: 53-83-70-06
35. *Christian Piccin, **Domaine des Groyes**, Villeneuve-de-Duras
    Tel: 53-94-75-49*
22. *Robert Gonthier, **Vignobles de Jeanneau**, 33790 Dieulivol Tel: 56-61-60-33*
21. *Pascal Gitton, **Château Lafon**, Loubès-Bernac Tel: 53-94-77-14
27. Michel Lazarétie, **Domaine Lamartigne**, Loubès-Bernac Tel: 53-94-77-24
14. André Delage, **Domaine de Lamothe**, Duras Tel: 53-83-75-14
16. Jean-Jacques Dubouchet, **Château Larégnère**, Loubès-Bernac
    Tel: 53-64-75-41
20. *Gilbert Geoffroy, **Domaine de Laulan**, Duras Tel: 53-83-73-69
 2. *Ercole Agostini, **Château Lavanau**, Les Faux Tel: 53-94-78-46;
    Loubès-Bernac Tel: 53-23-81-62
 6. *Blancheton et Fils, **Château la Moulière**, Duras 53-83-71-72
42. *Jean-François Thierry, **Château la Petite Bertrande**, St Astier-de-Duras
    Tel: 53-94-74-03*
43 Serge Lagroye, **Domaine du Petit Loubès**, Loubès-Bernac
    Tel: 53-94-77-24
44 Alain Lescaut, **Domaine du Petit malrome**, St Jean-de-Duras
    Tel:53-89-01-44
11. Armand Chilou, **Clos du Petit Ste-Foy**, Duras Tel: 53-93-35-50
 9. *Iréné Chassagne, **La Peyre du Bos**, St Jean-de-Duras Tel: 53-89-02-37*
 8. *Jean-Luc Carmelli, **Domaine de la Place**, St Jean-de-Duras Tel: 53-83-00-77*
24. *Jacques Guiraud, **Les Roques**, Loubès-Bernac Tel: 53-83-71-03*
15. *Maurice Dreux, **Domaine des Savignattes**, Esclottes Tel: 53-83-72-84
32. Cyprien Mourguet, **Domaine de la Tuilerie**, la Breille, Loubès-Bernac
    Tel: 53-94-78-32
 1. *Agostini et fils, **Domaine du Verdier**, St Jean-de-Duras Tel: 53-89-02-13*
 7. *Christian Boin, **Les Vergers**, Esclottes Tel: 53-83-77-39*
 4. *Bernard Bireaud, **Domaine du Vieux Bourg**, Pardaillan Tel: 53-83-02-18
45 Francis Mazéra, **Domaine Les Vignes d'Arnaud**, Loubès-Bernac
    Tel: 53-94-74-25

CÔTES DU MARMANDAIS

1. Vignobles Boissonneau (**Domaine des Géais**), Château de la Vieille Tour, 33190 St Michel-de-Lapujade Tel: 56-61-72-14
2. LES VIGNERONS DE BEAUPUY, 47200 Beaupuy Tel: 53-64-32-04
3. CAVE CO-OPÉRATIVE DE COCUMONT, 47250 Cocumont Tel: 53-94-50-21
4. Fernand **Lagaüzère**, Rizens, 47200 Sainte-Bazille Tel: not available
5. Monsieur **Simonnet**, Rizens, 47200 Sainte-Bazille Tel: not available
6. Robert Schult, **Château de Beaulieu**, 47250 St. Sauveur de Meilhan Tel: 53-94-30-40

CÔTES DE BUZET

1. LES VIGNERONS RÉUNIS DES CÔTES DE BUZET, Buzet-sur-Baïse, 47160 Damazan Tel: 53-84-74-30
4. Patrice Sterlin, **Château le Frandat**, 47600 Nérac Tel: 53-65-23-83
9. CAVE CO-OPÉRATIVE DE GOULENS-EN-BRULHOIS 47390 Layrac Tel: 53-87-01-65
2. Marie-Elizabeth Camblong, **Château la Hitte**, 47230 Lavardac Tel: 53-65-50-37
8. Daniel Tissot, **Domaine du Pêch**, 47310 Ste-Colombe-en-Brulhois Tel: 53-96-24-44
3. GFA du **Château Pierron**, Route de Mézin, 47600 Nérac Tel: 53-65-05-52
7. Bernard Thérasse, **Château de Sauvagnères**, 47310 Ste-Colombe-en-Brulhois Tel: 53-67-20-23

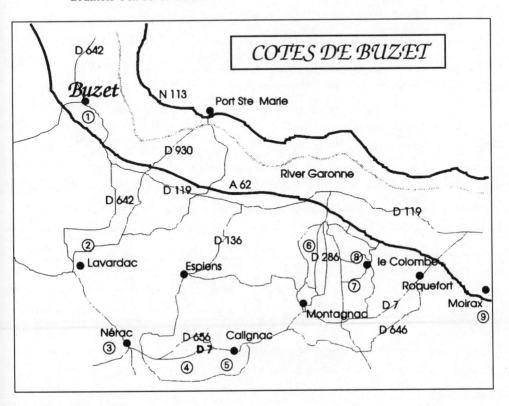

5.   Thierry Schellens, **Domaine de Tourné**, 47600 Calignac Tel: 53-97-15-00
6.   Jean Ryckmann, **Domaine de Versailles**, 47600 Montagnac-sur-Auvignon
     Tel: 53-97-10-53

Vin de Pays de l'Agenais

1.   **Cave Berticot** (see Côtes de Duras)
2.   **Cave les Peyrières**, Landerrouat (see Côtes de Duras)
3.   **Cave de Beaupuy** (see Côtes du Marmandais)
4.   **Cave de Cocumont** (see Côtes du Marmandais)
5.   **Cave Co-opérative de Buzet** (see Côtes de Buzet)
6.   **Cave Co-opérative de Goulens** (see Côtes du Brulhois)
7.   **Cave Co-opérative de Donzac** (see Côtes du Brulhois)
8.   CAVE DES SEPT MONTS, ZAC Mondésir, 47150 Monflanquin
     Tel: 53-36-33-40
9.   CAVE CO-OPÉRATIVE DU MÉZINAIS, 47170 Mézin Tel: 53-97-30-31
10. **Domaine de Campet**, 47170 Sos Tel: not available
11. **Maurice Perbos**, 47380 St Etienne de Fougères Tel: 53-01-06-03
12. **Perbos Fils Aîné**, Le Bourg, St Etienne de Fougères Tel: 53-01-06-09
14. Jean-Claude Pons, **As Gaillets**, 47440 Casseneuil Tel: 53-41-04-66
13. Jean-Pierre Richarte, **Les Oliviers**, 47140 Auradou Tel: 53-41-28-59

CÔTES DE BRULHOIS

1. CAVE CO-OPÉRATIVE DE GOULENS-EN-BRULHOIS, 47390 Layrac
    Tel: 53-87-01-65
2. CAVE CO-OPÉRATIVE DE DONZAC, 82340 Auvillar Tel: 63-39-91-92
4. Madame Orliac, **Château la Bastide**, 47270 Clermont-Soubiran
    Tel: 53-87-41-02
5. Monsieur Frémont, **Cavaille Haut**, 47270 Grayssas Tel: 63-39-68-39
3. Jacques et Jean Hébrard, **Domaine de Coujétou-Peyret**, 82340 Donzac
    Tel: 63-39-90-89
6. Roger Val, **Vignes de la Pujade**, 82340 Dunes Tel: 63-39-82-46

The Wines of Gascony
and the Landes

All the wines so far described once travelled by boat down one of the many rivers of the Aquitaine basin to Bordeaux, and thence onwards to their eventual markets.

This was not so with the wines of Gascony and the Béarn, which were rarely traded in Bordeaux, nor were they bought by the Bordelais for blending, like the other wines of the *haut-pays*. When they were ever anything other than *vins de pays* in the pre-phylloxera days, they were sent to the port of Bayonne down the river Adour and its tributaries.

The Adour rises in the high mountains, almost on the Spanish border, flowing north until it starts a long and gradual curve to the west, rather like the Loire. On the right are the vineyards of the Gers, then the Côtes de St Mont on either side. On its left bank are Madiran, Pacherenc and Tursan. Further to the south, a watershed divides the Adour basin from Pau. Through that town flows a *gave*, the local word for river, which travels north-westwards until it joins the Adour just short of Bayonne. The *gave de Pau* is the home of the wines called simply Béarn, while just over the hills on the left bank are the vineyards of Jurançon. Finally, in the hills overlooking yet another *gave*, which joins the Adour in the town of Bayonne itself, are the Basque vineyards of Irouléguy.

Until the late 1 970s, the vines grown on the right bank of the Adour produced thin white wines for distillation into Armagnac. Historically there were no table-wines of any commercial importance.

On the left bank of the Adour, in the vineyards of the Béarn and the Pyrenees, the situation was always different. Here there had long been a considerable production of red wine, based on the tannat grape (or moustroun as it is sometimes called locally). The wines from this grape have always been sturdy and rustic and the modern taste for more supple and fast-maturing wines has led to the gradual introduction of other grape-varieties to soften the rigours of tannat juice – usually the cabernet varieties or fer servadou (here called pinenc).

The only white wine from the area to receive fame in the outside world was Jurançon, traditionally sweet in style. There was no demand until after the Second World War for dry country wines. Even now, dry Jurançon has to be sold as Jurançon Sec, to distinguish it from the older, sweeter style.

Today, Gascony and the Béarnais produce a complete range of wines to suit all tastes, each with its own brand of rusticity and own *goût du terroir*. For example, in the home of Armagnac itself, the dry white wines in particular have had spectacular success.

WINES OF THE GERS: CÔTES DE GASCOGNE

The heartland of the once huge area of Gascony is the Armagnac country in the modern département of Gers. The western half of the county has always produced the more wine, because its sandier soil suits the production of wines to be made into Armagnac.

The Gers has long been somewhat self-contained. Until the middle of the nineteenth century the road system was primitive as the swamps of the Landes prevented effective land communications with Bordeaux. The navigable rivers led to Bayonne rather than the Gironde estuary; and those who designed the French rail network managed to skirt the district altogether, so that even today there are no direct mainline services in or out of the département. Add to these factors the fierce independence of the Gascon character, the adaptability of their terrain to so many different crops and thus subsistence-farming rather than the production of surplus crops for sale, and it is easy to see why the wine and even the brandy had few markets outside the area of production. The Gersois had neither the means nor the motivation to trade with the outside world.

While their fellow-Gascons in Madiran to the south and the Landes to the west made sturdy red wines to go with the hearty cooking of the region, the Armagnacois concentrated on the production of a rather thin and acid white wine for conversion into brandy, which does not call for grape-varieties of any distinction. The higher the yield the better. The ugni blanc has long been a dominant variety, as in Cognac where it serves a similar function. (It is confusingly also sometimes known as St Emilion, but has no connection at all with that fine wine-growing area.) It is much used as a blending wine in Italy, where it is called *trebbiano*.

For Armagnac production, the ugni blanc is backed up by the even more humble Baco 22 which is nowhere allowed into the making of quality table-wines. Baco traces its ancestry back on one side to the poor hybrids introduced in the immediate post-phylloxera era. Then there is the folle-blanche, also called picpoul. This grape also produces the acidic gros-plant wines of the Loire estuary. It was once the backbone of Armagnac, but it did not successfully lend itself to grafting after the phylloxera epidemic. In Gascony it is mostly to be found in the Bas-Armagnac, where it is still favoured by some of the quality producers.

The ugni blanc is an extremely high-yielding vine, and, equally importantly for brandy producers, it retains its acidity right through to the end of the harvest. The question-mark over ugni blanc today is that it has shown itself prone in Cognac to the fungoid disease called eutypiose, which is still awaiting an antidote. So far it has not spread to Gascony.

Listan is the name given locally to a grape better known as palomino, the principal constituent of sherry. It is hard to see why it has survived so long at this latitude, because it is low in sugar as well as acidity and tends to rapid oxidisation. It hangs on as a minor ingredient of a few Gascon wines.

Armagnac producers do not need quality stocks – the better the grape, the less useful it is for brandy. Perhaps this explains the hitherto limited use of the colombard grape, which modern techniques have demonstrated to be capable of producing an extremely quaffable crisp, white table-wine. The fashion for this grape has doubtless been fuelled by the success it has had in California, where it is now the most widely planted variety. We shall see that it is the colombard which has rapidly become the mainstay of the Côtes de Gascogne.

Everywhere you go in north-west Gers you see placards by the side of the tiny tracks leading to farms, advertising this *vin de pays*, as well as Armagnac and *foie gras*. Usually, but not always, the wine made is white and, as time goes by, it is more and more likely to be colombard-based. Some growers are experimenting with sauvignon to give the wine a twist of distinction which is sometimes otherwise missing. Others who are experimenting with gentle oaking of Côtes de Gascogne are also trying out the gros manseng, the basic grape of Jurançon.

Characteristically, Côtes de Gascogne has a citric smell to it, mixed with a whiff of apple. It is bone-dry and needs to be well chilled to show at its best. It often has a taste reminiscent of boiled sweets, the *bonbons anglais* again. It is light and there is no doubt about its ability to refresh one on a hot day, but for some people the character of the wine can pall. For others its charms do not stale, but for those who do not take to the acid-drop, nail-varnish-remover style, it is better left alone.

Côtes de Gascogne is fairly new to merchants' lists and the supermarkets both in France and further afield. It would be unfair to other producers to pretend that the three-legged Co-opérative called **Plaimont Producteurs** (with plant for wine-making at the three towns of **Pla**isance, St **Aignan** and St **Mont**) developed this wine single-handed, but they certainly did the lion's share of the work putting it on the map.

The co-opérative owes its dominant market position to André Dubosc who built it up from almost nothing during the 1970s. It was a trip to Germany in 1973 which put into Dubosc's head the idea that Gascony should be able to produce commercially viable white wines.

The members did not take him seriously at first, because they saw no need to diversify. Armagnac was thriving and, at the time, even expanding. In any case there was little confidence that the region could produce a quality wine. But when the Armagnac trade started to falter, the farmer-growers began to understand how much the world needed a large quantity of fresh, fruity, affordable wine, especially dry white wine. Côtes de Gascogne may be humble and variable in quality, but there is no doubting its market reputation as a by-word for fairly priced everyday drinking.

After the phylloxera there were practically no vineyards left in this part of Gascony. The surviving vines for making table-wine were allowed to grow wild and to climb like ivy into the fruit trees in the local orchards. Even today some vineyards still contain peach trees, producing what we call clingstone fruit but with a downy skin and red flesh – the Gascons call them *pêchers des vignes*. The first priority of the Groupement des Producteurs at Plaimont, formed in 1979, was therefore to rebuild the vineyard, then to adopt strict rules of production for all producer-members, and through marketing in bottle to develop an image for St Mont away from the traditional role of producers of sour wines for distillation.

Of the 2000 hectares belonging to 1350 different Plaimont members, 1200 (60%) produce grapes for Côtes de Gascogne, both red and white: 110,000 hectolitres out of a total production of 150,000. The red wines are essentially based on the tannat grape. They are full-bodied and deep in colour, with a generous and fruity nose. They are supple and meant to mature quickly, because they are given only four or five days' maceration. There is an astringency on the finish which is typical of the grape and the wines are quite attractive in a rustic kind of way. Dubosc does not agree with many producers of Madiran further south about the capacity of tannat wines to age. He thinks they can become dusty and dry out fairly fast.

The white Côtes de Gascogne wines are derived from ugni blanc, listan, but above all colombard. Dubosc is keen to develop colombard still further following a mutually beneficial exchange of know-how with Californian growers. Plaimont makes a whole range of wines bearing the name of the famous Gascon restaurateur, André Daguin, lighter and more easy-going in style than the mainstream wines of the Cave, and frankly intended for early drinking. The white wines are nearly 100% colombard. The Daguin range has found a ready market in France, especially in the restaurant trade.

Dubosc has realised the potential of marketing his wines through famous local restaurants, having persuaded no less a star than Michel Guérard to entrust to the co-operative the honour and responsibility of making a special wine from Guérard's own grapes. This was before Guérard planted his own vineyard at his home in the Tursan. His world-famous restaurant at Eugénie-les-Bains is less than half an hour's drive from St Mont.

Dubosc has been so successful with colombard that Plaimont have devised a blend called Colombelle, consisting of 70% colombard, 20% ugni blanc and 10% listan. It has the typical boiled-sweet taste of Côtes de Gascogne, with some citrus fruit and almonds. In the glass it develops a floral character, described by Dubosc as hawthorn and honeysuckle. Until bottling, the wine is kept chilled below a layer of carbonic gas in stainless-steel vats in order to preserve its young, lively character. Though not listed on their tariff, there is a wine under the name L'Abbadie de Léz, a full-bodied 12° white with more fruit and style than some other wines from this source. It is one of the better examples to be found in Britain. A rosé wine called Océanide is highly popular locally, having reached a level of production of 4000 hectolitres.

The makers of Côtes de Gascogne are legion, and almost every farm you pass on the road, as well as the many which lie deep in the backlands, seems to offer you wine to buy. Further east, a very similar product is sold as *vin de pays du Gers*.

One name which will come as no stranger to lovers of Gascony wines is Grassa: the family share with Dubosc the honour of having put the *vins de pays*, as well as some of its Armagnacs, on the world market. Pierre Grassa started his career in Bordeaux, but as a hairdresser and not in the wine business. He had left the countryside before the Second World War to seek fame and fortune, but after his war service, he met and married Hélène. Her parents, after flirting with life in the New World, took on the **Château de Tariquet** with a view to reconstituting the vineyard. When they found it there were but 5 hectares, all planted with the poor hybrid, noah.

Now Pierre and Hélène, with two of their children Maité and Yves, have carved out quite an empire near their birthplace of Eauze, and the family have four properties at which they make Armagnac, floc and wine. Besides Tariquet itself, an attractive small château distinguished by two small towers flanking the elegant façade, there are the **Domaine de Rieux**, the **Domaine de Plantérieu** and **La Jalousie**. Wines from all four are to be found in shops and restaurants in France and the United Kingdom. The vineyards are based on ugni blanc, colombard and folle blanche.

The Grassa wines are at the top of the Gascony league, always distinguished by freshness, the result of the most meticulous wine-making and plenty of fruit. The family also has a big business as *négociants* both in wines and brandies. For reliability and consistent standards, the Grassa wines are hard to beat and this no doubt explains their constant appeal to the trade in overseas markets.

The production of Armagnac and Côtes de Gascogne march hand in hand with each other, and spill over the boundaries of the Gers into the neighbouring département of the Landes. Thus near the mini-spa of Barbotan, in the heart of the best Armagnac production, Comte Laudet, now retired as the *régisseur* at Château Beychevelle in the Médoc, is making a very successful wine at his **Domaine de Laballe**. Although only a few kilometres over the county-boundary, it has to be called a *vin de pays des terroirs landais* by law. The same applies to the wines made by Albert

Danzacq at the **Domaine de Pagny,** of whose red wine it is not con-
descending to say that it goes marvellously well with charcuterie on a picnic. Doctor Garreau, whom we shall meet again later on, makes another
attractive *terroirs landais* wine at his château near Labastide, and at
Cazaubon there is even a co-opérative for those producers who are outside the boundary of the Gers and thus cannot call their wines Côtes de
Gascogne. Even so, these wines, like those of the co-opérative at Mézin,
are Gascon wines in all but name.

As with Armagnac, so with the table-wines: there is no association of
private growers, so it is almost impossible to say how many wine-
makers there are, or to begin to compile a list. Perhaps this is another
reflection on the independence of the Gascon character. There is no
mistaking the popularity of the style of these wines, however, and those
who have a bent for blowing their own trumpets seem to be able to find
good overseas markets for their product. For example, Hugh Ryman is
developing in partnership the white Côtes de Gascogne which
Monsieur Bordès makes at his five estates near Gondrin, halfway
between Condom and Eauze. Ryman markets one of these under the
name **Domaine le Puts**, but the same wine can also be found under
the Bordès name in supermarkets. Another wine often to be found in
the UK is Alain Lalanne's **Domaine de Lahitte** near Ramouzens, a
wine which is loaded with the pear-drops taste of colombard.

Gascon-born oenologists are turning their attention to the possibilities
of the Gers. For example, Jean-Marc Sarran has 20 hectares of vines
round his aunt's Auberge Bergerayre at St Martin d'Armagnac, between
Nogaro and Riscle. **Domaine de Bergerayre** (whose name has nothing
to do with sheep but is thought to derive from *bergue de l'aire*, an instru-
ment for threshing the corn) was always devoted to polyculture as a farm,
but Jean-Marc is interested only in the vines. He trained in Bordeaux and
returned to his native Armagnac to develop a pilot vineyard. His aim at
the time was to produce improved clones for the colombard grape. He
already has a deal of colombard planted in his vineyard and does not
intend to plant any more. He has plans to produce a finer wine than the
ordinary run of the *vin de pays* and thinks that the possibilities of colombard are limited; it lacks structure and personality, he says, and it is 'too
easy to drink'. He looks across the Adour to his friends in Madiran and
Jurançon, and wants to see what he can do with the grapes which they use
to make their high-class AOC wines, the *gros* and *petit manseng.*

Jean-Marc's first vintage was in 1992. With limited resources, and
with hindsight, too, he was wise not to begin too ambitiously. He made
a little of the wine himself, but, not yet having enough *cuves* of his own,
took most of his grape-juice to the co-opérative at Nogaro where the
wine was vinified. This co-opérative, of which Jean-Marc's uncle was
one of the founding fathers, is the only one in the Gers where you can
take your grape-juice already pressed.

His first wine was 60% colombard, 30% gros manseng and 10% arrufiac, a rare variety which we will meet again later in the Vic-Bilh. His

wine is, of course, served at the auberge. In developing his vineyard he will target particularly the export market, which he sees as ready for a new and improved style of Côtes de Gascogne based on the manseng grapes. When he has the equipment, he wants to give his wines a *macération pelliculaire*, as they do further south, and he is already experimenting with vinifying wine from the two manseng varieties in both new and old wood. The old barrels come from Alain Brumont in the Madiran, no less. He is keeping his mind open about the vexed subject of the use of new wood, which we shall see is such a bone of contention in the Jurançon, and he is not going to rush into any decisions.

Apart from the bottled wine in the restaurant, Jean-Marc gave me his *gros manseng* from both kinds of wood to taste. The wine from the old wood was very lively on the nose and palate, dry and without the pear-drop taste of colombard. Since the new wood had only been with the wine a short while, its effect was so far slight. No doubt Jean-Marc will have waited to see how these wines developed before attempting any *assemblage* of the two.

There are hundreds of keen wine-makers in the Gers apart from Jean-Marc Sarran, but I have picked him out as being particularly enthusiastic and almost evangelical in his sense of mission. Although he claims to have been one of the first to plant *petit manseng* in the Gers, he knows he hasn't got the *terroir* to make great wine, but he sees great possibilities in developing what he has got to the maximum. He feels that anyone can produce maize or sunflowers, or even wine from colombard, but a quality wine which really expresses its personality through the *terroir* gives the producer the chance also to stamp his personality on his work, and this appeals particularly to the Gascon temperament.

Condom is a centre for wine-production as well as home to large commercial producers of Armagnac. In fact the town has its own *vin de pays*, which is unusual in that there is more red wine sold under this title than white. For example, Monsieur Aurin has 55 hectares under vine at the **Domaine Meste Duran** just outside Condom. This is a big holding indeed by local standards and is largely given over to the production of red table-wine, the production of Armagnac having been abandoned some years ago. Monsieur Aurin is, however, a claret-lover and has forsaken the traditional grape-varieties of Gascony and planted his vineyard with the Bordeaux grapes, merlot and the two cabernets. He also makes some white wine, this time from the usual ugni blanc and colombard. The bulk of the white table-wine production in the Condom area is sold under the basic Gascony appellation.

FLOC DE GASCOGNE

Not the least of the pleasures of a wine-visit to this part of France is the joy of the landscape. The unearthing of treasures in the cellars of wine-makers whom no one else has yet discovered may be the principal object of the expedition, but it would be a mistake not to relax and delight in the subtly beautiful countryside. It is not a land of imposing châteaux after the style of the Dordogne, let alone the Loire, but rather of more modest manor houses, which the French call *gentilhommières*. Before the Revolution, when French society revolved around the court at Versailles, the socially and politically ambitious had neither the time nor the inclination to live in far-off Gascony. Conversely those who did tended to be more modest and less sophisticated. They felt less need to show off by constructing large châteaux which they could not afford to keep up.

Consequently, Gascony has a domestic and essentially regional feel. The architecture is simple, many of the smaller farm-buildings seem to be built of rather crumbly mud and straw called *torchis*, clinging with difficulty to the characteristic exposed timbers. The roofs are pantiled, and those which shelter brandy-casks have over the years developed a dark fungus caused by the rise of the fumes from the maturing alcohol in the *chais* below. The evaporation of the spirit which ascends sky-wards through the tiles is called *la part des anges*, or 'the share of the angels'.

For the wine-traveller the countryside of Gascony is a never-ending source of pleasure. Away from the Adour basin, the contours are gently undulating, giving the land a sculpted feel. The traditional subsistence-farming still endures here, and ensures constant variety in scenery. There seem to be more ducks and geese than there are people, the meat from these birds constituting the bulk of the protein eaten locally, while the fat is still used as a cooking medium in a land where there are few four-footed farm animals. Maize is a popular local crop because of the financial inducements of the Government to scrub up inferior vines and replant with other crops, and also because maize is the principal element of the poultry diet. With fierce competition from the USA, however, maize is gradually giving way to sunflowers, whose seeds produce an oil said to be far more healthy compared with other fats and oils because of the high proportion of polyunsaturates. Not that this worries the Gascons who manage to combine a large intake of goose- and duck-fat and still attain ages which are unrivalled anywhere else in France, or indeed Europe.

The survival of polyculture as a way of life explains the large number of wine-growers in the region and at the same time the tiny acreage which the average farmer devotes to the vine. All over Gascony you see boards advertising the sale of home-made *foie gras* and *confits*, as well as the wines and Armagnac made on the farms. You will also find that they offer a product called *floc*. Such is the degree of fantasy in the Gascon temperament that many have claimed to be the inventor of *floc*, so it is not certain whom one should believe. Did Henri Lamor of Sarclé, near Nogaro, invent it in 1974, as stated by C. E. Page in his informative book on Armagnac? Possibly, but that was the year of my first visit to the region and I seem to remember finding it already in circulation. Or is it perhaps an old peasant recipe from the sixteenth century, as claimed by Pierre Casamayor in his book on the wines of the region? Maybe it was Doctor Garreau, at whose château-farm near Labastide you can find a museum devoted to all manner of local produce, and whose publicity leaflets state that *floc* 'was born' at Château Garreau. The museum at the château is well worth visiting for its display of ancient wine-making implements and techniques.

I nearly forgot to explain what Floc de Gascogne is. It is the local version of Pineau de Charentes, an apéritif made from grape-juice which is not allowed to ferment and is therefore initially without alcohol. This juice is mixed with Armagnac at a strength which might vary from between 55° and 68° alcohol and in the proportion of about three parts grape-juice to one part spirit. The rules of production require that a maker of *floc* must have produced both the grape-juice and the Armagnac with which it is blended.

The addition of the spirit prevents any fermentation taking place. *Floc* can be based on either red or white grapes, and its colour will vary accordingly. In any event it should be served well chilled and even ice-cubes are permitted. If you like *pineau*, you will certainly like *floc*. It is very tempting on the kind of steamy sultry day which can be otherwise quite oppressive in Gascony in late summer. White *floc* is drunk either as an apéritif or with *foie gras* or desserts. Red *floc*, when not taken as an apéritif, goes well with ewes'-milk cheeses, melon (as a port substitute) and strawberries.

White *floc* is usually made from the same grapes as go into the wine for Armagnac; in a supporting role gros manseng, barroque and sauvignon are also found. (The Lafittes at Domaine de Boignières use an unconventional mix of sauvignon, sémillon and gros manseng.) Once blended the *floc* is aged in casks made from the local Gascon oak and bottled at between 16° and 18°.

The grape-juice for red *floc* comes from merlot, tannat, cabernet sauvignon, cabernet franc, malbec, gamay, and sometimes a variety called egiodola, which I have otherwise found only in the countryside of the Chalosse. Egiodola is said by Pierre Casamayor to deepen the colour of red *floc*.

The red version is made first by extracting the colour from the skins and pips, but this is done at a temperature either below or above that at which fermentation is possible, so as to prevent the final product being too rich in alcohol. Otherwise the simple method and the alcoholic strength is the same as for white *floc*.

The makers of *floc*, who now number many hundreds, have created their own *syndicat*, based in Eauze, and there is an Academy of Ladies and Troubadours whose sole object is the promotion of *floc*.

Just as *floc* is intended to be the local version of Pineau de Charentes from the Cognac area, so the Gascons have invented their own version of the champagne cocktail, though based on Armagnac, of course, and not on Cognac. Pousse-Rapière means literally 'rapier-thrust', and presumably the name is intended to describe the effect. Today Pousse-Rapière is the brand-name of a product marketed by Château Monluc in the north of the Gers. It is an orange-flavoured Armagnac, not unlike Benedictine and does not need to be of any great quality, because it is destined simply to lace a glass of sparkling wine which is then garnished with the peel of more orange. It is unwise to have more than one of these before a meal, especially a Gascon meal which is hardly likely to be a tee-total affair. A Pousse-Rapière lookalike is to be found in Britain under the name Le Touché.

CÔTES DE ST MONT

Largely through the pioneering work of the Plaimont co-opérative, an area of good-quality wine-making has sprung up between the Bas-Armagnac to its north and Madiran to its south. The Côtes de St Mont are on the brink of appellation contrôlée status for red, white and rosé wines grown on either bank of the Adour between Aire-sur-l'Adour in the west and Bassouès in the east. Nearly all the wines of St Mont are made by the **Plaimont Producteurs**, for there are only a handful of independent growers.

Alongside their Côtes de Gascogne wines, Plaimont have developed a range of higher quality wines based on the same grape-varieties as the wines of Vic-Bilh. Essentially what Dubosc has done is to create an extension of the Madiran, but with a view to making wines which are lighter and quicker-maturing, and therefore give a more immediate cash-return.

The red wines are at least 70% tannat (80% in the case of the premium Côtes de St Mont Rouge in the Collection Plaimont range). For this wine the tannat grapes will be vinified for as long as twenty days, as opposed to as little as eight in the case of the cheaper wine. The grapes are hand-picked, because it is felt that picking-machines are too rough with the fruit, tannat being particularly delicate as a grape. As at Madiran, the tannat grapes are allowed to macerate at a higher temperature than the cabernets and the pinenc, and the *vins de presse* are vinified separately. The premium wine is given the best part of a year in new barrels, one-third of which are renewed each year. The amount of *vin de presse* which goes into the final blend will depend on the character of the vintage and the requirements of the wine from the point of view of bouquet and taste.

The white St Mont is all dry, made from the same grapes as Pacherenc further south. Again Plaimont is creating its own extension of the Madiran vineyards. As there, it is the steeper west-facing slopes which produce the white grapes, about 200 hectares in all, yielding about 90,000 hectolitres of wine each year. Its rich aromatic character enables the wine to improve in bottle. There is also a St Mont rosé.

To confuse the situation, there is an even better range of St Mont marketed in all three colours under the name Les Hauts de Bergelle. The red and white versions are given three months in wood, which provides the wine with added structure and ageing power.

Finally, the Plaimont producers also undertake the vinification and bottling of the red wine from the Château de Sabazan, a pretty listed fifteenth-century manor just 3 kilometres outside Aignan, which has 15 hectares under vine. The wine is aged at the château for up to fifteen months in old wood. As might be expected, this unblended wine is the most characterful of the Plaimont wines.

Visitors to the Plaimont outlets may also find a variety of so-called *vins de table* on offer from the cask or vat. These may very well turn out not to be wholly 'French' wines at all – Monsieur Dubosc has been experimenting with making wine at Spanish vineyards, using their press, tanks and bottling-line as if he were a visiting chef preparing a meal in a colleague's kitchen. He then brings the resulting wine back to France either to sell as it is or to blend with French table-wines. On one occasion, where he found the plant at the Spanish winery too old-fashioned to be used for the kind of fresh young wines he likes to produce, he crushed the grapes and shipped the juice back to Gascony, selling it on as Spanish wine made in France. There is, of course, no question of any of this wine being sold under the St Mont appellation. All the same, he has found the French somewhat dubious about this idea, because Gallic producers and drinkers remain as suspicious of wines made elsewhere in Europe as they are of imports from California or Australia.

Dynamic though the Plaimont Producteurs are, good though the wines of the co-opérative may be, and much though the local growers owe to Monsieur Dubosc, the operation has its downside too. Speak to any of the independent growers I met and they will pour out their complaints about Plaimont.

Take Jean Garroussia, for example. He has 6 hectares to the east of Plaisance, right on the borders of the appellation at the **Domaine de Turet**. If you are driving in the hills of the Armagnac near Bassouès, you cannot miss the many signboards which he has put up to show you where he is. Garroussia *père* claims to have 'founded' the co-opérative, but when the latter laid down that the members must sell all of their crop through the Cave, the Garroussias left because they had plant of their own on which they needed to recoup their investment. Now the co-opérative is pressurising them to join again, and they complain of harassment. Madame Garroussia told us that two samples were submitted to the Cave for their approval, which is required so that the producer can use the appellation on the label. Though the two samples were from the same *cuve*, one was accepted and the other rejected, so much of their crop had to be de-classified.

This is a pity, because the Garroussias make good enough wine from the same varieties as are used by the Plaimont Producteurs. When the Cave withholds its blessing, the wine is sold as La Turenière. Although they suffered from the disastrously small crop of 1991 and the muddy harvests of 1992 and 1993, they are determined to persevere as independent growers and they have plans to build a *salle d'accueil* with a grant from the département. They have modern stainless-steel tanks, thanks to their bank who told them that they could borrow to buy a *cuve* every time they sold a cow. The wine is made biologically, without chemicals except for the Bordeaux Mixture which everyone must use to keep off the mildew. Their farm is run along the same lines, with only natural fertilisers for both vines and crops.

Madame Tonon had similar tales to tell about her husband's treatment at the hands of the co-opérative. Theirs is a much larger property – 25 hectares, which makes them one of the biggest growers in the area. The vineyards and their family house are called the **Château la Bergalasse**, and are in an outstandingly beautiful position, with views to the south over their own valley, and thence to the Pyrenees. The vines are immaculately tended and weeded, and the Tonons must be very sore that they are only a few hundred yards from the boundary of the Madiran appellation. They make some *floc*, which takes up 2 hectares of their vines. Of the remainder, about half goes to make St Mont, and the other half *vins de pays*. Both grades come in all three colours. These are excellent wines in their class and make an agreeable change from the Plaimont range, good though that is.

When I visited Madame Tonon, the property was just about to be inspected by the authorities who were in charge of the possible promotion of St Mont to AOC. She was concerned that they might be influenced to declassify some of her husband's land. This would mean not only that more of his wine might have to be sold as *vin de pays*, but also that quantitative restrictions which apply to AOC land would apply to the remainder of the vineyard too. On the other hand, she hoped that if the area was promoted to AOC, it would be easier to get labelling approval, because that would be in the hands of a more independent body.

I have not been able to visit Monsieur Fitan at the **Domaine de Braibert (5)**, near Riscle, a third independent grower, but a fourth has vineyards within both the St Mont and Madiran appellations, which may give him less reason to grumble. André Dufau's **Domaine de Maouries** is literally on the viticultural boundary at Labarthète. He told me that he thought the St Mont authorities discriminated against him as a private producer. He had just had some white St Mont rejected, on the grounds that it was 'too dark'. He thinks that the pre-eminence of the Plaimont name is likely to confuse the consumer, who will gradually come to regard that as the name of the appellation as a whole, instead of St Mont. He thinks this may be the intention of the Cave, and that the private growers might be effectively squeezed out altogether.

If these stories are not exaggerated, it is regrettable that the Cave does not allow more competition. The lessons from other areas where private growers exist outside the co-opérative, having sometimes broken away and started on their own, is that the quality of the appellation as a whole is increased, and the benefit of this rubs off on the co-opérative members just as much as on the private growers. On the other hand, one is left at the end of the argument with the undeniable quality of the Plaimont wines, and the undoubted achievement of André Dubosc which not even the most truculent of the private growers attempted to challenge.

One footnote is necessary to avoid confusion to readers. There is a company called Le Vignoble de Gascogne which gives its address as St Mont. This apparently has nothing to do with the cave co-opérative. It is a négociant which buys up and sometimes blends wines from various sources, and sells the resulting blends under its own invented names. The wines are mainly to be found in supermarkets and restaurants.

TURSAN

The *petit pays* of Tursan faces the limits of the Bas-Armagnac country across the river Adour and adjoins the westernmost vineyards of the Gers and Madiran. It is intensely agricultural and borders on the west the rich area called Chalosse. The countryside is gently undulating and shares much of the character of the Gers, although for the first time you start to see cattle - the beef of the Chalosse is famous throughout France and explains the fame of the various *daubes* which feature in farm-kitchens in winter. As in the Gers, the farmers grow a bit of everything, so that vines are but one of their crops. Hence the significance of the co-opérative: today **Les Vignerons de Tursan (1)** at Geaune is responsible for nearly all the wine production in the area.

At one time vines were grown throughout the Landes, but Tursan is today the département's largest surviving *vignoble*. Except for a few pockets of vines growing deep into the sandy soil close to the sea, the phylloxera took the same toll in the Landes as it did in other parts of the South-West. In earlier days fine wine was made here. The union of Eleanor of Aquitaine with the English Crown created a vigorous export market to England; the pilgrims passing to and from Compostella were enthusiastic ambassadors and salesmen; markets were opened up in southern Spain and the political links between Spain and the Netherlands from the sixteenth century onwards ensured a regular passage of commerce through Tursan and thus access to the markets of Rotterdam and northern Germany.

The river Adour afforded a perfect access to the ocean at Bayonne, and although the port exacted dues in return for the passage of wine, the burden was not too severe thanks to the influence of the Castelnau family from the Tursan, who had influence where it mattered in Bayonne. The production of wines within the Bayonne area itself also diminished gradually, so the taxes fell too.

In pre-phylloxera times, when there was little demand for dry white wines, the bulk of the production was probably red. It is also likely that the foundations of this wine were the tannat and cabernet franc grapes.

The latter is locally called sable rouge de Capbreton, a reminder of the former vineyards close to the Atlantic coast. Today these two grapes, with some cabernet sauvignon, dominate the *encépagement*, but in these days of quick turnover, the tannat is gradually losing out to the cabernets.

The white wine which was made in former times was derived largely from a grape called claverie, locally known as bouguieu. After the phylloxera this was replaced by another local variety, the barroque, a grape also used in the vineyards of the Béarn and Irouléguy, which suggests Spanish ancestry. But its Basque name in Irouléguy was 'bordolesa churia' which implies an origin in Bordeaux. Another possibility is that it is the place-name of a local settlement of monks, who may have brought the grapes back with them from the crusades, while some believe that the barroque is a cross between the folle blanche and sauvignon. Whatever the truth may be, it is curious that today the barroque has survived nowhere in any strength except in Tursan and the adjoining country vineyards of the Chalosse. Because it adapted particularly well to grafting after the phylloxera, one might have expected it to be more widely adopted. Today it represents at least 90% of all white Tursan, and white wine dominates the total production. Some sauvignon and gros manseng are added by the co-opérative.

Some commentators are downright rude about the barroque grape. Rosemary George calls it, 'Singularly uninspiring . . . the whites are solid and dry, without much real fruit, which is probably the fault of the grape-variety.' This is a little unfair. Jancis Robinson is more charitable, describing white Tursan as 'Full of flavour in a countrified rather than elegant way.' I personally have found white Tursan to be attractively perfumed and rather lively. I also think that both writers are wrong about the weight and strength of the wine: as of 1993 the white wines coming from the co-opérative were bottled at 11° alcohol and no more. It is refreshing to find a local grape such as barroque not only hanging on but flourishing and, like mauzac in Gaillac, still giving a pronounced local and quite individual character to the wine.

The revival of red Tursan is comparatively recent, coming even after the grant of VDQS status in 1958. The 1960 edition of Morton Shand's *A Book of French Wines* describes the red wines as 'of little importance' at that time but now they are tending to challenge the whites, and the Tursan rosé is also popular. To start with, tannat dominated the *encépagement*, but the proportion of cabernet is gradually increasing so that the wine can be marketed earlier, and is more supple and approachable. Again this could be a pity if the red Tursan were to become yet another Bordeaux satellite. The rosé wines are already made exclusively from the cabernets. It is important for the preservation of the character of red Tursan that the tannat presence is not allowed to fall further.

The co-opérative, called **Les Vignerons du Tursan**, enjoys a near-monopoly of Tursan production. Today it boasts 200 members with 800 hectares, but only about half the parcels of the vineyard qualify for VDQS. The present tendency is for the membership to decrease and the area of the vineyard to rise, but even so, simple arithmetic shows how small some of the holdings still are.

The co-opérative was formed in 1957 in the immediate lead-up to the grant of VDQS status to Tursan. It covers an area of thirty-seven communes within a rough square, whose northern boundary is the river between St Sever and Aire. The western edge is the main road from St Sever to Orthez. In the east it crosses and recrosses the road from Aire to Pau and in the south the frontier between the two départements of Landes and Pyrénées-Atlantiques serves also to separate Tursan from the vineyards of Béarn. The home of the co-opérative is roughly in the middle of the appellation area, in the town of Geaune which serves as a good centre for visiting this tranquil and deeply rural region. Geaune is also the centre of some of the better vineyards.

Co-opératives need dynamic directors to counterbalance the natural conservatism of the smaller growers and to galvanise their energies. Tursan does not lack one in Monsieur Paraillous. His marketing director is Monsieur Lacoste who was an admirable guide on a conducted tour, led by the vice-president, a Monsieur Lafenêtre. The Cave produces a remarkably wide range of wines – red, white and rosé. The half of the grapes contributed by members which do not merit VDQS status make *vin de pays des Landes*, and you can drive in and buy this straight from the vats. The basic grade of VDQS Tursan is sold in bottle as Paysage: the red is from 60% cabernet franc and 40% tannat. The tannat fruit and skins are given only five days' maceration and vinified separately from the cabernet which is given seven. Monsieur Lacoste says that this wine is for early drinking and can be drunk at cellar temperature, or even slightly chilled, and he claims for it an aroma of dry pine to remind you of the forests of the Landes. Is it my imagination that the texture too is slightly gummy? The rosé is made almost entirely from cabernet franc, with just a little tannat, and is good in hot weather: 'Ideal quaffing,' he says. The white is made entirely from barroque and can be drunk in the summer following the vintage, although it can keep for up to three years.

The better quality of the other ranges of wine produced by the co-opérative is due to variations in the mix of grape-varieties, and slightly longer maceration. Quality is also obtained from those growers who are willing to do a *vendange verte*, so as to reduce the yield to a maximum of 45 hectolitres per hectare. These growers get more money for their grapes, as an inducement to improve quality.

The names given to the various blends seem to change often. Carte Noire succeeded the previous Cuvée de l'Impératrice and has in turn given way to Pierre de Castelnau. The reds are mainly from cabernet franc with only 10% of tannat. The better whites usually have a little sauvignon and some gros manseng, and Monsieur Lacoste says that they would like to increase the proportions of these grapes if the rules allowed, although they have no intention of deserting the barroque.

One of the best areas of Tursan is round the village called Vielle-Tursan, a few kilometres north-west of Geaune, where there are panoramic views across to the Pyrenees. The grapes from the nearby Domaine de la Castèle are vinified separately by the co-opérative to make their flagship wine. This red wine is very largely cabernet, and the makers claim for it a thoroughbred quality, combining finesse with a solid structure. It is vinified for longer than the other wines, and is intended for medium keeping, say three years.

Monsieur Lacoste is confident that the vineyards of Tursan will expand as their economic viability overtakes that of other crops, such as maize, which are threatened by the removal of state protection and the fierce competition from the cereal belts of mid-America. If he is right, then it may be that the wine-growers of Tursan could follow the pattern of other vineyards in the South-West, and some of them may be able to break away from the co-opérative and start making and marketing their own wines. It is no criticism of this excellent co-opérative to say that the emergence of single-vineyard wines would be the biggest spur to improving quality within the appellation. Because of the virtual monopoly of the co-opérative, Tursan is almost a geographical brand-name. The success of nearby Madiran, for example, is largely due to there being a number of wines from different sources which provide variety within the appellation.

Tursan is bucking the trend which can easily be discerned elsewhere in the deep South-West. They are concentrating on lighter wines for early drinking, whereas in Madiran and Irouléguy producers are going for bigger and sturdier wines for longer keeping. It is not surprising that, in an area so dominated by the co-opérative, the accent should be on providing a quick cash return for the farmer-members. After all, they do not have to wait years to be paid for their maize. Tursan is also close to the Atlantic coast, and the huge summer holiday market which looks for hot-weather quaffing wines rather than hearty stuff more fitting for winter foods.

Such is the importance of the co-opérative that there seem to be only two independent producers of Tursan. Monsieur Dulucq and his son have 16 hectares of VDQS vines, a holding which they have expanded from the 6 they inherited. Their property, which is called the **Domaine de Perchade-Pourrouchet (3)**, is at Payros-Cazautets, two kilometres or so south-west of Geaune. The vineyard was replanted after the phylloxera at the turn of the century – Alain Dulucq's grandmother had to earn some extra francs by selling her *foie gras* and *confits* to pay for the new grafted vines. Otherwise the property was always exclusively devoted to the vine, and the family never went in for other kinds of farming, except to support their own household.

Like many growers, he produces two quality ranges of each of the three colours. His main production is sold as Le Gascon de Dulucq: the white is 100% barroque; the rosé 100% cabernet franc; the red half cabernet franc, 20% tannat, 20% fer servadou, and 10% cabernet sauvignon. His better range is called Château de Perchade. For the white he adds 10% sauvignon to the barroque, for the rosé and red he gives the cabernet franc 20% tannat and 10% cabernet sauvignon. All his wines are sold in bottle from the domaine, except for a little *vin de table* which he sells *en vrac*.

The vinification of the reds is traditional and the maceration lasts from seven to ten days according to the vintage, using both steel and cement. The wine is neither racked nor fined, simply drawn off the vats and put in old barrels for six months. He has tried new wood, but doesn't like the result. Certainly he won't hear of new wood for the white wines which are given short skin-contact as a nod in the direction of new techniques.

I asked Monsieur Dulucq why he did not belong to the co-opérative. He told me that he had actually *started* it, but when he was asked to give them all his crop he refused. He already had extensive equipment of his own, which he was not going to leave to rot, so he left. Initially there was some coolness of relations between the family and the co-opérative, but nowadays they get on quite well.

It may be politic of the co-opérative to foster good relations with its two private producers, because the second of them is none other than Michel Guérard, perhaps France's most famous chef, whose hotel-restaurant complex at Eugénie-les-Bains is only ten minutes' drive from Geaune. If you have a restaurant within a wine-making area, it must be a temptation to make your own, and Monsieur Guérard likes the challenge of novelty. When he bought as his family home the very pretty little eighteenth-century **Château de Bachen (2)** near the village of Duhort-Bachen, he decided to make his own white Tursan.

Michel Guérard's recipe for Tursan is as original as any of those he serves at Eugénie. The vineyard is planted 50% barroque, 25% mansengs (some of each), 12.5% sauvignon and 12.5% sémillon, the last-named to give the wine roundness and silkiness. He was helped in the creation of the vineyard by Jean-Claude Berrouet, the wine-maker at the famous Château Pétrus in Pomerol. His full-time wine-maker is the Anglo-Bordelais Thomas Stonestreet who was on holiday when I visited, but I was shown round by the very helpful Monsieur Dutoya, who is in charge of the grapes in the vineyards.

You would rightly expect the latest technology and equipment in the winery, but the cellars where the wine is stored are nothing short of breath-taking, like a renaissance chapel with barrels instead of pews, and a tasting-room like an altar at one end, rounded off with a romanesque abside. All this is housed in a Palladian construction of sumptuous style, designed by famous architects. The French have a wonderful way of coining phrases which you can take either to be admiring or just saucy. Certainly the epithet '*un petit bijou*' would not have occurred to me as it did to one grower in the Gers to describe the *chais* at Château de Bachen, but then it is a perfectly fair description, if you ignore the element of sour grapes.

Michel Guérard, whose first vintage was the 1988, reserves 20% of the production for his hotel complex. The rest is marketed through

Bordeaux agents. He also generously enabled me to sample his so-far experimental *moelleux*, made from the two mansengs, and he intends in due course to try making a little red for fun.

At present he makes two white wines for sale, one called simply Château de Bachen, the other Baron de Bachen, the latter distinguished by the generous oaking which it is given. Both wines are very fine, as may be imagined, but few would identify them at a blind tasting as Tursan. The unusual blend of grape-varieties conceals the wines' provenance well, but the standard of the wine-making is very high indeed. They seem made to accompany food, which may well have been Guérard's intention. It was a pity I forgot to ask him which of his recipes he thought they would go best with.

If more individual producers had the inclination as well as the capital to set up on their own, one might see a great leap forward in the quality of Tursan. The potential is there if the challenge can be met and markets established in the way that they have been in the pace-setting areas of Madiran and Cahors. It is interesting to find lighter wines being made next door to the South-West's heavy-weights. I do not agree that Tursan wines can be written off as unexciting – the strides forward made by the co-opérative in recent years give the lie to such a judgement.

OTHER WINES OF THE LANDES

Many people assume that the seemingly endless pine-forests of the Landes, so vividly evoked in the novels of François Mauriac, are primeval. It is quite a shock to learn that they are barely a hundred years old. Until the late nineteenth century, the whole area south of Bordeaux which is coloured green on the Michelin maps was a swamp with isolated island-pockets of sheep-pasture. The stilts on which the shepherds used to go about still feature in the more folkloric postcards of the region.

It was one of the poorest parts of France, but small vineyards were planted wherever possible, especially in the coastal strip where the soil was sandy. Here the vines were able to plunge their roots deep into the soil, which helped them to resist the phylloxera for a very long time. It was the custom to train these grapes to grow very close to the sand, which reflected the heat of the summer sun on to the fruit, thereby ensuring that they ripened well before the onset of the October rains.

These old-fashioned *vins de sable* are likely to prove rather interesting, if you can find them. Grown just behind the enormous dunes which pro-tect the land from the Atlantic rollers, the vines are in small but widely spread patches, which may explain the failure of the wines to develop commercially. Today the southernmost part of the forest, west of Dax, is the most likely area of exploration for the curious wine-lover, the towns of Capbreton, Vieux-Boucau, Soustons and Léon still producing small quantities.

In the small village of Messanges you will find Monsieur Thévenin.

His family has owned the **Domaine du Sable de Mallecare (5)** for generations and is still making a red wine which has the ability to age rather well. After twelve years in bottle, his 1979 was a bright ruby colour, pale and slightly brown at the edges, but with a delicate nose of soft fruits. It was rather like an old St Emilion which had lightened in body, and it had, not surprisingly, started to dry out a bit. But it had real style and quite a distinctive character. Monsieur Thévenin's wine is featured regularly at the Auberge des Pins just outside the small village of Sabres deep in the Landes, and not far from the local Landes museum. Another restaurant specialising in the local wines is the Hotel de la Poste at Magescq, on or nowadays bypassed by the N10 just short of Bayonne. It might also be worth trying Pierre Nadal at 14 Place La Fontaine, Biscarosse (Tel. 58-38-74-37).

Between Tursan and the forests lies the rich agricultural area of the Chalosse, where the rewards from rearing poultry are often higher than from producing a modest *vin de pays*. The vineyards were nevertheless extensive and commercially important in former times. The lower reaches of the river Adour ran alongside them and the district no doubt profited from the unnavigability of the water above St Sever, which meant that the wines of Madiran and Tursan were loaded on to boats there or at the port of Mugron.

No doubt the overseas demand for those wines helped the growers in the Chalosse to sell theirs too. The quality must have been appreciated because in 1800 the local wine was fetching 124 *écus* per *tonneau* at Bayonne, a good price when it is remembered that Jurançon was fetching 200 and Tursan 134.

Even at that time the vineyards of Chalosse were in decline, partly because of their invasion by the picpoul or folle blanche grape from nearby Armagnac. Quantities of it, laced with some of the Armagnac itself, were sold from quaysides which had previously known only the traditional wines of Tursan, Madiran and the Chalosse.

The boating activity on the river Adour must have been like that on the Lot. At the port of Mugron, carts loaded with barrels of Chalosse wine arrived overland, while from upstream at St Sever came small flat barges each carrying thirty barrels, the maximum which the shallow waters would take at that point. The people who ran the boats must also have been *négociants* in the wine itself, because they sent salesmen all over the world to find markets for the wines passing through their hands. The port was the focal point of local life, with its boat-builders, sailors, pilots, oarsmen, not to mention the barrel-makers and the special police station which the town had to provide. The sound of hammers and mallets on the sides of boat and barrel, the dry clip-clop of the horses pulling their loads along the tow-paths and the rumble of carts must have made the port a lively place.

The river is capricious, and repeated floods in the late eighteenth century forced the closing of the port of Mugron, though it continued for a while as an important storage centre for all the wines of the Adour basin. One of the largest warehouses still survives at Laurède at the farm called Larribère (Gascon for 'the river').

Today the river is silent, its customers having deserted to the railways and the motorways. The Chalosse vineyards suffered the same diseases as the others during the nineteenth century, although the spread of the phylloxera was slower than further north. This was due partly to the sandy nature of the soil which the aphids found difficult to penetrate, and partly because of the diffusion of the vineyards in small parcels over a wide area. Nevertheless, the quality of the wine did not recover until after the Second World War. In the first half of this century, what wine there was, based on American stocks such as noah and othello, was simply sold by its alcoholic degree, the poor wines fetching, for that reason, more money than the better grapes such as barroque. In 1968 the total vineyard was about one-third of what it had been a hundred years before.

It is not surprising that the local peasants have concentrated on other cultures in recent times. The farms where they raise wonderfully golden chickens and some of the best *foie gras* in France will have several hectares of grazing for the famous beef-cattle of the area as well as a few rows of vines, the surplus from which may go to the co-opérative called **Les Vignerons des Côteaux de Chalosse (1)**. There are a few private growers who sell their wine commercially, including Dominique Lanot who makes a very good rosé at **Domaine de Labaigt (6)** near Mouscardes. But the private growers probably do not have more than 10 hectares between them. It is the co-opérative which makes nearly all the wine. Established in 1962, it has about three hundred members whose average holding is less than 1 hectare. Three-quarters of the wine is sold *en vrac*, and only one-quarter is sold in bottle by the Cave. So these are real country-wines, although the rules of the *vin de pays* limit production to 70 hectolitres per hectare, as opposed to 80 in the case of the wider Landes appellation. About 22,000 hectolitres are made in a good year.

Jacques Lafargue is in charge, and he explained that most of the wine is made, appropriately enough, at their base in Mugron. There is another branch at Pouillon to the south-west and there are sales outlets at Dax, Léon and Orthevielle as well.

In pre-phylloxera times, 85% of Chalosse wine was white, but nowadays at the co-opérative only 20% is white, the remainder red and rosé in roughly equal proportions. There are two reds, one from cabernet franc and the other from tannat, the former given a relatively short maceration of five to six days. (The tannat is given rather longer.) The cabernet wine will benefit from keeping, but is ready to drink young, while the tannat wine needs more time.

The dry white, called Cuvée du Vigneron Blanc, is a curiosity because it is made from a purely local grape called arriloba, which I have not found anywhere else. Monsieur Lafargue thought that it may have originated in the Basque Country, but nobody I spoke to in Irouléguy seemed to have heard of it, nor does it seem to crop up in the old records of the Chalosse itself. The grapes are given an eight-hour maceration at 10° before fermentation, and the wine is made at the low temperature of 15°. It turns out quite flowery with a faint suggestion of muscat, and has more than a touch of *pierre de fusil*. There is also a *moelleux* made from the same grape but picked later, and two sparkling wines, one made by the *méthode champenoise*.

The rosé wine from Mugron is popular with locals as well as with the summer holiday-makers and tourists. It is made from an *assemblage* of tannat and yet another strange grape-variety called egiodola, which we met in the Gers as a minor ingredient of red *floc de Gascogne*. Monsieur Lafargue recommends his rosé as a party-wine – quantities are consumed after the favourite local semi-bullfights and rugby football matches.

Sometimes today it pays not to have an appellation contrôlée, for example when there is a ban on the plantation of more vines in AOC areas such as was introduced in 1992.

In this respect Monsieur Lafargue is lucky because his wines are simply *vins de pays* and therefore his growers are not subject to the ban. His aim is to. encourage growers to profit from grants available at departmental (county) level to plant the recognised varieties, so as to increase the proportion of *vin de pays* as compared with *vin de table*, which can come from any vine which happens to be in the vineyard. In this way he will also increase the proportion of wine which can be sold in bottle, which will in turn raise the image of the Chalosse and the incomes of its producers.

PRODUCERS

Côtes St Mont

1. PLAIMONT PRODUCTEURS (Cave Co-opérative), St Mont, 32400 Riscle Tel: 62-69-62-87 (also at Plaisance and Aignan)
2. Didier Tonon, **Château la Bergalasse**, 32400 Aurensan Tel: 62-09-46-01
3. André Dufau, **Domaine de Maouries**, 32400 Labarthète Tel: 62-69-63-84
4. Jean Garoussia, **Domaine de Turet**, Peyrusse-Vieille, 32160 Plaisance Tel: 62-70-92-57
5. Monsieur Fitan, **Domaine de Braibert**, 32400 Riscle Tel: 62-69-21-08

Tursan

1. LES VIGNERONS DE TURSAN (Cave Co-opérative) 40320 Geaune Tel: 58-44-51-25
2. Michel Guérard, **Le Château de Bachen**, Duhort-Bachen, 40800 Aire-sur-l'Adour Tel: 58-71-76-76
3. Alain Dulucq, **Domaine de Perchade-Pourrouchet**, 40320 Geaune Tel: 58-44-50-68

Landes

1. LES VIGNERONS DES CÔTEAUX DE CHALOSSE, Avenue René Bats, Mugron Tel. 58-97-70-75 (also at Route Stade, 40300 Pouillon Tel: 58-98-20-68; 59 Ave. G. Clemenceau, 40100, Dax Tel: 58-74-56-43; Route Mollets, 40550, Léon Tel: 58-48-77-97; Route Dax, 40300 Orthevielle Tel: 58-73-05-23)
2. Pierre **Nadal**, 14 Place Fontaine, 40600 Biscarosse Tel: 58-78-34-47
3. Jean-Claude **Romain**, Tastet, 40300 Pouillon Tel: 58-98-28-27
4. Jean Naslot, **Quai Angreilh**, 40500 St Sever Tel: 58-76-04-17
5. P. Thévenin, **Domaine du Sable de Mallecare**, 40480 Messanges Tel: not available
6. Dominique Lanot, **Domaine de Labaigt**, 40290 Mouscardes Tel: 58-98-02-42

The Wines of Vic-Bilh: Madiran and Pacherenc

Jean Dartigue stopped the engine of his tractor. Its fumes had not been helping me enjoy to their best the excellent wines of his son-in-law at the Domaine Taillerguet in Madiran. Seemingly everyone in the area had told me to search out Monsieur Dartigue, and although *midi* was fast approaching, he seemed pleased to rest for an hour and give me the benefit of his scholarship, for he is the acknowledged if unofficial historian of the Vic-Bilh.

Vic-Bilh, he explained, is not a person. In the old dialect of the Béarn *vic* meant a district, and administratively it corresponded roughly to a modern French canton. There were seventeen *vics* in Béarn. As a modern place-name Vic-Bilh has disappeared, although Vic-de-Bigorre and Vic-de-Béarn have survived. Vic-Bilh is better known than either, having recently revived as a centre for the making of excellent wines, both red and white.

'Bilh' means old, and the vineyards of the area date back at least to the third century, mosaics of that period having been found during the excavations at an old Roman villa in the district. Vic-Bilh is the most northerly of the *vics* of Béarn and straddles the boundaries of three modern départements – Gers, Pyrénées-Atlantiques and Hautes-Pyrénées. In very rough terms the northern and eastern boundaries correspond with the river Adour, the western boundary is the main highway south to Pau and the southern outpost is the small town of Lembeye, where the slope of the land starts to rise towards the watershed between the Adour and the *gave de Pau*.

The best red wines of this ill-defined area are called Madiran, which is the name of the small town (more of a village really) at the centre of its own appellation. Benedictine monks founded an abbey there in the middle ages. Jean Dartigue does not believe the official party line that they came from Marceillac in Burgundy, bringing with them the wine-making skills which they had supposedly learnt at the Clos de Vougeot. He has established that they came instead from Marcilhac-sur-Célé in the Lot, where a Sieur Sadirac gave several hectares of vines to the Church. Monsieur Dartigue is able to cite as his authority the *Calculaires de Madiran*, a sort of *Domesday Book* kept in the Bibliothèque Nationale. Casting his eyes into the blue skies of Gascony, Monsieur Dartigue said that in those days men gave their possessions to the Church to save their souls, but they do not do that any more because they don't always have souls worth saving!

Madiran was on one of the routes to St Jacques-de-Compostelle, and the settlement of the monks there is an example of the Church's pro-motion of stopping-places for pilgrims on their way to the shrine. St Jacques, the modern Santiago, was one of the most important of all medieval holy places and attracted more pilgrims than any other shrine in the Western Christian world.

The nature of these medieval wines is impossible to guess at, but cer-tainly their quality was good enough by the time of the Hundred Years' War for the English occupation forces to be sending Madiran back home. As with the wines of Cahors, wine-lovers in Holland and the Baltic coun-tries later became enthusiastic buyers of Madiran, the Low Countries alone taking 2000 *tonneaux* by the end of the seventeenth century.

The river Adour flows northwards only a few miles away from the town of Madiran, but, as we have seen earlier, it was not navigable until it was well on its way to Bayonne. The wines of the Vic-Bilh, therefore, had first to be carried on wagons overland to the ports of St Sever and Mugron before they undertook the three days' river voyage down-stream to Bayonne. Later, when the privileges of the port of Bordeaux had been abolished, some wines were carried overland by ox-drawn carts via Bazas to the Quai des Chartrons. It was only in 1992 that the last surviving wine-drover died, at the ripe old age of ninety-six.

The wine-writer Jullien described the production of Madiran in 1816 as limited to five communes, those of St-Lanne, Madiran, Soublecause, Lascazères and Castelnau. It is a strange coincidence that these small villages are all in Hautes-Pyrénées. It is hard to believe that even in those days Madiran was not being produced over the borders in the Gers and Pyrénées-Atlantiques. Today the centre of gravity of the vineyard has moved towards Maumusson, Viella and Aydie. The best wine seems to come chiefly, but not exclusively, from the eastern half of the appellation, the part lying eastwards of the Larcis stream.

In the period immediately before phylloxera, Jullien's estimation of Madiran was clearly high: he rated it as the best of all the wines of the Pyrenees. It was rich in colour, aged well in wood without deterioration and could be bottled for further development. Jullien estimated that the total area of the vineyard in his day was about 1400 hectares, which is about the same size as today, but the modern appellation area is much larger, extending over thirty-seven communes. There is thus still plenty of scope for development of the vineyard.

Monsieur Dartigue has been unable to find any evidence of what grape-varieties were planted until the first mention of tannat in 1820, though there is a reference to the white-wine grape picpoul a century earlier. There is no evidence to show whether before the beginning of this century tannat was the sole or even the principal red-wine grape of the region. At Domaine Barréjat there is a tannat vine which Denis Capmartin claims is over two hundred years old. It is certain that, post-phylloxera, tannat was very widely planted on new American grafts, but, as at Cahors, the stock was allowed to deteriorate. Hybrids were planted too, including baco, a great deal of very ordinary wine was made and all the growers relied on other crops for a living.

Madiran was one of the areas worst affected by the phylloxera plague. By the middle of this century, authentic Madiran was produced from only 6 hectares, a handful of enthusiasts having managed to retain, against all odds, a few pre-phylloxera vines. The French describe as *confidentiel* the production of a wine which is so rare as to be known only to a few connoisseurs and the local growers themselves. Madiran had certainly become a *confidentiel* wine, although the faithful managed to keep the sulphur-candle burning, as in Cahors, long enough to see full AOC status granted to them in 1948. As early as 1906 a primitive form of *syndicat* of producers had been created through the efforts of a Monsieur Nabonne and a few years later they won recognition for their wines over an area roughly corresponding with the modern AOC.

Before the outbreak of the Second World War, a few growers had started to bottle their own wines, the first time this had ever happened, according to Monsieur Dartigue. A co-opérative was started in Diusse in 1936. AOC status was applied for in 1942 and was granted in 1948. It was still to be some time before there was any real progress in Madiran as the bureaucracy was impossibly slow: it took a producer three months to 'get his label' (that is, be granted the authority to put his label on his bottles marked AOC Madiran) and the rules then gave him only six months to sell the wine. In those early years only 50 hectolitres were bottled under the new appellation. Though many farmers continued to uproot their inferior hybrid vines, they did not plant new ones and many switched entirely to the growing of maize. Even the 1960s saw little progress – as late as 1969 there were no AOC parcels in the commune of Maumusson, the quality stronghold of the modern *vignoble*, until Maurice Capmartin started to plant some tannat in that year.

The real force for revival in the post-war era was the co-opérative at Crouseilles, which had taken over from the first one at Diusse, so that it represented growers in the communes which were in the Pyrénées-Atlantiques and the Gers, but not those in the Hautes-Pyrénées. We shall see later that the latter have their own co-opérative elsewhere. By 1970 production had slowly climbed to 10,000 hectolitres, implying a total of about 200 hectares qualifying for AOC status. Then suddenly there was an explosion and both planting and production started to increase dramatically. In the commune of Viella alone 100 hectares were planted for the first time during the 1970s. By 1990 Madiran production had reached 60,000 hectolitres, six times the figure of only twenty years earlier.

If the production of Madiran was once *confidentiel*, that of the white wine called Pacherenc had until recently been miniscule. It has never had much exposure outside the region of production, although its commercial possibilities are now rapidly being grasped. Its AOC area is co-extensive with that of Madiran. Probably fewer than 100 hectares are given over to the growing of the grapes for this truly original wine, but while in 1985 there were only about six private growers making Pacherenc, nowadays nearly everyone makes a little. Pacherenc has its devotees, who would not agree with nineteenth-century critics who thought it inferior to Jurançon. Some even see it as the region's wine of the future.

The vineyards of Vic-Bilh are cradled in an elbow of the river Adour, but the strange feature of the local geography is that the valleys draining off the higher ground to the south do not run into the river at that point, but run parallel with the flow of the river and each other in a south-east/north-west direction. The hillsides separating these valleys stretch in three ridges from 8 to 12 miles long and a mile or two wide. In the south they may be as much as 1000 feet above sea-level and quite narrow and steep-sided, but they flatten out and widen as they sink north-west towards the Adour. These ridges between the streams are every now and then broken by small steep gaps, whose south-facing slopes, usually quite small parcels of land, are among the most favoured spots for vine-growing.

Such a topography tends also to produce an extraordinary geological variety and the landscape of Madiran lends itself to division into three broad categories of soil. On the western slopes of the ridges there is a tendency towards a clay-based subsoil which retains moisture well. It is here that the grapes are grown for the white wines of Pacherenc. On the eastern slopes, however, the soil is heavily endowed with iron and magnesium. A thick layer has built up through which neither rain nor the roots of the vines can easily penetrate. This is the home of the vine-stocks which produce the most intense, dark and tannic red Madiran wines.

Elsewhere, the soil can be a blend of sand and clay, mixed with tiny stones. The drainage system then allows the development of roots which can penetrate deep into the subsoil and extract moisture, however hot and dry the summer. But when the summer is wet or stormy, the surplus water drains away without the ground becoming waterlogged. Here the red wines, while firmly structured and still quite tannic, are rounder and more supple.

The influence of the Adour is also responsible for a micro-climate which lends itself marvellously to the late harvesting of grapes, and the Vic-Bilh specialises in the production of grapes which are picked late in the season. Although the influence of the Atlantic Ocean and the mountains of the Pyrenees yield a mild and moist climate overall, rainfall in the summer and the autumn is generally small. This is particularly so in the eastern and northern communes of the district, which perhaps explains why so much of the good wine comes from there. In 1992, when the vintage throughout the rest of France was brought in in heavy rain, the favoured areas of the Madiran had ten days of good weather at just the right moment.

The temperatures are mild too: with an annual average of $12^{1}/_{2}°$, winter and summer, night and day, they compare equally with other wine-growing areas of the South-West where the actual sunshine statistics are higher. Frost in spring is rare, but the season is rainy and May is one of the wettest months of the year. Summer does not usually arrive until the middle of June, but when it does come it is hot, often stormy, bringing with it the danger of hail. But above all it is the long autumns which help the *vigneron*, the weather in September and October being more stable and reliable than in the summer. The quality of the light and the strong penetrating power of the sun also contribute to the very particular *arrière-saison* which this region enjoys. So it is that the picking of the grapes can await their full maturity. This usually begins during the first fortnight of October, and, in the case of the Pacherenc grapes, can continue well into November, or even later.

The following table compares the annual climate in the principal vineyards of the South-West:

	Av. Tempersture (°C)	Rainfall (cm)	Sunshine (hours)
JuranSon	12.2	1155	1936
Vic–Bilh	12.5	900	1900
Cahors	12.5	824	2016
Gaillac	12.5	722	1950
Dordogne	12.5	764	2050

This *climat du terroir* has favoured the development of grape-varieties which respond to a late Indian summer. As with Cahors, Gaillac and Fronton, the character of each of the wines of Vic-Bilh derives principally from the adoption of one grape-variety which gives an unmistakable individuality to the wines. For Madiran it is the tannat, and for Pacherenc, to a lesser extent, the arrufiac. Although tannat does play a subsidiary role in the production of Cahors, it is otherwise mostly to be found in the extreme South-West, where it produces wines which are fiercely individual, typical of the Gascon characters who make them. Arrufiac is just about exclusive to the Vic-Bilh.

Tannat grapes dominate the red wines of the area, having gradually asserted their character over the cabernet franc and white grape-varieties, which at one time also went into the composition of the wine. Tannat is a tough sturdy vine, high, as its name implies, in tannins. It also matures late. It is naturally rich in alcohol and normally yields 3.5–4° acidity so that wines made from it tend to be slow-maturing and require long ageing. When the wines are young, the bouquet of fresh red and black fruit contrasts with the fullness of the tannins which some people find almost a shock; 'mouth-puckering' is a favourite word with the commentators. With time the tannins come round, developing a range of spicy aromas, a toasted flavour and a vanillin finish. The complexity of tannat wine is often accentuated by being aged in wood, which many producers nowadays consider essential if the wine is to be able to show off all its qualities.

When Madiran was first awarded AOC status, the rules required the tannat grape to constitute at least 30% but no more than 70% of the make-up of a vineyard. This was an exceptionally wide range which has subsequently been narrowed to 40/60. The balance is made up from the two cabernet varieties, and some growers use small quantities (rarely more than 10%) of fer-servadou, here called pinenc, which is also a permitted variety. We have, of course, met this grape at Gaillac and Marcillac in particular. Malbec, the mainstay of Cahors, and all other earlier constituent varieties have now been phased out.

The two cabernets, sauvignon and franc are basic to Bordeaux and its various satellites. While never allowed to dominate the tannat in Madiran, they nevertheless complement and serve to soften the tougher characteristics of that grape. Cabernet franc is here towards the southern limit of its range, and it does not sustain too much humidity. But there are years when its fresh fruitiness is a better foil for tannat than the more sophisticated and structured cabernet sauvignon.

The tough and unyielding characteristics inherent in the tannat grape are at the heart of the problem for modern Madiran-growers: how to preserve its essential rusticity, while at the same time making a wine which can be marketed within a reasonably commercial time-span. Here again the authorities have had to relax the full force of the AOC rules as laid down in 1948, which required at least three years of ageing before release on to the market. The period has now been reduced to one year.

There are two other ways in which the time-lag between vintage and sale can be shortened: reducing the percentage of the tannat grape (many growers do not use the maximum 60%, preferring to maximise the cabernet content); and shortening the maceration period of the grapes. This has the effect of reducing the amount of tannin extracted from the skins and pips, thus producing a wine which resolves what tannin there is much earlier than would otherwise be the case.

The tension in Madiran is between the two schools of production, which explains why, with a comparatively inflexible and uncompromising set of AOC rules, there is such a wide variety of wine. Nevertheless, because of the dominance of the single grape-variety, the production is much more homogeneous than, say, in Gaillac. It is hard to mistake Madiran for anything else.

Although the total production of Pacherenc is much smaller than that of Madiran (less than a tenth of it) there is in practice even more variety in the range of Pacherenc. This is partly due to differences in climate from year to year: as at Vouvray, dry hot years lend themselves to producing sweet wines, whereas in leaner seasons the wines are dry, or at least medium dry. Nowadays, however, producers aim to make a dry and a sweet wine each year. This they achieve in two ways: first by having a balance of grape-varieties which enables them to make both styles, and secondly by successive pickings from the same vines, the later grapes obviously having a higher natural sugar content than the earlier ones.

Traditionally the hallmark of Pacherenc has been the arrufiac grape, known elsewhere in Béarn as raffiat de Moncade. The rules of the appellation do not make it obligatory. In practice most producers use some, but the percentage can vary from 40% to nil. Didier Barré at Domaine Berthoumieu, for example, recognises its authenticity, but says quite simply that it is no good. Neither René Tachouères at Château Pichard nor Roger Castets at Domaine de Fitère has any either. André Dufau at Domaine de Maouries has 40% arrufiac in his white vineyards, perhaps because he is at the north-western end of the appellation where the soil might particularly suit it. It has to be said that the younger producers are tending to plant less and less of it, perhaps because they want to concentrate on the sweeter style of wine which can be made with the manseng varieties alone. It is to be hoped that this will not result in Pacherenc becoming a Jurançon lookalike, though the differences in *terroir* alone may be enough to prevent that.

The gros and petit mansengs make up the balance of the *encépagement* in most vineyards, though many growers like to have some petit courbu too. This last variety, which is losing ground in Jurançon because of its liability to rot and to the disease called *coulure*, is still admired by some Pacherenc makers because the rainfall is less in the Vic-Bilh, so the defects in the grape do not matter so much. All the same, it has the further drawback that it ripens earlier than the other local varieties, which disrupts the cycle of the harvest. Some growers overcome this by planting the petit courbu vines on more northwardfacing slopes so as to retard the ripening. The fans of this grape-variety like it for the perfume and freshness that it gives to young wines in particular. Its main use is in the dry wines.

The gros manseng is coming increasingly to be the mainstay of the Pacherenc makers. Its first pickings go into dry wine, and the later ones into sweet. The petit manseng is generally reserved for the sweet wines. It has a particularly tough skin and can remain on the vine late into the season, even into December, without rotting. Its reduced, evaporated extract is enormously rich and regularly attains 18–19° sugar balanced by acidity of five or six grams. The range of aromas which experts have been able to detect is bewildering, from pineapple and grapefruit, through spiced bread, roasting coffee, mango, elderflower and mint!

Sauvignon is occasionally used by some growers for the dry wines (Château Pichard again) to give freshness, acidity and bite. André Dufau (Domaine de Maouries) has some too, but he is going to give it up because, like petit courbu, it ripens early and in any case he does not think it suits the style of Pacherenc. At one time there were some sémillon vines grown here, but they seem to have disappeared, as has the chénin blanc which was authorised as a variety until the end of the 1950s.

The grapes in Vic-Bilh are grown, as in Jurançon, fairly high off the ground, to protect young shoots against the dangers of spring frosts. The Madiran vines are cultivated rather like a half-standard rose, while the Pacherenc vines are grown as in Jurançon with the shoots at eye-level along long wires. This means that the density of plantation is much less than elsewhere, usually between 2000 and 3000 plants per hectare.

The vintage must not begin until it is officially opened by the local Syndicat de Défense des Vins. This is usually some time during the first week in October, much later than one would expect at the latitude and almost entirely because of the frequency of late sunshine. In the run-up to the harvest, samples are taken from the vines every other day to assess the balance between sugar and acid in the juice of the grapes.

The actual making of the wines follows a fairly normal pattern. For the red Madiran, the length of the *cuvaison* fluctuates between both extremes. A short vinification of as little as four days is practised at the Crouseilles co-opérative for their quick-developing wines: whereas Alain Brumont at Montus and Bouscassé allows some of his red wines as much as five weeks.

It is obligatory that each grape-variety be vinified separately. After the *assemblage*, the young wines have to be aged for a period of one year before, by law, they can be released for sale. The name Madiran may only be used once the wines have passed a tasting test carried out under the auspices of the French wine authorities.

For the dry Pacherenc the vintage will take place during the first fortnight of October, but in a year where there are prospects for a sweeter end product it will be a month or more before the fermentation takes place.

One of the best ways of getting to know the wines of the Vic-Bilh is to order them with meals in the hotels and restaurants of the region, because they are seldom to be found away from Gascony, except in restaurants which specialise in the food and wines of the South-West. My wife Jeanne and I were introduced to them in 1974 by Maurice Coscuella, the patron of the Hôtel Ripa-Alta at Plaisance, a small town just east of Madiran. To accompany such delights as an omelette filled with crisped dice of skin from the specially fattened ducks of the region, and a ragoût of goose giblets in a wine sauce, Monsieur Coscuella persuaded us (without difficulty) to try the delicious Madiran made by the Laplace family in the small village of Aydie, and to accompany our dessert with one of their honeyed sweet Pacherencs. Such was the effect of Monsieur Coscuella's diplomacy, reinforced by his almost equal enthusiasm for the Armagnacs of the region, that we set off the next day with a letter of introduction to Monsieur Frédéric of **Domaine Laplace (14)**.

It took us the best part of a morning to find the Laplace farm. A working farm it was, because in those days the family relied not only on wine but on all manner of other crops as well for their livelihood. In fact, as we were to learn, it had been only a few years earlier that they had begun to bottle and market their own wine which had previously been sold off to the trade without even the benefit of appellation.

Nevertheless, wine-making had been in the family blood for generations, since 1759 in fact, and we were shown vines that went back to the phylloxera era and had somehow magically survived. The Laplaces were one of the small number of farmers who had managed to keep the local wine-making traditions alive and to help bring them back to life a hundred years after disaster struck in the 1880s. At the time of that first visit there was still something charmingly rustic about the production of wine at Domaine Laplace. Old Monsieur Frédéric Laplace (the estate is now run by his grandchildren) welcomed us into his living-room, which also served for wine-tasting, and there were more firearms and emblems of *la chasse* about the place than evidence of wine-making. Without removing his beret, which was perhaps only ever taken off for intimate family occasions, he gave us generously to taste of his wines, both red and white, and kindly posed for photographs to demonstrate his new electric pump which he had just acquired for carrying out the operations of *remontage*.

Madiran was even then a wine truly to be described as *confidentiel*: but Monsieur Laplace explained that, before the coming into effect of the new appellation rules, some Madiran, including his own, was made almost entirely of tannat, and the introduction of cabernet was a fairly new-fangled idea. He gave us a special *cuvée* of his 1967, of which he was particularly proud, to taste from an unlabelled bottle. It was, he said, made in the old-fashioned way. Seven years after the vintage it was still a fairly tough mouthful, but wonderfully full and rich, still tannic but with a long life ahead of it, and well able to keep at bay even the most fearsome of Gascon winter rains.

In the intervening twenty years the family has inevitably moved with the times, and we were very honoured to have had a rare opportunity of tasting the wine as it was made in the days when Alain Brumont was still at school. The Laplaces had only just introduced modern machinery on to the farm, including a highly innovative tractor. In South-West France tractors were comparative rarities until after 1960 – before that the land was ploughed with oxen or, more rarely, horses. In the old days nobody would have thought of de-stalking the grapes before making the wine, but it was not only the new rules which obliged the Laplaces to do this: the commercial pressures behind making quicker-maturing wines had a lot to do with it too.

Twenty years on, the family have 48 hectares under vines, roughly three times as many as when we first visited in their grandfather's day. Apart from the Brumont complex, this is the largest single property in the Vic-Bilh, although about one-third of the vines are a few kilometres away at St-Lanne and another third at Moncaup to the south-east. Four hectares are given over to the white Pacherenc grapes.

Since our 1974 visit the family have installed some modern plant to deal with their increased landholdings, gleaming stainless-steel vats having replaced the huge old wooden *cuves* which have fortunately been pre-served and still adorn the old *chais*. They are making three red wines, which I list in ascending order of quality, together with the *encépagements*:

	% Tannat	% Cab. Fr.	% Cab. Sauv.
Fleury-Laplace	50	40	10
Madiran Frédéric 　Laplace	60	20	20
Château d'Aydie	70	—	30

All the red wine grapes are vinified for twenty-one days in stainless steel. The Fleury-Laplace, formerly called Liseré d'Or, is matured in the steel, too, but the other two wines are transferred to new wood before their second, malolactic fermentation. The Château d'Aydie is given twelve to fourteen months in the wood, the Madiran Frédéric Laplace rather less. All three are bottled at 13° and kept for a further year in the cellars before sale. François Laplace says the Fleury-Laplace should peak at about eight years old, the other two at ten to twelve.

Of the red wines, the 1989 Liseré d'Or in 1993 was bright and deep in colour, with good 'legs' in the glass. All trace of purple had gone. There was plenty of the tannat's natural vanilla character and some toast on the nose. The attack was good and there was plenty of fruit. There was good style from the cabernets to balance the already retreating tannins. The wine could improve, but I was worried that it started to oxidise after half an hour, though this could have been an unlucky bottle.

The Madiran Frédéric Laplace from both 1990 and 1991 was domin-ated by the cabernets rather than the tannat, which was surprising, and François Laplace agreed. The nose of the 1990 was quite spicy with violets as well, the flavour was meaty and again there were the aromas of fresh toast.

As might be expected the Château d'Aydie is the best and most typical of these Madirans. Cloves and cinnamon were among the spices on the nose of the 1990, with some vanilla from the wood, but not too much. The wine was powerful but round on the palate with almost infinite pos-sibilities for development. The tannins were already beginning to soften.

There are two Pacherencs, dry and sweet with the following *encépagements*:

	% Arrufiac	% Gros M.	% Petit M.	% P. Courbu
sec	30	40	—	30
moelleux	30	20	40	10

Only the two mansengs are given skin-contact prior to fermentation. When this is finished, the wines are matured for a further year, of which the first six months are spent in new wood.

I was at first rather disappointed with the dry Pacherenc. The 1991 seemed to me to lack fruit, though it finished well, but a second bottle tasted a few weeks later in London was a great deal better than I had remembered the first one. The *moelleux* from the same year was quite a different matter. The nose gave but little indication of the power to come: in the mouth there was an astonishing range of rich, exotic fruits, pineapple and guava according to François Laplace. The finish was very powerful too, and long. A very fine sweet wine, though perhaps a bit 'wide screen' for some tastes.

François plans to concentrate more and more on the quality end of his range. Because of the present ban on planting new terrain in this AOC area, he is thinking of uprooting some of the less good red vine-stocks and replanting the same ground with petit manseng to increase his production of Pacherenc *moelleux*. This will reduce his red wine output, but he will cut the range to two, phasing out the Fleury-Laplace and concentrating on the two quality red wines.

Behind this strategy is his concern over the falling consumption of wine in France. There has been a 25% drop in the number of regular wine-drinkers, and also in the number of people who take wine only occasionally. There has been a 50% rise in the number who don't drink wine at all. He sees his market as being with the regular and discerning wine-drinker, rather than the occasional drinker, because the latter on the whole does not enjoy serious wine often enough to enable him to appreciate quality. Laplace recognises at the same time that quality wines from small appellations such as Madiran have to face strong mar-ket competition from overseas, so, apart from increasing quality he needs also to keep his prices keen. He is thus cautious about the future, and surprisingly enough welcomes the restriction on further planting, and does not mind that, in order to increase his production of Pacherenc, he must dig up some of his existing vines.

From the village of Aydie to Crouseilles cannot be more than five miles by road, but you will need infinite skill at map-reading and a highly developed sense of direction to find the way without getting lost. You will know when you get there because the small village is domi-nated by the recently restored Château de Crouseilles on high ground overlooking the surrounding countryside. This imposing estate was bought up by the Crouseilles co-opérative in 1981, replanted with tannat and cabernet and developed as their flagship wine.

Crouseilles is geographically at the heart of Madiran production, and the **Cave des Vignerons du Vic-Bilh-Madiran (24)** was founded in 1950. Few aspiring local growers had the capital to invest in the replanting of vineyards or the purchase of the necessary plant for the making of wines which would meet the quality tests of the new appella-tion. Co-operation among the growers was therefore the obvious answer, and it was not long before 90% of the total Madiran production was in the hands of the new co-opérative.

In the intervening years, more and more individual producers have

joined the handful who had started the revival. In the 1960s and 1970s
it was easier to finance the equipment of cellars at low rates of interest,
because the official policy was then to encourage the production of
quality wines. Some started from scratch, such as Alain Brumont; others
left the co-opérative to start on their own, such as Alain Oulié at the
Domaine de Crampilh. The percentage of Madiran produced by the
co-opérative has fallen to 40%, but this figure masks the increase in
wine actually produced for its members. There are 220 of these with
vineyards in the Madiran area, while there are other members for
whom the co-opérative makes wine as AOC Béarn and *vins de pays des
Pyrénées-Atlantiques* or *Conté Tolosan*. Their total surface under vine in
Madiran is some 450 hectares. Simple arithmetic dictates that the average member has something like only 2 hectares of vines, which would
obviously not justify setting up a quality vineyard on his own.

The Crouseilles co-opérative is as dynamic as it is successful, which it
needs to be to face up to the competition from the Plaimont producers.
A staff of twenty-two is needed to watch over a total stock of up to three
years' production. This includes some rosé as well as Pacherenc, but by
far the greater proportion is Madiran, and since this wine is by nature
slow-maturing, it is not surprising that the co-opérative has developed
techniques to turn over its stock more quickly. For example, in the case
of its Pot Gourmand, the wine is only vinified for four days, though the
blend is maintained at 50% tannat and 50% cabernet. The short *cuvaison*
emphasises the flowery bouquet and fleshy consistency of the wine,
keeping the power of the tannins in check.

Quite different is the Madiran which they call Folie du Roi. This
folie is a real *vin de garde*, and in good years the wine is so full-bodied
that it will last for ten years, which is extraordinary for a co-opérative
wine. It is based on specially selected growths of tannat, whose yield is
strictly controlled. The colour is a really deep ruby, and the nose is rich
in spices and red fruit. On the palate it is full and its firm structure is at
once apparent. The finish is round and long.

The same brand-name is applied to the sweet Pacherenc, which
remains almost as tiny a production as the ultra-sweet Moelleux
Automnal, made from grapes which are left on the vine until the last
possible moment.

The Madiran which the co-opérative makes from its own Château de
Crouseilles is, however, its best wine by a long chalk. First commercialised
in 1987, the château made a better wine the following year, which, as
everywhere, was a particularly successful vintage. This wine, a winner of
medals all over the place, is given new wood each year that shows up quite
fiercely on the nose. If the Folie du Roi is a keeper, it is hard to guess how
much time this wine needs in bottle. It is very good indeed and competes
worthily with the very best wines from private producers. But it must
have long cellaring. 1990 and 1993 were also good years.

The co-opérative also produces a range of wines which it reserves for
restaurants, many of which are not for sale either at the Cave or elsewhere.

Madiran and dry and sweet Pacherenc are each sold under the name of Comte d'Orion, while three Madirans are made for the owners of Domaine de Mourchette at Aydie, the Château de Gayon and the Domaine de Fauron, all for sale under the names of the properties. Declassified Madiran is sold as Vin de Fleur as a *vin de pays*. The range is completed with two Béarn wines, a red under the brand-name Poule au Pot, and the other sold simply under the Béarn appellation with a picture of the château at Pau on the label.

There is another less substantial cave co-opérative. It is at **Castelnau-Rivière-Basse (32)**, a small hill-town four miles north-east of Madiran and overlooking the valley of the river Adour as it runs northwards from Tarbes. This co-opérative caters for the Madiran growers in the département of the Hautes-Pyrénées. There are only twenty or so members, for whom the Cave makes about 2000 hectolitres of Madiran a year. Some rosé de Béarn is also made here and a tiny amount of Pacherenc from one grower. The Madiran is fairly tough and unsophisticated stuff, and not up to the quality of the other Caves. It is fortunate for the members that the cellars are on the main road to Tarbes, attracting a good passing-by trade, because this is the way that the Castelnau co-opérative sells much of its produce. It is unfortunate for the image of Madiran as a whole that many people will get their first taste of the wine from here.

Madiran and Pacherenc are also made by the **Producteurs de Plaimont (1)**, noted earlier in connection with the wines of St Mont and the Côtes de Gascogne. The branch at St Mont is near enough to the boundary with the Madiran and Pacherenc appellations to have attracted growers from there. Recent figures indicate that St Mont makes wine from about 225 hectares of Madiran and 45 of Pacherenc. Their Madiran and Pacherenc production is therefore about half the output of the Crouseilles Cave, enough to stimulate a lively competition between the two.

St Mont seem to favour a mix of grapes leaning more heavily towards tannat. Their Madirans, one sold under a Plaimont Tradition label and the other sold as part of the Collection Plaimont range, contain 65% and 70% tannat respectively. A good proportion of pinenc (alias fer servadou) helps underline the rustic character of the St Mont Madirans.

The Collection wine, after a *cuvaison* of fifteen to twenty days, is given on average nine months' ageing in new oak which certainly shows on the nose when the wine is young. It ages better than the cheaper and more basic Tradition wine. The tannat grapes which go into it are pruned much harder than the rules require, and come from vines at least fifteen years old. Production is only about three-quarters that which is allowed by law. The 1989 wine boasted 12.8° alcohol and could easily last ten to fifteen years.

The St Mont co-opérative also markets a Madiran exclusively to restaurants which comes from a property just south of Viella in the northern part of the appellation, sold under the name of Château Laroche. This wine is obviously made to mature earlier than the Collection wine, and seems to me to contain a higher proportion of cabernet. The strong aroma of cedar-wood on the nose certainly suggests this.

St Mont does not make a dry Pacherenc, preferring a half-sweet style. Like their rivals at Crouseilles they also make a premium ultra-sweet version which they call Pacherenc de St Albert because the grapes are picked very late, usually about 15 November, St Albert's Day. Experiments have also been made with a kind of *eiswein*, a technique from the Rhineland where the grapes are left on the vines literally until the frosts arrive. A few of the 1989 grapes were not picked until January the following year.

In François Laplace we have already met one of a band of five younger producers in the area who have been christened 'Les Jeunes Mousquetaires'. Today's D'Artagnan is Alain Brumont, the now famous grower who has done so much to revitalise the wines of Madiran, and whom our historian-friend, Monsieur Dartigue, calls *'une bonne locomotive'*.

Brumont lives at the **Château Bouscassé (43)** near the village of Maumusson, halfway between Madiran and St Mont. The property has been in his family for at least eight generations. He recalls his great-grandfather, a well-known local character who used to market his wines by giving three banquets a year, to which he would invite all the local bourgeoisie. Like his wines, the *foie gras* too was both home-made and vintage, and preceded course after course of *garbure*, chicken in the pot, *daubes*, roast meats, salmi of the local pigeon, *confits* of duck and goose, all in unlimited quantities and presented with typical Gascon generosity.

His grandfather made some Pacherenc as well as Madiran, and it seems that until the Second World War, Pacherenc was a word used to denote any white wine of quality. The word meant literally 'stakes in rows' (*piches en rang* in modern French) to differentiate from the former custom of planting vines at random and not in straight lines. Like everything on the farm, even the bottles were home-made. They came in two sizes: the *pichet*, which held 2 or sometimes 3 litres, and the *chopine*, which held half a litre.

The farm was typical of the system of polyculture: they reared and killed their own pigs, a ritual which is continued to this day and at which Alain is always present. They reared cattle, geese and grew all their own vegetables as well as making their own bread. Grandfather even kept bees to provide the wax for sealing the bottles of wine in the days before capsules. The honey was fed to the pigs, and they must have been delicious.

Bouscassé declined as a vineyard along with the others. Alain's father would not let him restore it, so in 1980 Alain left home and with neither money nor experience signed up to buy and replant a property called **Château Montus (43)**, which at the time produced no wine, though the *chais* were magnificent. He says he wanted somewhere which would be his own and where he could do as he liked. Perhaps inheritance problems at home might have inhibited his plans to make wine, even if he had been allowed to do so.

He reconstituted the vineyard at Château Montus in 1980, and in the meantime he has made things up with the family, who one hopes is proud of his success. He has moved back to Bouscassé and enlarged it beyond the dreams of his ancestors. The work which began in 1988 will not be completed for some years, but already there is a wonderful underground cellar in the Bordeaux manner, where the *barriques* of new wine are matured. There is, too, a new *maison de maître* of some magnificence built from local stone, a kind of Gascon Alhambra. Bouscassé is the headquarters of the Brumont enterprise, and it is here that he receives visitors.

The whole establishment remains self-sufficient as far as possible, the equipment used in the vineyards being made on the estate. Life is run on neo-feudal lines, all the twenty-two staff joining with the family for their midday meals. Alain calls and is called by the staff 'tu', though he remains very much the *patron*.

Alain Brumont is proud that, although he was always passionately interested in wine, he is entirely self-taught. He insists that he is not trying to do anything new: on the contrary his sole object is to try to re-create the wines of Madiran as they used to be. His wine is good because he is preserving his roots. He says that it was the generation which created the AOC rules which departed from tradition by allowing in the cabernet grapes and making lighter-style wines. That for him was the same mistake that was made at Cahors and other newer appellations. He is critical of St Mont, for example; he says that they had never in the past made wine there which was good for anything except distillation into Armagnac: now they are borrowing the Madiran grapes to make an imitation light-weight Madiran, which he says is false. For him tannat is the only Madiran grape, and the rules should be changed to exclude the cabernets. The other young musketeers would agree with him, though this is not a view shared by the smaller Madiran producers who do not have either the inclination or resources to make wines which take as long to mature as a 100% tannat wine does. Anyway, they say, it is all very well for Alain Brumont to go on about authenticity, but where is the evidence that Madiran was ever made exclusively from the tannat grape? It is little wonder that Alain has created a lot of waves in the area, despite the immense awe in which he is held.

He is on less contentious ground with his other hobby-horse, the use of new wood for maturing both the red and white wines, although here, too, the pretext of authenticity is fairly slim. Alain says that, in the old days, no one used anything except wood to store wine in, and of course that is true. But it was not *new* wood: in fact wine-makers would take careful steps to mature the barrels by cleaning them out to get rid of the tannins and flavours which the newness in the wood would give to the wine. His passion for new wood is something he acquired during his visits to Bordeaux, and of course he is only applying in the Madiran a technique which has now become commonplace all over the world. But for Brumont, wood is not just wood. He experiments with barrels from

Burgundy, Cognac and nearer home, conducting regular tastings to compare the effect of different barrel-makers on his wines. He gave me a taste of his *petit courbu* from three different *barriques*, each from a different barrel-maker, the grapes having been picked at intervals of one week for each of the three barrels. The results were amazingly different, not only because there was a fortnight between the first and the last, but because of the accents coming from the different woods.

Apart from his ebullient dynamism ('Maumusson will be the Napa Valley of the South-West,' he has boasted to the press), his novel approach is not limited to wine-making. The enormous financial investment he has made has come partly from loans on which he is paying 15% per annum – 'in wine'. At the end of seven years, the investor will have recovered his original capital. The operation is unique, in that it allows businesses to acquire a prestigious image through their association with a successful wine. He admits that, with him, much belongs to the banks. Nearly everything perhaps, except the essentials – his name, his reputation and his skill.

Behind all the blah-blah, there are two solid reasons for Alain Brumont's success: his amazing capacity for self-publicity and handling of the media; and, more important, the astonishingly high quality of the wines he makes. He says that wine is a rapport between the plant, the *terroir* and the wine-maker. But his endless pursuit of perfection through the development of new techniques is ample proof that the basic law, as stated by him, is not enough on its own. If it were, every grower in the Madiran would be making a Château Montus.

The Brumont enterprise now consists of three separate properties: Montus (34 hectares), Bouscassé (29 hectares and still growing) and a third called **Domaine Meinjarre (43)** (19 hectares). It is at the last-named that the grapes for Brumont's Pacherencs are grown, though the wine is sold under the name of either Montus or Bouscassé. The name Meinjarre is in effect used as a second red wine of Bouscassé: Brumont is anxious to escape the charge that his wines are expensive by producing what he calls 'a first-class Madiran for 20 francs'. He also says he is tired of providing other producers with an excuse for increasing their prices.

The Meinjarre is half tannat, half cabernet franc. It is vinified for ten days and given six months in barrels which have been previously used once for Montus, once for Bouscassé. The colour is not as black as the two bigger wines: the nose is of fresh plants, and in the mouth it is well built but light, rather silky. It is extremely good value. The name Meinjarre is also applied to a Rosé de Béarn from cabernet franc with some tannat.

Bouscassé and Montus each produce two wines: in each case one of them has a fairly traditional mix of grapes, and the other is 100% tannat. Perhaps this is the place to explain how, if the rules of the appellation call for not less than 40% or more than 60% tannat, it is apparently legal to make a wine which consists wholly of tannat. The reason is that the

rules do not require every red Madiran to contain the regulation balance of grape-varieties, but that each producer must have in his vineyards vines in those proportions. For a producer like Brumont,
therefore, who is aiming to make more and more wines with more and
more tannat, the production of less prestigious wines is an opportunity
to put to good use the grapes which he is obliged by law to plant, but
which he does not want to put into his premium wines.

The following are the specifications of the red wines from these two
properties:

	Ch. Bouscassé	Ch. Bouscassé Vieilles vignes	Montus	Montus Prestige
encépagement:				
tannat	60%	100%	70%	100%
cabernet franc	30	–	–	–
cabernet sauvignon	10	–	20	
fer servadou	–	–	10	
fermentation	4 weeks	5 weeks	4weeks	5 weeks
time in wood	1 year	1ear +	1 year	1 year +
time in barrels	twice-used	new	40% new 60% once-used	new

Each property gives its name to a dry Pacherenc, but only Bouscassé
a sweet one. Sweet Pacherencs must now be called *doux* to differentiate
them from sweet Jurançons, which are called *moelleux*. Both the dry
wines have arrufiac, Bouscassé complementing it with gros manseng
and a little sauvignon, Montus with petit courbu. Both wines are given
a cold maceration before being fermented in new wood and are matured
in it for six months.

The sweet Bouscassé is altogether more complicated. The wine
comes from 7 hectares of petit manseng, and 3 hectares of gros. Because
of the lower yield from the petit, this means that in terms of relative
volume, the wine is about 50% of each. Brumont copies the Jurançon
practice of getting his pickers to go over the grapes many times, so as to
ensure that all grapes which go into the wine are fully ripe. There will
normally be two pickings in October, and three or four each in
November and December. The October grapes will yield twice as much
as the November picking, which in turn will yield twice as much as the
December. Each month's picking is vinified separately, and each
month's wine separately bottled, with the month when the grapes were
picked proclaimed loudly on the label. Thus the later the month, the
sweeter and more expensive the wine. The October wines will be fermented and raised in barrels that have already been used once or twice,
the November wines half in new barrels and half in barrels that have
been used only once where they will remain for one year, and the
December wines in entirely new wood, again for one year.

In complete contrast, and to remind one that Bouscassé has vineyards that are mostly in the Gers, he makes a *vin de pays des Côtes de
Gascogne* from colombard and gros manseng which is meant to be
drunk within two years of the vintage. With his young red wines that do
not yet qualify for Madiran AOC, he makes a *vin de table* which he markets under the name Le Bigourdan. He says it can give lessons to plenty
of real Madirans. It is well structured, balanced and keeps despite a
fermentation of only five days.

This extraordinary man is hailed by French guides as 'the *vigneron* of
the decade', and his wines are regularly awarded higher marks in blind
tastings than the *crus classés* of the Médoc and the Sauternes. His
Bouscassé 1991 was voted one of the top ten wines in the world at
Montreal in 1994.

If he has plans for the future, he is keeping them under wraps. He
merely says that he aims to produce from Montus and Bouscassé the
best wines in Madiran, in a complete range to go with every course at a
meal. For most people that would be a bold ambition, but for Alain
Brumont it seems relatively modest.

What is so extraordinary about the development of the Vic-Bilh
wines is that, although Brumont is producing wines which aspire to
world-class, the other four young musketeers are not far behind him.
Two of them have vineyards, one on either side of Bouscassé. Jean-
Marc Laffitte to the north is the owner of the **Château Laffitte-
Teston (53)**, where he has built an underground cellar, not in imitation
of Alain Brumont, because that might be lèse-majesté, but certainly out
of the belief that only underground can his wines realise their potential
in the hot Gascon summers. His new tasting-room is very splendid too,
with panoramic views over his red wine vines.

Jean-Marc is and looks like a rugby-player. Large in all dimensions,
he has a wonderfully stentorian bass-voice, with a resonance that would
delight BBC audition panels. In 1975 he took over from his father
12 hectares of vines. He remembers his grandfather telling him that,
during the 1920s, white wine was the traditional drink in the local town
of Riscle, which then boasted no fewer than twelve bistros. Fortified
drinks such as Pernod did not come in until the 1930s and cocktails
never really made it to Gascony. But wine as a café drink declined in the
years before the Second World War. Jean-Marc thinks it could be
making a comeback as the fashion for whisky shows signs of weakness.

During the eclipse of Madiran, his forebears planted mostly poor-
quality hybrid grapes, though there are still 3½ hectares of really old
tannat vines more than seventy-five years old, from which Jean-Marc
today makes his premium red. He agrees with Brumont about the
supremacy of tannat in Madiran: without it there would be no Madiran.
He was keen to point out the necessity of keeping the vegetation of
tannat plants to a minimum. He explained that, with most grapes, the
more luxuriant the growth the softer the juice and the less intense. With
the tannat, the reverse is true. Excessive green accentuates the astringency

of the grape-variety. So reduction in yield produces more suppleness and softer tannins, rather than the opposite which is the case, say, with the cabernets.

Jean-Marc Laffitte is also a devotee of cement for maturing those wines which do not go into wood. He prefers it to stainless steel which he says is fine for fermentation because the temperature can be more easily controlled. It is the response of stainless steel to temperature changes which causes movement in the wine itself within the *cuve*, thus inhibiting the wine from throwing its deposits naturally. In cement the more constant temperature allows the more regular rejection of this matter.

As well as a red Côtes de Gascogne which he calls Domaine des Tuileries, and a rosé de Béarn which he sells under the Laffitte-Teston label, there is the usual range of two reds and a dry and sweet Pacherenc. The main wine, which producers in the area tend to refer to as their Générique, is from 70% tannat, the balance being made up by the cabernets equally. The vinification is from fifteen to twenty days according to the year and, after six months in *cuve*, is given eight months in not totally new oak. The premium wine, called Vieilles Vignes, is 100% tannat and is vinified for twenty-one days and kept in wood, mostly new, for thirteen months or so. This wine is, of course, for keeping, but the wines from this property do not seem as backward in style as some and Jean-Marc walked off with first prize for both his sweet and dry Pacherenc at the 1995 Madiran wine-fair. The Laffitte-Teston wines are reasonably priced.

Alain Brumont's other fellow musketeer-neighbour, this time on his southern boundary, is Patrick Ducournau, perhaps the most serious and scientific member of the band. Patrick has taken over the vines at **Domaine Mouréou (51)** from his father, having studied oenology at Montpellier and finished his training at Bordeaux. His father, who bought the property as recently as 1968, himself replanted its vineyard in association with some Laplace cousins. He now looks after the 100 hectares of cereals.

Patrick explained that in the old days the vintage was a relatively simple affair. You picked the grapes when you thought they were ready, pressed them and then put them to ferment. You then forgot all about them while you got in the maize. When that was safely in, the wine would be ready to rack and put into traditional huge old oak barrels for as long as you liked.

Patrick still believes, as does Alain Brumont, that the less you do to disturb the wine, once the alcoholic fermentation is finished, the better. Traditionally, new wine, especially that from the tannat grape, has always been drawn off the lees every six weeks or so to let some air into it to give the wine suppleness and to help soften the tannins. The aeration is important, but Patrick has always been concerned that this frequent disturbance of the wine does not allow the deposits to settle naturally, or even completely. He has therefore devised a technique of oxygenation by injection, which he is in the process of patenting jointly with the Laplaces. This can be applied to wine in barrel or in *cuve*. Patrick believes that this process makes for a more structured wine, and also makes the wine more proof against later oxidisation. It also clarifies the wine, avoids unnecessary filtration, and probably shortens the ageing process. During the oxygenation, it is important to keep the wine at a temperature between 12° and 18°. In the old days, they used to roll the barrels into the stables in winter and put them beside the cows, so as to raise the temperature to the right level.

Another neat idea of Patrick's addresses the problem of buying some new barrels each year. What he plans to do is to replace the flat ends to *all* his barrels *every* year, thereby ensuring that part of every barrel regularly includes new wood. This will save buying expensive new *barriques*, the high cost of which is largely occasioned by the curved rather than the flat surfaces. The flat ends represent a third of the surface area of the barrel, so annual renewal of the ends is equivalent to replacing a whole barrel after three years.

Patrick Ducournau has 14 hectares of vines, 2¹/₂ of which are set aside for Pacherenc. The petit manseng grapes for his *doux* are relatively new and were due to make wine for the first time in 1992, but the vintage was so poor that he made some dry wine with it instead. His 1994 is however another story.

The two reds come from quite different parcels of land. The Générique Domaine Mauréou is grown on soil where there is a lot of chalk, with an impenetrable subsoil which makes drainage difficult. It is planted with 70% tannat. The better land goes to make the premium wine called Chapelle Lenclos which is all tannat. These wines are very highly regarded indeed, and are much admired by young wine-makers all over the South-West. Patrick is less pessimistic about the *red* wines of 1992 than other growers, because it did not actually rain during the picking. The white grapes were picked in much more difficult conditions. Usually, his Pacherencs are of the same high quality as his reds, and it was interesting to see a dry wine made in a difficult year from petit manseng. Analysis would no doubt have proved it to be wholly dry, but there was no gainsaying the honeyed legacy of the grape-variety. Given some wood, this wine was delicious even only six months after the vintage.

Assessing the young reds was a much harder proposition, particularly when the *assemblage* had yet to be made. Ducournau had made a provisional blend from his Mauréou grapes – there was heaps of fruit with acidity to balance, but the whole was masked heavily by the tannins. This was even more so the case with the pure tannat wine from Chapelle Lenclos. Both were first-class wines in the making. A curiosity, because one would certainly otherwise not have the chance of tasting such a wine, was the pure cabernet franc which is part of the blend of the Mouréou red. This was like a rather overblown Bourgueil, with huge amounts of red fruits and cedar-wood.

Another typically modern range of wines is made by the fifth *mousquétaire*, Didier Barré, at the **Domaine Berthoumieu (3)**, deep in the countryside north of Viella. This is very much a family affair, where his father looks after the vines and Didier makes the wines and manages the business side of the operation. He takes less and less interest in the family's 35 hectares of cereals and more and more in the 24 hectares of vines. The property has been in the family since the eighteenth century, but there is nothing old-fashioned about Didier Barré. He is the joker of the *mousquétaires*, with a special brand of humour which the French call *malicieux*, which does not at all imply malice but a sort of roguish wit only to be found in the kind of quick-fire conversation in which the French excel. His infectious giggle masks the seriousness of his wine-operation, which puts Domaine Berthoumieu in the top flight of modern Madirans.

There are two Berthoumieu reds, the premium wine being called Cuvée Charles de Batz, which was an alias for the real life D'Artagnan. They compare as follows:

	Dom. Berthoumieu	Cuv. Ch. de Batz
encépagement:		
tannat	55%	80/90%
cabernet franc	15%	—
cabernet sauvignon	20%	10/20%
fer servadou (pinenc)	10%	—
fermentation tannat:	14 days	21 days
others:	10 days	cab. sauv. 12/15 days
remontage tannat:	daily	daily
others:	twice daily	twice daily
maturing	*cuve* or 3-year wood	new wood (3-year cycle)
length of *élevage*	1 year	1 year

The Berthoumieu wines seem to mature earlier than some of the other big wines of the region. The 1989 Charles de Batz was already nearly *à point* in 1993. The wine was very bright and a beautiful deep garnet colour, the nose highly perfumed. It was surprisingly soft on the palate, spicy with almonds and prunes. The finish was long. Perhaps the 1989s are coming round quicker than the 1990, or maybe the one year's difference is crucial to the ageing of these wines, but the same wine of 1990 was much tougher relatively. The nose was still loaded with vanilla, but Didier Barré said that the tannat gave a suggestion of vanilla even without wood. The flavour was toasty, with a hint of mushrooms and truffles. Perhaps this wine needs ten years, unless it suddenly starts to come round like the 1989. The 1991 and 1993 wines are lovely too.

The Domaine de Berthoumieu looks east over the valley towards Maumusson, where Didier has 2 west-facing hectares devoted to the Pacherenc grapes, in the proportion of 40% of each of the mansengs and 20% petit courbu. The dry Pacherenc is made from the first two pickings, and the newly made 1992 was very *bonbons anglais*. It was fresh and delicious. The *moelleux*, which is sold under the name Prestige d'Automne, is made from the third, fourth and fifth pickings of the grapes. After fermentation in stainless steel, it is transferred to new wood until the following June, when it is bottled. The 1992 was showing well as early as the spring of the following year, with a pronounced nutmeg character. The wood was not too prominent. The wine of the previous year was already wonderfully rich, but not as opulent and rather more subtle than some of the more heart-on-sleeve Jurançons we shall come to meet later. The 1994 is flowery, with citrus flavours and the taste of preserved fruits.

By now a pattern begins to emerge or, rather, be confirmed. The higher the tannat content of the wines and the longer the vinification and the more they are given oak, the longer the time they will need to mature. This may seem obvious but it must pose a problem for the producers of the tough new wines. Will the market wait for these wines, which are inevitably more expensive than the quick-maturing wines, to come round? Can they reasonably expect the trade to buy up their wines when young, and then either to sell them to a public with cellarage, or to keep the wines long enough to sell at their best?

Guy Capmartin is confident that the risk is not only worthwhile, but that there is no other choice or even future for Madiran. The style of wine which was being made during the earlier years of the appellation did not really catch the imagination of the market, so there were only two options: to move back down-market, which would have been a retrograde step and a betrayal of what so many local growers had worked for for so long; or to go for real quality.

In 1987, Guy bought up the old convent just on the edge of the village of Maumusson on the road to Viella. Although his father had been one of the pioneers of the 'middle-period' Madiran – i.e. post-appellation, but pre-Brumont – Guy was very much of the new school and wanted the freedom to experiment on his own. So he decided to start his own vineyard. The family remains very close: Guy is making and storing his wine back at Château Barréjat, the family-base which we shall visit presently.

The convent had only 1½ hectares of vines to start with, but Guy now has seven, of which one is reserved for Pacherenc grapes. The holding includes some old vines, going back to pre-phylloxera times, which he rents from an uncle. The holding has been renamed **Domaine Capmartin (45)**.

Of the red wine grapes, the statutory 60% tannat is fully represented, there is no fer servadou, and the balance is made up by roughly two parts cabernet franc to one part cabernet sauvignon. Guy might have preferred to find some other use for the non-tannat grapes which the law obliged him to have, but with only 6 hectares it was probably a sensible decision not to go in for rosé wines or Rouge de Béarn, which would have produced but a small commercial return. The result is, of course, that his red wines have rather less tannat in them than he would wish. Still, it is early days for this grower.

Guy Capmartin makes three red wines, the Tradition, which has only 40% tannat, the wine made from the very old vines which has 55% and the Cuvée du Couvent with 70%. The wines have a *cuvaison* of between fifteen to eighteen days, according to the vintage. The wines are all made in stainless steel, the Tradition grapes are then transferred to concrete, the *vieilles vignes* to old wood and the Couvent to new. All the wines are matured for twelve months, and the new wood is renewed over a three-year cycle.

With only 1 hectare of white wine grapes, Guy does not bother with a dry wine, except in a year like 1992 when he had no option but to use all the grapes to make a *sec*. His more normal *moelleux* is made from 60% petit manseng, 30% gros and 10% arrufiac. There are two versions, the better one having more petit manseng than the other and being sold under the Cuvée du Couvent label. The *moelleux* are made in wood, where Guy leaves them for six months before bottling them during the spring following the vintage.

Elsewhere in the Madiran, producers are often tempted to raise their prices in direct proportion with their own egos: Guy Capmartin is unusually unassuming for a Gascon, with a gentle twinkle in the eye and a quiet charm. Perhaps, therefore, there is a chance that his wines will continue to be as good value for money as they have been in his early years, because there is no mistaking their very high quality. His Madiran Cuvée du Couvent was rated by the unofficial classification sponsored by the *Guide Hubert* in 1992 as being one of the top five Madirans. All three 1990 reds, tasted in the spring of 1993, had a wonderfully transparent plummy colour. The Tradition had an attractive bouquet with prunes and *eau-de-vie* in evidence: on the palate there was a complex blend including soft fruits, cherries particularly, and spices. The wine from the *vieilles vignes* was still covered on the nose by the oak, and the wine was much more tannic and was going through a closed-up patch, but the Cuvée du Couvent had a marvellously explosive fruity bouquet, and the palate was rich in cassis, strawberries, currants and with overtones of truffle and mushrooms too. The finish was immensely long, although his 1992 and 1993 reds did not in my view come up to earlier standards.

Meanwhile back at **Château Barréjat (46)**, Guy's younger brother Denis has just taken over the reins from their father Maurice, and they will have a hard job to keep up with Guy. Denis will almost certainly follow the house-style established by his father who had been running the property since 1967. Before that time, his grandfather and forebears before him had sold the wine off to the trade and had not bothered with the appellation. His father was, in his time, as much of an innovator as the new *mousquétaires*; in fact he had formed his own band of *mousquétaires* which included our historian friend, Monsieur Dartigue at Domaine Taillerguet, as well as Brumont (no less) and Didier Barré's father.

It was Denis' father who had been the first to replant tannat grapes at Maumusson. But Maurice and Denis do not go all the way with the *nouvelle vague*. They accept the need for long maceration of the grapes, and for them twenty-one days is a minimum. But they do not believe in the *politique* of 100% tannat. Denis says that, over a period of years, the buyers of Barréjat wines have become accustomed to the 'middle-period' style, in which the tannat was softened by other varieties. He would lose a lot of sales by going over to the newer style of wine-making. In his heart of hearts, he doubts the value of new wood, but realises that if the property is to remain in the top league of Madiran-makers where it deservedly belongs he may not be able to afford not to swim with the tide.

Denis Capmartin makes only one red Madiran. Apart from a small hint of fer servadou, the vineyard is 60% tannat, and the rest, like his brother Guy's down the road, in the proportion of 2 to 1 cabernets franc and sauvignon. The grapes are vinified separately in stainless steel, concrete and sometimes fibre-glass. He says that the container is not important for the maceration, but it is for the *élevage*. Here he prefers concrete to steel because the wine can 'breathe' more easily.

This Madiran is generally forward in style and the 1990 which I tasted was no exception, even though that was a particularly 'big' vintage. There was a good toasted character to the nose, a feature which is often to be found in the better Madirans. The fruit on the palate was round as well as big, and the impression was of a wine which would soon be ready. This is an attractive and friendly Madiran.

Denis Capmartin also makes the usual pair of Pacherencs, and favours ten hours' *macération pelliculaire*. The wines are made in concrete, with the temperature at a cool 15°. He recommends his dry wine for drinking within the year. The one he showed us was beautifully fresh and aromatic, lively and what the French call *nerveux*, a word which underlies the basic truth that wine has a life of its own.

Denis Capmartin's *moelleux* is made from petit manseng and is usually lighter in style than some, discreet and even delicate. It has a rather classic elegance, restraint and *pudeur*. The 1994 has lovely depth.

The Barréjat vineyard is tended in an ultra-traditional manner. There is a parcel of pre-phylloxera vines from which new plants are still produced by layering. One of the oldest vines is said to be between two and three hundred years old, and certainly looks as if it must be. The average age of the vines is about forty years, reflecting the extensive planting which Maurice Capmartin carried out in the 1960s. His own father, that is to say Denis' grandfather, is ninety, but still prepares the ties which attach the vines to their stakes from willow bushes which he grows specially for the purpose. This is a tradition widespread in Gascony and the Béarn, and you can often see stumpy, heavily pruned little bushes adjacent to the vineyards or sometimes in rows behind the vines. You would hardly recognise them as willows unless you happened to be there in spring when the new shoots appear.

At Barréjat, we are only a short walk away from the **Domaine**

Taillerguet (42), where Maurice Capmartin's old friend Dartigue made the wine until a few years ago. He, too, has passed the job on, this time to his son-in-law, François Bouby. François has had a short apprenticeship as a *vigneron*, because he was brought up as a cattle-farmer in the Armagnac country, and had had no experience of growing vines or making wine. He is still able to keep his hand in at traditional farming, because Monsieur Dartigue had always had strings to his bow other than vines.

François does not look like the typical *vigneron*, if there is such a person. Tall and bearded, with slightly ascetic features, you might expect him to say he was a film-producer, or perhaps a potter. Nevertheless he has accepted the deep-end plunge of his marriage to Monsieur Dartigue's daughter and one of the oldest vineyards in the Vic-Bilh. Although small, it goes back to at least 1723, and the records fizzle out at that point. The 8 hectares produce a little rosé de Béarn, and there is a small production of Pacherenc. Without a preliminary maceration the vinification is in steel or concrete. The dry Pacherenc is bottled as soon as possible, and the *moelleux* given some new wood for six months. The white wines tend to be fresh and light; certainly this was the case with the 1992s and 1994s, but notes of tasting Taillerguet in earlier years confirm the same message. This is probably a more authentic style of Pacherenc, perhaps not the fashionable kind of heavyweight that comes from more prestigious producers today, but none the worse for that.

The red wines are equally traditional but surprisingly slow to come round. The two 1990 examples which François Bouby showed me, the one being the house Générique, and the other a premium wine given some oak, were both wonderfully bright, but a very deep purple. The bouquet was in each case meaty, with more tobacco and spices on the premium wine, where the oak was masking the tannins and giving a sense of false maturity. These wines needed another five years at least. François thought they lacked finesse, but perhaps that was just another way of saying that they were typical of a rustic style of wine-production which it would be a pity to lose. Not everyone has to keep up with the Brumonts and the Barrés.

My last visit in the Maumusson area was to Gilbert Dousseau, whose **Domaine Sergent (50)** is on the road to Viella. This property has a particularly beautiful situation on high ground with splendid views over to the Pic du Midi, an unmistakable needle-shaped mountain, one of the highest in the central Pyrenees. Dousseau's grandfather bought the vineyard before the First World War, and there are now 13½ hectares under vine, nearly 12 of which are devoted to red Madiran grapes, and the balance to Pacherenc. He has a little fer servadou to give some rusticity to the traditional tannat and cabernets blend. For his Pacherenc Monsieur Dousseau has only 10% arrufiac, the bulk being divided equally between the two mansengs. He also makes a little rosé de Béarn for his customers in the Basque Country and Holland.

The wine-making is modern at Domaine Sergent, though the

maceration periods for the reds are shorter than with the avant-garde producers. His Générique red is vinified for only eight days and is matured in stainless steel. His better *cuvées* are given fifteen to eighteen days according to the vintage and matured in new wood which is re-cycled over a four-year span. His 1993s promise very well.

Monsieur Dousseau told me that until 1975 he sold all his wine *en vrac*, and only in that year did he start to bottle his own wine. Even today he still sells from the cask his special blend for local buyers, shooting parties and the like, which has more cabernet in it and gets only eight days' maceration. This has to be de-classified as Madiran, but is a very good buy indeed. In fact all the wines from this property are remarkably good value.

The grapes for both the dry and sweet Pacherencs are given a prelim-inary maceration for twelve to fifteen hours, and vinified at a steady 18°. The dry wine is made in new wood and is bottled as soon as possible after a refrigeration to prevent tartaric crystals forming in bottle. The *moelleux* is then put into the same barrels to mature for a further four or five months before being bottled. In this way the same barrels can do double duty for both the whites. The 1991 which we tasted bore little evidence of the wood, which had nevertheless given the wine an added depth, without spoiling its unusual freshness and acidity.

It is not hard to see why, year after year, the same people come back to do the *vendange* at Domaine Sergent. Monsieur Dousseau reminds me a little of Pierre Boulez: perhaps it is the volubility. He has a mis-chievous twinkle in the eye and is an entertaining host. I always like to ask wine-makers what their ambitions are for the future: he told me that his was retirement. He hopes, however, that his daughter, who is studying in Montpellier, will take over the vineyard from him. His wife has already pinched a few rows of vines to plant her rose-garden against the back-drop of the Pic du Midi.

Before looking at some of the more remote vineyards towards the west of the appellation, mention must be made of the **Domaine Laougué (7)**, which is on the road east over high ground in the direc-tion of Madiran itself. The distinguished panel of tasters who adjudged the wines of Madiran for the *Guide Hubert* in 1992 put this wine in the top twelve of those which they sampled. The wine, quite apart from its quality, is also very good value, and can be found locally in the shops to whom the Dabadies are not too grand to sell direct. Their Madiran is quick-maturing too. The 1991 could only have been in bottle a month or two before I found it in the shops locally. It was attractively bright, with a little natural wood on the nose, perhaps a little stalky on the palate, but then it was still very young: good fruit and very attractive for early drinking.

In the far north-western corner of the appellation is the **Domaine de Maouries (2)**, where we have already met André Dufau wearing his St Mont hat. He is a man of many parts, because, during the winter when life in the vineyards is relatively quiet, he grows asparagus under plastic for the Christmas market: he has spent a lot of money on underground heating plant for the asparagus-beds, but has found that the cost of the electricity is so exorbitant that the plant lies unused. The asparagus nevertheless seems to thrive if the plants I saw were anything to go by.

Monsieur Dufau has his wife, two sons and a daughter to help him with his 21 hectares of vines, 3 of which are rented out to a neighbour. Because his land is partly in Madiran and partly in St Mont, he was able to highlight for me the demands of the two styles of wines. The St Mont has, oddly enough, more tannat, but the maceration period is only eight days. This compares with the twenty-eight days which he gives his Madiran grapes when the vintage is good and the grapes in perfect condition. He grows a little pinenc, which is compulsory in St Mont, but optional in Madiran. The Madiran may be matured for up to two years before being bottled, but the St Mont is put into bottle as soon as the market will take it from him.

His St Mont had a lot more weight than the Plaimont equivalent. The 1991 was still hard and tannic two years later, despite the shorter *cuvaison*. The Générique Madiran from the 1990 vintage was very dark, almost black in colour. Monsieur Dufau thought it had too much alcohol, but then he prefers a less potent style of wine. The nose was rich with blackberries and the palate with all manner of soft fruit. It needed time, though André Dufau does not believe in keeping his own wines too long before drinking them. The special *cuvée* from 1989, which had been given some new wood as a concession to modern practices, was highly spiced and rather mustardy. It had the characteristic toasty taste, and the finish was long. Their touch of rusticity makes these wines rather distinctive and refreshingly different.

The white St Mont, which had been rejected by the Plaimont coopérative as being 'too dark', had been bottled under the name Vin de Table, Cuvée de l'Ormeau. More interesting was his Pacherenc *moelleux*. The 1991 was still pale with greenish tints. Although the wine had been matured in some new wood, there was little evidence of this on the palate, and it was rather light and refreshing for a *moelleux*. The 1994 suggested apricot kernels and mangoes.

Two miles or so to the south of Domaine de Maouries, and just off the main road from Aire to Lembeye, stands the handsome **Domaine de Diusse (15)**. Among the vineyards of Madiran, this one is unique because it is not an ordinary agricultural enterprise but a Centre of Help Through Work for the mentally handicapped (Centre d'Aide par Travail). In the early seventies the property was derelict and was bought by this charitable foundation at auction. As a means of training the handicapped for re-introduction into the community, what better use for the property in the Madirannais than to plant a vineyard? There are now 12 hectares of red wine grapes, and two of white.

The other local growers do not know quite what to make of this enterprise, because it conforms to no known pattern of viticulture. But there is nothing dilettante or amateur about it: the whole operation is overseen by a fully qualified oenologist, who is even lent out to other local growers to advise them on how to deal with their own vineyards. All the same, I rather got the impression that the Domaine de Diusse was looked upon as not quite *sérieux*. This is all the more surprising in that the wines are marketed just as if they were the product of a conventional vineyard, and without any reference to the special nature of the work of the foundation. There is no special pleading for charity.

Perhaps the doubters should be given the same tour as I was by the chic and dynamic Madame Baillet. She explained that the charity encourages other industries such as stone-masonry, house-decoration and basket-making, but the vineyards were their main activity. The patients take part in all the activities of the vine-cycle: the growing of the grapes, the making of the wines, their bottling and their storage and *élevage* in the *chais* of the domaine. The vineyard aims to be self-sufficient and to support itself from the sale of its wines, even after paying the patients a 'wage' for their work, a concept which the foundation regards as basic to its relationship with the patients.

Nor can the wines of the Domaine de Diusse be criticised on the grounds of quality. They, too, were among the top twelve in the *Guide Hubert* tasting, and consistently win important medals in the international shows.

Although the vineyard as a whole is planted with tannat only to the extent of 40%, there is a deal of rosé wine made, which uses up the cabernet varieties, so that the red Madirans have always at least 55% tannat. The Générique wine is balanced with cabernet franc, while the next wine up the ladder is complemented by cabernet sauvignon. The latter is also bottled in a strange and unconventional tubby bottle which is being phased out. The wine is decreasing in production as the sale of the Générique wine rises. Both these wines are made and matured in stainless steel, and each of the vats is individually and electronically temperature-controlled.

Madame Baillet explained that the wine-makers at Diusse are not entirely persuaded about the virtues of new oak, though their premium wine called Privilège is given twelve to fourteen months in new barrels. She has quickly realised that you get little attention from the media unless your wine is oaked. The Privilège wine – 70% tannat, and the rest cabernet sauvignon – is from very ripe grapes, and she claims for it a jammy richness with crushed fruits. She is also proud of its fleshy texture.

The 2 hectares of white grapes include over one-third petit courbu and 30% arrufiac, unusually high proportions in each case. The vineyard is completed by 21% petit manseng, and 13% gros. Typically there is no petit manseng in the drier wine, but in 1992 all the white grapes were piled in because of the appalling weather at the time of the vintage. The *moelleux*, made from the petit manseng and the petit courbu, is given a preliminary maceration before fermentation, and is then made in new wood.

Most of the wine at the domaine is sold through trade channels, so it ought to be possible to find it in restaurants and shops in South-West France. It has been available intermittently in the United Kingdom.

Pacherenc de Vic-Bilh has always been a speciality at the **Domaine Crampilh (18)**, a little way further to the south-east. Alain Oulié's fore-bears have been making wine here through at least ten generations, and there are now 23 hectares of red grapes and 5 of white, which make this one of the larger properties in the appellation. Like so many other local farmers, the Ouliés went in for crops other than vines when the vineyards were in the doldrums, but they joined the co-opérative when it was formed and replanted their vineyard in the 1960s, though there are still some very old vines on the property which are reserved for their premium reds. The Oulié family has been independent of the co-opérative for some years now.

Alain Oulié gives the impression of being a traditionalist: he has the quiet reserve of the peasant farmer, but also a disarming smile. He prides himself on a balance between new techniques and the old, but he insists on the longest possible maceration, usually twenty-one days, for his red grapes. At the same time, he recognises the merits of new wood, though he still believes that only some of his *cuves* should be treated to it.

His generic red is slightly more tannat than cabernet franc, with a touch of cabernet sauvignon for good measure. It takes a while to come round though. His 1990, in the spring of 1993, was still unyielding on the nose, apart from a slight whiff of toast. The legs were good, and there were still lots of unresolved tannins.

In good years the wine from the old vines is nearly 100% tannat, and the 1990 had little to show except enormous body and tannins, which really grabbed you round the back of the teeth. The 1987, a lighter year, had only 75% tannat, and was given but ten days' maceration. It still had some way to go, though the nose was more open, with a distinct mushroom and truffle character. Because there are not many old vines, and their yield is smaller anyway, Monsieur Oulié can make only a little wine from his *vieilles vignes*, but he always tries to give some of it new oak, putting only a third of the intended *assemblage* into new barrels for twelve to eighteen months. He is another to believe that the tannat grape already has an element of vanilla built into its character, and he says this is reinforced by the soil in his particular part of the *terroir*. Professional tasters of his 1985 had sworn that his wine had been in new wood when it had not. He says his wooded 1990 will not be at its peak until after the end of the century.

Alain Oulié makes the usual dry and sweet versions of Pacherenc, because, he says, his customers insist. He would prefer to make only one wine and to leave the weather at vintage-time to determine whether it is to be sweet or dry. This was always the tradition in the area, as it was in the Jurançon, as we shall see. You would have thought that, with 5 hectares of white grapes, Alain Oulié could have easily managed to accommodate both styles in one year, but he says it is difficult to make anything except a dry wine in a bad year like 1992, when all the grapes produce a wine with too much acidity. He was doubtful about his 1992 *moelleux*, which he said was not really a *moelleux* at all, and he thought his *sec* was too acid. I thought he was being too self-critical. The dry wine was indeed very dry, but it was unusually flinty with a strong hint of citrus fruits.

The division into dry and sweet wines is something relatively new to Monsieur Oulié: the first time he made two styles was in 1988. His sweet 1991 was very fine indeed, with an archetypal bouquet of mountain honey and flowers: pineapple and apricots on the palate and the finish was very caramelly. Both the dry and the sweet 1994 are top rate.

The vines at Crampilh are on lower and flatter ground than some other vineyards, so Oulié is able to use machines to pick the grapes, although the older vines are picked entirely by hand, not out of respect but because tannat grapes from old plants are particularly delicate and need very careful handling.

Machines would be out of the question at some of the hillier properties, **Domaine de Pichard (27)** for example. The vineyard at this estate, which is towards the south-east corner of the appellation at Soublecause, was rebuilt in the 1950s by Monsieur Vigneau, one of the architects of the Madiran revival largely instrumental in the creation of the *syndicat* of private growers. Vigneau was the first grower, at least in modern times, to bottle his wine. When he had lived at Crouseilles he used to sell everything *en vrac*.

It is a family tradition at Pichard to have stocks of old vintages available for sale to customers, because in the old days a grower sold mainly to local buyers who wanted a range of wines for immediate drinking and who did not have the facilities for laying down wines for ten or more years. The custom is maintained today, because the family, now represented by Monsieur Vigneau's nephew René Tachouères and the latter's son Bernard, can sell you vintages going back to 1981. I know of no other property in Madiran, unless it be Château de Piarrine at Cannet, where there is such a choice of older vintages.

Of the 12½ hectares at Pichard, only the odd half is given over to Pacherenc, and that has a surprising 30% sauvignon content. Bernard Tachouères does not believe in a preliminary maceration before fermentation, because he feels it makes the aromas too volatile. They have tried and rejected new wood for fermentation, and prefer to make their white wine in concrete. Only when this has finished is the wine given two months in new wood and then bottled.

Of the red wine grapes, 40% is in cabernet franc, only a little less than the tannat. The rest is made up of 15% cabernet sauvignon. The tannat is generally macerated for fifteen days, the cabernets for twenty. The wine is aged in huge old barrels, which are a feature of the *chais*, and which are older than the building which houses them. In good years (the last until 1994 were 1989 and 1990) the Tachouères make a special *cuvée* from 70% tannat, and this is matured in new oak and sold as Château Vigneau Pichard in tribute to Bernard's great-uncle.

The wines from Château Pichard are generally spicy. The 1985 which

Bernard poured for me had some wood ash and vegetal aromas on the nose. The flavour was wonderfully ripe, with nutmeg and cinnamon and an underlying hint of prunes. I was also able to taste the 1981 at a local restaurant and it had the same intriguing spicy quality, still with a deal of fruit and a very long finish.

Another good property in this corner of the Madirannais is the **Château de Perron (28)** which is just the other side of a country lane from Château Montus. Both these properties have enormous placards announcing their names in letters as big as the hoardings at Hermitage. This is no doubt because they are just off one of the main holiday routes south into the Pyrenees.

Perron is a small but rather handsome château with a long history. Named after its founding family who arrived in 1645, it was probably a *rendez-vous de chasse*. The *chais* had already been built by 1734, and remain unaltered to this day, as well as being among the finest and oldest in the area. The courtyard of the château is attractive too, surfaced with the kind of local pebbles which are typical of the Pacherenc vineyards. At the time of the Revolution, Perron became a *bien nationale* and was sold off to the local peasants in small lots, including 50 hectares of vines in all. Even at the time of the phylloxera the vineyard was still producing 2000 hectolitres of wine, which suggests that it was still about the same size. There are a number of ambitious houses giving on to the Adour valley in this region, and only extensive vineyards would have justified the effort of their construction and the cost of their maintenance.

Richard Crouzet owns Perron today, and it was his father who bought it in 1945 when there wasn't a vine in sight. He rebuilt the vineyard in the 1960s, and there are now 11 hectares under vine in two parcels, 5 hectares immediately adjacent to the château and the remainder over the hill in the direction of Madiran.

I have often wanted to ask somebody why the rules of so many appellations specify a minimum density of vines per hectare, rather than a maximum. The uninitiated might assume that it would be better to plant vines further apart rather than closer to each other. Richard Crouzet was proud that he has the highest density of vines in the area, and explained that the closer you plant, the fewer the bunches of grapes each vine produces, and therefore the greater the concentration of juice.

Monsieur Crouzet is not at all the typical country wine-grower. He might easily have been produced by the English public school system, quite the *petit chatelain* in fact. He finds that the present day is a very interesting period in the history of Madiran – 80% of the vines are still in the hands of small family-makers, and those who rebuilt the reputation of Madiran are now retiring in favour of the next generation, who are technically much better trained than their fathers.

There is not yet any Pacherenc made at Château de Perron, because the vines are still immature, but the petit courbu and petit manseng will soon be ready. Meanwhile Monsieur Crouzet produces one single red wine from a vineyard which is classically composed of 60% tannat,

20% cabernet franc, 15% cabernet sauvignon and 5% fer servadou. Each variety is vinified separately for three weeks and the wine is then transferred to old wood to mature until it is time to bottle it, usually two years after the vintage. Crouzet uses new wood only when the vintage has been good enough to justify the extra expense, for example in 1989. In the spring of 1993 this wine had already thrown some sediment which is unusual in a Madiran so young. The colour too was mature and the bouquet was very claret-like in style with lots of cigar-box and some prunes. The fruit was rich and plentiful on the palate too, but there were some tough tannins still unresolved suggesting that the wine could have done with another year or two: not more perhaps because the style generally suggested a wine which was not intended for long keeping. Altogether this was an attractive Madiran which one could approach without too much trepidation.

One example of each of the constrasting styles of Madiran can be found in the tiny commune of Cannet in the north-east corner of the Madirannais. The **Château de Piarrine (38)** is a modern estate which was bought by Jacques Achilli in 1970: he built himself an impressive modern house and *chais*, having dug up all the old vines and replanted the vineyard. He told me that he had found some old merlot vines in the overgrown fields, and he showed me some old rootstocks to prove it.

Monsieur Achilli makes tough and uncompromising wines in what appears to be a traditional style. I say 'appears' because he was somewhat coy about sharing with me the secrets of his vinification, rather like a chef who is afraid that his customers will steal his best recipes if he tells them how a dish is made. He did, however, tell me that one of his 11 hectares is given over to gros manseng for the making of Pacherenc. He has planted some petit manseng too, but it is not yet producing. It may be that Monsieur Achilli is only a first-generation Gascon, but his stories are tall enough: he said that in 1992 he picked his Pacherenc grapes in December, and that usually he likes to defer the picking until January. I cannot be certain that this was an exaggeration because he showed us his 1992 *moelleux* which was indeed very dark for the year and is obviously going to be very fine. He believes in a long and cold vinification for the Pacherenc. He says that making this wine is like cooking a *daube* very slowly in a pot with a tight-fitting lid.

Jacques Achilli's red wines are as distinctive as his white: he believes that the wines of Cannet have a particular *goût du terroir* typical of traditional Madiran. His 1985, for example, is shot through with deep blue Victoria-plum glints: although it spent twelve months in wood, the vanilla has all gone, leaving a huge, deep-flavoured wine, full of fruit with good acidity and balance. But the wine still needs time to throw off the tannins which are still powerfully evident. This is not a wine for children!

A young grower, very much to be watched, is Martine Dupuy, who is in charge of the wine-making at her mother's **Domaine de Labranche-Laffont (52)**. Martine took first prize for her Madiran

Vieilles Vignes at the 1995 Madiran show. She makes lovely Pacherenc too: a dry version from one-third each of arrufiac and the two mansengs, and a sweet wine all from petit manseng. Her red Générique has 60% tannat and she gives 10–12 days vinification. The nose is powerfully floral, with hints of prunes and liquorice. Some of the old vines are pre-phylloxera and the wine from these is 85% tannat. It needs time; the tannins are tough and the structure very complex.

Very different is the kind of wine made a mile or so away by René Castets at the **Château de Fitere (39)**, an estate which has a magnificent orientation towards the south and west overlooking the valley where Martine's vines grow. The property had been in the Fitère family for many generations, when Roger Castets married a daughter of the house and thereby ensured the continuation of the farm. Roger himself fell ill in 1983 when his son René was only nineteen, so the latter was plunged into the deep end of wine-making at a very early age. It was not long before he expanded the vineyard from 16 to 23 hectares, of which only 1 is given over to gros manseng for the making of Pacherenc.

René and his wife have a baby daughter Karine, after whom they name their Pacherenc each year. They do not have enough white grapes to make two styles of wine, so they leave it to the character of the vintage to decide whether the wine is to be sweet or dry. The 1991, for example, is loaded with honey and almonds, with just the right touch of acidity to prevent it becoming cloying. The 1994 is just as good. It is quite one of the best Pacherencs I know. René Castets gives one-third of the grapes a preliminary maceration overnight, and the wine is then made in vitrified steel with the temperature strictly kept from between 16° to 19° and bottled in the August following the vintage.

The main production is, however, red, and there are three wines, from a vineyard which is 60% tannat, no less than 15% fer servadou, with the balance more or less equally divided between the two cabernets. René thinks that the fer servadou is particularly suited by the *terroir* at Cannet. The main wine, the Générique, represents almost the total production, apart from the wine which René makes from some very old centenarian vines. He gives the Générique only ten days' maceration in concrete, but the *vieilles vignes* wine gets twenty-one days. After the malolactic fermentation is finished the wines will be matured either in concrete or fibre-glass: René Castets does not believe in stainless steel. The wine is then left in the *cuves* for two years with *soutirages* every two months, and it is then bottled.

A little of the *vieilles vignes* wine has been made the subject of an experiment in new wood, and René will see how this goes before taking on any deeper commitment to oaking his wines. The 1990, his first year with new wood, certainly had a lot of vegetation on the nose, what René described as '*bois et sous-bois*', and the finish showed a lot of vanilla. Although the wine was tugh, it was easy to predict for it a brilliant future. The unwooded wines were both beautifully bright and agreeably forward, fruity, well developed and just about ready to drink.

André Beheity, the owner of **Domaine Damiens (11)**, is in charge of the publicity for the *syndicat* of local growers. This is another case of the owner's father having married the daughter of the former proprietor, the estate having been in the Damiens family for over a century. André himself comes from a long line of chefs. André expanded the vineyard in 1970 to create a holding of 12 hectares all in one parcel, right in the middle of the village of Aydie, not more than a stone's throw from the Laplaces. Three more hectares subsequently acquired make up a total of 15 hectares, all facing south-east. André explained that he has 3 more hectares available for planting when the rules permit, and he does not allow you to forget that he also has 14 hectares of cereals as a hedge against poor vintages. As a local farmer he is pleased that the tradition of mutual help continues at vintage-time, the growers all helping each other get the grapes in as and when each property is ready for picking.

His $1\frac{1}{2}$ hectares of white grapes are unusually strong in arrufiac: 50%, compared with 25% each for the two mansengs. For his Pacherenc he believes in rapid pressing without preliminary maceration: he does not think it appropriate to the style of the wine. He ferments a quarter of the grapes in new wood, and all of them at a temperature of 18°, although in a difficult year like 1992 he will adopt even lower temperatures. He bottles the wine during the February after the vintage.

For his red wines, he limits production to 45 hectolitres to the hectare for the better parcels, otherwise 55. He gives the cabernet grapes ten days, but the tannat anything up to twenty days according to the quality of the grapes when they come into the presses. The best *cuves* of tannat are given new wood.

André Beheity sums up the philosophy of so many of the younger producers in saying that you should not interfere with the wine unless absolutely necessary. The less you do to it the better. Over-sophistication can produce wines which are chemically perfect but have no character: he believes that it is the combination of the *terroir* and the grapes which makes a wine. This is why he is so scornful of the masses of Côtes de Gascogne which he says are promoted by technicians to prevent their being turned into alcohol.

André confesses to having tried a few years ago to make quicker-maturing, more commercial wines, but he decided they were not typical of Madiran so abandoned them. He echoes the *mousquétaires* in saying that the future is not in trying to make a wine which others can make more cheaply: concentrate rather on making the wine which Madiran can make best. This is a gamble which is totally logical, but one which the producers of Vic-Bilh cannot afford to lose. Good luck to them.

PRODUCERS

MADIRAN AND PACHERENC

24. *LES VIGNERONS DU VIC-BILH – MADIRAN, 64350 Crouseilles
Tel: 59-68-10-93
1. *CAVE CO-OPERATIVE PLAIMONT, 32400 St Mont Tel: 62-69-63-16
32. CAVE CO-OPERATIVE DE VINIFICATION, 65700 Castelnau-Riviere-Basse Tel: 62-31-96-21

19. Gilbert Terradot, **Château Arricau-Bordes**, 64350 Arricau-Bordes
Tel: 59-68-13-97
Château d'Aydie: see Laplace
46. *Denis Capmartin, **Château Barréjat**, 32400 Maumusson Tel: 62-69-74-92
4. Patrick Berdoulet, **Domaine Bassail**, 32400 Viella Tel: 62-69-79-33
31. Dulce Moutoue, **Domaine du Benguérats**, 65700 Madiran Tel: 62-96-33-55
54. Camille Larerrère, **Domaine de Bernal**, 32400 Maumusson Tel: 62-69-81-25
12. Georges Cazenave, **Domaine du Bernes**, 64330 Aydie Tel: 59-04-04-49
8. Yves Doussau, **Domaine Bernet**, 32400 Viella Tel: 62-69-71-99
3. *Didier Barré, **Domaine Berthoumieu**, 32400 Viella Tel: 62-69-74-05
25. Jean-Denis Bibian, **Domaine Bibian**, 65700 Soublecause Tel: 62-96-97-10
23. *Jean Boyrie, **Domaine des Bories**, 64323 Lasserre Tel: 59-68-18-04*
9. Pierre **Laborde**, Le Bourg, 32400 Viella Tel: 62-69-73-59
43. *Alain Brumont, **Château Bouscassé**, 32400 Maumusson Tel: 62-69-74-67
(Also the wines of Château Montus and Domaine Meinjarre)
48. Pierre Delle Vedove, **Domaine Brana**, 32400 Maumusson Tel: 62-69-77-70
45. *Guy Capmartin, **Domaine Capmartin**, 32400 Maumusson Tel: 62-69-87-88
La Chapelle Lenclos: see Mouréou
16. Edmond Préchacq, **Domaine Cousteau**, 64330 Mont-Disse Tel: 59-04-02-46
18. *Alain Oulié, **Domaine du Crampilh**, 64350 Aurions-ldernes
Tel: 59-04-01-61
11. *André Beheity, **Domaine Damiens**, 64330 Aydie Tel: 59-04-03-13
58. Daniel Lartigue, **Domaine Dastugues-Camblong**, 64330 Viella
Tel: 59-68-20-18
15. ***Vignobles du Domaine de Diusse**, 64330 Aydie Tel: 59-04-00-52
39. *Roger Castets, **Château de Fitère**, 32400 Cannet Tel: 62-69-82-17
49. René Dessans, **Domaine Grabi´ou**, 32400 Maumusson Tel: 62-69-74-62
34. *Dominique Boucher, **Château de Guissan**, 65700 Castelnau-Rivière-Basse
Tel: 62-31-95-91*
26. Lucien Remon, **Domaine d'Héchac**, 65700 Soublecause Tel: 62-96-35-75
17. Adrien Hourcadet, **Domaine Hourcadet**, 64350 Aurions-ldernes
Tel: 59-04-01-98
36. Joseph Ghirardi, **Domaine Jaourou**, 65700 St-Lanne Tel: 62-31-96-93
52. *Yvonne Dupuy, **Domaine Labranch-Laffont**, 32400 Maumusson
Tel: 62-69-74-90l
35. *Marius Ducoussou, **Domaine Laburthe**, 65700 St-Lanne Tel: 62-31-95-15*
41. *Maurice Ponsolle, **Domaine de Lacave**, 32400 Cannet Tel: 62-69-77-38
53. *Jean-Marc Laffitte, **Château Laffitte-Teston**, 32400 Maumusson
Tel: 62-69-74-58
47. Pierrette Carsana, **Domaine Laffont**, 32400 Maumusson Tel: 62-69-74-63
44. Michelle Capdevielle, **Domaine Lalanne**, 32400 Maumusson
Tel: 62-69-74-65
7. *Pierre Dabadie, **Domaine Laougué**, 32400 Viella Tel: 62-69-90-05
14. ***Vignobles Laplace**, Château d'Aydie, 64330 Aydie Tel: 59-04-01-17

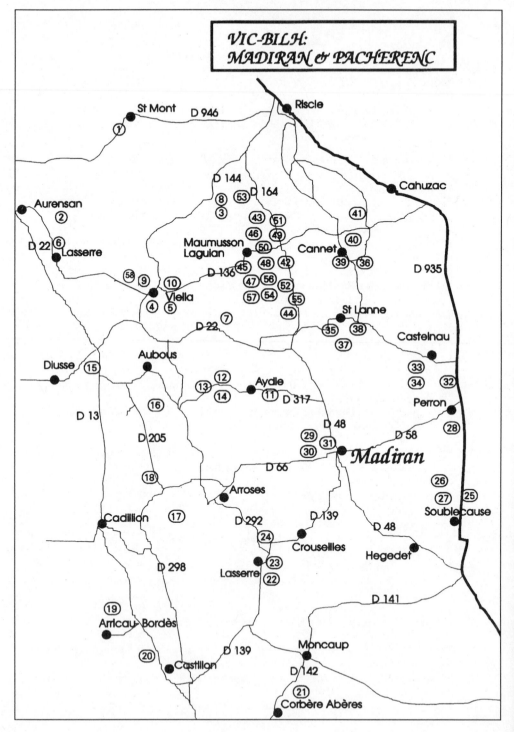

VIC-BILH:
MADIRAN & PACHERENC

33. Guy Lacouterie, **Château Larrauzet**, 65700 Castelnau-Riviere-Basse
     Tel: 62-31-98-94
29. Raymond Galbardi, **Domaine Larroque**, 65700 Madiran Tel: 62-96-35-46
30. Claude Louit, 65700 Madiran Tel: 62-69-72-19
 2. *André Dufau, **Domaine de Maouries**, 32400 Labarthète Tel: 62-69-63-84
57. *André Terrade, **Domaine Margalide**, 32400 Maumusson Tel: 62-69-77-71*
     Domaine Meinjarre: *see Bouscassé*
20. Monique Gaye, **Domaine Mesté Bertrand**, 64350 Castillon Tel: 59-68-14-57
56. Daniel Saint-Orens, **Domaine Mont-Blanc**, 32400 Maumusson
     Tel: 62-69-82-51
     Château Montus: see Bouscassé
22. *Michel Arrat, **Domaine de la Motte**, 64323 Domaine de la Motte
     Tel: 59-68-16-98
40. Michel Charrier, **Domaine du Moulié**, 32400 Cannet Tel: 62-68-77-73
51. *Patrick Ducournau, **Domaine Mouréou**, 32400 Maumusson
     Tel: 62-69-78-11 (Also La Chapelle Lenclos)
37. *Jacques Maumus, **Cru du Paradis**, 65700 St-Lanne Tel: 62-31-98-23
28   *Richard Crouzet, **Château de Perron**, 65700 Madiran Tel: 62-31-93-27
21. Denis de Robillard, **Château Peyros**, 64350 Corbères Tel: 59-02-45-90
 6. Jacques Brumont, **Domaine Peyrou**, 32400 Viella Tel: 62-69-90-12
38. *Jacques Achilli, **Château de Piarrine**, 32400 Cannet Tel: 62-69-77-66
27. *René Tachouères, **Domaine Pichard**, 65700 Soublecause Tel: 62-96-35-73
10. Pierre Lannusse, **Domaine du Pouey**, 32400 Viella Tel: 62-69-78-25
13. Claude Lanux, **Domaine Poujo**, 64330 Aydie Tel: 59-04-01-23
50. *Gilbert Dousseau, **Domaine Sergent**, 32400 Maumusson Tel: 62-69-74-93
42. *François Bouby, **Domaine Taillerguet**, 32400 Maumusson
     Tel: 62-69-73-92
55. Henri Polesel, **Domaine Tichané**, 32400 Maumusson Tel: 62-69-89-70
 5. A. et C. Bortolussi, **Château de Viella**, 32400 Viella Tel: 62-69-75-81

The Wines of the Pyrenees:
Béarn, Jurançon and
Irouléguy

BÉARN

The old county of Béarn separates the Basque Country from Gascony. It was once part of the Kingdom of Navarre, and its principal city, Pau, was the birthplace of its most famous son, Henri, who later became Henri IV of France. Everywhere you go you will find his name, usually taken in vain for commercial purposes. The image is good: his christening with the wine of Jurançon and cloves of garlic was an excellent start to a PR campaign which included promising all Frenchmen a *poule au pot* for every Sunday lunch. A famous restaurant named after him in northern France created the *sauce béarnaise* in his honour. He was an attractive monarch who propelled France firmly into the seventeenth century, but he was too good to be true and, like John Kennedy, was felled by an assassin with his work barely started.

Undoubtedly he would have helped to put the wines of his home county on the map. The vineyards themselves are thought possibly to date back to before the coming of the Romans, but certainly they were producing wines of quality by the time Henri IV was born. In 1587 the port of Bayonne was opened to river traffic, including the flat-bottomed boats navigating with difficulty the *gave de Pau*, just like the boatmen on the river Lot. The river became navigable far upstream from the city of Pau, nearly as far as Lourdes.

As was the case with the other wines from the far South-West, access to the sea opened up overseas markets, particularly in England and Holland. The situation of the Béarn, away from the perpetual battle-grounds further to the north and east, enabled it to develop a lively commerce in relative peace. The Somport Pass became an important link between Spain and France, and with the wars between the French and the English making transport difficult and dangerous down the Garonne, the *gaves* became busy waterways.

When the region was invaded by Wellington on his return journey from the Peninsular Wars in 1814, it must have been with some relief that the local inhabitants discovered the English army to be quite different from their medieval precursors. By respecting the lives and property of the Béarnais, they were taken to heart by them, to such an extent that, following the demobbing of the troops in 1815, many stayed behind or even returned to the South-West and founded an extensive English colony there. It is said that up to 4000 English people once lived in Pau, about a third of the then population. Their Anglo-Saxon passion for plumbing, drainage and pure drinking water has left its mark on the infrastructure of the town, and it was the English influence that brought about the building of the Boulevard des Pyrénées, with its spectacular views over the mountains to the south.

Like the vines of the pre-phylloxera era, the English take-over of Pau is now little more than a legend. It was real enough at the time, however, and as recently as the 1930s Dornford Yates was setting his nostalgic novels there, and it was a Miss Bunbury from that city who became the wife of Alfred de Vigny. A special version of sauce béarnaise, named after the Palois, the inhabitants of Pau, was no doubt intended for the English to eat with their lamb, flavoured as it was with mint rather than tarragon. The English period at Pau is strangely paralleled in modern times by the modern rush of English expatriates to the Dordogne.

Part of the English folk-memory of Pau was the wine of Jurançon. Not that the wine has ever been widely drunk in England, but it has almost certainly enjoyed a bigger reputation here than it has in France, at least until recent times. The same cannot really be said about the more humble wines of the Béarn, those which are not entitled to call themselves Jurançon or Madiran.

Madiran growers, as we have already seen, cannot call their white or rosé wine Madiran, so that the co-opérative at Crouseilles, for example, will make and market pink and white wines for its members under the AOC Béarn, or, if they do not comply with the rules for Béarn, *vin de pays des Pyrénées-Atlantiques*. Similarly, there is no such appellation as red Jurançon, so red wine made by Jurançon growers is also sold as Béarn.

Apart from the *vin de Béarn* which is made by the Madiran and Jurançon growers, there is the area exclusively given over to the Béarn appellation, centred on the co-opérative at Bellocq, a small village on the south side of the *gave de Pau* just west of Orthez. The castle, which overlooks the river, is in ruins today, but it was once the home of Jeanne d'Albret, the mother of Henri IV, and by all accounts a formidable dragon indeed. According to one historian, there was nothing feminine about her – except her gender.

It will come as no surprise to learn that here too the phylloxera virtually wiped out the vineyard, the former grape-varieties being replaced by poor quality, high-yielding hybrids. Again the enterprise of an enthusiast led gradually to the reconstruction of the vineyard, and the formation of a co-opérative in 1947 was largely due to the oenologist Henri Meyer. His work coincided with the sudden popularity in Paris after the Second World War of pink wines, and the rosé de Béarn was an instant hit. VDQS status was granted in 1951 for wines of all colours, and this was followed by full AOC status in 1975.

The growers of Bellocq may have been a trifle lucky to win their battles for recognition so early, but at the time they faced little competition from Madiran and Jurançon, whose own wines are nowadays much superior, but were then still to emerge from obscurity. There were many growers in Madiran and Jurançon who had no ambitions then to develop fine wine-making and were only too glad to find a market for their wines through the Bellocq co-opérative.

The true Béarn appellation area centred round Bellocq is particularly attractive and merits some time off from wine-tasting. The roofs are of red slate, like those of the Dordogne, and Salies-de-Béarn has more than a slight feel of Sarlat about it. It generates a sense of historical prosperity, due to the revenue from the salt made locally which goes into the curing of *jambon de Bayonne*: no ham is worthy of the *Bayonne* name if it is preserved in any other salt.

Béarn red wines, whether made at the co-opérative or at Jurançon or Madiran must be produced from our old friends tannat, cabernet franc and/or pinenc (fer servadou). Some cabernet sauvignon is used for bouquet and suppleness, and there are local black-skinned varieties of the manseng and courbu sometimes added for local colour. Henri Ramonteu used to use a little manseng noir, which is a high-yielder and gives a deep colour and a specific *goût du terroir* to the wine. It is sad that he is tearing up his red wine grapes to make room for more white, but he is not allowed to increase the total area of plantation, as we have seen.

Tannat is the grape which gives Béarn, along with all the other wines of the deep South-West, its particular character. The better wines from the Bellocq co-opérative use 50-60% tannat, the balance being made up from the two cabernets. In the case of their best wine, named after Henri IV, the whole of the complement is cabernet sauvignon, and this wine needs a certain amount of keeping to allow the hard edges to soften. Their Cuvée des Vignerons, sold also under the name of Gaston Phoebus, another local hero, is more immediately accessible; half tannat, only 15% cabernet sauvignon and 35% cabernet franc. There are no hard and fast rules about these percentages, the laws allowing each wine-maker freedom within the range of permitted grape-varieties. For example, Richard Ziemek-Chigé at Jurançon makes one red Béarn under the Mirabel label entirely from an equal blend of the two cabernets, and another exclusively from cabernet franc. The latter has the characteristic grassy, curranty bouquet and flavour of the grape, suggesting a southern version of Marcillac.

The Crouseilles co-opérative at Madiran markets its red Béarn under the names Poule au Pot and Vin de Fleurs. It manages a fairly heady 12°. The Jurançon co-opérative makes two red Béarns, one called Beau Vallon which is intended for early drinking, and the other called Collection Cave, which requires five or six years to reach its prime.

It is rare to find Béarn from a producer outside the co-opérative or the Madiran and Jurançon areas. I believe there is only one independent property and it belongs to the Lapeyre family, who own the **Domaine de Guilhémas**, on the edge of the old town of Salies-de-Béarn. The family have 11 hectares, all in one parcel beautifully situated with full southern exposure a short drive out of Salies. Until very recently the grapes were pressed at the vineyard, but now there is new plant back at Guilhémas so that the pressing and the vinification can be done under the same roof.

The wines are made in two parallel ranges, the one not necessarily better than the other, just different. Under the title Domaine de Guilhémas, they make a red which is 50% tannat, 30% cabernet sauvignon and 20% cabernet franc. The 1990 won a gold medal in Paris: it is very dark in colour and has quite a meaty nose. In 1993 there were still a lot of tannins to resolve, but the wine was full of promise. The red made under the title of **Domaine Lapeyre** was similar in style, but it is given a year in wood which had yet to work its way through. The 1989 won a *prix d'excellence* in Strasbourg. These wines are both keepers: they get fifteen to twenty days of maceration in a good year, although the weather was so poor in 1991 that the period was reduced to only ten days. Later vintages have enhanced the reputation of these wines.

The Guilhémas rosé is from equal proportions of tannat and cabernet franc; the Lapeyre has more tannat. They are both very pale with a distinct strawberry character and are most attractive.

Both whites are dry: the Guilhémas from 80% gros manseng and 20% rousselet de Béarn, and the Lapeyre in precisely the reverse proportions. Monsieur Lapeyre gave us to taste some pure rousselet, because this is a grape-variety not met with outside Béarn. It was very appealing, with some pear-drops on the bouquet, but a great deal of fruit. It was long in the mouth and very dry.

White Béarn is a much smaller production than the red or rosé. It used to be made at Madiran, from the two mansengs and petit courbu, but these vines have been turned over to make Pacherenc. Similarly, no white Béarn is made at Jurançon for obvious reasons.

The white wine produced at Bellocq is rather different. Its interest lies in the fact that it is made entirely from the arrufiac grape, here called Raffiat de Moncade. Moncade is the name of the ruined tower which is all that is left of the palace at Orthez, where the viscounts of Béarn had their court. The old bridge at Orthez over the *gave de Pau* is reminiscent of the bridge at Cahors, only it is smaller (it is sadly disfigured by the railway line which runs alongside it).

The fame of the Tour Moncade at Orthez is perpetuated in the name of the local vine. Although this is an ancient variety, its present pre-dominance is new, because it seems that, after the phylloxera, the white wines of Béarn were made largely from barroque and claverie varieties. Raffiat gives the wine an individuality which sets it apart from the other wines of the South-West. Long may it survive.

The rosé wine which made Béarn wine fashionable in the post-war years has declined although it retains its popularity with the tourist trade in summer. For the Béarnais this is perhaps a pity because their rosé is their best wine. They make a very good one at Crouseilles in the Madiran, a blend of tannat and cabernet sauvignon, better made than the rival version produced at Bellocq, which markets one wine based on tannat and another on cabernet, but any of these pink wines makes good summer drinking at a picnic by the side of the fast-flowing *gave de Pau*, chilled in the cool mountain waters.

Perhaps it was inevitable that Béarn should be squeezed between the born-again wines of Jurançon and Madiran, but one admires the Lapeyre family in particular, who are managing to make wines which are distinctive and not carbon copies of either. The co-opératives remain good sources of wines for fairly priced everyday drinking.

JURANÇON

The vineyards of Jurançon are an extension of those of Béarn, occupy-ing the slopes of the saddle of hill-country which divides the *gaves* of Pau and Oloron. At Bellocq the vineyards were relatively low-lying, but as the ground follows the rivers towards the snow-capped mountains, the terrain gets rougher and more contorted, vines often being found at an altitude of 1000 feet or more in the Jurançon.

The vineyard is named after what is today a suburb of the town of Pau on the south bank of the *gave*. The making of wines here had been in the hands of the abbeys during the middle ages, but the bourgeoisie of Pau came to take an increasing interest in them and it became fashionable for prominent citizens to have a few hectares of vines just outside the city gates. The officially delimited appellation area starts in the suburbs of the modern town. It includes a number of communes to the south and east of the town, but any trace of viticulture must have disappeared from these villages with the phylloxera. Today the vineyard is almost all to the west of the main road out of Pau south into the Pyrenees.

The town of Gan marks its eastern limit. It is here that the Cave des Producteurs de Jurançon is based. On the right of the road which runs west from Gan through Lasseube to Oloron, well-watered intimate valleys run north-west in the direction of the *gave de Pau*. It is on the steep slopes of these valleys, those which face south-east and south-west, that much Jurançon is made. Most of the remainder is made in the neighbourhood of Monein to the west, where the ground is lower. Some detect a difference in the style of the wines as a result. They say that the wines of Monein have less acidity.

Looking south from the Boulevard des Pyrénées in Pau, you can see very easily that the hills on the other side of the river which hide the vineyards from sight are really the first foothills of the high Pyrenees beyond. Their contours contrast sharply with the flat table-land to the north of Pau, and the geology of the terrain is noticeably different as well. The Pyrenean chain was the result of some tremendous subterranean upheaval millions of years ago, and even the edges of such a gigantic movement have left a marked and irregular stamp on the face of the countryside. Sharp and twisted outcrops of rock break through a subsoil of clay mixed with chalk or flint, and a generous mixture of shingle washed down by mountain glaciers.

The climate is unusual too. The spring is even longer and wetter than in Madiran, and the Indian summer longer and usually drier. The higher altitude exposes the vines to the risk of spring frosts, so the plants are traditionally trained to grow tall, *en hautains* as they say. Stakes between 1.5 to 2 metres high are driven into the ground and the vines trained and pruned to climb them; then they are made to shoot sideways along wires, so that the grape-bearing shoots are kept well off the ground and away from the influence of pockets of low-lying, freezing air. This system also allows the maximum aeration of the grape-bunches in the ripening season, but has the disadvantage of exposing the vines to a greater risk of disease than with more usual methods of cultivation.

Historians have traced the trade in these wines back to the year 988, but undoubtedly it was the creation of the navigation channel at the mouth of the Adour and the opening of Bayonne to trade upstream which gave the impetus to local wine-production. The wines of Jurançon were transported to Bayonne either by mule trains or down the *gaves* in flat-bottomed boats. These were made from hollowed-out tree-trunks, bound together with the twining stems of clematis.

The timely arrival of Henri IV added a boost to the reputation of the wines and his parliament enacted laws to protect the reputation of the wine. The best parcels of land were identified and rated so that taxes could be efficiently and justly collected, and, as at Gaillac, the importation of wines from outside the region was prohibited so as to prevent adulteration.

The best overseas markets were in the Low Countries and England, where Jurançon was much prized at the court of Charles II. Later it was exported to America. Scandinavia, too, must have known about Jurançon, because a butt of the wine was supplied from the royal cellars at Stockholm to celebrate a peace treaty in 1397. Writers as well as princes have fêted the wine: Colette wrote, 'When I was a young girl, I was introduced to a passionate Prince, domineering and two-timing like all the great seducers; Jurançon.'

Nineteenth-century writers detected the perfume and flavour of truffles in Jurançon, and agreed that the wine improved with age. It was distinguished from German wines by having more body, though less sweetness. The red wines were highly esteemed too, but, as we have seen, these are now sold as *vin de Béarn* and may not call themselves Jurançon.

In those days, there were about 3000 hectares under vine, rather a lot when you compare it with a mid-1950s figure of only 300. But then the phylloxera had intervened, although its effect at this latitude was rather less severe than it had been further north. Indeed there are pockets of pre-phylloxera vines still surviving today.

Traditionally the wines of Jurançon have been sweet in style. The southern latitude usually guarantees a late vintage, sometimes lasting well into November and December. The heat of the sun is reinforced by the hot wind which blows over the mountains from Spain in autumn, drying the juice within the skins and producing a marvellous concentration of fruit and sugar. Such a dry ripening season does not encourage the development of botrytis, the fungoid agency which pro-duces such honeyed sweetness in Monbazillac and Saussignac. If rot does develop, it will almost certainly be because the weather has been wet, and the autumn sun and mountain wind have failed to perform. Also the grape-variety most used for the production of sweet Jurançon has such a thick skin that *pourriture noble* cannot easily penetrate it. It is a fallacy therefore to believe that the character of sweet Jurançon derives from *pourriture*.

The vagaries of the climate cause sharp differences in quality and even style from one year to the next. This hardly helps the presentation of a consistent image, nor the planning of a grower's cash-flow. Little wonder, therefore, that wine-makers have developed the production of dry wines in parallel with the traditional *vins moelleux*. To avoid the confusion which two quite different styles of wine might have pro-duced, the title Jurançon Sec was created in 1975 to distinguish them.

The quality of many great wines derives from the character of one grape-variety, though strictly speaking in Jurançon it may be two. I say 'may' because there are two grapes, the petit manseng and the gros, which, although they share a name may not share parents. We have met them both before in Vic-Bilh, so it will come as no surprise that petit manseng is the mainstay of the sweet wines, while gros manseng is the bulk ingredient of the drier wines. Other grape-varieties which may be included by law but which are decreasing in terms of actual use are the petit courbu, camaralet and lauzet, which together account for only about 5% of the total production. The last-named pair are now quite rare, but the petit courbu hangs on despite its tendency to disease and rot, because some producers value its touch of vivacity and its young freshness.

The sweet Jurançon wines are usually a blend of the two mansengs, although more and more producers indulge the ultimate luxury of a wine made from petit manseng alone. The dry wines are usually a blend too, but the preponderating vine is the gros manseng. The petit is a small yielder: the fruit is tiny and the vegetation opulent so this variety gives only about 15 hectolitres to the hectare, compared with 45 or so for the gros. The old-fashioned method of growing the vines so far off the ground effectively keeps down the yield from both kinds of grape, so that neither attains in practice the quantities permitted by the appellation rules. These allow 50 hectolitres for sweet wines and 65 for the dry.

The same rules require a minimum of 11° alcohol for the dry and 12¹/₂ for the sweet Jurançon. In practice these figures are regularly exceeded, more especially for the sweet wines where it is not uncommon to find wines packing up to 15°, plus a few more of unconverted sugar. But to compensate for and to balance this alcoholic strength, the wines have a remarkable acidity which enables them to age gloriously and prevents them from cloying on the palate. Even a dry Jurançon, which can be drunk with pleasure while still only a year or so old, will benefit from two or three years in bottle when it will develop a rich and perfectly balanced bouquet.

As in the past, it is the sweet wines of Jurançon on which the fame of the vineyards rests. There is no reason to control the start of the *vendange*, because picking is delayed for as long as possible, sometimes until the fall of the first snows. Even then the grapes are not picked all at once. In some of the best vineyards – some do not bother or do not have the resources – the vines may be gone over three or more times as the grapes which are really ready for picking are taken off the plants, leaving the rest to go on maturing. In Jurançon the term *passerillage* is used to denote the successive cropping and the resulting shrivelling of the overripe grapes, without rot.

Because the vineyards are so high above sea-level and the vintage takes place so late, the weather is always a hazard, much more so here than in other regions further north. Good dry wines can be made in most years, but for sweet Jurançon the vintage label is of some importance. For instance very little was made in 1992, when it scarcely stopped raining between the end of September and Christmas. Many growers even used their petit manseng to make dry wine because of the lack of sugar. Three good recent years for the sweet wines were 1988, 1989 and 1990, before that 1985, 1978 and 1971. Old-timers speak with tearful nostalgia of the 1956s (surprisingly) and a trio of glorious years in the 1920s – 1926, 1924 and 1921 – which was perhaps the greatest of all. Fingers are being crossed for a potentially great 1995.

Simply to describe a Jurançon as sweet gives no idea of its individuality. A mature wine will be a deep golden colour. Writers have long vied with each other to describe the exotic character of the bouquet and flavour of these wines. Pineapple, guava, nutmeg and cinnamon have all been detected; mango and quince have suggested themselves to others, but all are agreed about the honey and wild flowers. Wines of a great year will keep indefinitely, darkening as they age. A sweet Jurançon can be drunk as young as four years old, but ten is usually regarded as a minimum.

One of the first things you will discover in this area is that there are two kinds of wine-maker: those who use new wood to make and age their wines in, and those who don't. Jurançon is not unique in this respect, but the difference in wines which have been given wood and those which have not is possibly more marked here than in any other region. The use of wood is relatively recent, so its effect on a slow-maturing wine such as Jurançon is still not certain in the long term. This adds a certain piquancy to the assessment of what are already spicy wines.

The post-phylloxera history of Jurançon follows a familiar pattern. The local grape-varieties were more resistant to the plague than others, but the vineyards nevertheless declined sharply. This was due not so much to the disease but the cumulative effect which it had on other vineyards, depressing the market in wines from the South-West, and dragging Jurançon sales down with the rest. Three wars also took their toll in terms of heavy loss of life to the local community. By the end of the Second World War, the standards of wine-making had fallen very low, excessive sugaring being practised to induce extra sweetness without bottle-age. Poor hybrid plants were widespread in the vineyards.

As elsewhere the revival was due to a handful of enthusiasts for whom the making of true Jurançon was more a way of life than a living. Alongside them there grew up the co-opérative at Gan, called **La Cave des Producteurs de Jurançon (A)**. It was founded by the same Henri Meyer who had done so much to put the wines of Béarn on the map. Today the three hundred members of the co-opérative are responsible for over half of the total production, according to Monsieur Vallin, the wine-maker currently in charge. Three-quarters of the production is in the hands of less than one-third of the membership, so if the total of 530 hectares implies a vineyard of less than 2 hectares per member on average, there are 200 members with only 140 hectares between them. It is easy to see how attractive the facilities of a co-opérative are in such a situation.

The members' vineyards are planted overall with 80% gros manseng, 15% petit manseng and 5% petit courbu. There are also token plantings of lauzet and camaralet. Because the yield from the petit manseng is only half that from the gros, the amount of wine produced from it is only about one-tenth. The co-opérative is currently producing about 21,000 hectolitres of AOC wine a year, equivalent to 2.8 million bottles.

As with all modern co-opératives, rigid standards of quality are enforced, and nowhere is this more necessary than in the supervision of the condition of the grapes which come into the presses, particularly those which are late-picked. The Cave is at the eastern end of the appellation, so growers in the vicinity bring in their own grapes, which are then appraised for weight and sugar-content according to variety. These factors determine the price paid to each member for his grapes. Members will previously have submitted samples to the Cave for them to assess the balance of sugar and acidity, and the computerised records of this information enable the co-opérative to tell each member when he should pick.

Members whose vines are at the western end of the appellation near Monein have their produce transported in their labelled hods by special lorries to the Cave, to minimise the risk of oxidisation.

The terrain is such that neither pruning nor harvesting by machine is often possible. All picking, not just that of the late-ripening grapes, is done by hand. The co-opérative boasts that it insists on *passerillage*. With some of the smaller growers this may be something of a pious hope, especially if the maize harvest is still waiting.

The plant at the Cave has recently been replaced with the most modern stainless-steel fermentation tanks, so that the temperature of the vinification can be rigorously controlled. Monsieur Vallin prefers an unusually high 22°. According to him, this is quite cool enough to preserve the freshness and young fruit in the wine.

Monsieur Vallin says that the official policy is not to encourage members to make red and pink Béarn, but he does not discourage them either because he likes to keep his own hand in at making something other than white wines. The rosé, some of which is bottled under the name Peyresol, is made from half tannat and half cabernet franc. It has some presence and body, with persistence and substance to the finish. It is very pale and rather good.

Monsieur Vallin also told us that it is one of the most exciting aspects of an oenologist's work at a co-opérative, as opposed to a private *chais*, to be able to be concerned in such a wide variety of wines: at Jurançon they have a range of no fewer than sixteen including a number of properties in private ownership for whom they make and market the wine under the names of the vineyards.

With many co-opératives, the range of wines tends to change quite often. The people in charge of marketing obviously feel that they can stimulate demand by new titles, unusual bottle-shapes, attractive brand-names and other presentational gimmicks. An account of their wines at any given time is therefore likely soon to be out of date, but the Cave at Jurançon does seem to retain a continuity which its customers have come to expect.

Take the three dry whites, for example. Two are inexpensive and account for the bulk of their overall production. The Brut d'Océan has a slight prickle: it is lively, what the French call *nerveux* and aromatic. It is made from 100% gros manseng. The Grain Sauvage has rather less acidity, but the only year I have tasted recently was the difficult 1992, which may account for the flatness of the wine compared with the Brut d'Océan. It tasted rather as if the rain had got into it.

The third dry wine is infinitely better and much more interesting. I found it to be one of the best of all dry Jurançons readily available, well able to compete with wines from some prestigious independent growers. It is called Peyre d'Or, and the raw material comes from members who can be relied upon to produce a consistently richer juice from successive pickings. Though chemically quite dry, it has a honeyed nose with lots of the exotic fruits which one associates with the sweeter styles of wine. Monsieur Vallin thinks this would be good with food, perhaps a fish or chicken in sauce, and he says that the 1990 will not be at its peak until 1996. The 1995 should be excellent in time.

There are three *moelleux* wines which are not aged in new wood: the basic Cordon Viguerie and Apéritif Henri IV, and the much more interesting Prestige d'Automne. The last named is by far the best of the three. It is made from 100% petit manseng. After three years this wine was already very rich, but it will improve with age. The 1990 may even outstrip the excellent 1985, and the 1995 both of them.

Croix du Prince is the name reserved for the *moelleux* aged for four months in new wood. Monsieur Vallin is sitting on the fence about his new barrels. He says that wood undoubtedly helps to intensify the finish of the wine, but, even where it is not excessive, it still modifies the character of the wine and can to that extent be considered unnatural. Here the wood was by no means aggressive, the 1988 showing well after five years, but with a good future ahead of it.

Of the five single-domaine wines which the Cave makes and markets, the Château des Astous belongs to it. It is a rather handsome small château half-way between Pau and Gan on the west side of the road. The vineyard is planted with 100% petit manseng, and if the château is elegant, the soil is poor and shallow with rock near to the surface. Not surprisingly the wine has an attractive suggestion of minerals, even steel, to offset the sweetness. The 1989 was very attractive as early as 1993.

The Domaine des Terrasses provides grapes for both dry and sweet wines, being planted with 75% gros manseng and 25% petit. This was the only *moelleux* made by the Cave in 1992. The wine from the previous year, when the crop was drastically reduced by frost, seemed dumb on the nose, but there was some richness from the petit manseng. Better in every way is the Château de Navailles. Monsieur Vallin had given the 1990 four months in wood which was hardly noticeable. He said that 1990 was such a rich year that the wine could take a lot of wood without its showing too much. This wine was long and persistent in the mouth and very good.

The co-opérative also makes the wine from Château Lasserre, near St Faust, and also Château Coute.

The general impression left by the wines of this co-opérative is that the everyday drinking wines, both dry and sweet, though well made and perfectly acceptable, lack excitement, but the premium wines and those made for the individual domaines are of a high standard.

THE EASTERN VINEYARD

Behind the Cave co-opérative a small road climbs to a horseshoeshaped ridge of high ground, some 1350 feet above sea-level, which runs parallel with the main road south from Jurançon. It starts to veer west just behind Gan and eventually north through the small village of La Chapelle-de-Rousse. Eventually it winds downhill and emerges at Laroin, not far from Madame Hégoburu's excellent vineyard at Domaine de Souche. The landscape in this lost corner of the Béarn must be some of the most dramatic and picturesque of all French vineyard scenery, with the curving amphitheatres of vines set against the chalky blue and the snow of the Pyrenees, and a picture-postcard sky.

Along this road there is a cluster of some of the finest growers in this part of Jurançon. The first you come to is **Château Jolys (48)**, the property of Robert Latrille. The château is a rather pretty eighteenth-century manor house with a typically Béarn-style grey slate roof. Its Cave goes back to the fifteenth century. Monsieur Latrille and his mother left Algeria after independence in 1959, and it was she who decided on arrival in France that they would buy Château Jolys as their home. At that date there was not a single vine on the estate.

Had he stayed in Algeria, Monsieur Latrille would have pursued his business career. He knew something about making red wine, but nothing about white. His neighbours thought he was quite mad when he started to plant a vineyard, not a small experimental affair, but 36 hectares. Even today it is by far the largest single Jurançon vineyard.

Monsieur Latrille is no peasant-grower. He is very much the *patron* in manner, and in the efficient, business-like way in which he runs his estate. It sounds almost a boast when he says it is twenty years since he sat on a tractor-seat. He has a full-time *viticulteur* and a secretary, and he has himself trained up his *maître de chais*. But he likes to get away from his paper-work, and nothing gives him greater pleasure at week-ends than to spend some of his time alone talking to his vines.

The vineyard is divided into three roughly equal parcels surrounding his château, mostly on steep slopes facing south-east and south-west, which is quite normal, but some facing north, which is not. The locals were amazed that he should plant north-facing vines, but he says he does well enough with them except when there are frosts about in the spring. He grows only the two varieties of manseng, two-thirds of the vineyard in gros, and one-third in petit. He says there is a symbiosis between the mansengs and the terroir of the Béarn, and that no other grapes ought to be allowed in the appellation. He is rude about the petit courbu. He told an agricultural expert who was trying to persuade him to plant some that 'advisers don't have to foot the bills'. He says you can lose a lot of production if the petit courbu gets the *coulure* in the spring, or the rot in the autumn. The risks are that much greater in the Jurançon where the annual rainfall is bigger than the other vineyards of the south-west.

The vines are planted *de haut en bas*, that is to say in vertical rows following the gradient of the ground, rather than in horizontal terraces. As practically everywhere in the Jurançon, harvesting by machine is impossible because of the steepness. He employs six full-time pickers and likes to complete the operation as quickly as possible. He dispenses with more than one *trie*. For maintenance of the vineyards he has a special four-wheeled tractor to cope with the steep slopes.

He likes the grapes to arrive at the *chais* whole and uncrushed. They are hand-sorted to eliminate unripe ones, the stems from the bunches, earth and other unwanted matter. They are mechanically de-stalked and then given twelve hours' maceration at a low temperature before they are fermented. They are pressed four times, the juice from the last pressing being thrown away. Monsieur Latrille would like to be able to throw away the third pressing too, and sometimes he does, but, as he says, '*il faut faire du vin*'. The two (or three) pressings then go into stainless steel for the alcoholic fermentation. The temperature is controlled in the vats so as not to rise above 19°. At the end of the fermentation, the wine is filtered and refrigerated for a week. This is to prevent the formation of crystals at a later date, which, though in no way harmful to the wine, put off the customers. The wine then goes back into steel again for six months, at the end of which it is filtered and bottled.

There are three styles of Château Jolys. First there is a *sec*, from 95% gros manseng. Monsieur Latrille gave me a tasting of his 1992 just after it had been bottled. It is a good, commercial, typical style of dry Jurançon. It had not at that time developed much bouquet, but it was a fresh wine, and not too high in acidity, as many wines of that very difficult vintage were.

Then there are two *moelleux*. The first is made from equal proportions of the two mansengs, and I confess to having found the 1991 rather dull. Perhaps it was the year, because the 1990 version of his other *moelleux*, made from 100% petit manseng, was extremely good indeed. It is called Cuvée Jean and has the rich and exotic flavour of ripe peaches and mangoes. This is the only wine to which Monsieur Latrille gives any new wood. He says he is not entirely sold on the use of new wood, but realises its commercial attractions. Again it was the businessman speaking.

Monsieur Latrille is everyone's idea of an old-fashioned Frenchman, with his exaggerated courtesy and flattery. He speaks in a loud, clear voice, and, when he gets going on the subject of his beloved wines, he might be delivering a speech from Racine. He may be a covert monarchist. His greatest hero is Henri IV, so that, when he designed his tasting-room, he insisted that its picture-window should command a view of the Château of Pau where Henri IV was born.

The future rather worries Monsieur Latrille. Jurançon is an expensive wine to make because of the low yields from the vines. He exports over a third of his wine, and growers in Australia and California for example are easily able to undercut him with wines of good quality. That was how he lost the renewal of his contract with the Orient Express, and highlights a problem for growers like Monsieur Latrille with 36 hectares of vines, and a great deal of wine to market each year. Smaller growers who can sell all their produce locally do not have to worry, because the French consumer, at least in the provinces, won't buy anything except French wine. You very rarely see any other in a supermarket.

Take Monsieur Labat at **Château de Rousse (44)** up the road for example. He has only 7 hectares, and Madame told us that they rely almost entirely on recommendation by word of mouth, most of their customers being private buyers. Favourable comment in some of the French guides also helps them sell to local restaurants and shops as well. Monsieur Labat's property is very striking indeed, the vineyards being planted in natural amphitheatres called *cirques*, the rows of vines looking in certain lights like the banks of seats in a classical theatre. The effect of a *cirque* is to concentrate the heat of the sun which shrivels the petit manseng almost into currants.

The château was once an old hunting lodge in the time of good King Henry, and it has been in the Labat family for five generations. They have a son who is an oenologist working in Bordeaux, so continuity seems assured. When they replanted some of their land, the Labats found some remains of old vines growing *en désordre*, that is to say not in rows but at random, which is how vineyards used to be many years ago. Tests on these vines proved that the vineyard too went back to the time of Henri IV. It was reconstituted after the phylloxera in about 1890 and some of the gros manseng vines go back to that time. Grapes are the only crop from the property nowadays, though formerly the Labats used to grow maize and some fruit, especially strawberries, but the market in both is not what it was, because of competition from over the Pyrenees.

The vineyards are 50% petit manseng, 40% gros and 10% petit courbu. Madame Labat agreed that the petit courbu was difficult (she used the colourful word *fragile*), especially since it ripened earlier than the rest of the grapes and upset the rhythm of the *vendange*, but her husband valued it because it brought a particular perfume and finesse to the wine and was worth growing in limited quantities for that reason. They start picking the petit courbu as a rule in mid-October, and *passerillage* of all the varieties continues until the end of November.

For a relatively small property, the wine-making at Château de Rousse is quite up-to-date, perhaps influenced by the oenologist in the family. The fruit for their dry wine, a blend of gros manseng and petit courbu, is given skin-contact overnight before maceration which takes place in stainless steel. Madame Labat said they saw no need to control artificially the temperature within the *chais*. The *sec*, especially in a good year like 1990, benefits from some ageing, and Madame thought that that particular wine would not be at its best until 1996.

There are two sweet wines, made identically except that one is given new wood, which is only used once. The wine stays there for between eight and twelve months, the length of time depending on the vintage. These wines are mostly petit manseng, but there is a little of each of the other grapes as well. I tasted the 1988 vintage of the oaked version, and found that the wood had gone altogether, leaving a wonderfully per-fumed wine, honeyed and exhaling exotic fruits, and it had a touch of caramel at the end. The oaked wine has a black label and the other *moelleux* a white one.

Given wine of such quality, one wonders what argument there can possibly be against the use of wood. Richard Ziemek-Chigé nearby at **Clos Lamouroux (52)** is in no doubt at all. He considers the use of new wood an abomination. 'My customers do not want a *jus de planche*,' he says. 'A wine with a *goût du terroir* like Jurançon needs neither disguise nor help.' He calls wine made in new wood '*un vin d'optimiste*: in five years it may be good. You can taste five different wines from different appellations, grape-varieties and styles of vinification: if they've been put into wood, they all taste the same. It is a fashion like mini-skirts.'

You have to take Monsieur Ziemek seriously, because, without bene-fit of wood, his wines are very good indeed. He has recently taken over Clos Lamouroux from his father-in-law, Jean Chigé, in whose family it has been for 300 years. As with so many other properties in the area, the vineyard went downhill gradually in the first half of this century, and the family diversified into other crops. The wine was sold *en vrac* to merchants in Paris. In 1950 reconstitution of the vineyard started with 10 hectares and the oldest vines go back to that time. A further 2¹/₂ hectares were added in 1975. The family have recently purchased another property with only 3 hectares called **Clos Mirabel**, a little way away over the hills to the north-east. Both properties have enjoyed a considerable reputation for many years. Clos Mirabel's name is now exclusively reserved for the red Béarn which they have always been keen on making at Clos Lamouroux, and which is mentioned in the sec-tion on Béarn. All the white wine from both properties is sold under the Lamouroux label.

The manseng grapes are the only white ones which Monsieur Ziemek uses. He grows twice as many petit manseng vines as gros. But since the one yields so much less than the other, the balance in terms of wine is more like 60/40.

Monsieur Ziemek does not believe in Jurançon Sec. He doesn't make any unless the poor quality of the vintage prevents him from making anything else, as it did in 1992. He believes that Jurançon is essentially and exclusively a sweet wine. His vines enjoy perfect exposure to the south. In good years the grapes contain so much sugar that, if it were fermented out as it would have to be for a dry wine, he would end up with too much alcohol.

What he does at Lamouroux therefore is to make two wines. The first is half-sweet, half-dry, with only 10% petit manseng. This is made and matured for one year in stainless steel. The second wine is much sweeter and is made entirely from petit manseng grapes from older vines. This is vinified in steel and then aged in *old* wood for a year. This is a really fine wine, quite one of the best in the appellation.

Monsieur Ziemek is a firm believer in *passerillage*. He says that, because the grapes are grown so high off the ground, even retired people can pick them. He has a party of regular pickers who come back year after year. They include a general, two colonels, a doctor, a retired police inspector and thirty others for whom Madame Ziemek has to prepare lunch. Perhaps their fidelity has something to do with Madame's cooking?

Jean-Marc Grussaute, who lives nearby on the crest of the ridge above Lamouroux, has no problems with the harvesting of his grapes either. Like many of the smaller growers he manages to twist the arms of his family and friends to pick the 4 hectares which he currently has in production at his **Domaine de Larrédya (43)**. The name Larrédya seems to have two meanings in the local patois: twilight, a romantic name for a wine, especially a sweet one; it is also the name given to the old wooden tiles of which the roofs in the region used once to be made.

Jean-Marc is one of the younger growers in the Jurançon, though the property has been in his family since the beginning of the century. The family used to belong to the co-opérative, but he left to make his own vintage for the first time in 1988, having trained in oenology at Blanquefort for two years after his *baccalauréat*. He has since planted another 1¹/₂ hectares, but the grapes are still too young to produce wine.

I tasted his 1992 *sec* just after it had been bottled in April 1993. The picking season had been wet throughout, and Jean-Marc freely admitted that the wine would not turn out as well as his 1991. It was well perfumed and lively, but it lacked the essential fruit which is the characteristic of Jurançon. The 1991 was much richer and much better than even that year might have suggested. Jean-Marc explained that, up on the ridge where his vines are, they had not had the spring frosts which had afflicted the vineyards lower down, and he even preferred his 1991 wines to his 1990, generally held in the district to have been an exceptional year.

Like so many growers, he makes two sweet wines. His basic *moelleux*, two-thirds from gros manseng, is made in stainless steel, but matured in old wood for twelve months. It is fairly quick-maturing and not intended for long keeping. The 1991 Sélection des Terrasses, on the other hand, which is all from petit manseng, had ten years or more life ahead of it, according to Jean-Marc, who preferred it to his 1990, which he described as *flatteuse*, too easy to drink. The 1991, which had been given rather less wood, was the better balanced, perhaps for that reason. He is not as hooked on the use of wood as some of his young colleagues, but he likes the depth which it gives to the finish of his petit manseng wines.

Grussaute's immediate neighbour is Jean-Bernard Larrieu at **Clos Lapeyre (42)**. In fact their boundary runs down the middle of one of the cirques.

Like the Labats up the road, the Larrieu family had diversified into other cultures, particularly strawberries, when the Jurançon vineyards went into decline, though they have had 10$^{1}/_{2}$ hectares under vine over three generations at least. Like the Grussautes they too joined the co-opérative, but young Jean-Bernard had ambitions to make his own wine, so they left. It is perhaps not a coincidence that both Grussaute and Larrieu prefer to vinify their wines at 22°, like the co-opérative does, higher than is the fashion elsewhere. They both give a proportion only of their dry wine grapes a pre-fermentation maceration.

The Larrieu vineyard at Lapeyre is divided more or less equally between the two mansengs. Some very old gros manseng is used to make a special dry wine called *Vitage Vielh*: Larrieu gives this ten months in new wood, but has not yet begun to market even the 1990 which he said (1993) needs another five years to show its best. He explains that these old vines yield wine of exceptional richness, which he thinks will benefit from the new wood. It certainly promises very well.

The mainstream *sec* won a Paris medal. It was also picked out by Gault-Millau in their annual wine-review as having 'perfumes of ground almond and aniseed: well-rounded on the palate with good freshness, long and plenty of extract'. Both the 1991 and 1992 were partially allowed a second malolactic fermentation, which Larrieu thinks particularly beneficial in less good years.

As usual there are the two sweet wines: a *moelleux* to be drunk as an apéritif or 'at four o'clock'. This is given six months in not quite new barrels, and is thus a good commercial *moelleux*, in which the wood is not too prominent. This should prove to be Larrieu's best-selling wine. The sweeter wine, called Clos Lapeyre Selection, is made with anything up to 100% petit manseng, according to the year. The 1991 won another Paris medal. Larrieu's sweet wines demonstrate his flexibility in the use of wood. He is prepared to use his full armoury of techniques according to the particular vintage, and is not dogmatic in any way about using oak. For example the 1992 *liquoreux* which we tasted from the cask had had only five months in wood, but the year was so dubious that perhaps this was already enough. The 1991 had however already lost all trace of wood on the nose, and was excellent.

For family and friends the Larrieus also make a *vendange tardive* ultra-sweet wine. The 1991 was made from grapes picked on 2 and 3 December and in two later *tries*. These took place during a fortnight of dry weather when the sun was hot during the day, but there were frosts at night. This wine, which Jean-Bernard does not commercialise, at least not yet, is very much after the style of the very concentrated sweet wines made by Henri Ramonteu, whom he much admires.

All the growers on this horseshoe of high ground seem to make excellent wine. Two others whom I must mention are Henri

Lapouble-Laplace, whose **Clos Thou (46)** petit manseng 1990 is out-standing, and Philippe de Nays who, at the family **Domaine de Nays (45)**, makes what Australians call 'fruit-driven' wines.

MONEIN

Henri Ramonteu, unlike most of the local growers, is a relative newcomer to Jurançon, though his family had lived not far away at Lacq, the big centre for natural gas on the *gave de Pau*. In 1957 they bought the **Domainé Cauhapé (4)**, pronounced 'Quarpay'. This is one of the most westerly of all the Jurançon properties, and is a few miles the other side of the town of Monein, which is itself a half-hour's drive from La Chapelle de Rousse. As the rivers lose height in their journey to the ocean, the land too is more gentle and less mountainous. The town of Monein is at only half the height of Jean-Bernard Larrieu's vineyard.

The countryside at Cauhapé is almost gentle, so much less steep that it is possible to grow vines in traditional rows without terracing. Today there are 25 hectares of them, which makes this the second largest estate after Château Jolys. When the Ramonteus moved in, there were only four hectares, very run down and planted mostly with poor hybrid varieties. There were however a few very old gros manseng plants over ninety years old.

Henri Ramonteu is to Jurançon what Brumont is to Madiran. Always passionate about wine, he too is largely self-taught, though he did his *stages* at Bordeaux. He took over the reins at Cauhapé only in 1981, at just about the same time as Brumont was replanting Montus. He has the same vivacity and energy as Brumont, the same persuasiveness and the same over-brimming self-confidence. He is an irresistible salesman of his own wines, as well as a powerful spokesman for Jurançon as a whole. He is held in the same kind of awe tinged with envy as Brumont, and he is just as fearless at sweeping away the cobwebs from the process of wine-making. His influence on the new generation of Jurançon *vignerons* is no less impressive than Brumont's in Vic-Bilh.

Ramonteu makes only white wines: he used to make some Béarn Rouge from cabernet franc and manseng noir, but he has scrubbed up the vines to make room for more petit manseng which now accounts for 40% of the vineyard. The remainder, except for a tiny amount of petit courbu, is gros manseng.

He makes the same three basic wines as his fellow-growers, a dry and two sweet wines: there are however a number of variations on these main themes which he makes in small quantities either experimentally, or for the very top end of the wine-market. His basic dry wine is widely available in France and in the United Kingdom, and is perhaps the best known of all the dry Jurançons. Even in bad years like 1992, Ramonteu is able to make a good basic *sec*, and this wine accounts for 70% of all his dry production, about 50,000 bottles, or 375 hectolitres, a year.

In addition to this, he makes a dry wine which is fermented in new wood and left there for six to seven months. The barrels are replaced over a four-year cycle. Two years after the vintage the 1991 still had a lot of wood on the nose, and may take some time to come to a balance.

Then there is another dry wine which is made exclusively from the old vines. This is not given any new wood at all. Monsieur Ramonteu allowed me to taste his 1990, and it was wonderfully fat, but supple too. The finish was long and spicy. I liked this by far the best of the dry wines.

These dry wines are made almost entirely from gros manseng, but he also makes a dry wine exclusively from petit manseng, which would be an extraordinary conceit with any wine-maker other than Ramonteu. The early picking of the grapes, in mid-September, a month before they are normally harvested, ensures that there is a shortage of sugar in what is essentially a sweet grape. This wine is given six to seven months in new wood, with regular *batonnage* to give extra elegance and fat. This is an interesting experiment: the wine is totally dry, but nevertheless embodies suggestions of a sweetness that is not allowed to happen. A kind of *botrytis interruptus*.

Perhaps it is with the sweet wines that Ramonteu has really broken new ground. Depending on your point of view, you may prefer to say that he has rediscovered, Brumont-like, what real Jurançon is all about. His basic *moelleux* contains, surprisingly, no petit manseng, being made wholly from the gros. Ramonteu explained that this is essentially the same wine as his basic *sec*, but the grapes are picked three weeks later, and come mostly from older plants. The yield is therefore lower and more concentrated. His 1992, newly made, had some elderflower on the nose, and the sweetness on the palate came as an explosive surprise. These wines always have good acidity and finish, and will please experts and beginners alike.

Then there is the sweet wine called Vendanges Tardives, said by Ramonteu to be his best-selling sweet wine. It is made from equal quantities of the two mansengs. The 1990 was picked on 10 November, which gives some idea of the lateness of the harvest in a good year. It is given one year in wood, though not all of it new. This is a truly exotic wine, always with the right touch of acidity to balance the tropical fruits and honey on the palate. Ramonteu described this wine as the 'natural expression of Jurançon'. It truly is very fine. The 1995 should be a worthy successor.

All of which leaves few superlatives for the two most extraordinary of the Cauhapé wines, both made exclusively from petit manseng, of which they are named respectively the Noblesse and the Quintessence. The 1990 Noblesse was picked after severe frosts, and the grapes registered 20° sugar as they came in from the vineyard. This wine was given eighteen months in new wood. The nose was astonishingly rich and the volume of exotica on the palate was almost overwhelming: my notes record bananas as well as mangoes. This wine was rated fifth in the world in a Gault-Millau tasting of sweet wines, behind only Yquem,

Coutet, an Alsace Vendanges Tardives and a German Trockenbeeren-auslese. I found this wine more harmonious than the Quintessence, which, though the nose was a little more restrained and thus perhaps even more seductive, was really rather over the top. The wood was also still more aggressive even though the wine was a year older than the Noblesse. For the 1989 the grapes were picked on 12 December and there were two *tries* after that during a period of severe frost and snow. The grapes registered 24° sugar.

Monsieur Ramonteu may think me carping and perhaps old-fashioned, but I do not think it is any coincidence that the wines of his which gave me most pleasure were those which had been given least wood. For my taste, many were over-oaked, though I freely admit they were young and they may achieve a better balance when they are more mature.

Henri Ramonteu has a kindred spirit in his close friend, Charles Hours, the proprietor of **Clos Uroulat (12)**, whose seven and a half hectares of vines are tucked away at the back of beyond between Cauhapé and the town of Monein. Charles Hours too is a relative new-comer to Jurançon, having bought the Uroulat farm, which then had but half the present area of vines, only in 1983. Perhaps it was easier for him, as a virgin-*vigneron*, rather than some other established grower, to set up the Association des Clos, Domaines et Châteaux de Jurançon, which he did in 1991, to promote the interests of the individual pro-ducers in the area. The association has already done a great deal to make it easier for visitors to find their way round the intricate network of tiny lanes which join the vineyards together, by putting up signposts in strategic spots. Charles Hours is planning a *route des vins*, and hopes that Jurançon will be able to join in a pan-European Scheme for *routes des vins*, now being organised by the Champagne-makers.

Hours is in his mid-thirties, of good Gascon build, with an efficiency and clear-mindedness which he may well have acquired in his early career of administration. Like all good Gascons, he likes talking to peo-ple: he says that working all day in the vineyards is a lonely job, so he welcomes the opportunity to chat to prospective customers at his *chais*. Vines were in the family, because his grandparents ran a grape-nursery. Young Charles abandoned his desk-job, trained in wine at Talence and came to Jurançon where he already had two distant cousins established as wine-growers: their vineyards are quite close to Uroulat.

Uroulat is one of the relatively few estates where petit courbu survives in any quantity. Here it represents 15% of the vineyard. Charles Hours recognises its drawbacks but, like Monsieur Labat at Château de Rousse, he likes it for its acidity and spicy freshness. Otherwise the vine-yard is planted with 50% petit manseng and 35% gros. The fact that he makes only 240 hectolitres on average each year from his 7½ hectares demonstrates the relatively low yields from the vines in this part of the world. Charles Hours believes above all in improvement in quality. He points out that, if you come to Pau and order a bottle of Bordeaux which is poor, you will not condemn all Bordeaux on the strength of one bottle, because you know perfectly well how good a great Bordeaux can be. But if you order a bottle of Jurançon, perhaps for the first time, and it is not of top quality, you will tend to write off Jurançon and may not give it another try.

Monsieur Hours makes only two wines. The *sec* he has named Cuvée Marie after his baby daughter. The 1991 and 1992 were both very dry indeed, and the influence of the petit courbu was apparent. The 1991 was the more perfumed, but the frosts in the spring had cut the quantity, and rain in the autumn had made the harvest difficult.

He offered me some of his 1992 *moelleux* from the wood, and, like so many of these wines in their first few months of life, it was vividly perfumed with apples and pears. This bouquet wears off during the summer after the vintage, and the wine then rests before developing the characteristic nose of honey, flowers and exotic fruits. The 1991 was already really delicious, not one of the sweetest I tasted, but admirable as an apéritif or with foie gras. Ramonteu had already made the point to us that, although a *moelleux* was excellent with foie gras, the sweetest wines were not really suitable: they should be reserved for desserts, but then again not the sweetest of food because the sugars in the wine and the food would compete rather than complement each other.

The 1990 *moelleux* from Uroulat came top in a blind tasting run by *Que Choisir?*, the French counterpart of *Which?* magazine. You will get some idea of the quality of the wines which Hours is producing from the fact that it beat that of his friend Ramonteu as well as Châteaux Filhot and Bastor-Lamontagne from Bordeaux. '*Très gourmand*' was how he described it.

He ferments and matures both his wines in wood, half of it new. The new wood is renewed on a five-year cycle. The wines are bottled one year after the vintage. He does not himself favour a *macération pelliculaire*, because he believes strongly that the drinker 'should not see the maker behind the wine'. This approach perhaps explains why his wines are less technicoloured than some of the other sweet Jurançons, but what they may lack in power they make up for in their classic elegance and aristocratic style. It is not surprising that they are to be found on the tables of such distinguished restaurateurs as Arrambide at St Jean Pied-de-Port, Guérard at Eugénie-les Bains and Verge at Mougins. Monsieur Hours described his attempts at exporting his wine as '*symboliques*'. Like many other small growers, he finds a sufficiently ready market on his doorstep although he has recently been able to establish outlets in the UK.

While we were enjoying our tasting of his wines, Charles Hours produced a list of his association's members. I asked him about one name which was conspicuous by its absence from his list, that of Madame Migné, whose wines from her Clos Joliette had acquired an almost legendary importance in the folklore of Jurançon. He explained that she had died as recently as 1992. He described her as 'L'Arlésienne' of the Jurançon, a powerfully formidable character who was as one-off as her wines, which she would keep in wood (old, of course) for ten years before bottling them. He wished he had been able to buy her property when it was put up for sale after her death, but he had had to content himself with some of her wines. He generously presented to me a bottle of 1974 Clos Joliette *sec*, which it may well be sacrilege ever to open.

Two other growers close by to Clos Uroulat could not be more different from each other, either in their style and personality or their attitude to wine-making. Casimir Capdevielle at the **Domaine Capdevielle (14)** is sixtyish and the first real country-style grower I had come across in Jurançon. He brought it home to me how young most of the others had been. My time spent with Monsieur Capdevielle was pure joy. He has naughty, dark eyes and a most infectious giggle which is irresistible. He twinkled his way through the story of his vines, which had been in the family for five generations. Of his 5 hectares, one went back to pre-phylloxera days, all his gros manseng there being ungrafted. He has just the two manseng varieties, 3 hectares of the gros, and 2 of the petit. He makes a dry wine and a *moelleux*, both exclusively from gros manseng, and a *liquoreux* entirely from petit manseng.

The *vendange* takes family and friends only two afternoons, fifteen people picking between lunch-time and nightfall. He does not believe in picking in the morning, because the grapes are often covered in dew which the hot wind from over the mountains must first dry off. He doesn't bother with *passerillage*, gathering all the grapes at one go, usually towards the end of October.

The vinification is ultra-traditional: no *macération pelliculaire*, for example. The wine is made in stainless steel and matured in old wood, the dry wine for six months after the fermentation is finished, and the sweeter wines twelve months longer. He does not believe in the use of new wood which he says hides faults in the wine and is unnatural.

Until 1988 he used to make only one sweet wine, blending the two manseng varieties. His customers, tasting the two different constituents of the blend separately, persuaded him to leave them that way, and he does this now exclusively. This must surely be the right decision. Although his *moelleux* is very good, and the blend would surely also be good too, the 100% petit manseng *liquoreux* is absolutely outstanding. Nowadays it is rare to find a wine of this quality which is spared new wood. Monsieur Capdevielle manages to sell his whole production by word-of-mouth reputation, and has never shared with anyone else any of his turnover, which is perhaps why his wines are such good value as well as being first class in quality.

Pascal Labasse at **Domaine Bellegarde (15)** could hardly be more different. Young, a prototype athlete, genial and passionately new-wave as a wine-maker, he is a fervent admirer of Patrick Ducournau in the Madiran. In 1986 Pascal took over from his father who had been a member of the co-opérative. In the dark days of the phylloxera, the family had emigrated to the United States, where they settled in New

Orleans. It was his grandfather who had eventually decided to return to France and buy the 13 acres of Domaine Bellegarde.

The vineyard is nowadays roughly 60% gros manseng, and 40% petit. All the wine is vinified in steel, except for a little petit manseng with which Pascal makes a private *cuvée*. Temperatures are strictly controlled throughout. He makes one dry wine, some of which is given eight or nine months in new wood, and a *moelleux*, some of which sees new wood, and some does not. He is not dogmatic on the subject of wood, though he prefers to use at least some for wines which are intended for longer keeping. It depends too, he says, on the vintage, so that the number of new barrels he will buy each year varies.

Of two vintages of the classically made *sec*, I tasted the 1992 almost immediately it had been bottled: it had the usual apples and pears bouquet of the young wines of the region, and was not as high in acidity as some wines of that year. The 1991 had much more fruit, and the nose was indeed more like that of a *moelleux*. Pascal thought that, eighteen months after the vintage, it was only just starting to lose what had once been an excess of acidity. Both vintages were bone-dry.

The 1991 which had been given some wood was redolent of tobacco and spices. The oak was not too prominent. Pascal thought this wine needed two or three years' keeping to show of its best, and it certainly seemed to hold out the most promise of the dry wines of his that I tasted.

His *moelleux* is called Cuvée Thibault after his young son. This is the wine by which he would like his vineyard to be known. He showed us the 1991 and 1990, both bottled at 14°. He thinks this wine is really typical of the appellation. He did not think the 1991 had more than ten years ahead of it, preferring his 1990, which was more honeyed. Curiously, and unlike most other local growers, Pascal says that 1988 was the best of the recent vintages, preferring it to both 1989 and 1990, which he said were '*trop flatteuses*'.

I was privileged to taste some of his private *cuvée*, which he has only just started to market and is called Sélection Petit Manseng. He only makes a few hundred bottles of this and then only in good years. Bottled at 15° with a lot of residual sugar still in it, it is obviously trying to emulate the Noblesse and Quintessence styles of Henri Ramonteu. For my taste this wine, or at least the 1989 which we tasted, was better than either, because the wood was less aggressive. Pascal thinks it could last a century. He explained that you need perfect conditions to make a wine of that kind. The weather has to be right throughout the autumn, the grapes have to be perfectly healthy and above all dry, and the mountain wind must have almost dehydrated them to the condition of currants. Exceptionally this wine is vinified in the new wood, where it stays for a further eighteen months.

Pascal Labasse thinks that the future of the Jurançon appellation lies in the petit manseng grape. He reminded me of the enthusiasm of Ducournau for the tannat, saying that there is too much competition in the dry white wine market for an area of small growers, if they are to earn a decent living from their properties. I put this point to Monsieur Vallin at the cave co-opérative, who vehemently disagreed. Once again there is an inherent conflict of viewpoint: the small private producers are selling to a quality-market, whereas the co-opérative's *raison d'être* is to find a market for wines made by non-specialists for whom the grape is only one of many crops. For the co-operator, the quick returns from crisp, dry wines are much more attractive than the potential of twice the money if you are prepared to wait for it. For this reason, Monsieur Vallin thought that the backbone of the Jurançon trade would continue to be the dry wines. He was quick to point out that dry wines represented 80% of the co-opérative's output; and that in some years, such as 1992, many producers had been able to produce nothing else. It happens that Pascal Labasse did: not just a sweet wine, but his wonderful Sélection Petit Manseng.

The yield from the tiny berries of the petit manseng is so small that many growers find it wasteful to blend it with wines from the higher-yielding varieties. An unblended petit manseng wine will fetch half as much again as an ordinary *moelleux*. Hence the tendency for producers to make two styles of sweet wine, one predominantly based on the gros manseng and the other, de luxe wine 100% petit manseng. Christian Lihour for example at **Domaine de Castéra (20)** does just this, his 1991 *moelleux* containing only 5% petit manseng and his *liquoreux* no gros at all. They are both absolutely typical of their styles and of excellent quality, the *liquoreux* in particular being especially rich, with tons of spicy fruit on the nose, and very long and complex.

Lihour, however, belongs to the no-new-wood school, and the wine-making is just as it always was in Father's day. In fact it was Father who welcomed us to this property, on the east side of the Monein valley, with its six hectares of vineyards beautifully exposed to the full strength of the early afternoon sunshine. Lihour Senior was busy mixing cement for the new bottle-store when we arrived, and explained how it was his grandfather who had bought the property at the depth of the phylloxera crisis in 1895. The gros manseng had, according to him, always been the traditional mainstream grape of the region, the petit manseng having been introduced as an ameliorator. He remembered that in the old days, both varieties were grown alongside one another, and would be harvested and vinified together. Nowadays the vineyard is 75% gros and 25% petit. They would like to grow more of the latter, but do not plan ever to have more than 10 hectares in all.

The wine is all vinified in concrete where it is left to mature for one year before bottling. The *sec* is wholly made from gros manseng, and even in a bad year like 1992 it manages to avoid excessive acidity and give generously of the typical honey and flowers bouquet of the appellation. Unlike some of the dry wines of this part of Jurançon, there was no suggestion of pear-drops. The 1991 won a gold medal in Paris.

Both the *vendange* and the marketing are essentially family affairs.

Lihour estimates that 70% of the wine is sold to private buyers, mostly in the region, a little goes to restaurants and the better kind of shops while as much as 20% is sold abroad, some to the UK.

Nearly half of all the private Jurançon producers are based on the town of Monein, and I have so far mentioned only a few. Others who consistently produce wines of top quality include the highly respected **Domaine Bru-Baché (10)**, on the outskirts of the town and on the road leading north to Mourenx. Georges Bru-Baché retired in 1994, handing over to his nephew Claude Loustalot. These wines regularly score high marks in the French guides such as Larousse and Hubert. The 1990 Cuvée des Castérasses *sec* is described in the one as 'deep, golden yellow, foreshadowing correctly a complex bouquet in which strong perfumes of wood mix with the aromas of citrus fruits. On the palate the bouquet is confirmed, with grapefruit and vanilla.' Hubert says of the same wine, 'The colour is golden, the nose spicy, creamy and well-developed. The flavour is full and rich, with a finish which is lively and aromatic.' Equally fine is the *moelleux*, which also goes under the name of Castérasses, and the 1990 is said to have hints of liquorice, to be rich without being heavy, and to have a text-book balance. This estate is outstanding, and the wines are frequently available in the United Kingdom. They are much admired by the musketeers of Pacherenc.

Further up the road in the small village of Lahourcade is the domaine of the Barrère family. Until his death a few years ago, Alfred Barrère was one of those who could truly be said to have kept Jurançon alive during the difficult years of the 1960s and 1970s. **Clos Cancaillaü (2)** was a byword for quality in the realm of the traditional sweeter wines, while he marketed through the *négociant* Etienne Brana, whom we shall meet presently in Irouléguy, a Jurançon *sec* under the name of Clos de la Vierge. Alfred's daughter Anne-Marie has taken over the reins at this respected estate, and now markets the dry wine herself. She maintains her father's traditions with respect, including an insistence on old wood rather than new. She is beginning to nod in the direction of newer styles of wine, and it may be an irony that the historical fame of the Barrère wines could be branding her with an 'old Jurançon' image. For example, another grower who would agree with most of what she is doing is Jean Lacoste, who maintains at **Domaine Nigri (16)** the old-fashioned style of Jurançon *sec*, forswearing both new wood and controlled temperatures during fermentation. But he succeeds in making a virtue of his conservatism.

SOUTHERN JURANÇON

Not all the good growers come from the two areas we have so far visited. No survey would be complete without the inclusion of at least some of the growers on the southern edge of the appellation. If you take the road south from Lasseube you will find signs off to the left to the **Clos Guirouilh (31)** which you reach by a few kilometres of winding lanes through very pretty countryside. The terrain here is much hillier than at Monein, and there is a real feeling of already being in the Pyrenees.

Monsieur Guirouilh would be recognisable anywhere as a farmer from the deep South-West, slightly balding under his rarely removed beret, and with a soft charm and welcoming smile. His farm used to include other crops and they raised cattle too. But even during the worst years of Jurançon they never gave up wine-making, because it was something the whole family could do and it was a crop which did not need outside labour. In those days, most of the vines were rather nasty hybrids and nothing special was made in the way of wines, although there are still a few pre-phylloxera ungrafted gros manseng. Monsieur Guirouilh agreed that these gave fine wine, but they were difficult to manage in poor years.

Today, Monsieur Guirouilh does nothing but make wine, and his vineyard covers 10 hectares. He likes to make a little red and rosé, and for this purpose he uses equal quantities of tannat and cabernet franc for both colours. The production of red is small, however, because it fluctuates in quality more widely from year to year than the white, and customers like a consistency which is not always possible.

For his dry white wine, Monsieur Guirouilh uses 90% gros manseng and 10% petit courbu. He is not in favour of *macération pelliculaire*: he thinks it produces a heavier wine, and he likes his *sec* to be light in style; he does not expect it to be rich and complex like a *moelleux*. So he makes it traditionally in stainless steel and when the fermentation is finished, it is racked and transferred to beautiful forty-year-old barrels, each containing between 20 and 30 hectolitres. He has seventeen of these, and the wine stays in them until twelve months after the vintage when it is bottled. Monsieur Guirouilh demonstrated some of the 1991, which had been in bottle for six months. The nose was very floral, and there was just a hint of honey among the various fruits on the palate, though the flavour was quite dry. I was so taken with this wine, delicate and light though it was when compared with some of the blockbusters enjoyed elsewhere, that I think it may well be the best dry Jurançon I have come across.

The Guirouilh *moelleux* is equally distinguished. It is made from roughly equal quantities of the two mansengs, the proportions varying slightly according to the character of the vintage. Some of the petit manseng is vinified and matured in new wood, but the remainder, together with all of the gros manseng, is made in stainless steel and then transferred to old wood. After eighteen months the wine is bottled. The *assemblage* is usually arranged so that about two-fifths of the petit manseng comes from the new barrels, and three-fifths from the old. It is then blended with the gros manseng, and the final wine is then bottled.

Monsieur Guirouilh confirmed to me his extreme caution with new wood. '*Le plus une femme est maquillée, le moins elle est jolie,*' that is to say, 'The more make-up a woman wears, the less pretty she is.'

Nevertheless this does not prevent him from making in good years a 100% petit manseng wine which is made and matured in new wood for eighteen months. I tasted both the 1990 and the 1991, and in neither case was the wood aggressive. There was just the extra touch of caramel and richness with the earlier year which was a much better vintage. He seemed to have got the knack of balancing the oak perfectly.

Jean Guirouilh told us that most of his neighbours were members of the co-opérative. Near him the only other private grower was Serge Hondet, who sadly was unable to confirm his appointment with me because it was the end of term at his daughter's school, and she had the lead in the school play. Not wishing to cause a family row I moved on instead to **Clos Mondinat (49)** some way away to the east, almost due south of Gan in a deeply rural valley in which this was the last farm. As I drove up to Mondinat, I could see the vines, planted *de haut en bas*, clinging to the stony mountainside, and wondered how ever it was possible to cultivate, let alone harvest the grapes from plants on such a slope. Monsieur Mondinat told me that, although he would dearly love to double the present vineyard of 3 hectares, his real priority was to terrace the existing vines. This seemed to me a Herculean task, but you could tell from the glint in his eye that the Mondinat family were determined one day to achieve it.

The three existing hectares are divided approximately in the proportion three to one between gros and petit manseng respectively, with just a little petit courbu. Only in a bad year like 1992 does he bother making any dry wine. He concentrates rather on a *moelleux* from the gros manseng and the petit courbu. The *vendange* is done at the end of October, usually with the help of friends and local farmers. Because he is not far off one of the main roads south into Spain, he has little difficulty selling most of his output at the door, though he has eager buyers among the locals and gîte-renting holiday-makers. The path to his cellar is made possible by Monsieur Hours' excellent signposts.

The old-fashioned vinification would cause a few eyebrows to go up at oenology schools. It is done entirely in huge old barrels where the wine is left on its lees for eighteen months before it is bottled. Needless to say there is no question of *macération pelliculaire* or temperaturecontrol. Given the primitive conditions, the 1990 and 1991 were very good, though one has to admit that modern technology can make life easier for the wine-maker.

Monsieur Mondinat then told me that all his petit manseng is reserved for an old-fashioned *liquoreux*, which is given what he called 'just a suggestion' of new wood. He said this almost apologetically, as if he had committed some awful sacrilege. We were about to taste this when his son burst into the Cave and whispered something hurriedly in his father's ear. They both left precipitately, and I was left wondering what to do next. A little way off there was a painful moo-ing sound, and soon Monsieur Mondinat returned a little worried-looking, but announced that we would now resume the tasting of his *liquoreux*. Almost immediately his son was back, and they both rushed out of the Cave once again. More moo-ing, which suddenly ceased and then the truth about what was going on suddenly dawned. Worried that some calamity had befallen either mother or calf, Jeanne and I packed up our note-books and camera and prepared for a suitably commiserating departure. But Alexis Mondinat returned, his face wreathed in smiles to announce that, although it had been a breach-birth, all was well. In the excitement he forgot to pour out his *liquoreux* to celebrate, and we took our leave without ever tasting it.

It was a fitting close to a tour of the Jurançon to visit a working farm, where wine was only one of the activities, and was being made in the way it must have been in the days before concrete vats, let alone stainless-steel ones were invented. While waiting for news from the cowshed, I had taken an opportunity to poke around in the wine-shed and to see bottles in their bins going back to 1964, 1943 and 1929, still unlabelled and covered in cobwebs which blew about slowly in the spring breeze. I noticed too the sulphur-candlesticks hanging from a beam in the company of an old pipette, and there was something very comforting about the rows of huge old barrels which must have seen some remarkable vintages in their times. It is probably wishful thinking to believe that Clos Mondinat will stay as it is: there is Alexis' son, who one day soon will be ready to take over the vineyard, terrace it as it ought to be, and to plant those 3 hectares of new ground with the treasured petit manseng; and there will be nowhere near enough room in the present *chais*.

The last ten years have seen a complete re-birth of Jurançon. Today's wine-makers have grasped the demand for a quality-product in this field, as public taste is beginning to discover that not all white wines need to be made from the sauvignon and chardonnay grapes. Pierre Latrille was right to identify the difficulty in the Jurançon of producing wines which compete in quality with the best from the New World and Australia at an equally competitive price. This difficulty is compounded in the short term by the difficult vintage of 1991 and the disastrous ones of 1992 and 1993. It is to be hoped that the growers will not make the mistake which Cahors did in 1974 and use the small yields of these two years as an excuse to jack up the prices of the wines; this seems unlikely in view of the large amount of wine sloshing round the Chartrons unsold. In a difficult trading period, the growers may be fortunate that such a large proportion of their market is on their doorstep. Local custom will probably prove more loyal than the international market, ever keen to switch from one fashionable novelty to another. As the world begins to emerge from recession, the outlook for Jurançon looks set fair in the long term, especially if 1995 proves to be the fine year it promises to be.

IROULÉGUY

Rising in the beechwood forests of Iraty high in the Pyrenees, the river Nive runs down a picture-book mountain valley to the pretty town of St Jean-Pied-de-Port on its way to Bayonne. Locally, the word port means pass, not port, and the pass in question is the Col D'Ibaneta, beyond which lay the former abbey of Roncevaux, famous in the middle ages and 3000 feet up in the Pyrenees. This was the easiest way over the mountains for the pilgrims going to St Jacques-de-Compostelle, so the Church took care to establish vineyards for an enormous passing trade.

We are now in the French Basque Country, part of the former Kingdom of Navarre, which once straddled the Pyrenees. The greater part of Navarre lay in what is now Spain, but it was partitioned between France and Spain at the time of the Treaty of the Pyrenees in 1659, when the mountain range became the effective border.

The vine seems to have been grown here since records were kept, and the monks of Roncevaux, precluded by the altitude at which their abbey stood, built two dependent priories down in the Nive valley, one at Irouléguy and the other in the neighbouring village of Anhaux. When partition split Roncevaux on the Spanish side from its satellites in France, the abbots ceded their vineyards to the local farmers. Today the same land yields wines which still rejoice in the extraordinary name Irouléguy.

As well as those of Roncevaux, other wines of the Nive created a reputation which spread to the best tables of Bayonne, the estates of the Vicomte d'Etchaberry being especially highly rated. By the end of the nineteenth century the vineyards had extended as far downstream as Itxassou and in 1906 they covered 470 hectares. Even by that year the phylloxera had not arrived this far south, but the mildew had, and 1907–9 inclusive were three disastrous vintages. Irouléguy went into steep decline and the *coup de grâce* in the form of the phylloxera struck in 1912.

The former vineyards reverted to pasture, the farmers pulling up their vines rather than replanting with new immune stock. The *vignoble* shrank to a nucleus of three villages: St Etienne-de-Baïgorry, Irouléguy and Anhaux.

A few makers of quality wines persevered between the two world wars, and they were the force behind the formation of a local *syndicat* in 1945 whose object was to secure both finance for the reconstitution of the vineyard, and an appellation contrôlée for Irouléguy. Their efforts were rewarded with partial success in 1952 when VDQS status was granted to the three main villages and for a total of 293 hectares. The immediate result was the creation of the co-opérative in the same year and the completion of its cellars and plant two years later.

The VDQS umbrella was extended to six communes in 1962, and the area covered by the modern AOC, established in 1970, now extends to three more.

At this stage the Cave was producing about 1500 hectolitres of wine each year, of which about one-third was rosé. The rest was red and there was no white. By 1976 production had topped 3000, and by 1990 4000 hectolitres.

In the bad old days before Appellation, the wines of Irouléguy, unless consumed locally, were sold off to the trade for blending. None would have been bottled at source. With the advent of the co-opérative and proper legal protection for the appellation, a greater interest was taken in the marketing, because the *raison d'être* of the co-opérative was to obtain the best possible prices for its members' wines. It was unfortunate that the first year in which the Cave bottled its own wines co-incided with the disastrous vintage of 1977 when only 301 hectolitres of wine were made. Nowadays all the wine is sold in bottle except for any which has to be de-classified under the rules of the appellation.

Until 1986, there were just two red wines and two rosés, the better grades being sold under the banner of the full title of the Cave, **Les Maîtres Vignerons d'Irouléguy**. The basic wines of the Cave are today sold under the names Gorri (meaning red) d'Ansa and Argi (meaning pink) d'Ansa. Ansa was the name of an old *petit pays* which included but was larger than the present AOC area.

The total extent of the vineyards is still very small, so visitors to the region have to look hard to find the vines, except on the slopes of the Arradoy mountain which dominates the village of Ispoure just north of St Jean. Only a few years ago there was only 1 hectare under vine in Ispoure; now there are 55.

The Irouléguy vineyards occupy two quite distinct types of soil, one a mixture of clay and chalk with alluvial deposits washed down from the mountains in pre-history; the other a red sandstone. The latter is porous but still manages to retain some humidity. It is poor stuff, so the vines planted in it take longer to mature, but are more consistent in quality year on year. Most of the vines are grown on steeply graded terraces, some of which rise to over a thousand feet above sea-level.

As in Jurançon, the vines are grown away from the ground, *en hautains* or *demi-hautains*, to protect the grapes from spring frosts. The grape-varieties are tannat and the two cabernets, the style of the wine depending on the relative percentages of the three grapes and the soil conditions of the vineyard. As might be expected, the higher the proportion of tannat, the tougher the wine and the better its ability to age.

The combination of the terrace-system and the high trailing of the vines makes for a low yield per hectare. The forty-nine members of the co-opérative have 136 hectares under vine (1993) of which 124 produced grapes then mature enough for wine-making. As with many other co-opératives, the bulk of the production is in the hands of relatively few growers, many having less than 1 hectare. At Irouléguy eighteen members make 80% of the crop. The enterprise produced 4345 hectolitres of wine in 1992, at a yield of 35 hectolitres to the hectare. The previous year was a disaster because of spring frosts and the yield was only just half the 1992 figure.

In a normal year about 45% of the production is rosé, a wine which is highly popular with the holiday-makers flocking to the Atlantic beaches not far away. The basic Argi d'Ansa, made from 70% cabernet and only 30% tannat, is vinified for twenty-four hours only and comes in a tall white bottle. The Cave also produces a superior pink wine called Les

Terrasses de l'Arradoy, the name of the mountain already mentioned. Half tannat and half cabernet, this wine is vinified at low temperatures and bottled during the month of March following the vintage. The bouquet of blackcurrant derives from the cabernet grapes, and the wine has fair length as well as freshness. It is bottled at a heady 12.5° alcohol and makes a siesta-inducing accompaniment to a picnic in the mountains on a hot day.

The red wine called Gorri d'Ansa was first produced in 1987 and is made from 60% tannat and 40% cabernet franc. It is very dark in colour with garnet highlights. There is plenty of ripe fruit on the nose, and the makers claim for the wine a perfume of violets with cinnamon. The grapes which go into it are all harvested by hand, because the terrain is not suitable for machines. The wine is said to be at its best after five years and, like all red Irouléguy, goes well with red meats, spicy dishes and cheese.

The co-opérative set up a pilot vineyard just outside St Etienne-de-Baïgorry as long ago as 1961 and called it Domaine de Mignaberry (which means 'old vines'). Today it covers some 25 hectares and is planted with 80% tannat and 20% cabernet franc. Until 1986 the wine from this property was blended, but since then it has been vinified separately. The grapes, though red, are picked in *tries*, as in Jurançon: this is to ensure that the fruit is as ripe as possible. The wine is like the Gorri d'Ansa, only more so, partly because it is given a slightly longer vinification. Its power, which comes from an alcoholic strength of 12.5° as well as the high content of tannat, is tempered by the six months or so which it spends in oak. One-third of the barrels are replaced each year, so the wood is relatively new. The wine is bottled during the late summer following the vintage. The Cave believes this to be its best wine. After four years, the 1989 was a ripe colour, but not yet browning; it was a bright deep ruby. There was some oaky vanilla on the nose and a clear suggestion of almonds as well as ripe fruit in the mouth. The finish was good, rather peppery with cinnamon and hints of other spices. Beside it the 1990 was still hard, but has developed well since.

A rather different style of wine is made from 9 hectares of land on the slopes of the Arradoy mountain, laid out on very steep terraces indeed, so all operations are carried out by hand. The harvest, as elsewhere in Irouléguy, is often carried out by people who have been working in hotels during the summer season and before they move on to the ski resorts in the mountains.

This vineyard, called Iturritze, is in single ownership, but the wine is made and matured at the co-opérative. The *encépagement* is one-third tannat and one-third each of the cabernets. The resulting wine is light in colour for an Irouléguy, and the bouquet has a distinct cabernet style, spicy and cedary. It spends six months in wood. This is a wine which will mature quicker than the Mignaberry, perhaps reaching its best three to five years after the vintage. Michel Berguignan, who has been president of the Cave since 1986, told me in 1993 that the 1990 was just approaching the 'maximum of its expression'.

More traditional in style is the last of the Cave's single-domaine wines, called Domaine Mendisokoä, meaning 'corner of the mountain'. Its 7 hectares are in the lee of the mountain called Iparla, whose peak is on the Spanish border. Mendisokoa made its début as recently as 1990, so it is early to judge it. Made from tannat (60%) and cabernet (40%), it is a big, chewy and well-structured wine, with aromas of truffle and farmyard as well as the vanilla reflecting six months in wood. Five years is the forecast for its peak.

The Cave recommends that its reds should be served at room temperature, and like all tannat-based wines should be uncorked at least two hours before they are served.

Until recently, all Irouléguy was either red or pink. The local *négociant* Etienne Brana bought the last barrel of white wine from the cooper at Irouléguy in 1957. In the pre-phylloxera days however, there was plenty of white wine made. As well as the two mansengs that we met in Jurançon and Vic-Bilh, and which are called in the extraordinarily bizarre language of the Basque Country *ichiriota churi*, the wine-makers also grew barroque, the mainstay of modern Tursan. With a tentative revival in the making of white wine, the barroque has not been revived, but the mansengs have staged a come-back. The co-opérative has experimented in making a dry wine from 60% gros and 40% petit manseng, the first vinification having taken place in 1991. Pale in colour when first made, it will darken to look like a lime-blossom tea. It has the characteristic bouquet of exotic fruits and flowers, which one would expect from the grape-varieties, but with citrus fruits (pear-drops) as well. The wine is bone-dry and with a long finish, but is not for keeping. It is to be enjoyed young when fresh. The wine is marketed under the name Xuri (meaning 'white') d'Ansa. The production is still tiny, all of it coming from one grower who has only 2 hectares.

Berguignan would like his members to plant some petit courbu to increase the production of white wine, which they are at present prevented from doing. Berguignan thinks this is unfair to smaller expanding vineyards which have a ready market for their wine: he says it doesn't matter much to Bordeaux which has a glut of unsold wine.

Until 1990 the co-opérative had competition from only one private grower, Peio Espil, who has a particularly handsome Basque family house in the centre of Irouléguy village itself. His front door opens directly into a huge ground-floor area which acts as a tasting-room. An old pony-trap furnishes one of the corners, and in former times the family used to sit thirteen down to meals at the vast refectory table. The property is called **Domaine Ilarria**, which means 'Domaine des Landes', and it has but 6 hectares of vines, some of which are on the site of the old priory built by the monks of Roncevaux. Three hectares are in production, including some plants more than seventy years old, and three are planted with new vines, from which Espil is making some rosé.

Ilarria has been in his family for hundreds of years, and they have all been devoted to Basque tradition, still speaking the language *en famille*.

They have some very old vintages tucked away and are proud of the longevity of Irouléguy wines. Monsieur Espil told me that some centenarian bottles were found in the cellar of President Poincaré after his death.

The Ilarria vineyards are planted with 50% tannat and 50% cabernet franc, with some cabernet sauvignon mixed in. Monsieur Espil prefers to plant his vines in vertical rows, *de haut-en-bas*, rather than in terraces. He says that the planting of terraces disturbs the ground too much.

Espil makes two red wines, one from 80% tannat, the other from 100% tannat. The latter is called Cuvée Bixintzo, the Basque name for St Vincent, the patron saint of Irouléguy. As might be expected from their make-up the wines are tough and unyielding when young, and Espil does not believe in compromising with short maceration periods in the vinification. He gives the tannat fifteen days and the cabernets twenty. The wine is made in concrete vats and, after six months, is transferred to wood, some new, some old, where it stays for eighteen months. The resulting wines take four years to throw off the purple colour of their youth, remaining dark and dense as they age, with layers of fruit and a long finish.

With his small production, Monsieur Espil does his own marketing, his red wines being taken up by the best restaurants specialising in the food of the South-West. Espil says he would like to plant some petit manseng when he is allowed to do so: he is not the first, nor the last grower in the far South-West to be aware of the growing market for sweeter white wines.

Perhaps Irouléguy is in the course of emulating Madiran: as the reputation of the wine increases, so individual growers seem prepared to launch out on their own independently of the co-opérative. Pierre Espil himself predicts this and even now he is no longer the sole private producer. Jean-Claude Errecart has left the co-opérative and is making wine on his own from his 9 hectares at **Domaine Abotia** in the lee of the Arradoz mountain. With only 30% tannat and a short *cuvaison* of 8–10 days, his wine is intended for early drinking, but he has a substantial investment in plant to recoup.

Closer to the Espil style is Michel Riouspeyrous who lives just opposite him in the village of Irouléguy itself. The property is called **Domaine Arretxea** and there is much more tannat than at Abotia. There is a pink wine from at least 70% tannat, as well as two reds, one given a liberal oaking and called Cuvé Haitza after the Basque word for oak tree. *Cuvaisons* are short at the moment but Michel may lengthen them to extract more from the fruit. He is a promising 'green' grower, who takes as much care of his home-grown compost as he does of the vines.

Another newcomer I was told about is called Hillau, and he is based at St-Etienne-de-Baïgorry, but he only started in 1994, so it is too soon to judge his efforts. Finally, there is Jean-Claude Berrouet, the wine-maker from Pétrus, who has just bought a parcel in the district. The Basque vineyards are already familiar territory to him from the days when he helped the Brana family set up their own vineyards **Domaine Brana** at Ispoure just behind St Jean.

The Branas first set up in business as négociants at Ustaritz in 1897. They moved to St Jean-Pied-de-Port in 1920. When his father died, Etienne Brana was faced with the choice of progressing his ambitions to play the saxophone in the army band, or of taking over the family business, and the art of music was the loser. In 1974 he created a distillery for the making of eaux-de-vie from pears, plums, raspberries and marc. The pears came from his own orchards which he had planted at St Jean. He claimed his pears had a very particular individuality due entirely to the *terroir*. His eaux-de-vie became and remain famous worldwide, and are ranked by gourmets as among the best in France.

But Etienne Brana had one more ambition, and that was to plant his own vineyards at Irouléguy: it became an obsession which took feverish hold on both him and his son Jean. In 1983 they bought a few hectares on the slopes of the Pic d'Arradoy, a holding which they have since expanded to its present 20 hectares. The gradient of the terraces on which these vines have been planted is no less than 65%. Excavations of 200 metres of soil separate the lowest from the highest vine-rows, and this land had to be reclaimed metre by metre from the scrub and undergrowth which was strangling it. The Branas needed more than an obsession to overcome that sort of difficulty. They needed a purpose-built caterpillar tractor made to work the slopes, and to build terraces like the Swiss had done many years before in the canton of Valais. Jean's father, Etienne, went to Switzerland to study their techniques of growing grapes in vertical conditions, and also to Marcillac in the Rouergue where vines are grown in terraces, as we have seen.

Given the idealism of the enterprise, the site for this dream-vineyard was perfect. Facing south and south-west, with some of the vines at a height of over 500 metres above sea-level, the grapes receive every bit of sunshine there is, each one being as it were in the front row of the dress circle, with uninterrupted views of the mountains. Their health is assured by the warm winds which blow from Spain at vintage-time, dispersing the fogs of autumn and preventing the development of rot. The ultimate proof of the Branas' dedication lies in the minuscule yields which such a vineyard can achieve; 12 hectolitres to the hectare is said to be the average. One is reminded of Château Yquem where it is said that the fruit of a whole vine is needed to make one glass of wine. The economics of such an exercise mean inevitably that the wine produced is always going to be expensive, the sort of wine which the finest Gascon chefs in Paris will want to have on their list for their most demanding patrons.

Etienne Brana was assisted devotedly by Jean, who had put in two years working at Château Pétrus in Pomerol: it is hardly possible to think in terms of higher standards than that, and Jean was fortunate in the encouragement and practical advice which he received from Berrouet.

To round off this pioneering enterprise, the Branas have constructed the most magnificent cellars at the vineyard, part of them built underground into the mountain-side. They were designed by the same architects who had built the Palladian-style winery for Michel Guérard at his Château de Bachen near Eugénie-les-Bains in the Tursan. Above the doors the stone-work carries an inscription, reminiscent in its exotic Basque lettering of the inscriptions on the palace-tombs at Petra. It translates as 'Taste some of this good wine and you will have a good life.' There is space inside to make and store wine from a further 8 hectares of vineyard which have already been planted but have not yet matured.

But what of the wines themselves? Planting of the vines started in 1985, so that some wines were made, perhaps a little early, in 1989. The vineyard is roughly two parts red to one part white. The red wines come from cabernet franc (40%), cabernet sauvignon (30%) and tannat (30%). They grow in both the kinds of soil described above and are planted in the order of their ripening, that is to say the cabernet franc at the top, then the cabernet sauvignon, and, on lower ground, the tannat which is always the last of the red grapes to ripen. All vineyard operations are carried out by hand, needless to say. The *cuvaison* of the red wine varies from between ten and fifteen days. The wine is matured in old wood for twelve months before bottling in the spring two years after the vintage. The barrels come from Château Beau Séjour-Bécot in St Emilion.

Brana explains the relatively low tannat content of his wine by saying that traditionally Irouléguy was made up of the two cabernets and that tannat is a relative newcomer to the area. Espil disagrees and offered to show me some tannat vines belonging to a neighbour of his which he said were well over one hundred years old.

The Brana red is a deep ruby colour, absolutely clear and bright, a credit to the quality of the wine-making. The nose is dominated by red fruits and cassis and is both powerful and complex. On the palate, there are all the right tannins, 'those which ensure some fat but also suppleness to the wine,' as Martine, Jean Brana's sister, points out. The cabernet grapes ensure elegance and finesse, as well as a long finish. There is a second wine from the younger vines called Harri Gorri, which has all the Brana hallmarks of quality.

The white wine is no less remarkable than the red, though perhaps it astonishes less because of the proximity of so much Jurançon. There is only one wine and it is completely dry, deriving from gros manseng (30%) and, interestingly enough, petit courbu (70%). As at Jurançon the grapes are gone over by the pickers several times to ensure that only the ripest go into the presses. Brana allows skin-contact with the juices to give more perfume to the wine. Fermentation is temperature-controlled by the most modern methods and is stopped by refrigeration. The wine is neither racked nor fined, and is bottled on its lees during the spring after the vintage. In a year like 1992, when the harvesting was done in the rain throughout, the wine was allowed a malolactic fermentation in February to help counteract the high acidity.

The colour is surprisingly golden for a dry wine. The bouquet shows more than a hint of citrus-fruit and wild flowers, also some gun-flint and vanilla. On the palate the flavour is big with some fat, excellent overall balance and the finish is long and elegant. Jean Brana recommends that this wine be drunk at the surprisingly high temperature of 13–15°.

It is very sad that Etienne Brana died in the spring of 1992 at the early age of fifty-five. At least he lived to see the realisation of his dream, a folly comparable in its audacity with the opera house at Bayreuth. Jean and Martine continue with the good work, under the eye of their experienced mother, and the enterprise could not be in better hands. Jean had been undecided whether he wanted to enter into the family business before the vineyard had been created. He was not so attracted by the *négociant* and distilling trades. It was his time spent with Coste at Bordeaux which inspired him to want to make wine, and perhaps it was this ambition which finally brought about the planting of vines at Ispoure in partnership with his father.

It is interesting to compare the Espil and Brana wines. Espil gives the impression of growing his grapes and making his wines out of pure love. Perhaps he is not under the same commercial compulsion as the Branas who have recently invested enormous sums in their experiment. The Branas' wines will be ready to drink earlier, as a rule, than Espil's, but many wine-lovers will not be sad about that. Espil's are less compromising and more rustic, the Branas' more sophisticated and supple in style. All Irouléguy, however, is tough and sturdy, intended to accompany the spicy country dishes of the Basque Country, such as the salmis which they make from the pigeons called *palombes* which are slaughtered in droves when their migration seems to take them straight to the barrels of Basque guns; or the dishes of diced veal or lamb, spiced with the local hot red peppers.

Irouléguy has not yet caught up with Madiran, but the style of the wines are not dissimilar, nor is the enthusiasm of its wine-makers any less infectious.

PRODUCERS

BÉARN AOC WINES

1. CAVE CO-OPÉRATIVE , Bellocq, 64270 Salies-de-Béarn
    Tel: 59-65-10-71
2. GAEC Lapeyre, **Domaine de Guilhémas**, Salies-de-Béarn Tel: 59-38-10-02
3. Richard Ziemek-Chigé, **Clos Mirabel**, 64110 La Chapelle-de-Rousse,
    Jurançon Tel: 59-21-74-41

Caves Co-opératives at Crouseilles and Castelnau-Rivière-Basse (Madiran) and
Gan (Jurançon) q.v. Also private growers at Madiran, including Château
Bouscassé, Château Laffitte-Teston and Domaines Laplace, Domaine de
Diusse, Domaine de Crampilh, Château de Perron, Domaine Sergent,
Château Arricau-Bordes and Domaine de Maouries (all Madiran, q.v.).

JURANÇON

A. *CAVE DES PRODUCTEURS DE JURANÇON, 53 Avenue Henri IV,
    64290 Gan. Tel; 59-21-57-03

38. Rose Bascougnet, 64110 St Faust   Tel:59-83-07-18
22.. Giselle Bordenave-Montesquiu, **Clos Bayard**, 64360 Monein.
    Tel: 59-21-31-36
47. Alexis Bazaillacq, **Domaine Bazaillacq**, La Chapelle-de-Rousse,
    64110 Jurançon Tel:59-83-06-30
15. *Pascal Labasse, **Domaine Bellegarde**, 64360 Monein Tel:59-21-33-17
27. Jean Muchada, **Clos Bellevue**, 64360 Cucqueron Tel:59-21-34-82
21. *Pierre Bordenave, **Domaine Bordenave**, 64360 Monein Tel:59-21-34-83
19. Gérard Bordenave-Montesquieu, Quartier Ucha, 64360 Monein.
    Tel: 59-21-43-49
33. André Peyroutet, **Domaine Bory**, 64290 Aubertin Tel:59-82-70-11
36. Jean Bousquet, **Domaine Bousquet**, 64110 St Faust. Tel: 59-83-05-56
10. *Claude Loustalot, **Domaine Bru-Baché**, 64360 Monein, Tel: 59-33-36-34
37. Henri Burgué, **Domaine Burgué-Bats-Louran**, 64110 St Faust.
    Tel: 59-83-05-91
39. Jean Séré, **Domaine Burgué-Séré**, 64110 St Faust Tel:59-83-06-40
30. Patrice Limousin, **Domaine de Cabarrouy**, 64290 Lasseube.
    Tel: 59-04-23-08
24 *Henri Cambot, Quartier Laquidée, 64360 Monein Tel:59-21-42-50*
14. *Casimir et Didier Capdevielle, **Domaine Capdevielle**, 64360 Monein
    Tel:59-21-30-25
20. *Christian Lihour, **Domaine de Castéra**, 64360 Monein Tel:59-21-34-98
17. Alain Labourdette, **Clos Castet**, 64360 Cardesse Tel:59-21-33-09
4. *Henri Ramonteu, **Domaine Cauhapé**, 64360 Monein Tel:59-21-33-02
35. *Pierre Saubot, **Domaine du Cinquau**, 64230 Artiguelouve.
    Tel. 59-83-10-41
32. Isabelle Bordenave-Coustarret, **Domaine Coustarret**, 64290 Lasseube.
    Tel: 59-21-72-66
13. Marie-Jeanne Hours, **Cru Crouzeilles**, 64360 Monein Tel:59-21-40-76
23. *Francis Gaillot, **Domaine Gaillot**, 64360 Monein Tel:59-21-31-69
5. Henri Laborde-Ganadé, **Domaine Ganadé**, Route de Pau, 64360 Monein
    Tel: 59-21-31-67
29. Jeanine Tavernier, **Clos Gassiot**, 64360 Abos Tel:59-60-10-22

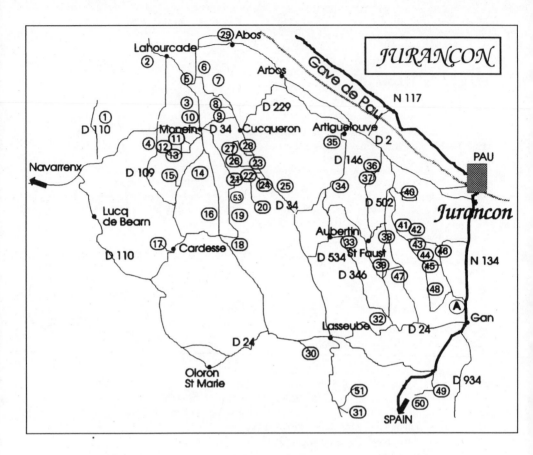

9. Jean Guirardel-Cazaubeilh, **Domaine Guirardel**, 64360 Monein.
   Tel: 59-21-31-48 (formerly **Clos Prat**)
31. *Jean Guirouilh, **Clos Guirouilh**, 64290 Lasseube Tel:59-04-21-45
51. Serge Hondet, Quartier Rey, 64290 Lasseube. Tel:59-04-22-95
50. Jean Cours- Husté, **Clos Husté**, 64290 Gan Tel:59-21-75-52
48. *Pierre-Yves Latrille, **Château Jolys**, La Chapelle-de-Rousse,
   64110 Jurançon Tel:59-21-72-79
41. *Michèle Pissondes, **Domaine Labrée**, La Chapelle-de-Rousse, 64110
   Jurançon. Tel. 59-21-74-45
28. Francis Riuné, **Clos Lacabe**, 64360 Cucqueron Tel:59-21-30-92
52. *Richard Ziemek-Chigé, **Clos Lamouroux**, La Chapelle-de-Rousse,
   64110 Jurançon Tel:59-21-74-41
42. *Jean-Bernard Larrieu, **Clos Lapeyre**, La Chapelle-de-Rousse, 64110
   Jurançon. Tel: 59-21-50-80
43. *Jean-Marc Grussaute, **Domaine Larredya**, La Chapelle-de-Rousse,
   64110 Jurancon Tel:59-21-74-42
 1. Jean Estoueigt, **Domaine Larroudé**, 64360 Lucq-de-Béarn.
   Tel: 59-34-35-92
18. Gaston Mansanné, **Domaine de Malarrode**, 64360 Monein.
   Tel: 59-21-44-27
49. *Alexis Mondinat, **Domaine Mondinat**, 64290 Gan Tel:59-21-71-53
53. Jacques Balent, **Domaine de Montesquiou**, 64360 Monein.
   Tel: 59-21-49-44

7   *Alfred Moussou, Quartier Loupien, 64360 Monein Tel:59-21-31-76*

45. *Philippe de Nays, **Domaine de Nays-Labassère**, La Chapelle-de-Rousse, 64110 Jurançon Tel:59-21-70-57

16. *Jean Lacoste-Nigri, **Domaine Nigri**, 64360 Monein Tel:59-21-42-01

8. *Albert Nomboly, **Domaine Nomboly-Traydou**, 64360 Monein. Tel: 59-21-35-98

26. Patrick Peyrette, **Domaine Peyrette**, 64360 Cucqueron Tel:59-21-31-10

11. Alfred Hours, **Domaine Peyrette-Lasserre**, 64360 Monein. Tel: 59-21-48-65

3. Annie Peyroutet, **Clos Orgambide**, 64360 Monein Tel:59-21-42-99

34. Pierre Bascourret, **Domaine Reyau**, 64290 Aubertin, Tel: 59-82-70-18

25. Jean-Louis Ricarde, **Domaine Ricarde**, 64360 Monein Tel:59-21-30-47

44. *Joseph Labat, **Château de Rousse**, La Chapelle-de-Rousse, 64110 Jurançon Tel:59-21-75-08

40. *Yvonne et J.R. Hégoboru, **Domaine de Souche**, 64110 Laroin. Tel: 59-06-27-22

46. *Henri Lapouble, **Clos Thou**, La Chapelle-de-Rousse, 64110 Jurançon. Tel: 59-06-08-60

12. *Charles Hours, **Clos Uroulat**, 64360 Monein Tel:59-21-46-19

2. *Anne-Marie Barrère, **Clos de la Vierge**, Lahourcade, 64150 Mourenx. Tel: 59-60-08-15

6. Vincent Labasse, **Domaine Vincent Labasse**, 64360 Monein. Tel: 59-21-31-02.

IROULÉGUY

1. LES MAÎTRES VIGNERONS D'IROULÉGUY, 64430 St Etiennes-de-Baïgorry Tel: 59-37-41-33

2. Peio (Pierre) Espil, **Domaine Ilarria**, 64220 Irouléguy Tel: 59-37-41-33

3. Jean et Martine Brana, **Domaine Brana**, 64220 St Jean-Pied-de-Port Tel: 59-37-00-44. Shop at 6 rue de l'Eglise Tel:59-37-25-97

4. Jean-Claude Errecart, **Domaine Abotia**, 64220 Ispoure Tel: 59-37-03-99

5. Michel Riouspeyrous,**Domaine Arretxea**, 64220 Irouléguy Tel: 59-37-33-67

6. M. Hillau, 64430 St Etienne-de-Baïgorry Tel:59-37-23-76

After-taste

A recurring refrain from growers is the problem which they face from three difficult vintages in a row. Many areas were badly hit by frosts in the spring of 1991, and, although these were not nearly so serious as the catastrophic freeze in April 1956, they were enough to reduce the crop drastically, because the poor summer weather did not encourage enough new growth in the plants.

1992 was a horribly wet vintage, which followed a dismal summer. Most areas made a lot of wine, but, compared with the wonderful run of years ending in 1990, the quality of the harvest was mediocre. 1993 was an equally dim year though marginally less wet at vintage-time, noticeably less so in Gascony and the Pyrenees. 1994 was better, but that is not saying much and is nothing to write home about.

These problems are not peculiar to the South-West, but the local growers, unlike those in Bordeaux, do not have stocks from earlier years on which they can rely for cash-flow. Furthermore they are now in a position where, for a few years, they will have only wines from off-vintages to sell. With a glut of Bordeaux wine which it will take some years to clear, the country growers of the South-West may have to sell off their wines at sacrificial prices in order to survive. The 1995 vintage, which promises so well in most of the area, may have come just in time to save money.

Even so, I have been particularly struck by the improvement in standards of wine-making which have enabled skilful growers to make good wines in vintages which, twenty years ago, would have been written off. The principal problem in the short term is for producers to turn their produce into cash. For this they need to consolidate their hold on their local customers, but, perhaps more importantly, to establish a wider market-base for their wine. Although there is a fashion for the wines of

Madiran and Jurançon, where total production is still small enough to ensure a quick turnover, Gaillac, Fronton, Bergerac and the smaller vineyards of Aquitaine need sales in Paris, the North and West of France and overseas to sustain production and enable further growth. It is no longer enough for wine-makers to rely exclusively on their local markets. *Les grandes surfaces* are stocked with wines from all over France, and sometimes, *horribile dictu*, Australia and California, which can vie in terms of quality and price with the local product. The South-West needs a strategy to equal the quality of the best imports at a price which will be competitive with other French wines.

I believe that, first and foremost, wine-makers must guard the originality, the *typicité* of their own product. If a wine is to sell as Gaillac, it should be identifiable as such. There are plenty of wines on the market which are agreeable, but relatively few whose origin can be tasted in the glass. Growers will fail to sell wines as, say, Gaillac or Duras, if they taste like petits Bordeaux, because Bordeaux can make and sell them more cheaply, usually better and under a name which requires no promotion. I believe that this explains the success of many of the younger wine-makers, who are determined to stake their future on the *goût du terroir*, their local grape-varieties and traditional methods of vinification. It is also the reason why I believe that the Cave at Rabastens for example is short-sighted in encouraging growers to replace their traditional mauzac and len de l'el grapes with sauvignon.

Secondly, producers need to be wary about the seduction of new oak, another factor which, in all except the finest wines intended for long maturing and keeping, can smother the individuality of the wine. There is a place for these techniques in Cahors and Madiran, as producers like Brumont have clearly demonstrated. Even, though perhaps more controversially, the wines of Jurançon have sufficient weight and concentration to benefit from this treatment. But the wiser of the wine-makers in Fronton accept and even make a virtue of the fresh fruitiness of their wines which would be destroyed by the use of new wood. It would be no bad principle for growers to presume that new wood is unsuitable unless proved by experiment to the contrary.

The third temptation is to turn investment round faster by shortening the period of maturation and *élevage* of the wines. Growers who understand their *terroir* and their grape-varieties will know how far they can go in this respect. If the cornerstone of policy is to be the integrity of the appellation, it follows that it is a nonsense to try and produce a *primeur* in Cahors; also that the distinctive grape-varieties, such as n´grette in Fronton, auxerrois in Cahors or tannat in Madiran should in future be required to form a larger rather than smaller part of the *vignoble*. Longer ageing implies a greater investment by the grower and thus higher prices to the consumer, but the wines of the South-West are good enough to face that challenge, and they are too good to allow themselves to be engulfed by the international tide of anodine and characterless wine. The rebirth of the vineyards of the South-West came about because of the demand for middle-range wines which were more affordable than the best of Bordeaux, but better than the average product available off the shelf of supermarkets. To ensure that they do not fall into the wine-lake, growers will need to apply the highest standards and avoid the short cuts.

The Grape-Varieties of South-West France

Each grape is a principal or sole variety in the wines shown in capital letters: otherwise the grape is a supporting variety. Grapes in italics are dying out.

ABOURIOU: COTES DU MARMANDAIS, vdp St Sardos

ALICANTE: vdp Agenais

ARRILOBA: vdp Côteaux de Chalosse

ARRUFIAC: PACHERENC DU VIC-BILH, COTES ST MONT, vdp Côtes de Gascogne, BEARN

AUXERROIS: CAHORS, vdp COTEAUX DE QUERCY, vdp THEZAC- PERRICARD, Gorges de Millau, Fronton, Bergerac, Pécharmant, Côtes de Duras, Côtes du Marmandais, Côtes du Brulhois, Floc de Gascogne

BARROQUE: TURSAN, Floc de Gascogne

BOUCHALES: vdp Agenais

CABERNET FRANC: Entraygues, ESTAING, Gorges de Millau, Gaillac, BERGERAC, PECHARMANT, COTES DE DURAS, COTES DU MARMANDAIS, COTES DE BUZET, COTES DU BRULHOIS, Fronton, LAVILLEDIEU-DU-TEMPLE, vdp. COTEAUX ET TERRASSES DE MONTAUBAN, vdp ST SARDOS, TURSAN, vdp COTEAUX DE CHALOSSE, BEARN, Madiran, Irouléguy.

CABERNET SAUVIGNON: Entraygues, ESTAING, Gaillac, BERGERAC, PECHARMANT, COTES DE DURAS, COTES DU MARMANDAIS, COTES DE BUZET, COTES DU BRULHOIS, Floc de Gascogne, COTES ST MONT, Tursan, Béarn, Madiran, Fronton

CAMARALET: Jurançon
CHENIN BLANC: ENTRAYGUES, ESTAING, GORGES DE MILLAU
COLOMBARD: vdp COTES DE GASCOGNE, FLOC
COT (see Auxerrois)
COURBU, NOIR: Béarn
COURBU, PETIT: Pacherenc du Vic-Bilh, Jurançon, IROULEGUY
DURAS: GAILLAC, Gorges de Millau
EGIODOLA: Floc de Gascogne, vdp Côteaux de Chalosse
FER (FER
   SERVADOU):   MARCILLAC, ENTRAYGUES, GAILLAC, Côtes du
                      Brulhois, BEARN, Côtes St Mont, Madiran, vdp Agenais
FOLLE
   BLANCHE: vdp Côtes de Gascogne, FLOC DE GASCOGNE
GAMAY: Entraygues, GAILLAC, GORGES DE MILLAU,
                      COTEAUX DE GLANES, Fronton, LAVILLEDIEU-
                      DU-TEMPLE, vdp Côteaux et Terrasses de Montauban,
                      vdp St Sardos, Floc de Gascogne
GAMAY ST LAURENT (see Abouriou)
JURANCON A
   JUS BLANC: vdp Côteaux et Terrasses de Montauban
JURANCON
   NOIR: vdp COTES DU TARN, vdp Agenais, vdp Coteaux de
                      Quercy
LAUZET: Juranson
LEN DE L'EL: GAILLAC
LISTAN: vdp Côtes de Gascogne
MALBEC (see Auxerrois)
MANSENG, GROS: vdp Côtes de Gascogne, Floc de Gascogne, COTES ST
                      MONT, Tursan, Pacherenc-du-Vic-Bilh, JURANCON,
                      Irouléguy
MANSENG, NOIR: Béarn
MANSENG, PETIT: COTES ST MONT, PACHERENC DU VIC-BILH,
                      JURANCON
MANSOIS (see Fer)
MAUZAC: GAILLAC, Estaing, Gorges de Millau, vdp Comté
                      Tolosan
MÉRILLE: Fronton, vdp Agenais, vdp Comté Tolosan.
MERLOT: Cahors, Gaillac, vdp Thézac-Perricard, Estaing, vdp
                      Côteaux et Terrasses de Montauban, BERGERAC,
                      PECHARMANT, COTES DE DURAS, COTES DU
                      MARMANDAIS, COTES DE BUZET, COTES DU
                      BRULHOIS, Côteaux de Glanes
MUSCADELLE: Bergerac, Monbazillac, Saussignac, Rosette, Montravel,
                      Gaillac, Côtes de Duras,
MOUSTROUN (see Tannat)
NEGRET DE
   BANHARS   Estaing
NEGRETTE: Estaing (?), FRONTON, Lavilledieu-le-Temple
ONDENC: Gaillac
PINENC (see Fer)
PINOTOUS
   D'ESTAING: ESTAING

RAFFIAT DE MONCADE (see Arrufiac)

ROUSSELET DE BÉARN:	BEARN
SAUVIGNON:	Gaillac, BERGERAC, Monbazillac, Saussignac, MONTRAVEL, COTES DE DURAS, COTES DU MARMANDAIS, COTES DE BUZET, Floc de Gascogne, Tursan, Pacherenc-Vic-Bilh
SÉGALIN:	Côteaux de Glanes
SÉMILLON:	Gaillac, BERGERAC, MONBAZILLAC, SAUSSIGNAC, ROSETTE, MONTRAVEL, COTES DE DURAS, Côtes de Buzet, Floc de Gascogne
SYRAH:	GORGES DE MILLAU, GAILLAC, Fronton, LAVILLEDIEU-DU-TEMPLE, vdp COTEAUX ET TERRASSES DE MONTAUBAN, vdp ST SARDOS
TANNAT:	Cahors, Gorges de Millau, Lavilledieu-du-Temple, vdp COTEAUX ET TERRASSES DE MONTAUBAN, vdp ST SARDOS, Floc de Gascogne, COTES ST MONT, Tursan, vdp COTEAUX DE CHALOSSE, MADIRAN, BEARN, IROULEGUY
UGNI BLANC:	COTES DE GASCOGNE, FLOC DE GASCOGNE

Wine and food pairing chart (fill level of glass indicates suitability: full = highly recommended, half = suitable, empty = not recommended).

Wine	Shellfish, other fish grilled or fried	Fish with sauce	Garbures, potées, pot-au-feu, etc.	Foie gras	Charcuterie	Salades composées	Mushroom dishes	Entrées, light poultry and veal dishes	Offal, poultry – roast or in heavier sauces
Dry white (1) — Entraygues, Estaing, Millau, Gaillac, Landes, Côtes de Gascognes, Mousseux Brut	full	full	empty	half	full	half	empty	empty	empty
Dry white (2) — Bergerac, Montravel, Duras, Marmande, Buzet, Brulhois, St Mont, Tursan	full	full	empty	empty	full	full	empty	empty	empty
Dry white (3) — Pacherenc, Jurançon sec, Irouléguy	full	full	empty	half	half	full	empty	empty	empty
Medium white — Bergerac, Moelleux, Rosette, Côtes de Montravel, Gaillac Moelleux, Gaillac Mousseux demi-sec	empty	full	empty	full	half	half	half	full	empty
Sweet white (1) — Gaillac doux, Saussignac, Haut-Montravel, Pacherenc doux	empty	empty	empty	full	empty	empty	empty	half	empty
Sweet white (2) — Monbazillac, Jurançon, all *vendanges tardives*, Gaillac Mousseux doux	empty	empty	empty	full	half	empty	empty	empty	empty
Vins rosés	empty	empty	half	full	full	half	empty	full	half
Red (1) — Fronton, Tursan, Gaillac, Primeur	empty	empty	full	half	full	full	full	half	full
Red (2) — Marcillac, Estaing, Entraygues, Millau, Marmande, Brulhois, Landes, *Vin de pays*	empty	empty	full	half	full	full	full	full	full
Red (3) — Gaillac, Bergerac, Duras, St Mont, Béarn	empty	empty	full	half	full	empty	full	full	full
Red (4) — Buzet, Cahors, Pecharmant	empty	empty	half	empty	full	empty	half	full	full
Red (5) — Madiran, Irouléguy	empty	empty	half	empty	half	empty	half	half	full

Column headers (foods):
- Cassoulet
- Grilled and roast meats, confits magret
- Daubes, salmis, game
- Soft white cheese from cows' milk
- Hard., blue or goats' milk cheeses
- Roquefort and hard ewes' milk cheeses
- Fresh fruit and fruit-based desserts
- Sweeter desserts and patisseries

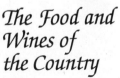

The Food and Wines of the Country

The South-West has its own complete repertoire of cookery, as well as its all-embracing range of wines. This table may help those who are unfamiliar with the food or the wines of the region, or both, to marry the two to the best advantage.

The table concerns itself only with combinations and not with the merits of either the wines or particular foods on their own. There are four grades:

 denotes an ideal marriage

 a good one

🍷 a possible one

🍷 a bad one

Bon appétit!

Bibliography

French Titles

JOSE BAUDEL. *Le Vin de Cahors*. (Les Producteurs des Côtes d'Olt.) 2nd edition 1977. Parnac.

MELLE BAYNAC. *La Crise Phylloxérique et ses conséquences dans le Canton de Luzech*. 1884.

PIERRE CAPDEVILLE. *Le vin de Cahors des Origines à Nos Jours*. (Editions Milan.) 1983. Toulouse.

PIERRE CASAMAYOR. *Vins du Sud-Ouest et des Pyrénées*. (Editions Daniel Briand/Robert Laffont.) 1983. Toulouse.

HENRI DUFOR. *Armagnac, Eaux-de-vie et Terroir*. (Editions Privat.) 1982. Toulouse.

ADRIEN ESCUDIER. *Histoire de Fronton et du Frontonnais*. (APAMP.) 1992. Toulouse.

EDOUARD FERET. *Bergerac et ses vins*. 1903. Paris. Nouvelle édition 1994.

BERNARD GINESTET & JEAN-PIERRE DEROUDILLE. *Bergerac/Monbazillac*. (Jacques Legrand.) 1987. Paris.

PIERRE GOMBERT. *Le Vallon de Marcillac*. (Editions B. J. Photo.) 1990. Rodez.

DR JULES GUYOT. *Rapport sur la viticulture comparée du Sud-Ouest de la France*. 1863.

A. JULLIEN. *Topographie de tous les vignobles connus*. 1816.

ALEXIS MONTEIL. *Description du Departement de l'Aveiron*. (Editions Pour Le Pays d'Oc.) 1802 Rodez.

PHILIPPE SEGUIER. *Le Vignoble de Gaillac*. (Editions Daniel Brand.) 1991. Toulouse.

VARIOUS CONTRIBUTORS. *Le Vin de Bordeaux et du Haut-Pays*. (Editions Montalba.) 1977.

English Titles

MICHAEL AND SYBIL BROWN. *Food and Wine of South-West France*. (B. T. Batsford.) 1980. London.

ROSEMARY GEORGE. *French Country Wines*. (Faber & Faber.) 1990. London.

HUGH JOHNSON AND HUBRECHT DUIJKER. *The Wine Atlas of France*. (Mitchell Beazley.) Revised reprint 1989. London.

EDMUND PENNING-ROWSELL. *The Wines of Bordeaux*. (Penguin.) 4th edition 1979. London.

JANCIS ROBINSON. *Vines, Grapes and Wines*. (Mitchell Beazley.) 1986. London.

P. MORTON SHAND. *A Book of French Wines*. (Jonathan Cape.) 1960 edition. Also 1964 edition revised by Cyril Ray. London.

Glossary

The following terms appear in the text, and are here translated or defined in case their meaning is not clear.

appellation contrôlée (AOC) a statutory, legally controlled area of élite wine-production.

argileux clayey, consisting of clay.

assemblage the creative blending of wine from different barrels by the same wine-maker.

ban de vendange official permission to start the grape-harvest.

barrique barrel or cask, nowadays usually containing 225 litres.

batonnage breaking up with a stick (or similar) the solid matter thrown to the surface of a vat during fermentation.

blanc de blancs a white wine made exclusively from white grapes.

blanc de noirs a white wine made exclusively from black grapes.

bonbonne demi-john (a measure of about 10 litres).

botrytis cinerea a fungoid disease which rots the skin of grapes. In Monbazillac, a pre-condition of fine sweet wines.

bouquet the aromas produced by wine in the glass, other than the basic smell of wine. Often translated as 'nose' for short.

bourbe the deposit from the juice, fruit, stalks and skins of grapes during the early stages of vinification.

bourgeon the bud of the grape-vine.

bourru rough, unsophisticated.

brut bone-dry (of sparkling wine).

calcaire limestone.

cassis blackcurrants.

cave wine-cellar.

cépage grape-variety.

chai(s) a storehouse for wine: a winery.

champenoise as in Champagne.

chapeau the cake-like solid mass which forms from the matter thrown to the surface of a vat during fermentation.

chaptalisation the artificial sweetening of wine by the addition of sugar.

chêne oak.

clos a vineyard, strictly speaking enclosed by a wall.

collage the fining of wine: the process of forcing all solid particles suspended in the wine to the bottom of the tank or barrel.

cru a wine selected from the best.

cuvaison fermentation of grapes and their skins to make red or rosé wine.

cuve a vat, either open or enclosed, and of whatever material.

cuvée a consistent blend of wines from the same source.

débourbage the racking or settling of the must prior to fermentation.

demi-muid a barrel of 300 or 400 litres.

douelle the stave of a barrel.

ébourbage à froid removal of waste matter from the newly pressed grapes by refrigeration.

éffeuillage the thinning of the leaves on a vine to promote maximum exposure of the grapes to the sun.

égrappoir a machine for removing the stalks (**égrappage**) from the bunches of grapes.

élevage the maturing of wine after fermentation ends.

en espalier grown on a trellis.

encépagement the balance of different grape-varieties in a vineyard, or in the final wine.

engrais natural manure or artificial fertiliser.

étiquette a label.

fagots, derrière les, from a secret supply, hidden from general view.

finesse the opposite of roughness: a quality of elegance and softness.

flatteur plausible.

floraison the flowering of the grapes.

foudre a large barrel, a wooden tun.

fouloir a machine for crushing grapes, often combined with an égrappoir (q.v.) for removing the stalks, when it is called an égrappoir-fouloir.

fût a cask.

gouleyant easy to drink, a wine which goes down well, quaffable.

goût du terroir a taste deriving from a combination of soil, locality, grape-variety and climate which is exclusive to a particular wine.

gras rich, buttery, fleshy, literally fat.

grave (of the soil) gravelly, made up of tiny stones.

greffe a graft.

gris a *vin rosé* so pale that it is 'grey' rather than pink.

hectare 10,000 square metres (about 2.5 acres).

hectolitre 100 litres (about 11 dozen bottles).

INAO French National Institute for Appellations Contrôlées (q. v.).

liquoreux the sweetest grade of wines, not to be confused with liqueur.

macération the leaving of the skins, stalks, fruit and juice of the crushed grapes in contact with each other, either before or during fermentation.

macération carbonique a method of wine-making where the grapes are not crushed but are allowed to disintegrate by themselves under a layer of carbonic gas.

macération pelliculaire or **préfermentaire** maceration at cool temperature before fermentation is allowed to begin (white wine only).

madérisation excessive oxidisation of wine, producing an effect not unlike the smell and taste of Madeira.

maître de chais cellar-master.

malolactic (fermentation) a second fermentation of wine after the first alcoholic fermentation has finished, which converts the malic acid in the wine into milder lactic acid.

méthode champenoise the way of making still white wine into sparkling wine, as practised in Champagne.

mildiou mildew

millerandage uneven swelling of the grapes, so that some never achieve a size bigger than a small berry. Usually a result of a cold summer.

moëlleux mellow and full; usually denoting a degree of sweetness.

must the contents of a *cuve*, liquid and solid, during fermentation.

négociant a dealer in wines.

nerveux vigorous and lively.

paille (vin de) wine produced from dessicated grapes, sometimes laid on straw and often indoors away from the sun and rain.

passerillage Over-ripeness of grapes without botrytis.

pays (vin de) the highest-ranking table-wines after appellation contrôlée (q.v.) and VDQS (q.v.). Not to be confused with:

pays (vin du) any local wine.

perlé containing tiny bubbles, giving a slightly prickly sensation on the tongue.

persistance length of finish in a wine.

pierre-à-fusil gun-flint.

pigeage the breaking up of the *chapeau* (q.v.) to give the fermenting wine more access to the solids. Formerly done with the feet, now by do-it-yourself substitutes.

porte-greffe root-stock.

pourriture rot (see botrytis).

primeur wine made for drinking within a year after vintage.

rafle the wood and fibre, as opposed to the fruit, in bunches of grapes.

récolte harvest, crop.

régisseur the manager of a vineyard.

réglisse liquorice.

remontage the circulation of the wine in the vat by pumping it back into the top of the container to submerge the chapeau (q.v.).

rendement yield (quantitatively).

robe (du vin) colour, appearance.

sable (vin de) wine grown in extremely sandy conditions.

saignage drawing off the pink juice from the fermenting red wine grapes to produce vin rosé.

serpette pruning-knife.

sommelier wine-waiter: person in charge of wines in a restaurant.

soutirage the 'racking' of wine, by drawing it off its lees to clarify and oxygenate it.

tonneau a large cask, a hogshead.

tri (or trie) the selective picking of overripe grapes: also hand-sorting of grapes prior to crushing.

typicité the individuality which distinguishes a wine from others.

ullage the volume of air created in a cask or bottle by evaporation; also the topping up of the container to refill it.

vendange the grape-harvest.

vendange tardive late harvesting of overripe grapes.

vendange verte the picking of whole bunches of unripe grapes in midsummer, to promote concentration and quality in the bunches which are allowed to remain.

vigne a vine-plant.

vigneron a vine-grower/wine-maker.

vin de garde a wine requiring ageing before it is drinkable.

vin de goutte the wine which runs free after fermentation without pressing.

vin de négoce a blended wine produced by bulk-buyers.

vin de presse the wine which results from the pressing of what is left after the free-run wine has been run off.

Vin Délimité de Qualité Supérieur (VDQS) a statutory, legally controlled area of wine-production, not so highly-rated as areas of appellation contrôlée, but ranking above the vins de pays.

en vrac in bulk: in large containers other than bottles.

Index